Children of the Dictatorship

Protest, Culture and Society

General editors:
Kathrin Fahlenbrach, Institute for Media and Communication, University of Hamburg.
Martin Klimke, New York University Abu Dhabi.
Joachim Scharloth, Technische Universität Dresden, Germany.

Protest movements have been recognized as significant contributors to processes of political participation and transformations of culture and value systems, as well as to the development of both a national and transnational civil society.

This series brings together the various innovative approaches to phenomena of social change, protest and dissent which have emerged in recent years, from an interdisciplinary perspective. It contextualizes social protest and cultures of dissent in larger political processes and socio-cultural transformations by examining the influence of historical trajectories and the response of various segments of society, political and legal institutions on a national and international level. In doing so, the series offers a more comprehensive and multi-dimensional view of historical and cultural change in the twentieth and twenty-first century.

Volume 1
Voices of the Valley, Voices of the Straits: How Protest Creates Communities
Donatella della Porta and Gianni Piazza

Volume 2
Transformations and Crises: The Left and the Nation in Denmark and Sweden, 1956–1980
Thomas Ekman Jørgensen

Volume 3
Changing the World, Changing Oneself: Political Protest and Collective Identities in West Germany and the U.S. in the 1960s and 1970s
Edited by Belinda Davis, Wilfried Mausbach, Martin Klimke, and Carla MacDougall

Volume 4
The Transnational Condition: Protest Dynamics in an Entangled Europe
Edited by Simon Teune

Volume 5
Protest Beyond Borders: Revisiting Social Mobilization in Europe after 1945
Edited by Hara Kouki and Eduardo Romanos

Volume 6
Between the Avantgarde and the Everyday: Subversive Politics in Europe, 1958–2008
Edited by Timothy Brown and Lorena Anton

Volume 7
Between Prague Spring and French May: Opposition and Revolt in Europe 1960–1980
Edited by Martin Klimke, Jacco Pekelder, and Joachim Scharloth

Volume 8
The Third World in the Global 1960s
Edited by Samantha Christiansen and Zachary A. Scarlett

Volume 9
The German Student Movement and the Literary Imagination: Transnational Memories of Protest and Dissent
Susanne Rinner

Volume 10
Children of the Dictatorship: Student Resistance, Cultural Politics, and the "Long 1960s" in Greece
Kostis Kornetis

Volume 11
Media and Revolt: Strategies and Performances from the 1960s to the Present
Edited by Kathrin Fahlenbrach, Erling Sivertsen and Rolf Werenskjold

Volume 12
Europeanizing Contention: The Protest against 'Fortress Europe' in France and Germany
Pierre Monforte

Volume 13
Militant Around the Clock? Left-Wing Youth Politics, Leisure and Sexuality in Post-Dictatorship Greece, 1974–1981
Nikolaos Papadogiannis

Volume 14
Protest in Hitler's 'National Community':Popular Unrest and the Nazi Response
Edited by Nathan Stoltzfus and Birgit Maier-Katkin

Volume 15
Comrades of Color: East Germany in the Cold War World
Edited by Quinn Slobodian

Volume 16
Social Movement Studies in Europe: The State of the Art
Edited by Guya Accornero and Olivier Fillieule

Volume 17
Protest Cultures: A Companion
Edited by Kathrin Fahlenbrach, Martin Klimke and Joachim Scharloth

Volume 18
The Revolution before the Revolution: Late Authoritarianism and Student Protest in Portugal
By Guya Accornero

Children of the Dictatorship

Student Resistance, Cultural Politics, and the "Long 1960s" in Greece

Kostis Kornetis

berghahn
NEW YORK • OXFORD
www.berghahnbooks.com

First published in 2013 by
Berghahn Books
www.berghahnbooks.com

© 2013, 2016 Kostis Kornetis
First paperback edition published in 2016

All rights reserved. Except for the quotation of short passages for the purposes of criticism and review, no part of this book may be reproduced in any form or by any means, electronic or mechanical, including photocopying, recording, or any information storage and retrieval system now known or to be invented, without written permission of the publisher.

Library of Congress Cataloging-in-Publication Data

Kornetis, Kostis.
  Children of the dictatorship : student resistance, cultural politics, and the long 1960s in Greece / Kostis Kornetis.
    pages cm. — (Protest, culture and society)
  Includes bibliographical references.
  ISBN 978-1-78238-000-9 (hardback) — ISBN 978-1-78533-033-9 (paperback) — ISBN 978-1-78238-001-6 (ebook)
  1. Student movements—Greece—History—20th century. 2. College students—Political activity—Greece—History—20th century. 3. Ethnikon Metsovion Polytechneion (Greece)—Student strike, 1973. 4. Greece—Politics and government—1967–1974. 5. Greece—Social conditions—20th century. I. Title.
  LA788.7.K67 2013
  378.1'98109495—dc23
                                                                                2013015977

British Library Cataloguing in Publication Data

A catalogue record for this book is available from the British Library

ISBN 978-1-78238-000-9 hardback
ISBN 978-1-78533-033-9 paperback
ISBN 978-1-78238-001-6 ebook

Στον πατέρα μου

Contents

List of Figures ... ix

Acknowledgments ... xiii

List of Abbreviations ... xvi

Transliteration ... xviii

Introduction ... 1

CHAPTER 1. A Changing Society ... 10
    Greece in the 1960s 10
    Universities between Progression and Regression 12
    Student Activism 14
    Tediboides and *Yeyedes:* Youth Culture 16
    Generation Z 19
    Continuities and Ruptures in Contentious Politics 23
    The Lost Spring 26

CHAPTER 2. Phoenix with a Bayonet ... 37
    The Colonels' Takeover 37
    Passivity, Consensus, Resistance 42
    Tidying Up the University 48
    '68 as a Point of Reference 53
    Life Is Elsewhere: Greek Students Abroad 60
    Home-Grown Revolutionaries 71
    The Terrible Solitude of Rigas Feraios 77
    The Historical Generation Retires 83

CHAPTER 3. A Mosquito on a Bull ... 95
    Competing Youth Cultures 95
    A Rebellious Subjectivity 99
    Heirs and Defectors 105
    Tale of Two Cities 111
    Political Opportunities 115
    Incubator Chambers 116
    Technocracy and Its Discontents 127
    Marx's Children 129
    The "Other" among Student Groups 140
    Libidinal Politics 148

CHAPTER 4. Cultural Warfare — 158
   Media and Publishing Strategies   158
   The Arrival of the 3 M's in the Colonels' Greece   162
   Cinema as a Gun   169
   A Window on the World   174
   "Tickets to Freedom": Theater   181
   The Musical Culture Wars   189
   Reinventing Tradition   196
   A Singing Movement   199
   A Collective Falling in Love   202
   Gendered Militancy and "Sexual Revolution"   204
   Revolutionizing Everyday Life   213

CHAPTER 5. Ten Months that Shook Greece — 225
   The 1973 Reforms and Student Radicalization   225
   The Movement Gains Prestige   228
   "Anything but May '68": The Law School Occupations   230
   The Cost of Participation   241
   A "Glocal" Movement   246
   The Mission of the Youth   251
   "This Is What Revolution Must Be Like": The Polytechnic Events   253
   The Copycat Occupation   280
   After the Revolution   286
   Metapolitefsi and Beyond   292

EPILOGUE. "Everything Links" — 312
   Events   317
   Medium-Length: Utopias and Outcomes   322
   Future's Past: Cultural Changes   325
   Conclusion   328

Bibliography — 335
   Interviews   335
   Periodicals   336
   Archives   336
   Published Sources   336
   Secondary Sources   337
   Film   357
      Documentaries   358
      Television Documentaries   359
   Sound   359
      Music   359
      Sound Documents   359

Index — 360

Figures

Figure 1.1. Change in Student Numbers in Greek Institutions of Higher Education, 1960–1973.   13

Figure 1.2. Teddy boy with his hair buzzed off, publicly humiliated by the police in the late 1950s. Members of this particular subculture, indicative of common patterns of socialization in Greece as elsewhere, received very harsh treatment by the authorities.   17

Figure 1.3. Funeral of the assassinated left-wing MP Grigoris Lambrakis in Athens, 28 May 1963. The funeral marked the politicization of an entire generation.   20

Figure 1.4. Protesters during the so-called July events in Athens in the summer of 1965. The *Lambrakides* were amongst the most fervent participants in the protests, alongside workers. Future analysts described those events as an "early '68."   27

Figure 1.5. University of Salonica students holding a placard with a drawn image of the dead student leader Sotiris Petroulas, July 1965. Petroulas' death sent shock waves and radicalized student militants.   29

Figure 2.1. 21 April 1967. The coup d'état has just taken place and tanks are rolling in front of the Parliament.   38

Figure 2.2. 22 April 1967. The "revolutionary government" is being sworn in by King Constantine II, in the middle—with a stern look indicating disapproval. Second to his right, on the left lower corner, is Colonel Georgios Papadopoulos, the *primus inter pares* of the regime.   39

Figure 2.3. The regime's symbol: a phoenix emerging from its ashes, with a soldier bearing a fixed bayonet rifle in its base. The phoenix was endlessly reproduced in the public sphere—from coins and schoolbooks to cigarette matches. The caption reads "Long Live 21 April 1967."   41

Figure 2.4. Propaganda sign of the regime reading "Always walk to the Right, 21 April Avenue," demonstrating its extreme communistophobia.   54

Figure 2.5. "Parallel Lives, Parallel Images." Caption of the centrist newspaper *Ta Nea* comparing the events of May 1968 in France to the events of July 1965 in Greece on the basis of "moral panic," 29 May 1968. Notice the images of the occupied Sorbonne and of Daniel Cohn Bendit in the right column. 56

Figure 2.6. A tragic conclusion to the "armed struggle." The car in which Maria Elena Angeloni and Giorgos Tsikouris died on 2 September 1970, when the bomb they attempted to leave outside the US embassy detonated prematurely. 81

Figure 2.7. Athens Military Tribunal. Members of a clandestine organization—probably Rigas Feraios—are transferred handcuffed from the court back to prison, 1968–1969. By 1971 underground resistance had been wiped out. 83

Figure 3.1. Funeral of former prime minister George Papandreou, 3 November 1968. Alongside poet George Seferis's funeral in 1971, it was one of the few recorded incidents of mass protest during the first years of the dictatorship. 111

Figure 3.2. Police arresting a protester during Papandreou's funeral. In the background one can discern advertisements for one of the anticommunist military films that were financed by the regime. 113

Figure 3.3. Leaflet distributed by the Maoist-Stalinist student organization AASPE (Anti-Fascist, Anti-Imperialistic Student Front of Greece) calling for a "general strike." 139

Figure 4.1. Headline of the antiregime daily *Thessaloniki* reading "Freedom … Freedom," and with small letters in the subtitle "in Spain." This was a typical strategy of the newspapers during the Junta, testing the boundaries of censorship. 160

Figure 4.2. Scene from Thanasis Rentzis and Nikos Zervos's movie *Black-White*, 1973. The student protagonist enters a record store in Athens and stares at a poster of Frank Zappa, while in the background one can hear a song by Deep Purple. The film shows the extent of familiarization with Western pop culture, including progressive rock. It also contains direct references of a "cinéma-verité" kind to the rising student movement. 174

Figure 4.3. Projecting the repressed desire for freedom onto the screen. This was the 1970 advertisement for the film *The Straw-*

berry Statement, which dealt with student uprisings on US campuses. The film caused a sensation and was subsequently banned. 178

Figure 4.4. The avant-garde theater group Elefthero Theatro performing John Gay's *Beggar's Opera* in 1970. The group, which decided to abolish the *director-dictator* in a symbolic antiauthoritarian move, exemplified the fusion between politics and the arts. 187

Figure 4.5. Dionysis Savvopoulos being filmed by one of his collaborators, director Lakis Papastathis, during the legendary sessions at the Kyttaro Club in 1971. Kyttaro was a meeting point of the political and the countercultural. 192

Figure 4.6. Marisa Koch performing in a video clip of the early television shows. The fusion between the traditional song ("Armenaki"), Koch's hippie attire, and the psychedelic background was part of a conscious strategy to "harm" tradition. 197

Figure 4.7. Regent General Georgios Zoitakis—with glasses—and Brigadier Dimitrios Ioannidis—the notorious Head of ESA and latter day "invisible dictator"—championing a folk dance during Orthodox Easter in 1971. Regime figures never missed a chance to demonstrate their skills in the folk dances *tsamikos* or *kalamatianos* in public. 199

Figure 4.8. Change in Male and Female Student Numbers in Greek Institutions of Higher Education, 1968–1973. 205

Figure 4.9. A female student is dragged by the hair by two policemen around the time of the Law School events in February 1973. Misogyny and a particularly harsh treatment of women protesters were part of the regime's repressive repertoire. 211

Figure 5.1. An antiregime student, Makis Balaouras, during the "Trial of the Eleven," with visible evidence of police brutality on his face. The fact that this photo was allowed to be published by a magazine such as *Epikaira*, alongside other images of arrested students with bruises, shocked the public but also indicated the controversial nature of the regime's "controlled liberalization." 229

Figure 5.2. Students barricaded at the terrace of the Law School building, Athens, March 1973. Notice the growing visibility of women among the protesters, partly due to the forced conscription of their male peers. 239

Figure 5.3. Junta's amnesty, summer of 1973. Political prisoners are returning home by boat from the remote islands to which they had been sent into exile. On their way out many praised the role of the students as a catalyst for their release. 247

Figure 5.4. 15 November 1973. An estimated ten thousand people gathered around the Polytechnic. This second day of occupation is typically described as a "celebration." 258

Figure 5.5. Students writing anti-Junta slogans on a bus in front of the occupied Polytechnic, 14–16 November 1973. The central streets around the Polytechnic were jammed with traffic, which the students exploited in order to distribute leaflets and write slogans on trolleys and buses, calling everyone to come and demonstrate against the dictators. 262

Figure 5.6. A tank is about to crush the Polytechnic gate where students are barricaded, morning hours of 17 November 1973. The bloody ending of the ten months that shook Greece. 277

Figure 5.7. After the Revolution. The crushed gate of the Polytechnic in daylight. Next to the bulldozed Mercedes of the school's dean, a gate column with the graffito "NATO Out." Other gate columns bore the inscriptions "USA out" and "Allende." 279

Figure 5.8. Constantine Karamanlis is being sworn in as prime minister and head of a Government of National Unity in the morning hours of 24 July 1974 in the presence of General Gizikis. Certainly not the revolutionary outcome many of the Polytechnic protagonists had imagined. 293

Figure 6.1. Everything links. Antidictatorship rally in the United States in 1974, associating the Junta with the war in Vietnam. In the third-worldist frame of the "long 1960s," Greece and Vietnam were grouped together as victims of US imperialism. 313

Figure 6.2. A powerful *lieu de memoire*. Thousands of young people demonstrating within the Polytechnic yard one year later, November 1974. The democratic transition was already underway, and the Polytechnic acted as a legitimizing event of the entire process. 327

Acknowledgments

This book took many years to come to fruition. Partly because of its sheer length—the original comparison with Spain had to be left out for logistical reasons—and partly because of the major modifications that the exigencies of the book project demanded. In this long and painful process, I was accompanied throughout by the wise advice and guidance I had received during my Florence years. My then supervisor, Luisa Passerini, remained a powerful inspiration and a precious interlocutor throughout these years. Antonis Liakos, a mentor and a friend, continued to be a solid point of reference, always offering me extremely detailed and insightful comments. Donatella della Porta, always generous in her praise and fair in her criticism, never ceased to be a point of reference, as we kept discussing the student movements of the 1960s in terms of their afterlives at present. Conversations with Katherine Fleming on historiography have been invaluable, while Nancy Bermeo, Karen Van Dyck, and Philip Carabott remained inspiring forces and sources of instruction for the entire project and its cultural and political nuances.

I would like to thank the publisher Marion Berghahn for her trust and my *Genosse* Martin Klimke for inviting me to participate in the intellectual adventure of the book series on *Protest, Culture and Society,* which he coedits, alongside Joachim Scharloth and Kathrin Fahlenbrach. Even though our collaboration proved to be at times tense, due to disagreements regarding the form and content of the manuscript, it always remained within the boundaries of mutual respect and appreciation. In the end, I believe that Martin helped me make a much better and more readable book. My gratitude also goes to the three reviewers of the manuscript, James Green, Nikos Papadogiannis, and Dimitris Papanikolaou. I was honored to receive their feedback, criticism, and praise, as all three men have been, in different ways and capacities, precious intellectual fellow travelers throughout the years. I am particularly grateful to Efi Avdela for discussing my ideas in her graduate seminar, as well as to Natalie Bakopoulos, Ciara Foster, Sakis Gekas, Kostis Karpozilos, David Konstan, and Constantina Zanou for reading and commenting impeccably on parts of the book. Katerina Lambrinou, apart from reading excerpts of the manuscript, was so kind as to share some of her own archival material with me, for which I am deeply grateful. Paige Sarlin should be singled out for her invaluable feedback but also for being the "godmother" of this intellectual child. I am thankful to Ruth Homrighous, Lydia Carr, and Kristine Hunt for their valuable help with editing the manuscript at different stages. I am indebted to Elizabeth Berg for her helpful advice and support throughout the editing process. The final version of the book is the outcome of the careful editing and proofreading of Heidi Broome-Raines, to whom I am grateful.

I would like to thank Chrysafis Iordanoglou, Nikos Kaplanis, Dimitris Katsoridas, Dimitra Lambropoulou, Dimitris Livieratos, Michalis Sabatakakis, and my beloved aunt Dona Korneti for their precious help in locating and contacting possible interviewees. The private collections of Olympios Dafermos, Giorgos Chatzopoulos, Minas Kokkinos, and Alkis Rigos proved to be of great help. Vangelis Karamanolakis of the ASKI Archives, Dimitris Bacharas and Giorgos Tsaknias of ELIA, Vangelis Angelis from EDIA in Athens, as well as Anna Lee Pauls of Firestone's Rare Collections at Princeton offered me great help both in terms of finding material and of facilitating my use of it. I am also grateful to Constantin Georgoulis, the late director of the Fondation Hellénique in Paris, for entrusting to me the material he had collected from events and activities organized by Greek residents during the Junta years. Thanks also go to Olga Balaoura, Iason Chandrinos, the Floros Archives, Thanasis Kalafatis, Giorgos Kotanidis, Myrsini Lionaraki, Lakis Papastathis, and Aristotelis Sarrikostas for their kind permission to reproduce photographs of the period from their personal collections, as well as to Margarita Markoviti for patiently and carefully assisting me to select them.

I am indebted to Maria Andronikou, Apostolos Ververidis, and Alexis Efkleidis for their love, encouragement, and intellectual stimulation throughout the years. I am also grateful to the old friends from Florence, Giorgos Antoniou, Javier Arrupe, Maud Bracke, Elias Dinas, Lisa Francovich, Sakis Gekas, Antonio Garcia Espada, Nicky Koniordos, Hara Kouki, Alexis Rappas, Javier Rodrigo, Eduardo Romanos, Nikos Skoutaris, Aphroditi Smagadi, and Vasilis Tzevelekos for helping me in various stages of the manuscript and above all for remaining faithful companions throughout the years.

Tassos Anastassiadis, Konstantina Andrianopoulou, Giorgos Andritsos, Patricia Barbeito, Vangelis Calotychos, Davide Deriu, Karen Emmerich, Elena Hamalidi, Reguina Hatzipetrou-Andronikou, Alban Jacquemart, Eleni Kallimopoulou, Eirini Karamouzi, Damian Mac Con Uladh, Vasilis Letsios, Anna Papaeti, Neni Panourgiá, Paris Papamichos Chronakis, Eleni Papargyriou, Panos Poulos, Vasiliki Rapti, Kostis Smyrlis, Katia Stasinopoulou, Katerina Stefatos, and Gonda Van Steen, all contributed to the book through their valuable ideas and constant encouragement.

I would also like to thank my colleagues and friends at Brown University and New York University for their support, and in particular, Rina Bliss,

Keith Brown, Deborah Cohen, Stephen Gross, Johanna Hanink, Nancy Jacobs, Byron MacDougall, Jo Labanyi, Despina Lalaki, Mary Nolan, Stratis Papaioannou, Robert Self, Naoko Shibusawa, Larry Wolff, and Vasira Zamindar. Special thanks go to Enric Bou and the Department of Hispanic Studies for funding part of the editing process, as well as to my precious "intellectual friends" Cornel Ban and Oddny Helgadottir for boosting my morale in various stages of the manuscript submission process. I would like to single out the pillar of my tenure at Brown, Elsa Amanatidou, for her relentless and multifaceted support throughout the book-writing saga. A special thanks also goes to Chris Chappell for his continuous interest in the book and for the extra care he took of the paperback edition.

This book belongs to the extraordinary individuals who shaped it through their memories, which they generously shared with me, regardless of whether they were painful or not. A special tribute goes to those, like Nikitas Lionarakis, Andrianos Vanos, and Angeliki Xydi, who passed away very prematurely. Their vibrant voices still resonate in my mind.

Finally, I would like to thank my family, and especially my sister, Elsa, for her sensitivity and care, and my mother, Penny, who offered me endless affection, understanding, and enduring support whenever I was in need of it. First and foremost, however, I dedicate this book to the memory of my late father, Michalis, who consciously cultivated and generously sponsored my love for history. He inspired this passion himself through his incredible gift of storytelling, which I so terribly miss.

Abbreviations

Armed Resistance Organizations

ARF	Aris—Rigas Feraios, militant "front" organization of Rigas
DA	Democratic Defense (liberals)
DEA	Democratic Committees of Resistance (Trotskyist)
K29M	29 May movement (Paris-based)
LEA	Popular Revolutionary Resistance (Paris-based)
PAK	Pan-Hellenic Resistance Movement (fusion between leftists and liberals)
PAM	Pan-Hellenic Antidictatorship Front (communist-led)

Clandestine Organizations

A-EFEE	Antidictatorship EFFE (communists)
EDE	Revolutionary Internationalist Union (Trotskyists)
EKKE/AASPE	Revolutionary Communist Movement of Greece/ Anti-Fascist, Anti-Imperialistic Student Front of Greece (Stalinist-Maoists)
KNE	Communist Youth of Greece (KKE's youth section)
KOS	Communist Organization of Students (KKE-Esoterikou's youth section)
OSE	Organization Social Revolution (Leftists)
PPSP/OMLE	Progressive Student Unionist Party/ Organization of Marxist-Leninists of Greece (Marxist-Leninists)

Miscellaneous

ASPIDA	Officers Save Patria, Ideals, Democracy, Meritocracy (alleged left-wing conspiracy within the Army)
CCO	Coordinating Committee of Occupation (during the Polytechnic events)
EAM/ELAS	National Liberation Front/National Greek Popular Liberation Army (the left-wing resistance movement during the German occupation)

EAT-ESA	Special Interrogation Unit of the Hellenic Military Police
EKNE	National Movement of Young Scientists
EPON	United Panhellenic Youth Organization (EAM's youth organization)
GSEE	General Confederation of Greek Workers
IDEA	Sacred Bond of Hellenic Officers (paramilitary conspiratorial organization of anticommunist officers)
KYP	Central Service of Information (Greek Intelligence Agency)
OPLA	Organization for the Protection of the People's Struggle (EAM's secret police unit)

Official Organizations and Societies

EKOF	National Social Student Union, extreme right-wing student organization
EKIN	Hellenic-European Youth Movement
EMEP	Society for the Study of Hellenic Problems

Political Parties

EDA	United Democratic Left
EK	Center-Union (liberals)
ERE	National Radical Union (conservatives)
KKE-Esoterikou	Communist Party of the Interior (post-1968)
KKE	Communist Party of Greece

Student Unions

EFEE	National Student Union of Greece
EPES	Association des Etudiants Hellénes à Paris
FEA	Student Committees of Struggle (unofficial committees of antiregime students)
FEAPTH	Society of Students of the University of Salonica

Terrorist Organizations

17N	Revolutionary Organization November 17th
ELA	Revolutionary People's Struggle

Transliteration of Greek Characters into Latin Characters

After G. Mavrogordatos, *Stillborn Republic. Social Coalitions and Party Strategies in Greece, 1922-1936,* Berkeley: University of California Press 2003, xxi.

GREEK	LATIN	GREEK	LATIN
α	a	ν	n
β	v	ξ	x
γ	g	ο	o
δ	d	π	p
ε	e	ρ	r
ζ	z	σ	s
η	i	τ	t
θ	th	υ	y
ι	i	φ	f
κ	k	χ	ch
λ	l	ψ	ps
μ	m	ω	o
αυ, ευ, ηυ	av, ev, or af, ef, depending on pronunciation	μπ	b if initial, mb otherwise
γκ	g if initial, ng otherwise	ντ	d if initial, nd or nt otherwise
γγ	ng	ου	ou
γχ	nch		

Introduction

In 2010 the well-known British Pakistani writer and political activist Tariq Ali commented that "were there a Michelin Great Protest guide, France would still be top with three stars, with Greece a close second with two stars."[1] Ali was referring not only to the 2005 riots in France and the 2008 civil disturbances in Greece, but to a *longue durée* structure of civil disobedience in the two countries that dates back to the 1960s and 1970s. If the most emblematic moment in France's recent protest culture remains May 1968, the absolute vertex for later developments in Greece's political activism was the student occupation of the Athens Polytechnic in November 1973. The culmination and the most spectacular of all resistance activities, it took place in the country during the seven years of the Colonels' dictatorship (1967–1974). The uprising lasted three days and came to a bloody conclusion as it was crushed by the regime's tanks; at least twenty-four people were certified dead and another fifteen went "missing."[2]

The "Polytechnic," as it became known, has inhabited a central symbolic space in Greek society ever since the democratic consolidation took place the following year. With its memorialization it became the major legitimizing incident of the democratic transition, as evidenced by the fact that the first post-Junta elections were scheduled for 17 November 1974; this specific date was thus appropriated and transformed into a national symbol. Before long, 17 November was established as a day of national celebration.[3]

The responses to the uprising and its commemoration were not uniformly positive. On one side of the spectrum, a pro-regime faction insisted on promoting its own revisionist version of events. As early as the summer of 1975, during the trials of the Polytechnic massacre, some of the accused and their apologists claimed that the 1973 events had either been staged or caused no losses at all (or both) and were, therefore, void of significance.[4] According to the so-called "epic fraud" theory, still exceptionally popular among the rising extreme right in Greece, no one was harmed on 16 and 17 November 1973 since the police were extremely careful and protective of the rebelling students.[5] Others argued that the existence of but a single, poor-quality piece of footage of the tank crushing the Polytechnic gate testifies to the fact that this was all studio work. For further evidence that the events never took place, extreme right-wingers have often invoked ex-premier Spyros Markezinis's stubborn denial of the fact that the occupation had turned into a bloodbath during his last days in office. During the course of the current research various individuals of different social and political standings repeated to me this outrageous conspiracy theory, in particular the skepticism about the existence of casualties. In the present political context of the economic crisis, and with the Neo-Nazi party Golden Dawn becoming increasingly popular, this kind of revisionism is acquiring new momentum.

On the other side of the spectrum, and in terms of left-wing culture, the Polytechnic occupation came to haunt future generations, as it was looked upon as the ultimate archetype of resistance, militant action, and self-sacrifice. Many different political actors—predominantly the entire palette of the Greek Left—struggled to interpret its "true" meaning; a standard topos of the postauthoritarian era was that the Polytechnic's "message" and aims have been unfulfilled, if not betrayed. Every Greek student mobilization since then (from the mass student movements of the late 1970s and 1980s to the December 2008 riots) has implicitly or explicitly evoked the Polytechnic as a model.[6] Therefore, the history of the Polytechnic is typically seen as a set of events that provides keys to understanding contemporary (youth) rebellions. For that reason, Mimis Androulakis, a former student leader during the dictatorship period and currently a politician, argued that the so-called Polytechnic Generation acted like a group of "vampires." Through its deification, he explained, his generation absorbed younger age groups in its own past rather than allowing them to develop their own genuine rebellions.[7]

More interestingly still, it remains imprinted in Greek collective memory that it was the students of the Polytechnic who brought down the Junta. In the summer of 2011, during a surge of protest against the austerity measures taken by the government to deal with its trouble-ridden economy, a slogan launched by the Greek *indignados* went "Bread, Education, Freedom: The Junta did not end in 1973"—both appropriating the Polytechnic uprising's most famous catchphrase (see chapter 5) but also perpetuating the common belief that it was the student movement that brought down the regime in 1973 (instead of 1974). Despite the symbolic and actual work that the Polytechnic did to discredit the regime's putative democratic evolution—as will be demonstrated in this book—this interpretation is strikingly inaccurate. It testifies, however, to the fact that the Polytechnic Generation still possesses a certain mythical aura in Greek society.

A more cynical view from both the Right and the Left concerning the members of the eponymous generation is that, from the mid-1980s onwards, they became conformist, betraying their youthful ideals and acquiring in exchange important positions of power in Greek society. Since the Polytechnic was often described as a "late '68," this development was likened to the '68ers taking positions of power in many Western countries. However, in Greece, as elsewhere, for every government minister there were dozens of protesters who disappeared after the flash of the moment. Moreover, on top of being criticized for "cashing in" on its past militancy—a critique that was accentuated throughout the 1990s—the Polytechnic Generation has currently come under attack as being politically accountable for the vast economic and political crisis that hit Greece after 2009. As the "Polytechnic" became a metonym for the entire period of the *Metapolitefsi,* namely, the period since the fall of the dictatorship, its original glorification (going hand-in-hand with the theory of a model democratic transition) gave way to its current demonization (fitting well with the recent tendency toward blanket rejection of the entire post-1974 political legacy).

This permanent attraction to and constant criticism of the Polytechnic Generation were triggers for the present book, inspiring my desire to both analyze in depth and demystify its history. The hegemonic role that this emblematic movement played and continues to play in Greece, at least in the sphere of the imaginary,[8] renders its close study of paramount importance in order to understand both the events themselves and their afterlives on the collective and individual level. Naturally, by the time of this research, a great semantic distance has separated past and present, involving a period of dramatic sociopolitical transformation that has inevitably altered the way former activists think of themselves. The transition from authoritarianism to democracy, from minority to mass politics, from socialism to yuppieism, and from armed struggle to institutionalized positions in the power structure of the state all resulted in fragmented identities. To be sure, the abrupt post-1989 passage from a bipolar to a multipolar world, the loss of a solid point of reference such as the Soviet Union, and the marginalization of communism and the metanarrative of the class struggle were all hits too direct not to have personal ramifications. The return to normalcy and the various failings of utopia caused a whole class of malaises: depression, alienation, radicalization, marginalization.

Former activist *Katerina[9] shows herself to be quite conscious of the distortions, not so much of memory as of perspective, which these changes inflicted: "If someone had asked me in '74, I would surely have said different things" (*Katerina, interview).[10] Certainly, if the interviews had taken place at the present conjuncture they would have been conditioned and filtered through the prism of the current economic and political crisis, a fact that is characteristic of the contingent nature of oral testimonies. To paraphrase oral historian Alessandro Portelli, this is a typical case in which the distance between "myself narrated" in the past and "I narrator" in the present is inflicted by history itself.[11]

Talkin' 'bout My Generation

British historian Arthur Marwick famously argued that the best way to look at the 1960s is as an extended chronological period, the "long 1960s," that began in 1958 and continued until the international oil crisis in 1974.[12] Even though Marwick had Italy, France, Britain, and the United States in mind, this kind of chronology would also make sense for Greece, despite political scientists' insistence on the contrary. An entire conference dedicated to this period took place in Athens in 2005, presenting the Greek 1960s as a "short decade" due to the imposition of the Colonel's dictatorship in 1967 that violently interrupted its course, but also—in a Hobsbawmean sense—due to the acceleration of events that led to a density of time.[13] My view is, however, that the pre-Junta period is inextricably linked to the actual dictatorship years. This period must be understood not only in terms of ruptures, but also of continuities, and as such it must be studied in order to achieve a true understanding of the evolution of social actors.[14] Rather than fostering a total segregation from the world and international developments—as is often argued—the Junta unwittingly provided the complex and intricate terrain for the unfolding of the Greek "long 1960s."

This book explores how from 1971 onward a young generation of students, aided by the regime's loosening, came to an open confrontation with the Colonels and, in so doing, replaced the preceding generation of activists whose antidictatorship actions had failed because they were largely conditioned by the predictatorship past. In contrast to their predecessors, people who were teenagers in 1967 would in the early 1970s opt for mass protest instead of individual clandestine action, thus exploiting the political opportunities offered by the regime and leading to the apogee of student resistance in 1973. Although the ostensible focus of the study is on protagonists of contestation, this is not to suggest that the Polytechnic Generation dominated student circles during these years. Its members were rather a strict minority, while the vast majority of students remained indifferent. My aim in the chapters that follow is to reconstruct the developments in Greek society and university life, including the emergence of these distinct generational groups, and to trace the continuities and ruptures in patterns and cultures of protest.

This book does not draw clear-cut epistemological distinctions between "youth" (usually a description of biological age) and "students" (a social category), partly because in the context of the 1960s these categories tended to conflate. In period literature, the term *youth culture* encompasses the full spectrum of young people, the predominant group and spearhead of which were indeed students. In addition, university revolts all around the globe reinforced the idea of the student body as a solid category of a supranational character.¹⁵ Still, since young people as a demographic group is much larger than just university students, and as class (and other) divisions matter, it is important to note that the focus of this study is firmly on university students, middle-class or otherwise.

A further goal of the present book is to catalog the cultural and ideological features that antiregime students had at their disposal to disrupt the relative consensus that had been created over five years of dictatorial rule and to create new meaning. The authoritarian regime's partial liberalization in the early 1970s allowed for the reinforcement of their mobilizing structures. The particular mass culture that these students developed and appropriated drew on a strong current of radical youth politics coming from abroad, coupled with the transformation of their everyday realities. This conclusion challenges a certain left-wing historiographical paradigm that both stresses the stupefying effects of mass culture and looks at exposure to Western ideas and foreign imported models of life as destructive, paralyzing, and disorienting for Greek students. An illustrative example is offered by Giorgos Giannaris's *Student Movements and Greek Education,* a standard work regarding the history of student activism in Greece:

> In the first years of the dictatorship, youth interests were focused on football, games of chance, new songs—mainly Anglo-Saxon ones—dress (bell-bottoms and later on blue jeans, turtleneck sweaters, and, for the working classes, leather or plastic suits, most often black ones)—long hair and beards, sexual activities, entertainment in general. ...
>
> In other words, the satisfaction of basic desires ... Radio, cinema and in general paraphilology and the Press, newly arrived television, etc., led student consciousness to a foreign, that is, imported and therefore unfamiliar, way of life, carelessness, inertia, things that the Junta systematically promoted. These were the elements that aided the regime.[16]

By looking at elements such as mass culture, subcultures, cultural appropriation, and mimicry as positive registers in the evolution of the Greek student movement, the present book positions itself against such theories.

This book also explores the relationship between international and local dimensions while drawing parallels with other Western movements and student experiences. The distinct characteristics and ultimate demands of the Greek movement were determined not only by internal politics but also by a broader flux of information and semantic codes, such as dress, taste in music and literature, and rhetoric and slogans. My main point here is that the student mentality, marked by both students' domestic situation and an adversary as concrete as a military Junta, was nevertheless enhanced by an awareness of other contemporary student movements abroad. In an implicit comparison of the Polytechnic uprising to the '68 movements, my book contends that this generation of Greek students was its own avant-garde, in terms of both self-perception and action repertoire.

While a number of fundamental differences distinguished the mobilized Greek students of '67–'74 from the generation of '68 elsewhere, my hypothesis is that in Greece the student movement came in on a wave of cultural as well as political rebellion, a fact that likens it to the gestalt of '68. Despite—or maybe because of—the presence of the dictatorship, Greek students shared many similarities with "the children of Marx and Coca-Cola," as Jean-Luc Godard had characteristically labeled the French youth in 1966. It is precisely for this reason that the Greek case, alongside the ones of the student movements under the Iberian dictatorships in Spain and Portugal, deserves to be studied within the wider paradigm of the international "long 1960s"—a fact that has been more or less ignored by the dominant bibliography so far.[17]

By analyzing the distinct characteristics of the Polytechnic Generation and discussing its similarities to and differences from the preceding generation—which I call Generation Z—this study examines connections between culture and politics, public and private, past and present. Since Greek students were representative of a social movement, following '68's "explosion of subjectivity,"[18] it is crucial to investigate the role of individuals and their memory of the period in question. Accordingly, I trace the specific dynamics at work in the upsurge of student activity in Greece in the early 1970s, its present representation by protagonists, and the interrelatedness between these different accounts. I aim to reconcile the age-old division between structure and agency in an attempt to account for both structural conditions and individual perceptions. In addition, my focus on subjectivity exposes "the mutual influences and tensions of the relationship between individuality and collectivity, experience and memory in the process of shaping the individual."[19] Here, I follow Luisa Passerini's rule of thumb according to which oral sources facilitate the exploration of memory under authoritarianism and the variations of subjectivity in history rather than making these difficult, as is often assumed.[20]

Accordingly, my aim is not to look only at the facts, but to explore the psychological and symbolic dimension: the unconscious, the imaginary, projections, compensations, and dismissals of the actors in question.[21] In other words, I am trying to situate the social processes of that period in an appropriate context through cultural analysis. In contrast to the binary perception at work in people's self-representation that tends to juxtapose the organized with the spontaneous, Greece with the outer world, and right-wing background with left-wing influences, my project shows that these features were largely intermingled and interrelated. Finally, the complexity of the events renders it difficult to do justice to the subject matter without narrowing the research in geographical terms as well. As Athens, followed by Salonica, clearly played the vanguard position within the movement, the student revolts that occurred at the Universities of Patras and Ioannina have been left aside in the present study.

This volume departs significantly from the existing research into the Polytechnic, through its systematic approach to the student experience by a nonparticipant, its focus on oral history combined with new theories of social movements, and its in-depth examination of the cultural climate of the period. It does not align itself with the theory that there is necessarily strict continuity in the student movements from the 1950s onward due to a cycle of protest. Although this cycle existed in the early 1960s, it was violently interrupted by the arrival of the Colonels, only to be succeeded by an entirely new cycle later on. In analyzing the student movement that evolved during the latter period, this book resists presenting the movement as a single, unified ensemble of progressive students and instead attempts to highlight its black spots alongside its coherent moments.

The contribution of the present book is that, apart from tackling a complicated issue in a complex, methodological way, it reaches beyond the Greek case and calls for a "thick description" of social phenomena as a possible way of confronting various histories of student revolts. It attempts to carve out a middle ground; thus it neither classifies the Polytechnic as a solid Greek '68, arguing for its consistency with the greater European experience, nor insists on the exceptional nature of the Greek case. It should be stressed that although Greece and other countries are implicitly or explicitly compared, the beliefs and actions ascribed to each country have obviously been shaped by the political and sociocultural peculiarities of the respective countries and their individual histories and conditions. Still, by juxtaposing the experiences and memories of students and by measuring the results of their real or perceived contact with the international environment, this study argues for a mutual striking feature: even in a semiperipheral authoritarian country of the Mediterranean, new youth cultures emerged, which apart from being driven by local necessities bore the strong imprint of the 1960s protest waves. Finally, the book offers an archaeology of origins regarding the international influences on Greek youth that can be useful in order to understand more contemporary political events that are taking place in the country.

Notes

1. Tariq Ali, "Why Can't We Protest against Cuts Like the French?" *The Guardian*, 19 October 2010.
2. Leonidas Kallivretakis, "Eponymous dead of the Polytechnic."
3. It is noteworthy that the so-called Polytechnic Generation—namely, those who had participated in the antidictatorship student movement of the early 1970s—acquired its signifiers from the actual *location* of the uprising rather than the year, in contrast particularly to the movements of 1968.
4. See *The Trials of the Junta. The Full Minutes. The Polytechnic Trial*, Athens. Also see Giannis Katris, *The Birth of Neofascism in Greece:* 40.
5. Already in December 1973 pro-regime circles circulated a theory according to which the Polytechnic was a myth created by a handful of journalists.
6. Especially during the three weeks of civil disturbances that followed the murder of a fifteen-year-old student by a policeman in the center of Athens in December 2008 and their relation to the "revolutionary past" in general and the Polytechnic in particular, see Kornetis, "No More Heroes."
7. Androulakis, *Vampires and Cannibals*.
8. I am using the term *imaginary* as a concept that denotes something that is not necessarily "real" but rather is contingent on the imagination of a particular social subject. The original term *l'imaginaire*, coined by Jacques Lacan, implies illusion, seduction, and fascination but not inconsequentiality.
9. Names preceded by an asterisk are pseudonyms, respecting the interviewee's wish to remain anonymous.
10. I have translated extracts from interviews I have conducted and the titles of Greek sources in the text and endnotes. Passages in English cited from Greek and other non-English sources are my own translations unless otherwise indicated. Quotations accompanied by the interviewee's name in parentheses refer to interviews which I have conducted and will not be referenced by an endnote. The date of each interview can be found in the bibliography. Quotations taken from published accounts will be endnoted, however. In terms of Greek names, see the note on transliteration. I have kept intact, however, first names of Greek personalities who in foreign reports of the time were called with the English equivalent of their first name, namely George instead of Georgios, and so on. I have also respected the transliteration that certain people prefer for their names even when it does not comply with the one I chose for the book.
11. Portelli, "Intervistare il movimento," p. 131.
12. Marwick, *The Sixties*. It is important to note that the idea of the extended decade has been used by several historians prior or parallel to Marwick, even though the term has been popularized by him. See, for example, Carmelo Adagio et al., *Il lungo decennio*, and Axel Schildt, Detlef Siegfried, and Karl Christian Lammers, *Dynamische Zeiten*. Also look at Kornetis, "'Everything Links'?"
13. See Rigos, Seferiadis, and Chadzivasileiou, *The "Short" Decade of the '60s*.
14. On this see Tsoukalas, "The Greek Decade of the 60s: 'Short' or 'Long'?," in the same volume.

15. Della Porta, "1968. Zwischennationale Diffusion und Transnationale Strukturen," p. 142.
16. Giannaris, *From EPON to the Polytechnic*, p. 337.
17. A major example of the tendency to leave these countries out of a general appreciation of the European Sixties is provided by Schildt and Siegfried, *Between Marx and Coca-Cola*, a collective volume that focuses solely on Western and Northern Europe.
18. This concept was introduced by Luisa Passerini in "Le mouvement de 1968."
19. Anastasia Karakasidou, book review of *Historein*, special volume on "Heterodoxies," *Journal of Modern Greek Studies*.
20. Passerini, "La memoria europea," p. 86.
21. See Passerini, *Storie di donne*, p. 45.

Chapter 1

A Changing Society

This chapter aims to reconstruct the conditions of the university and the country prior to the Junta. By looking at the period leading up to the dictatorship, it attempts to trace the identity of those students of the mid-1960s, some of whom were the first to experience the impact of authoritarianism in 1967. The pre-Junta period is inextricably linked to the actual dictatorship years in terms of continuities and ruptures, and is crucial for providing an understanding of the context and the evolution of the social actors concerned. The chapter focuses on Generation Z, an age-group that was shaped by the civil war and post–civil war experiences, and in particular the political assassination of left-wing MP Grigoris Lambrakis in 1963.

Greece in the 1960s

The Communist defeat in the Greek Civil War (ca. 1944–1949) by the National Army, with the initial aid of Great Britain and the subsequent decisive intervention of the United States, produced a deeply divided society in its wake. Even though schisms were not something new for Greek society and politics—ever since World War I a major cleavage existed between royalists and republicans—this time the armed nature of the civil conflict led to the creation of a semi-apartheid system for the defeated, entirely lacerating the social fabric. Over 100,000 people had to leave Greece for the countries of the Eastern Bloc. Communists and sympathizers were treated as internal enemies or, as anthropologist Neni Panourgiá aptly put it, "dangerous citizens."[1] Up until the mid-1960s thousands of left-wingers and "fellow-travelers" were interned in remote islands for reeducation purposes. "National-mindedness" (*ethnikofrosyni*) became the official state ideology, in juxtaposition to the supposed unpatriotic Left.[2] The extreme communistophobia that prevailed must be understood in the context not only of the long-lasting legacy of the Greek Civil War but also of the Cold War itself.

Still, despite the deleterious effects of the aftermath of the civil conflict, Greece experienced some improvements in the early 1960s both in terms of democratization and modernization.[3] The United Democratic Left (EDA), a political party that gathered the heritage of the communist-led wartime resistance and advocated for democratization after the civil war, gradually became a significant political player starting with a spectacular electoral result in 1958.[4] More importantly, the first non-right-wing governments since the early 1950s led by George Papandreou's Center Union (EK) from late 1963 to mid-1965 introduced some liberalization, including the softening of anticommunist legislation, the gradual closing down of internment camps and the first repatriations of exiled communists from the Eastern Bloc. Despite this liberalization, however, the Communist Party of Greece (KKE) continued to be banned under Law 509 of 1947 on the implementation and circulation of ideas aiming at the overthrow of the political system.

Nonetheless, Greece's incomplete democracy and the remnants of the civil conflict—very apparent after the summer of 1965 when the prime minister came into an open conflict with the king, causing a constitutional crisis and a parliamentary turmoil that lasted for about two years—managed to establish the groundwork for the arrival of the Colonels in 1967. Moreover, even despite Papandreou's introduction of a limited liberalization, in reality the post–civil war status quo of curtailed democratic rights and limited social expression extended up to 1974: it was only *after* the collapse of the Colonels and the restoration of democracy in 1974 that the long-lasting post–civil war era came to a close, at least on an institutional level, with the decriminalization of communism and the rehabilitation of the exiled and imprisoned left-wingers. Novelist Alexandros Kotzias's term "The Greek Thirty Years' War," coined in order to describe this entire period of extreme polarization, is quite accurate.[5]

In structural terms, the country was still suffering from economic underdevelopment and social backwardness. Its socioeconomic outlook was comprised of a dominant peasantry, a relatively weak working class, a large petty bourgeoisie, an oligarchy of compradors, and a small-scale commodity-type production, coupled with delayed industrialization. There was a postwar economic boom that was facilitated by foreign investment, but its effects were to be fully experienced relatively late in Greece in comparison with the Western European countries. In the late 1950s, despite skyrocketing industrial production and US capital investments in exchange for military presence,[6] the desperate need for jobs led to a considerable export of labor, mainly to West Germany and to a lesser extent to Belgium. Greeks were among the most numerous "guest workers."

At the same time, Greece was changing rapidly in the long 1960s and moving toward modernization. The unprecedented urbanization and social dislocation that the country experienced in the post–civil war era was accompanied by a complete reconfiguration of the urban landscape.[7] This period also witnessed a rapid increase in US imported consumer culture, enabled by the "economic miracle" of the 1950s. Modern electronic devices and cars—luxuries a decade earlier—had become normal commodities by the early 1960s.[8] While large segments of the urban population joined the expanding public sector workforce, the establishment of a welfare state became an expressed aim of both the right-wing government of Constantine Karamanlis (1955–1963) and the centrist ones of George Papandreou (1963–1965). Although welfare was never fully achieved, its anticipation increased the expectations of a better future, while the introduction of more consumer goods was supposed to make Greeks pay less attention to politics. Prosperity and mass consumption, however, two of the main features of postwar Western Europe, were not consolidated prior to the Colonels' dictatorship. In contrast to their counterparts in other Western European nations, Greek youth of the 1960s spent their teen years without television, as this medium was purchased en masse only in the following decade.[9] By the early 1970s, televisions and stereos, major sources of mass culture in the Western world, had already become standard necessities, their purchase having been made possible by payments in installments.

Another interesting change regarding not only the Greek economy but the society as a whole is the fact that the country started becoming a tourist destination in the 1960s. Partly thanks to major blockbusters such as Jules Dassin's *Never on Sunday* (1960) and Michael Cacoyannis's *Zorba the Greek* (1964), Greece and its islands were becoming touristic attractions. But again, it was during the years of the dictatorship when the country's tourism really took off. Whereas Greece received 394,000 tourists in 1960, the number of tourists entering the country totaled 2.5 million in 1972,[10] which coincided with the development of commercial air travel. Apart from high-class tourism and as was the case with Ibiza in Spain at about the same time, several Greek islands, including Crete, Mykonos, and Samothrace, became hippie "headquarters," where liberal habits in terms of clothing and sexual behavior were openly pursued. This upset both the regime's moral standards and the traditional local societies of the time—bringing them, however, in direct contact with the outside world.

Universities between Progression and Regression

What was the situation in the Greek universities in the "long 1960s"? Similar to other European countries, by 1967, Greek universities had witnessed an unprecedented increase in student numbers that began in the early 1960s, mainly due to the demographic boom of the postwar years and the post-civil

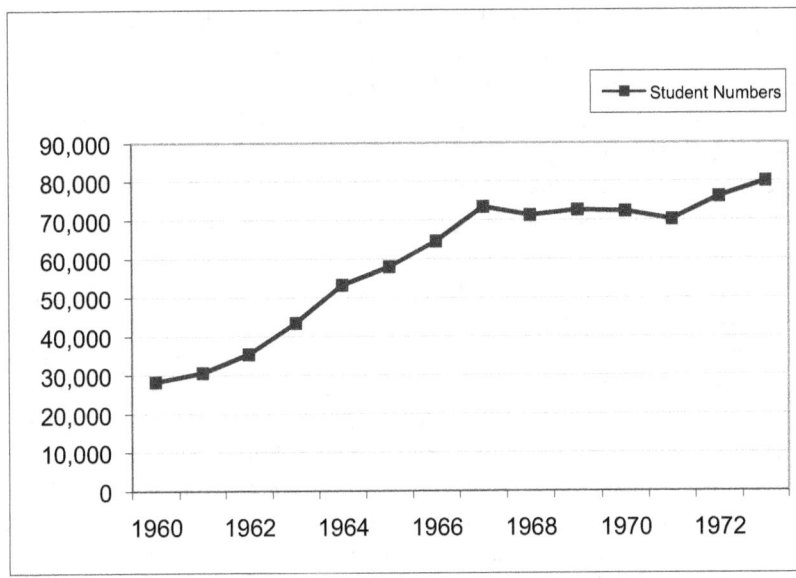

Figure 1.1. Change in Student Numbers in Greek Institutions of Higher Education, 1960–1973. (Source: ESIE)

war era that led to a rising concentration of youth in big cities. These phenomena enhanced the perception of the youth as a separate social category. Altered demographics boosted the youths' "awareness of constituting a distinct community with particular interests."[11]

Rising production needs created a demand for specialized technocratic personnel who could take up careers in the rapidly expanding public sector. The student population almost tripled from 28,302 in 1960–1961 to 80,041 in 1973. In order to cope with these changes, more student places were created, including a university in Ioannina and another later on in Patras.[12] The greatest increase in student numbers occurred in the years 1963–1965, when the student population grew from 35,000 to 53,300 (figure 1.1).[13] This shift was facilitated by the educational reform carried out by the liberal EK government that came to power in 1963, whose intellectual guru was pedagogue Evangelos Papanoutsos. The reform removed several social obstacles to entering higher education, the most important of which was tuition fees. It also initiated the National High School Diploma (*Ethnikon Apolytirion*), an examination of students by blind peer review that bypassed personal relations and favoritism, enabling gifted students from the countryside to study for a degree.

The same reform gave a progressive push to Greek education for the first time since the end of the civil war. It significantly reduced ideological propaganda in school curricula and favored the use of the vernacular Greek (*dimotiki*) over the artificial, purified version (*katharevousa*) that had been constantly promoted by the Greek state until then. More importantly, the Center Union government under Papandreou abolished the certificate of civic mindedness (*pistopoiitikon koinonikon fronimaton*).[14] This was a document issued by the police regarding a citizen's political affiliation, meant to stigmatize "unpatriotic" left-wingers and exclude them from all public jobs, aid, scholarships, and professional permits.[15] The certificates had been a university entrance requirement ever since the end of the civil war whose legacy was clearly a long-lasting one.

By 1968–1969, 71,259 students were enrolled in institutions of higher education: 48,758 men and 22,501 women. Women had begun entering the universities in larger numbers only in the mid-1960s as a result of more flexible family strategies and the enhanced possibility of entering the job market on favorable terms as graduates. Approximately one-third of all students came from the two large urban centers (25,460 from Athens and 6,944 from Salonica), while the rest were from the provinces.[16] Naturally, students from the countryside had more freedom of action than those living with their parents, though they came to university less politicized. In their recollections, these students stress the differences between themselves and the city kids. One emphasized the effects of these cultural differences: "I used to be, you know, the kid from the provinces, and I felt like a bit of a bumpkin. Naturally, it took me a while to demythologize some of my fellow students who were very nicely dressed, who were from Athens and had a different attitude" (Mavragani, interview).

The educational reforms contributed to the change in the social composition of the university population. For the first time, young people of lower middle-class and working-class origins entered the universities in large numbers. The proportion of students from lower middle-class families (children of merchants, shopkeepers, and so forth) rose from 10 percent in 1959–1960 to 13.2 percent by 1969–1970, while the portion of students from a working-class background grew to 14.6 percent from 8.3 percent. The representation of students from farming families also increased from 24.5 to 27 percent. By 1969–1970, the categories of workers, employees, and merchant-sellers (according to father's occupation) had increased from 27.6 percent to 41.5 percent in only a decade.[17]

Student Activism

The political consequence of the increase in student numbers was that students gradually acquired social force to affect politics. University life had been a source of friction for a long time prior to the dictatorship, and complaints about government education policies were a standard feature of Greek politics throughout the postwar era as various governments neglected the growing funding and personnel needs of higher education institutions. So while in the 1950s the university had been the battleground for the nationalist cause of the "unification" of Cyprus with Greece, in the 1960s it became the terrain par excellence for exercising pressure on the state to democratize and distribute funds more fairly. A cycle of protest began that would last until the 1967 coup.[18]

Those born during World War II or the civil war proper were also the ones who caused the first great disturbances on university campuses. The Greek democracy was weak and repressive, and its pluralist system was restrained by right-wing regimes of enforced consent, patronized by the United States, and sustained by the Crown, the army, and the Orthodox Church. Still, marginal avenues of political action such as the EDA remained open, even if they were semilegal and checked by extraconstitutional factors such as the "para-state." According to anthropologist Neni Panourgiá the latter term "denotes the machinery of the underground, unacknowledged, and (thus) lethal structure of persecution, character assassination, and extermination of political dissidents that allowed the official state to maintain its modicum of legality."[19] The spectacular rise of the EDA reinforced such practices and increased the fear and prejudice against these so-called cryptocommunists and everything they represented—most of all, ties to the Soviet Union and the outlawed Communist Party of Greece (KKE), whose headquarters were in Bucharest, Romania.

The 1960s were marked by political disturbances and growing unrest. The 1961 electoral results, produced by violence and fraud engineered by segments of the National Radical Union (ERE), the right-wing party in power, fueled the so-called unyielding struggle of the recently created coalition of several liberal parties to form the Center Union. From this time forward, student activists dropped strictly educational issues and became the linchpin of a political struggle aimed at breaking the monopoly of the three successive right-wing governments that had ruled the country since 1952. Prompted by the arbitrary use of police powers, including the frequent invasion of university campuses, student activism gained momentum by advocating for democracy in university administration and in access to knowledge. This was the 114 Movement, a name that refers to the article of the 1952 constitution according to which the implementation of the constitution is guaranteed by the citizens themselves. Student activists interpreted this article as giving citizens the right to act in situations in which a government was not respectful of the constitution. That 114 was the second-to-last article of the constitution was taken as an indication that it summarized the spirit of the whole document. Student activists reappropriated the vague formulation of the article to vindicate their right to resist and to spearhead the movement for more democratic rights.

This movement was coupled with the demand in the early 1960s to increase government funding for education. The students' main slogan was "15 percent," the amount of the budget for educational expenses that they demanded the government provide.[20] The 15 percent was also known as the "dowry to education," a reference to the tax imposed to pay for Princess Sofia's dowry in her marriage to the Spanish prince Juan Carlos de Bourbon in 1962. Students took this opportunity to juxtapose the luxurious dowry with the poor state of education. Other attempts to organize student action were channeled by the Bertrand Russell Youth Committee for Nuclear Disarmament, which from 1963 organized meetings, peace marches, and talks. The committee became very popular, demonstrating that a politically militant mass of young people was looking for new spaces and means of expression beyond the restrictions of the existing political parties.

Tediboides and *Yeyedes:* Youth Culture

By the mid-1960s, teen life in Greece was as explosive as it was elsewhere in Europe and the United States, a development that Greek authorities viewed with great disapproval. Various elements of international youth culture had penetrated the repertoire of Greek youth and style. Already in the late 1950s, a "teddy boy" subculture existed in Greece, whose members went for fringes, frills, Brylcreem, and cinema.[21] The *tediboides,* small bands of male adolescents, who were not necessarily working class, loved stealing cars and achieved considerable notoriety for throwing "yogurt bombs" at their teachers and elderly women. The phenomenon of "societal provocation," as it was characterized by the press, was coupled with the appearance of the first rock and roll bands.[22] In order to cope with the teds, the infamous Law 4000 was introduced, according to which young rebels were immediately arrested, were given a buzz cut by the police, and were marched through the streets carrying humiliating placards. Colonel Ioannis Ladas, who would later on become a leading member of the military junta of April 1967, remembered with pride partaking in this ritual in the past: "Allow me to tell you on this issue, especially since I have dealt with it in practical terms, that when I used to arrest them and shave their heads, I didn't do it in order just to cut their hair, but in order to stop this mentality which was destructive for themselves and for the Motherland."[23] The extremity of the reaction on the side of the state—probably comparable to ones in the Soviet Bloc—and the moral

A Changing Society | 17

Figure 1.2. Teddy boy with his hair buzzed off, publicly humiliated by the police in the late 1950s. Members of this particular subculture, indicative of common patterns of socialization in Greece as elsewhere, received very harsh treatment by the authorities. (From the author's collection)

panic that was generated around the "teddies"—shows that something about this youthful rebellion was deeply unsettling for the authorities and the social norms of the time in Greece.[24]

Alongside the rebellious though not politically dissident male teenage gangs, a sexual openness emerged for the first time among female adolescents, often manifested in forms of sexual exhibitionism such as performing stripteases at parties; exhibitionism of this type became a standard feature in films made during this period.[25] The miniskirt, a symbolic step toward female aesthetic and ultimately sexual emancipation, also became fashionable in Greece. By the mid-1960s Beatlemania was widely diffused, and Richard Lester's *A Hard Day's Night* (1964) became a box-office hit. Greek youths who followed this trend were referred to as "yé-yés," in Greek *yeyedes*.[26] The journal *Modern Rhythms* (*Modernoi Rythmoi*), which was influenced by the French radio station Salut les Copains, reported that the first concert by the rock group Forminx in May 1964 in Salonica was met with "seismic enthusiasm" by the youth. Apparently, the band mimicked what was happening abroad with the Fab Four and Johnny Hallyday.[27]

Still, the fact that postwar economic hardship already seemed a distant and unpleasant memory to growing sections of the urban population during the 1960s was a key element behind the introduction of commodities such as stereos and a standard pocket money, two of the preconditions for the emergence of a youth culture. Although this did not translate into more private space for the young within the traditional Greek home, young people in Greece did become regular consumers for the first time. Subcultures were gradually becoming sources of inspiration and the material of an extended financial activity. Historian Antonis Liakos notes that as the consent of the bourgeois classes after the war was guaranteed through the ideology of the "affluent society," contestation expressed itself not in the sphere of production but in consumption—"Not at the time of work but during leisure. Not as a break with parental working culture but as a solution of its contradiction on an imaginary level," and thus a symbolic one.[28] In a standard filmic representation of this generation, the young hero concludes that his generation's priorities are a new flat with modern furniture and electrical equipment, a car, and plenty of night life.[29]

By the mid-1960s, a distinct youth culture had formed in Greece for which music expressed rebelliousness. The commonly expressed view that "rock and roll did not exist before the 1980s in Greece" has already been rejected by other historians who convincingly argued that in the 1960s everyone bought rock and roll records and was eager to listen to the few specialized radio programs for this music.[30] Myrsini Zorba, a secondary school student at the time, recalls, however, that she did not possess a stereo at home: in the mid-1960s, a stereo was still a means of turning private into communal space. At the same time, movies such as Jean-Luc Godard's *Masculin Féminin* and Michelangelo Antonioni's *Blow Up* (both 1966) made the youth more familiar with consumerist trends and pop culture, as well as with representations of "rive gauche" Paris and "swinging" London youths. Another favorite for young audiences at the time was Mike Nichols's *The Graduate* (1967), with its depictions of sexual exploration and the very popular ballads of Simon and Garfunkel.

In terms of music, and apart from the romantic lyricism of the so-called New Wave in Greek music—that to some extent copied the French chanson of the early 1960s[31]—there was a Greek rock scene singing in English and copying the foreign model, at the same time leaving out of their lyrics any social dimension. An interesting exception to this was provided by the *poète-chansonnier* Dionysis Savvopoulos and his song "Vietnam Yé-yé", in which yé-yé culture (the innocent pop movement that originated in France in the late 1950s) was married to a political subject matter, thus circulating a typically ambivalent message. Nevertheless, the official Greek Left rejected "US imported" cultural models such as rock music as corrosive and destructive of the youth and disliked the fact that youthful potential was being expressed through "collective hysteria" instead of channeled into political action.[32]

Generation Z

The year 1963 was key for youth politics. The assassination in May in Salonica of Grigoris Lambrakis, an independent left-wing MP and member of the Greek branch of Bertrand Russell's Peace Movement, marked the peak of post–civil war repression and the beginning of the end of conservative premier Constantine Karamanlis's days in power. The result of the emergence of a massive "para-state" mechanism based on violence and the intimidation of left-wingers, the assassination acted as a generational unifying event. The "five days of May" started with the attack on Lambrakis and climaxed with his overcrowded funeral service in Athens. This sequence of events played a major role in politicizing a new student generation. Anna Frangoudaki, a Humanities student at the time and professor of education at present, describes how a human chain of young people during Lambrakis's funeral embraced her, somehow ascribing a role of destiny to this automatic rite of passage to the Left: "As if by fate the chain opened up and a girl said "Come on in, come with us," and from that moment on I belonged to the Greek Left" (Frangoudaki, interview).[33]

Lambrakis soon became the symbol of a pioneering movement that was created in early June 1963 and was named after him: the Democratic Youth Movement Grigoris Lambrakis, later renamed "Lambrakis Youth," or simply "Lambrakides." The slogan among the youth of the time was that Lambrakis was still alive, "o Lambrakis Zei." The letter Z, first initial of the word "lives on" in Greek, became common in graffiti as a symbol of the Lambrakis Youth. According to the left-wing composer Mikis Theodorakis, the leader of the Lambrakis Youth, this letter also resembled the thunder that castigates

Figure 1.3. Funeral of the assassinated left-wing MP Grigoris Lambrakis in Athens, 28 May 1963. The funeral marked the politicization of an entire generation. (Source: EMIAN, Society for the Study of the History of the Leftist Youth)

the enemies of the people.[34] This graffiti further inspired the title of Vassilis Vassilikos's book *Z* (1966), which became the basis for the screenplay of Costa-Gavras's renowned political film *Z* on the same affair (1969). Since the dead Lambrakis became the key figure in the collective representation of left-wing youths of this time, I describe this generation as "Generation Z."

Generation Z mainly comprised people who were born roughly between 1944 and 1949, while the subsequent cohort—the "Polytechnic Generation"—was made up of people born between 1949 and 1954. These two groups, although part of the same biological generation, reacted to various political stimuli in distinct ways and tend to represent themselves differently in current accounts. As Karl Mannheim has famously argued, a generation is a social (rather than a biological) phenomenon, entailing a common location in historical time and space, which creates a predisposition towards a particular mode of thinking, acting, and experiencing. According to sociologist Jeffrey Olick, generations are not normative periods but rather subjectively defined cohorts that exist "if and only if a number of birth cohorts share a *historical experience* that creates a community of perceptions."[35]

A major axe that shaped the historical experiences of these two generational units was the 1940s and their aftermath. Even though movement historian Catherine Saint Martin argues that "Lambrakis became the hero of a generation, which … was searching for another message from that of hatred and blood that was unleashed by the Civil War,"[36] the fact remains that Generation Z was shaped by the civil war and post–civil war experiences. The latter provided formative elements in the imaginary and memory of its members, who often portray themselves as people who did not experience youth. They further tend to represent the assassination of Lambrakis in 1963 but also the imposition of the Junta 1967 as the linear continuation of the civil war. Similarly, Mikis Theodorakis argued in the *Lambrakides' Manifesto* (1966) that the generation born during the occupation remained a hostage of the legacy of the civil strife: "[This generation] grew up within the flames of the civil war. It matured within Karamanlis's Middle Ages. What have the governors responsible for our country offered it up to now? What possibilities to educate itself, fulfill itself or create? Quite the opposite, they put it within a 'free prison,' without democratic rights and liberties, and with the only right to remain blind—jobless and desperate."[37]

Triantafyllos Mitafidis, born in Salonica in 1947, has very strong memories of these years: "The main feature of our childhood," he says, "was being terrified." Mitafidis speaks as though he had personally experienced the violence of the civil war, though he was a newborn at the time. What is more, his perception is that of a prolonged civil conflict up to the 1960s, a long, drawn-out period of repression: "I was born during the civil war. It was the generation that was born toward the end of the occupation and at the same time inside the civil war, and was brought up with those images of the fratricidal struggle. … That generation had no respite." (Mitafidis, interview).

Anestis Evangelou's poem "Generation of the '60s" is often quoted as representative of this climate:

> Between the poison of the adder
> And the wolf's tooth
> Within the mist and the fear
> With panic
> And under the gaze of the stool pigeons
> We came to know the world
> For this reason our words are poor
> Without exaltations, with no music
> And our verses are usually bleeding[38]

In contrast to Mitafidis and Evangelou's bleak depictions of that period, however, it has to be noted that by the mid-1960s a certain relaxation was *in statu nascendi*. The Lambrakis Youth biweekly paper *I Genia Mas* [Our Generation] and the journal *Ta Tetradia tis Dimokratias* [Notebooks of Democracy] offer characteristic tokens of this tendency, which often involved ridiculing the seriousness of everyday repression. In a telling article in the former, Giannis Theodorakis mocked the outrageous character of the die-hard anticommunist legislation and the supposed sound patriotism that it promoted:

> Let's say that you are a Medical School graduate and that you want to be appointed as a rural general practitioner. You must be around twenty-five. Meaning that in 1941 you were one year old. An infant during the occupation. A child during the civil war. But the first thing that the state will ask you is where were you and what were you doing during the decade 1940–1950. It is a "DECLARATION" according to article 4, paragraph 3 of the Law 516/1948 and you must respond to the questions. Here are some of the questions: "Where did you reside since 1 May 1941.... Were you ever a member of a communist organization (especially KKE, EAM, AKE, ETA, OPLA, EPON etc.)?"[39]

Still, the fact remains that this generation's activism came at a price. Christina Vervenioti recalls the difficulty of being a student activist in the years before 1967: "Even before the Junta came, the universities were not open enough [for us] to organize a gathering or a demonstration.... We were already having a hard time" (Vervenioti, interview). Similarly, Thanasis Athanasiou, a Commercial School student, attributes a sort of heroic status to political activism prior to 1967: "In that period if I did not spend one night in jail it was an exception. I've visited all the jails of Attica.... So, to be organized in the Lambrakides during this epoch was indeed something heroic. Because you were in direct danger. It was no joke.... Surveillance and arrests were everyday phenomena" (Athanasiou, interview).

The Lambrakis Youth's repertoire of action included extensive rallies, open discussions, and peace walks, with a focus mostly on educational and cultural issues. Their goal was to create not just a political but a cultural mass movement. Chapters of the Lambrakis Youth created two hundred "cultural societies" throughout the country. According to one contemporary account, the organization, whose members numbered about two hundred thousand, "planted flowers and trees in the mountains after a fire, donated blood to the Red Cross, formed cultural centers, libraries, discotheques of classical music."⁴⁰ By April 1965 the Youth numbered 37,000 members and could mobilize up to 100,000.⁴¹

The Lambrakis Youth movement brought about critical innovations in traditional left-wing politics and was the Greek equivalent to the Anglo-Saxon New Left that was on its rise during the same period. It was an organization open to everyone and with a declared independence, despite its clearly defined political engagement. Its original organizational structure moved beyond the rigid political tropes of the time. Crucially, for the first time since the end of the war and in a period in which women in their twenties were supposed to be preoccupied with marriage, female participation reached high levels. According to sociologist Magda Nikolaidou, Greek women of the 1960s "were treated as second-class citizens" and were not supposed to study or work.⁴² Men were still considered superior and acted as the breadwinners of their households, and women were considered to be destined for housekeeping. This was the background against which the female Lambrakis Youth members, the Lambrakisses, acted and to which they reacted, though their activity never translated into any significant separate women's organizations or radical feminist demands.

Eventually, the Lambrakides coexisted in the pre-electoral campaigns of 1963–1964 with the Youths of the Center Union and occasionally with members of the tiny, idiosyncratic Progressive Party. The youth arm of the conservative ERE was rather uninspiring, leaving a large space to the National Social Student Union (EKOF), an extreme right-wing, all-male student organization with a solid pedigree of violence and aggression, including the bullying of students its members considered not "nationally minded" enough.

Continuities and Ruptures in Contentious Politics

The mid-1960s were marked by the appearance of a new intellectual current in cinema, music, theater, the fine arts, and writing and literary criticism, all of which converged easily to left-wing ideas concerning innovation, creation, and humanism. The intellectuals who backed the Lambrakides were among the first to articulate a critique of the Communist Party orthodoxy. The avant-garde journal *Pali* [Again], founded by surrealist poet Nanos Valaoritis in 1963, adopted new aesthetic paradigms in literature, attacked literary orthodoxies, and published risky texts that explored taboo issues such as homosexuality.⁴³ Equally innovative was the *Epitheorisi Technis* [Art Review], founded as early as 1954, which was supervised but not controlled by the left-wing EDA. As literary critic Aris Marangopoulos observes, this small, elitist circle concerned with liberating itself from party discipline and discovering Ernst Fischer, Gyorg Lúkacs, Bertolt Brecht, Emma Goldman, Antonio Gramsci, the Frankfurt School, Jean-Paul Sartre, and Rosé Garaudí failed to touch on the improvement of everyday life and to render it a left-wing demand.[44] Its social criticism and progressive currents in creative writing were accessible only to restricted intellectual circles. Quite influential, though less daring politically, was the journal *Epoches* [Seasons], founded in 1963 and financed by the well-known liberal publisher Christos Lambrakis. In its editorial board it catalogued some of the most prestigious intellectual figures of the country, such as George Seferis, Giorgos Theotokas, and K. Th. Dimaras.[45]

Overall, Greece was experiencing a cultural renaissance of sorts. For the first time, the possibility of linking elite with popular culture was regarded as a tangible project. Theodorakis's attempt to popularize poetry by setting it to music is an illustrative example of this tendency. Similar ideas were expressed in painting, theater, and cinema. All this fitted neatly with the Lambrakides' idea of an everyday street culture, open and accessible to all. In fact, the Lambrakis Youth were the first generation of activists after the civil war to explicitly link culture to politics. In addition, they were in favor of peaceful means of protest, placing themselves within Bertrand Russell's campaign and sharing similarities with the contemporary civil rights movement in the United States.

Students within the Lambrakis Youth's ranks were also creating a break with the official Communist Party line. The first Maoist organization was formed during these years around the journal *Anagennisi* [Renaissance], which fought for the revival of the communist movement in Greece. This tendency, called "antirevisionist," attributed responsibility for the revisionist turn of the international communist movement to Nikita Khrushchev's reforms. It admired Nikos Zachariadis, the controversial former general secretary of the Greek Communist Party in the 1930s and *líder máximo* of the "Democratic Army" during the civil war (1946–1949), as he remained supposedly faithful to the true nature of the movement. Alongside this, a Third-World movement grew out of the political awareness caused by the Vietnam War and the guerrilla struggles in Latin America. Ho Chi Minh and Che Guevara made their way to Greece in the form of political groups that defined themselves without reservation as "anticapitalist," and "anti-imperialist" while accusing EDA of being "legalist" and "defeatist."

Last but not least, the Lambrakis organization supported gender equality in its male and female sections. Greek society at the time was not ready to digest the coexistence of the sexes in this organization, which was indeed a breakthrough within the stalemate of the archaic postwar social structures.

Things had started to change as the massive urbanization and the new needs of developing Greek society brought more women into universities and workplaces. By the early 1960s, female presence in the auditoria had increased significantly, though at the beginning of the decade the student body was still predominantly male. High schools remained segregated in order to preserve "in a variety of ways the traditional concept of the role of women."[46] Pictures of student demonstrations up to the mid-1960s reveal few women among the left-wing youth.[47] Salonicean Lambrakissa and later-day feminist Zogia Chronaki laments the preferential treatment of her brother by her family and its gender bias in terms of restrictions:

> Kostis, a boy, was coming home at 4 o'clock in the morning because he was sitting at [the bar] Doré to solve the global problems of history and the Left, and I had to be back home at 9. . . . In petit-bourgeois or working-class households it continued to be enforced that girls should not go to demonstrations. So, on top of everything, we had to clash with the parents too. (Chronaki, interview)

The Lambrakis Youth included a relatively large number of women in its ranks, but men continued to hold most of the leading positions within the organization. Chronaki remembers being the only woman in EDA's student bureau: "I remember that in the hierarchy I had reached the bureau of the Student Section. . . . I think I was the only woman there" (Chronaki, interview).

In the Lambrakisses' imagination and discourse the worshipped generation of the 1940s had opened the way for the interaction of women and men on an equal footing, and this was regarded as an established practice. During the German occupation, the provisional guerrilla government of the mountains granted women the right to vote in 1944, almost a decade before the official Greek state did so (1952). Still, the assertion of many female left-wingers in the 1960s that wartime women had become agents of their own political fate for the first time was more legendary than real.[48]

Lambrakis women were often accused of low morals and sexual promiscuity, which alarmed well-to-do Greek families. A famous expression of the time (attributed to the publisher Helen Vlachou, who had a particular bias against the Lambrakis Youth) that was reverberated by the head of the ERE, Panagiotis Kanellopoulos, described them ironically as "the Lambrakis girls with the black tights." The Lambrakisses were accused of having a predilection to entrap well-to-do bourgeois boys and respectable army officers.[49] At the same time that Lambrakis Youth women were portrayed as loose, the movement itself was sufficiently rigid to hinder its own liberal and progressive character and evolution. The attempt to impose a Soviet-style moral discipline, for example, contrasted with the liberal ideas of the movement at large. A Lambrakis had to be "honest, hard-working and virtuous."[50] The official organizational stance considered the development of sexual relations between men and women as a step that would of necessity lead to marriage, though this assumption was habitually disregarded. Puritanism also dictated the rejection of long hair for the boys and pants or smoking for the girls in the name of the struggle against the American lifestyle.[51] Mikis Theodorakis, in particular, openly rejected the youth who were wearing blue jeans—whom he contemptuously dubbed "blue jeanists."[52] Pictures of Lambrakis Youth demonstrations of the mid-1960s show primarily male protesters in clean-cut, buttoned-down outfits, their ties and suits hardly distinguishing them from previous generations. This generation tried but did not manage to break social conservatism and provoke an overall break with the hegemonic value system.

The Lost Spring

The pioneering aspects of the Lambrakis Youth movement were curtailed by the fact that the organization did not retain its autonomy for long: by the end of 1964 it had fallen under the control of the Communist Party, which decided to merge it with the youth organization of EDA. Giannis Velopoulos, a law student and founding member of the Lambrakis Youth, recalls his disillusionment with these developments—a standard feature in people's memories of this moment: "I was cautious regarding the merging, I remember. I believed that the Lambrakis Youth should continue its activities undistracted and should not merge with any communist youth. Young people wanted to act on their own, without patrons."[53] Interestingly, members of the hard-core faction of the EDA Youth were not enthusiastic about the fusion either and contemptuously dubbed the environmentally conscious Lambrakides "caterpillar-collectors." The fact is that from that point on, the latter were continuously subjected to political manipulation.[54] By 1967, Mikis Theodorakis himself had felt compelled to resign a couple of times from the movement's leadership.

Another turning point for the Lambrakides and the progressive movement of the 1960s was the so-called July events, which signaled an "organic crisis" marked by the "massive withdrawal of support for the structures of representation, and an abrupt increase in political demands."[55] The unconstitutional sacking of Prime Minister Papandreou by King Constantine in late June 1965, when the sovereign refused him the right to assume direct

Figure 1.4. Protesters during the so-called July events in Athens in the summer of 1965. The *Lambrakides* were amongst the most fervent participants in the protests, alongside workers. Future analysts described those events as an "early '68." (Photographer: Aristotelis Sarrikostas)

control of the Ministry of Defense, created a power vacuum that was partly filled by a series of successive unstable governments by Center Union defectors, supported by the Crown. This triggered general upheaval, in which the participation of the youth was crucial. There was a huge wave of protests, strikes, and riots over the following seventy days, during which students and workers collaborated in striking harmony. The more than four hundred open-air rallies, numbering several hundred thousand people,[56] the libertarian attitude of the demonstrators, the largely anarchic means of protest, and the fact that half of Athens was set on fire made future analysts describe those events as an "early '68."[57]

Although this was the first time after the end of the civil war that the people rose up in such a manner and political mobilization provided a challenge to the prevailing social order, the methods used to mobilize the crowds and to express their grievances were conventional. Even though strikes and rallies became more and more frequent, acts of revolutionary violence such as bombings or property occupations were hardly present. In fact, right-wing politician and intellectual Panagiotis Kanellopoulos, who came to lead the

Greek caretaker government that was supposed to lead the country to elections at the time when the Colonels' coup took place, believed that the period of intense mobilization had ended long before the military intervention.[58]

Thus the protesters' repertoire of action remained highly predictable, even if several activists simultaneously framed it as a clear-cut "revolutionary situation," a term appropriated by later researchers using Marxist analytical categories.[59] According to their line of thinking, July 1965 provided the "objective conditions" for a revolution, namely, an uprising of the masses against the repressive state. The "reformist" communist leaders of the time, however—namely, the EDA and the exiled KKE—missed the opportunity to channel popular dynamism toward a direct confrontation with what they considered the bourgeois establishment and the right-wing state.[60] The absence of the organized Left and its lack of initiative was attributed to the old left-wingers' defeatism and their obsession with being victimized. This "missed revolution" motivated some people, such as Stergios Katsaros (a student at the time), to go radical. Katsaros recalled that following the events of July, "a quite solid Guevarist team was formed within the EDA Youth" of fifty to sixty members who used leaflets to propagandize their views. "We had the violent rupture on our minds," he said.[61]

The death of Sotiris Petroulas, a student leader flirting with third-worldism who was killed during a demonstration in the center of Athens on 21 July 1965, reinforced people's rage and instantly became a generational symbol. Petroulas was "the first victim of our generation," Katsaros recalled in his memoir.[62] Mikis Theodorakis's "Song for Petroulas," a hymn written in the second person, "was sung by the crowds during Petroulas's funeral,"[63] according to the composer himself. An emotional response to the event, the song linked the dead student directly with Lambrakis ("Lambrakis has taken you over to him"), concluding: "Sotiri Petroula / Lead your People, / Lead us Forward."

The flipside of Petroulas's tragic death was the humor of the popular uprising of 1965. Apart from the various slogans against the king and the influential Queen Mother Frederica, those concerning the so-called apostates (the defectors of the Center Union that had tried to form a majority with the support of the Right) were also daring compared to the rigid discourse and ethics of the time.

The Lambrakides movement, which started in 1963 and continued until 1967, was organically connected to the antidictatorship student movement. During the dictatorship years (1967–1974), students assumed that they formed a group with the right and duty to speak out on political issues. This belief was built upon the political involvement of this earlier generation of students and the fact that for over ten years student mobilizations had

Figure 1.5. University of Salonica students holding a placard with a drawn image of the dead student leader Sotiris Petroulas, July 1965. Petroulas' death sent shock waves and radicalized student militants. (Source: ASKI, Archives of Social and Cultural History)

played a crucial role in street politics—if one were to add to the Lambrakides their direct predecessors. One effect of students' growing participation in street politics was the transformation of the popular imagination concerning them. The students, who occupied a privileged category due mainly to their abundant free time, soon became a point of reference in the struggle for a different future. A certain image of youth action in Greek society became widespread, one that would be reinforced and would acquire a more universal character following the coup. *Avgi,* the daily newspaper associated with the EDA, was quick to recognize its potential: by 1965 it had two separate rubrics exclusively dedicated to the Lambrakides.[64] It is no coincidence that those of the later generations looked on these student activists with awe. Humanities student Vera Damofli remembered, "I wanted to go to the university and experience such action" (Damofli, interview). Architecture student Kleopatra Papageorgiou elaborated:

> I had in mind that I would study and that I would definitely enter the university or the polytechnic. In the same way I had had in mind ever since I was little, that when I would become a student I would participate in the student movement.... And therefore when I would be at the university, one of my fields would be science and studies and the other one would be a matter of the Left, you know, and the social movement. (Papageorgiou, interview)

The Lambrakides were praised and feared, to the point that Premier and Minister of Education George Papandreou and others suspected them of being about to stage a revolt—a possibility that became an urban myth later used in the Colonels' own line of argument. In the spring of 1965, Papandreou sent out a circular to all schools with warnings about the Lambrakis Youth's alleged attempts to win pupils over and initiate them into communism, with instructions to punish such incidents with great harshness. Decree 1010, regarding "politicized students," gave schoolmasters the right to expel students involved in "political activities," and Papandreou flirted with the idea of banning the organization altogether for good measure. The demonization of this generation reached such heights that publisher Helen Vlachou argued the Greek Parliament should be shut down in order to "send all the 114 rats back to their basements to play pinball."[65] That a conservative publisher of a high caliber such as Vlachou would make a public argument that entertainment (pinball) was a better alternative to political participation (114) was an unprecedented occurrence, which demonstrated the extent to which the dynamism of the new generation alarmed certain circles. Vlachou went so far as to prophesy a left-wing coup, with the Lambrakides, previously compared to rats in her animalizing vocabulary, now in the forefront hailing the dictators.[66]

This was a generation aware of its distinctiveness. It is no coincidence that the main student paper of the Lambrakis Youth bore the title *Our Generation*. Present-day publisher and former militant Giorgos Karambelias, born in Patras in 1946, juxtaposes the setbacks and defeatist tendency of older generations to this one's fresh approach and will for confrontation:

> There was a new generation coming out, which did not carry the fear of the old people. Oh, the old ones had been in exile, in prison, all

those who instructed us, and they had begun to obey the logic of how to get beaten up less, that was the logic of the Old Left. There was a new generation coming out which wanted to be more aggressive.... We felt that we could go on the offensive, though in reality it only happened after the fall of the dictatorship. (Karambelias, interview)

To say that the new generation wanted to take the offensive in the 1960s is probably an overstatement. It is accurate, however, to say that it rejected the attitude of victimization that had been characteristic of left-wing culture in Greece since the 1940s. Karambelias expresses all the regret of his generation, which regards the coming of the Junta as the end of its growing political and social emancipation. Fondas Ladis, another exponent of this political generation, wrote shortly after the coup: "A whole people camped on the streets. This is where we ate, where we fell in love—we rarely slept. We all together became a lion, we wanted to eat governments, kings, and much more. With the dictatorship the streets fell empty. It looks as if all these things that filled up our eyes were nothing more than a giant newspaper that was suddenly blown off by the wind."[67]

The mid-1960s were regarded by the Left as a rebirth after years of stagnation, a "spring," to quote novelist Stratis Tsirkas's term, that would be violently interrupted by the dictatorship in 1967.[68] The well-known translator and writer Kostas Tachtsis pointed to the limits of the Greek "renaissance," however, stressing the backward aspects of Greece's avant-garde of the mid-1960s compared to the Western ones:

> In the West, to the sound of the music of the Beatles, and under the influence of psychedelic drugs that were sold without restrictions at the time, various liberation movements had erupted: youth movements, feminist, homosexual, black movements; the flower generation was also about to appear, rock would turn into pop, and I had experienced all that, partly as a participant—albeit in my own way—partly as a mere observer.
>
> What did I find upon my return to Greece? The same provincial hell, parochial ideas, and unsolved contradictions that I had left behind some years earlier. Young workmen and students were on the streets demonstrating to the sound of Theodorakis's hymns, to the slogans "114," "bread-education-freedom"; in the tavernas the first generation of the "kamakia" [predatory Greeks courting tourists] were dancing the syrtaki—self-absorbed, unselfconscious—with the tourists looking on. They called this "a spring," they called this a "renaissance."[69]

Shortly before the coup, the universities were once again the theater of protest and violence. When policemen stormed into Salonica University in early April 1967 to disperse a student protest, the press unknowingly predicted a long chain of violations that were about to take place from that point onward, not only on university premises but across the whole country. An article in the daily *Makedonia* reported:

> The university asylum was violated in its entirety yesterday. For the first time in the history of the Aristotelian University, policemen entered its historical building in full uniform, in order to violently chase the students out of it ... with the blessings of the Rectorate. ... Greece, and all the more so Greece of intellect and science, is ridiculed on an international level for the unacceptable tactics of some of its representatives and the crude use of material violence against the student youth. The worst has come to the worst.[70]

An interesting analogy is provided by the Rolling Stones concert in Athens's Leoforos Alexandras Stadium on 17 April 1967, just four days prior to the coup, in front of almost ten thousand young people. When at one point the group's manager threw a bouquet of red roses to the audience, the communist-phobic police interpreted this as a political gesture and interrupted the concert. The event ended up in complete chaos; the lights of the stadium were shut down, Stones members were harassed by the police, and fans were beaten black and blue. Although the Center-Left opposition newspapers criticized the savage beatings of demonstrators during political events, they seem to have been of the opinion that these *"yeyedes"* deserved what they got.[71] A part of the press not only viewed the long-haired boys as entirely unpoliticized, but on the contrary accused them of being "passive," of "never shaving," and of "sleeping in caves."[72] Accordingly, a distinction was made between apolitical *yeyedes* and politicized youth.[73]

This split in the pre-1967 generation continued after the coup took place. The more politicized students inevitably got involved in serious resistance activities, while their apolitical counterparts remained passive, despite the fact that they retained a counterculture style. However, the division would be put in question some years after the imposition of the Junta, in the early 1970s, when a new generation would absorb the characteristics of the apolitical counterculture and couple them harmoniously with a new type of politicization, reinforced by the regime itself. The long-haired, bearded boys and the girls sporting a Joan Baez look would not appear as laughable outsiders but rather as the protagonists of a major social and political battle.

Notes

1. Panourgiá, *Dangerous Citizens*.
2. See in this respect Elefandis, "*Ethnikofrosyni:* The Ideology of Terror and Incrimination."
3. Here it has to be noted that modernization as a term is not connoted solely in a positive way. For a critical reelaboration of the term see the Introduction in Fehrenbach and Poiger, *Transactions, Transgressions, Transformations*.
4. In the 1952 political elections, the EDA received 10.6 percent of the vote without gaining a seat in the parliament due to the majority electoral system, introduced under US pressure. Six years later, the EDA emerged as the main opposition party with 24 percent of the vote, alarming the political system. See Clogg, *Parties and Elections*, 17–55.
5. See Kotzias, *Usurpation of Authority*.
6. Between 1950 and 1965 the country's industrial production increased five times, while in more or less the same years its annual growth rate was over 6 percent. See Karakatsanis, *The Politics of Elite Transformation*, 3.
7. See in this respect Lambropoulou, *Construction Workers*.
8. See Karapostolis, *Consumerist Behavior*.
9. See Komninou, *From the Market to the Spectacle*, 136–37.
10. See Mouzelis, *Modern Greece*, 50. Also see the *Economist*'s analysis, "Swallows Winging South," 31 July 1971.
11. See Passerini, "Youth as a Metaphor for Social Change in Fascist Italy and America in the 1950s," 319. Although Passerini discusses specifically the United States in the 1950s, this development was shared by most postwar European societies.
12. See Antonis Liakos's excellent synopsis of the theoretical and empirical coordinates any study of the student movement requires in "Thoughts on the History of the Student Movement," 330, and Mavris, "University Crisis." ESIE, *Statistical Yearbook for 1968–69*, 5. Besides the two old universities and the Polytechnic in Athens, there were six other independent institutions of higher education in Salonica and Athens. These were the School of Arts, the Geoponiki, the Commerce School (ASOEE), and Panteios School (Political Sciences), all of them in Athens, and an industrial school in each of the two cities.
13. Anderson, *Personality and Stance*, 86.
14. Samatas, "Studying Surveillance in Greece," 183. Panourgiá calls it *certificats de civisme*, *Dangerous Citizens*, 234.
15. Samatas, ibid. The certificate was required even in order to obtain a passport to travel or a driver's license.
16. National Statistical Service of Greece, *Statistical Yearbook for 1968–69*, 5, 29; Liakos, *Appearance of Youth Organizations*, 66.
17. Ciampi, *The Radicalization of Youth*, 73.
18. For the notion of cycles of protest, see Tarrow, *Democracy and Disorder*.
19. Panourgiá, *Dangerous Citizens*, 122.
20. Linardatos, *Civil War to the Junta*; Saint Martin, *Lambrakides*, 45.
21. Hebdige, *Subculture*, 50.

22. The advent of rock and roll in Greece followed the screening in 1956 of the film *Blackboard Jungle*, featuring Bill Halley's mythical hit "Rock around the Clock" (1955), which was welcomed with particular enthusiasm.
23. Ladas, *Speeches*, 9–24.
24. For a comprehensive analysis of the phenomenon of the *tediboides* see Efi Avdela, "Corrupting and Uncontrollable Activities."
25. These films often deal with juvenile delinquency, and the female need for sexual emancipation tends to be presented as immoral or fatal. See Paradeisi, "Depiction of Youth."
26. This term was introduced by French journalists from the Beatles' song "She Loves You," whose refrain was simply, "She loves you / yeah, yeah, yeah." It soon became synonymous with young people who dressed, talked, and behaved in a pop fashion, and in Greece it acquired negative connotations.
27. Papanikolaou, "Shaping the Youth," 6.
28. Liakos, *Appearance of Youth Organizations*, 71.
29. Actor Kostas Voutsas in Giannis Dalianidis's *Teddyboy, My Love*, 1965. See Delveroudi, *Greek Cinema*, 170.
30. Kallivretakis, "Problems of Historicizing the Rock Phenomenon," 170. Alongside Petridis's famous radio program and some pirate stations, the most popular radio station transmitting rock music was AFRS, the station of the US military base outside Athens, which suggests the extent to which the US military presence went hand in hand with cultural transmission.
31. See Kornetis, "The Greek 'New Wave' Music of the 1960s."
32. Katsapis, *Sounds and Echoes*.
33. Interestingly, Lambrakis's funeral turned out to be such a landslide moment that the exiled KKE accused the EDA's leadership of not assessing correctly the "moods of the wide masses" and for overlooking "the opportunities that emerged for the direct overthrow of the government." See "Πολιτική απόφαση" [Political Decision] 5th Plenary Session, October 1963, *KKE. Official Documents*, 299.
34. Foreword to Lendakis, *Neofascist Organizations*.
35. Jeffrey Olick, "Collective Memory," 339, emphasis mine. Karl Mannheim, *Essays on the Sociology of Knowledge*, 291. See also Claudine Attias Donfut, *Sociologie des générations* and the study of Howard Schuman and Jacqueline Scott on the distinct imprints that the same historical events produce in different generations, "Generations and Collective Memories."
36. Saint Martin, *Lambrakides*, 56.
37. Theodorakis, *Lambrakides' Manifesto*, 50.
38. Quoted in Zafeiris, *We, the Travelers*, 9.
39. Giannis Theodorakis, "Πιστοποιητικά κοινωνικών φρονημάτων" ["Certificats du civisme"], *I Genia Mas*, 14 August 1965, 4–5. A year later, Leonidas Kyrkos, one of the EDA's leading members, wrote an article in the same paper in defense of the Lambrakis Youth, whereby he delivered an outspoken attack on the destructive "stupidities of Decemberology [Δεκεμβρολογία]," by which he meant the state-sponsored demonization of the 1944 December events (in which the Greek communists clashed with and were ultimately defeated by the British-backed government forces).

See Kyrkos, "ΔΝΛ: Την προστατεύει το έργο της και τα ιδανικά της" [DNL: Its Service and Its Ideals Are Protecting It], *I Genia Mas,* 10 December 1966, 10. I am grateful to Katerina Lambrinou for pointing both articles out to me.
40. Vassilis Vassilikos, "L'affaire de l'assassinat du deputé grec Lambrakis," *Le Monde,* 28 April 1967.
41. Vernardakis and Mavris, *Parties and Social Coalitions,* 102. Also see Papadogiannis, "Greek Communist Youth and the Politicisation of Leisure," 56.
42. Nikolaidou, "Working Woman."
43. See Arseniou, "The Emergence of a Hybrid Avant-Garde."
44. Aris Marangopoulos, "Children of Marx," 22.
45. As far as student writings are concerned, the journal *Panspoudastiki,* founded in 1956 by a group of left-wing students, was a step forward in terms of increased radicalism and political autonomy, as it promoted the creation of a left-wing student body free from strict party control.
46. Eliou, "Those Whom Reform Forgot," 68.
47. For a detailed analysis of the role of the few women in university politics during this period, see Lendakis, "Αναφορά πάνω στις γυναίκες αγωνίστριες της εποχής" [Report on the Women Fighters of the Time], *Eleftherotypia,* 19, 20, 21, and 23 March 1982.
48. See Alki Zei's semiautobiographical account of a communist woman's itinerary during the occupation and the civil war period, *Achilles' Fiancée.* Also see Hart, *New Voices.*
49. Papathanasiou et al., *Lambrakis Youth in the 1960s,* 341.
50. Saint Martin, *Lambrakides,* 185.
51. Ibid.
52. Katsapis, *Sounds and Echoes,* 307.
53. Papathanasiou et al., *Lambrakis Youth in the 1960s,* 375.
54. Likewise, student attempts to break party monopoly and to acquire an independent voice through the journal *Panspoudastiki* and the National Student Union of Greece were short-lived.
55. I borrow this Gramscian term from Robert Lumley's thorough analysis of the Italian case in the 1960s and 1970s. See *States of Emergency,* 9.
56. See Lendakis, *Neofascist Organizations,* 123, and Katris, *Birth of Neofascism,* 228.
57. Vernardakis and Mavris, *Parties and Social Coalitions,* 239–67; Petros Efthymiou, "Η ηχώ στην Ελλάδα" [The Echo in Greece], in *May '68, 30 Years After,* special section in *To Vima,* 10 May 1998. For the different "temporalities" of the '68 movements, including their designation as "early" or "late" manifestations of the same protest wave, see Kornetis, "Everything Links."
58. Bermeo, "Classification and Consolidation."
59. See Psyroukis, *History of Contemporary Greece;* Livieratos and Karambelias, *July Events '65.*
60. This does not mean, however, that the KKE leadership was oblivious to the potential of such moments.
61. Stergios Katsaros, Εμείς οι γκεβαριστές [We, the Guevarists], quoted in IosPress, *30 Years Che: Tribute to Che Guevara,* no. 4, *Eleftherotypia,* 9 October 1997.
62. Katsaros, *I the Provocateur,* 40.

63. Theodorakis, *Poetry Put into Music*, 143.
64. Γενιά της Δημοκρατίας [Generation of Democracy] and Λαμπράκηδες [Lambrakides]. See Papathanasiou et al., *Lambrakis Youth in the 1960s*, 339.
65. Quoted in Theodorakis, *Lambrakides' Manifesto*, 26.
66. Vlachou, "Επίκαιρα. Ιδέες" [News. Ideas], *Kathimerini*, 26 August 1965.
67. Ladis, *Mikis Theodorakis*.
68. *The Lost Spring* is a semiautobiographical novel about what was the beginning of the end of the gradual recovery of more individual liberties for left-wingers and of the cultural uplift that took place after 1963.
69. Tachtsis, *Terrible Step*, 371. I owe the reference to Papanikolaou, "Singing Poets," 98–99.
70. "Το αστυνομικόν κράτος απέβαλε το προσωπείον" [The Police State Took Off Its Mask], *Makedonia*, 12 April 1967. At the same time, *Makedonia* reported on the violent suppression of a demonstration of building workers in Athens: "Αιματοκύλισε τους οικοδόμους η κυβέρνηση" [The Government Caused Bloodshed among the Building Workers], 13 April 1967.
71. Kallivretakis, "Problems of Historicizing the Rock Phenomenon," 171.
72. Ibid. These were the terms used by Dimitris Psathas, a well-known writer and playwright, in his column in the liberal newspaper *Ta Nea*. Interestingly there were positive reviews of the concert in right-wing papers. See, for example, A. Miliadis, "Οι Ρόλλινγκ Στόουνς κατακτούν την Αθήνα" [Rolling Stones Have Conquered Athens], *Apogevmatini*, 18 April 1967. Also see Katsapis, "Sounds and Echoes," 365–67.
73. For left-wing and in particular Mikis Theodorakis's criticism of the yé-yé culture as "poisonous" and destructive for the nation, see Katsapis, "Sounds and Echoes," 349.

Chapter 2

Phoenix with a Bayonet

Chapter 2 proceeds to analyze some of the elements of the new regime, including its ideology and practices, as well as the institutional changes that it brought about in the universities. This chapter further provides an overview of resistance organizations and groupings, their discourse, and their relationships to one another. Apart from focusing on what was occurring in Greece, a central part of the chapter addresses Greek students abroad, mainly those living and studying in France and Italy, who were both inspired and perplexed by their contact with the '68 revolts. The chapter concludes that it was hard for those students who were the continuation of the Lambrakides and were involved in so-called dynamic action to adapt to the new conditions created by the Junta and to switch to successful forms of defiance, as they had already exhausted their creativity in previous years.

The Colonels' Takeover

The seizure of power by the Colonels in April 1967 was the peak of a series of political irregularities that had characterized Greek public life since at least 1961. The turbulent and chaotic state of affairs and the high probability that George Papandreou's liberal EK would win the elections scheduled for 28 May alarmed certain middle-ranking circles in the armed forces, but it also made it easier for them to declare a state of emergency. The transition of Papandreou Junior, Andreas, from a bourgeois liberal standpoint to a neo-Marxist one had greatly alarmed the Crown, the Right, the armed forces, and the US embassy. The reform currents brought by the EK and the changing dynamics in the country and its policies, both domestic and foreign, had made the Papandreous unwanted figures for the bastions of post–civil war Greece. The deadlock deepened with the 1965 crisis, the Cyprus imbroglio, and the allegations of a left-wing conspiracy codenamed ASPIDA [Officers Save Patria, Ideals, Democracy, Meritocracy] within the armed forces directly implicating Papandreou Junior, which served to aggravate the already unstable climate prior to the scheduled elections. The 1967 putsch matured in this crisis of the post–1949 power structure.

The army in particular underwent a partisan politicization, while closed circles within its ranks, such as IDEA [Sacred Bond of Hellenic Officers], had demonstrated their willingness to directly intervene in politics since the early 1950s. Segments of this group, mostly low-ranking officers, orchestrated the 21 April coup, taking by surprise a group of generals planning to do the same. According to political scientist Ioannis Tzortzis, these officers "acted for their own interests to save the position of the army in the power structure of the country, endangered as they saw it by the balance shift that had occurred in Greek politics from the early 1960s … that questioned the post–Civil War status quo."[1] For a long time preceding the coup, various left-wing politicians and the press had frequently referred to the possibility of imminent intervention by the army and the danger of a dictatorship, as if attempting to exorcise this possibility. Despite these warnings, when the "nation-saving revolution," to borrow the Junta's own term,[2] took place, it became evident that the political parties had made no preparation whatsoever for such an eventuality. Most prominently, EDA, the front of the exiled communists, proved entirely unprepared to respond to the task of coordinating a coherent resistance due to the partially clandestine conditions within which it had to operate; and this despite its being the only body with solid organizational structures.

Figure 2.1. 21 April 1967. The coup d'état has just taken place and tanks are rolling in front of the Parliament. (Photographer: Aristotelis Sarrikostas)

The coup took place after the country was declared to be in a state of siege, putting into action the NATO-inspired military plan "Prometheus," which had been drawn up in order to prevent a possible communist attack from the north. The parliament was disbanded, martial law was declared, and preventive censorship was imposed on the press so that newspapers could only print what they were given from the government news agency, resulting in identical headlines. All the provisions of the 1952 Constitution granting freedom of thought, expression, and the press were suspended. The new regime took control of the machinery of the state and began censoring all mail and indiscriminately tapping telephones.

The authoritarian Junta immediately implemented a near-ubiquitous system of oppression, inhibition, and exclusion in order to ensure law and order. Vice-General Odysseus Angelis, new chief of the army, announced the main articles of the martial law on 27 April 1967. These forbade open-air meetings of more than five people, gatherings in halls other than cinemas and theaters, antinational propaganda (including publication or dissemination of any news likely to disturb public order), and possession of arms or explosives of any sort. All arms had to be handed over to the police within

Figure 2.2. 22 April 1967. The "revolutionary government" is being sworn in by King Constantine II, in the middle—with a stern look indicating disapproval. Second to his right, on the left lower corner, is Colonel Georgios Papadopoulos, the *primus inter pares* of the regime. (Photographer: Aristotelis Sarrikostas)

forty-eight hours, and all hunting licenses were annulled. Equally forbidden was the temporary harboring of persons not normally resident in the area (unless their presence was declared to the police), possession of amateur radio transmitters or other means of communication, and the hoarding of food and other essentials.[3]

The Junta's mechanisms of detention and coercion violently interrupted any political process and were extended with particular harshness to the wider policing of civilian social life. About three thousand left-wingers, stigmatized as "nonpatriotic," were put in prison, and more than eight thousand were sent to concentration camps on remote islands, a practice that had never been fully abandoned after the end of the civil war. Brigadier-General Stylianos Pattakos, a member of the dictators' troika alongside Colonels Georgios Papadopoulos and Nikolaos Makarezos, made the ludicrous comment in June 1967 that "the deportees [were], on the whole, enjoying a very pleasant time, swimming in the sea and sun-bathing, and being well-fed," which contradicted his own remark that "political prisoners are not men—only beasts" only a couple of weeks later.[4] At the same time, the use of systematic torture became standard practice and was mainly carried out by the Special Interrogation Unit of the notorious Military Police (EAT-ESA).

Apart from wide networks of surveillance and the mechanisms of suppression, the Colonels counted on the inability of civil society to react and on the long-time democratic deficit. In many ways, the Junta reproduced the repressive mechanisms that had served the upper classes before the coup, so that the Colonels' regime was the ideological continuation and coherent reproduction of earlier elite political dominance. Most regime figures were of peasant or lower-class origins—a fact that often fuelled the regime's rhetorical hostility toward hard-core capitalists, upper-class circles, and their endeavors and habits. However, no particular measures were taken to reduce the latter's advantages or influence. Still, as political scientist Nancy Bermeo justly notes, the coup was not the result of a military-capitalist-bourgeois coalition and had not emerged to oppose redistribution of funds and a fall in GDP.[5] Therefore, the Colonels' dictatorship should not be considered a "bureaucratic authoritarian" regime, following Guillermo O'Donnell's famous typology.[6]

The Colonels' ideology was an extreme version of the post–civil war ideological superstructure of the Greek state, which was based on fierce anticommunism and a mystical glorification of the "Greek Spirit." In their chauvinistic world view, "Greece of the Hellenic Christians" was exalted as morally, culturally, and socially superior to any other in the Western world. But the nation was undergoing a crisis, due to moral corruption, political feudalism, and communist erosion; the revolution's goal was to lift the patria

Figure 2.3. The regime's symbol: a phoenix emerging from its ashes, with a soldier bearing a fixed bayonet rifle in its base. The phoenix was endlessly reproduced in the public sphere—from coins and schoolbooks to cigarette matches. The caption reads "Long Live 21 April 1967." (Source: ELIA, Greek Literary and Historical Archive)

from its lowest ebb and reinstate it in all its splendor.[7] The Colonels made frequent references to this idea of "national renaissance" and they chose as their symbol the mythical phoenix emerging from its ashes, with the addition of the silhouette of a soldier bearing a fixed bayonet rifle (what journalist Bayard Stockton called "phoenix with a bayonet").[8]

In a speech in late April 1967, and in order to underline the urgency of the matter, Papadopoulos made an analogy between Greece and a patient on her deathbed who needed to be sedated and operated on:

> I spoke of an operation. The time of the patient's recovery as well as the duration of the operation depend on the seriousness of the illness, and at this moment I could not say that I am in a position to know. Also it depends on the capacity of the organism to respond and to reinstate itself in good health.[9]

The rejection of the corrupt "old establishment" was peppered with the promotion of family, country, and religion as a panacea against corruption and decadence. The moral code imposed on education was guided by these principles too, coupled with iron discipline in terms of behavior and outlook. Boys had to maintain a "decent appearance," be clean and well mannered, and have short hair. As for women, they were forbidden to wear miniskirts and had to dress "correctly" and avoid undesirable places.[10] Schoolchildren and their teachers were expected to go to church every Sunday, and all Greeks had to stand at attention each time the national anthem was played.[11]

Passivity, Consensus, Resistance

The imposition of the coup was followed by stagnation. King Constantine II, responsible for the legitimation of the dictators in the first and crucial hours of the coup, staged an aborted countercoup on 13 December 1967 and after its failure went into self-imposed exile in Rome. Political elites, who came to be referred to as the "old political world,"[12] remained on cold terms with each other throughout the dictatorship years due to mutual suspicion, a lack of consensus on how to confront the regime, and opposing visions regarding the country's political future. Shortly after their release from house arrest, the party leaders George Papandreou (leader of the Center Union) and Panagiotis Kanellopoulos (leader of the right-wing ERE and the acting prime minister at the time of the coup) condemned the regime. As Bermeo points out, it was hard to legitimate the regime when Kanellopoulos, the leader of the largest conservative and highly pro-capitalist party in the country, unambiguously opposed the coup.[13] After Papandreou's death in autumn 1968, his heir apparent, Georgios Mavros, adopted the same position of sheer rejection. Soon Mavros and Kanellopoulos would take on the role of defending the accused in the trials of the Junta's arrested opponents. At the same time, Evangelos Averoff, ERE's ex-minister of foreign affairs, followed an idiosyncratic line, trying to "build bridges" with the regime. Constantine Karamanlis, the founder of ERE and premier for eight consecutive years, continued to live in Paris, waiting for the right moment to return to involve himself in the country's political affairs. Finally, Ilias Iliou and Leonidas Kyrkos, EDA's main leaders, were immediately imprisoned and were unable to coordinate any serious action.

To many ordinary people, the coup came as an unexpected, traumatic event. This fact is vividly illustrated by former militant and present-day historian Antonis Liakos in his short autobiographical story "The Missed Date," in which he recalls that the coup meant for him the cancelation of a date with a woman he had planned for 21 April. By underscoring the violent impact of the event on a personal rather than a political level, Liakos challenges the boundaries between the two: "Why was the cancellation of a personal choice not a political matter?" he wonders.[14] In purely political terms, on the other hand, left-wingers had been told by the EDA party leadership that there was nothing to worry about. Zogia Chronaki underlines this point: "Then all of a sudden a dictatorship took place. It took the Left by surprise too, since *Avgi* came out a day before with the seven reasons why a dictatorship would not occur" (Chronaki, interview). That *Avgi*, EDA's main newspaper, discussed whether a coup was possible demonstrates that there was a growing uneasiness about this eventuality, however, even if it was not considered to be imminent.[15]

The issue had been raised many months prior to April 1967 by prominent politicians, including former prime minister George Papandreou. His son Andreas and composer Mikis Theodorakis, however, both expressed their faith that in case of a coup d'état, the Greek people would risk their lives and resist. The commonly repeated statement, "Resistance began on the very first day," does not accurately reflect the marginality of early resistance attempts, however.[16] A significant number of people did indeed loathe the regime, but they did not know how to act. Initially, there was a shared belief that the dictatorship would not last long. The gradual realization that the regime was more resilient than expected instigated a fatalist attitude. Writer Evgenia Fakinou expressed this feeling: "What would happen if it were as resilient [a dictatorship] as that of Franco in Spain? We would spend all our life like that."[17] Franco's regime was a recurrent negative point of reference that indicated the terms in which people tried to foresee the regime's endurance.

Marios Chakkas's short story "The Fish Bowl," about a left-winger who fluctuates between going underground and staying at home, captures the reigning indecision between action and passivity that tormented many left-wingers:

> Unconsciously he started cutting slices from the corner of the bread while at the same time optimistic thoughts came to his head: "Bah, this situation won't last long. Soon they'll fall." ... "How are they going to fall," he heard a voice inside him [ask], "on their own like ripe fruit or by shaking the tree hard?" "People will oust them," he corrected, a bit embittered, because it was certain that he considered himself one of these people and so he did not leave himself out of it.

After much going back and forth, the symbolic end to Chakkas's story has its protagonist deciding to return home to feed his fish in its bowl, alluding to people's reluctance to give up the routine of their everyday lives in order to resist the regime.[18]

In 1968, a year after the imposition of the dictatorship, the actress Melina Mercouri said in an interview in London, "If I had a bell I would ring it to wake up the whole country,"[19] pointing to the need to raise consciousness among the Greeks. Most Greeks remained frightened and, with the exception of some organized circles, passive. One explanation for the lack of reaction is that resistance organizations "fail[ed] to provide a convincing alternative proposition and relevant ways of action."[20] At the same time, pre-dictatorship political forces had lost their credibility precisely because they had failed to prevent the coup. Another deterrent seems to have been the consequences, as well as the memories, of the civil war and people's fear of a recurrence. All these explanations suggest, however, that resistance is a natural reaction in times of crisis and that in cases of lasting oppression something must block people's natural impulse to resist. The fact is that ordinary family men and women do not easily override fear or put their lives at risk for a problem that they do not even believe they can redress. Michalis Sabatakakis, a high school student when the coup took place, recalls the paralyzing effect of fear. His narrative strategy employs a typical interpretative model based on the opposition of "in those days" to "now":[21]

> What the ones who haven't experienced this cannot feel, namely, those of a certain age and younger, is the brutal political climate of the dictatorship. That is, there are no parties, there is no Parliament. It is the feeling that every single thing is heavily policed. It is the fear. The basic thing is fear. Because the man, you know, who until '67

was going out to the streets with great ease in order to demonstrate during the July events, is [now] scared. (Sabatakakis, interview)

Rather than searching to figure out how to lead a clandestine existence, the majority of people who were against the regime exercised a sort of "passive resistance," as it was popularly described at the time. They did so not through civil disobedience, despite abortive attempts to boycott or isolate the regime, but mainly through the circulation of caustic jokes about the Colonels. These jokes castigated the absurdity of the appearance and discourse of Papadopoulos and Pattakos, two of the regime's major figures. Similar to other authoritarian contexts, wit and laughter were an outlet for people to express their discontent and provided a temporary release from the repressive social norms dictated by everyday life in an authoritarian regime.[22] As Luisa Passerini has argued, "laughter is a principal way of asserting subjectivity,"[23] and this is reinforced in an overtly repressive context. As journalist and politician Giannis Dimaras notes, "Jokes were the hidden weapons of subjugated people from '67 to '74," the famous "weapons of the weak."[24] Dimaras's emotional conclusion that when people "plunged their arrows in the poison of satire the tanks started to tremble" is a gross exaggeration, however.[25] In later days, and particularly in the wake of the Polytechnic uprising, Mikis Theodorakis, a symbolic figure of antiregime activity, seemed very pleased with the fact that "the bitter days of passive resistance are over for good."[26]

Greek passivity must not be understood as wholesale support for the regime, however. The passive stance of a large part of the population, former activist and movement historian Olympios Dafermos notes, "was never transformed to a consensus and even less so to active support."[27] Political scientist Nancy Bermeo argues that the regime did not find legitimization, partly because of the nature of Greek political institutions and political culture. The army was not a united whole, and politicians belonging to rival parties agreed to cooperate, a development that Bermeo attributes to the country's long parliamentary tradition. Greece's democratic political culture, which encompassed liberal nineteenth-century constitutions and the early adoption of universal male suffrage, ensured the rejection of authoritarianism, she claims.[28]

On the other hand, evidence suggests that several old sections and new subgroups of Greek society took a passive stance because they were tolerant, if not supportive, of the Colonels' regime. Social isolation was not as total as is often described, and one can speculate that the lower classes' apathy was not just the result of fear of the violence of the military regime.[29] Analysts maintain that rising welfare also partially accounts for the people's passivity. The regime benefited from a relatively good economic performance at least up to 1972, despite inflation and foreign indebtedness.[30] In the words of a foreign journalist, "Greece, the country that for years had sent its starving unemployed abroad to find jobs, suddenly experienced a labor shortage. The number of private autos and telephones more than doubled, as did the consumption of electricity."[31]

In addition, the Junta cancelled farmers' debts, paid higher salaries to civil servants, issued more permits for building construction, and offered greater allowances and loans to the average petit-bourgeois Greek. The Colonels drew considerable support in rural areas, not least because of their efforts to build infrastructure, including roads and the introduction of electricity. Apart from that, the regime's close cooperation, even under unfavorable terms, with foreign multinational companies, including Esso Pappas and Aristotle Onassis's enterprises, seemed to many a step toward modernization. The Colonels privileged the tourism sector, boosting the national GDP and profiting from the reigning "peace and quiet" despite the persistent attempts of antiregime organizations in Greece and abroad to boycott it.

The lack of credibility that the democracy suffered in the years following 1965 as the country was experiencing a serious crisis of parliamentarianism is yet another reason that accounts for popular consensus. A large part of the population welcomed an extraconstitutional solution, because they had experienced permanent crisis, the disintegration of the political system, the continuous alternation of short-lived governments, and widespread tension and fanaticism. In the end, it seemed to many that accountability and public order had replaced political fanfare and popular unrest, and for the traditional voters of the Right, the difference initially did not seem that great. Helen Vlachou, one of the few publishers to suspend publishing activity altogether throughout the dictatorship, attributed the pervasive indifference to the Junta to the fact that most people were profoundly unhappy with the pre-1967 state of affairs and were therefore willing to give the new regime a chance: "People in the streets showed no interest and no concern about the outcome of things. In reality this stoic acceptance of a situation was no one's victory but a defeat of all politicians of all colors, since the previous one seems to not have satisfied most of them. 'Let them try' was the slogan that reigned."[32]

According to conservative economist George Pesmazoglou, "The greater part of the people initially tolerated the coup ... because they were afraid that communism or anarchy would prevail."[33] Historian Nicholas Doumanis argues that far from proving a fascist inclination in the Greek national character, this was rather an indication that people wanted a strong government that could affirm its proper public responsibility by showing the real capacity to implement its decisions.[34] For the American anthropologist Michael Herzfeld, however, it was "downright embarrassing to be told by

Greeks [that they] need[ed] a strong government and therefore deserved the junta." Such comments seemed to him to be part of the dominant ideology in the period of the Colonels.[35] A military officer at the time replied to one person's affirmation that the Junta did not enjoy any form of support from the Greek people: "I don't agree. If the Greek people had spit on us we would have been drowned in their saliva. They don't do it, though."[36] So it may be said that apart from generating genuine discontent, the regime also enjoyed considerable consensus among people who saw authoritarianism's firm grip as a necessary political response to endemic social problems.

There were some segments of the Greek populace that did make systematic attempts to resist. After the initial shock, the few left-wing ringleaders still at large made efforts to create clandestine nuclei of action. Over thirty official groups started operating, thus keeping the antiregime activities largely fragmented. Resistance never gained much momentum. The groups' numbers remained small, and they failed to establish links with the people. In short, they were not the products of the new dynamics created by the establishment of the Junta but rather, to borrow the analysis of sociologist and former activist Gerasimos Notaras, "the continuation of the past," and "thus … obeyed its logic."[37] In general, resistance in the form of minor clandestine actions had no strategic aim other than that of demonstrating reaction against the regime.

The three major operating organizations were Democratic Defense (DA), the Pan-Hellenic Antidictatorship Front (PAM), and the Pan-Hellenic Resistance Movement (PAK). PAM, a direct derivation of EDA and the Communist Party, was the quickest in printing brochures and a journal—*Machitis* [Fighter]—containing information on resistance activities. Its members engaged in ongoing moral debates on the ethics of violence and whether the group should turn to more radical and "visible" acts of resistance. It utilized such tactics on a limited level but abandoned them after Antonis Brillakis, PAM's leader, was accused of personally causing the death of a passer-by in Athens who was killed by an exploding bomb during the first months of the Junta. DA, on the other hand, was clearly oriented toward "dynamic" action, though the social profile of its members might have suggested otherwise. It was an organization mainly composed of middle-aged professors, doctors, and lawyers without a clear left-wing orientation. Its repertoire was confined to placing bombs, with great attention given to avoiding victims.[38] Lastly, PAK, founded in March 1968 by the recently released Andreas Papandreou, professed revolutionary action, hinting at a struggle not only against the Junta but for general social change, including liberation of the Greek nation from U.S. imperialism.[39] Papandreou's son Nikos points out, "It was natural that Andreas Papandreou would place his attempt … within the general context of this period," namely, "the paradigm of the liberation movements from Cuba to the Congo and the resistance of the people of Vietnam against the huge power of the United States," which explains the use of the word "liberation."[40] In other words, PAK's rhetoric was influenced by third-worldism, and in particular by Latin American city guerrilla theories.[41]

Attempts to create a unified or at least a coordinated body of resistance out of the three organizations failed miserably despite constant appeals to the need for unity among the antidictatorial forces during the first years of the coup. The very nature of the resistance methods resulted in additional division and fragmentation within the organizations.[42] Later years brought a whole range of negotiation strategies and an interplay with the regime that further duplicated the initial division between active and passive resistance. What is more, the politicization of everyday practices and the emergence of new collectivities with their own contestatory strategies created spaces of political agility that eventually transcended the dichotomy between hard-core resistance and passive acceptance.

Tidying Up the University

On 30 April 1967, the major pro-regime newspaper with the almost ironic title *Eleftheros Kosmos* [Free World] published the news that the regime was dismantling EDA, the Lambrakis Youth, and EREN and EDIN, the youth organizations of the ERE and the Center Union. A week later, the same paper quoted the order of the chief of the general staff, Vice-General Odysseus Angelis, to dismantle 279 more societies and clubs, constituting a strong blow against the right to build societies and preserve networks and spaces of sociability. The new regime quickly dismantled the whole structure of student representation and participation at higher institutions. Student elections were banned, the archives of the old student unions were confiscated, and new student councils were directly appointed by the government, with their constitutional charters modified in order to ensure compliance with the new order.[43] Konstantinos Kalambokias, the Junta's first education minister, explained: "Instead of devoting themselves to education, students have become tools of the parties through their youth organizations."[44]

Georgios Georgalas, the Junta's main ideologist and a former avowed communist, described the "detoxification" of the new generation, which had previously been exploited by communism and party politics, as one of the coup's main aims.[45] According to a newsreel of the time, "Young people, restless and directionless, were led to chaos." In an attempt to cure this malady, all pre-1967 student ringleaders were either imprisoned or exiled. By 1970,

140 students had been tried by martial courts and expelled from university.[46] Zogia Chronaki remembers this as a very bleak period: "[There was] a shutting down. Half of my friends were underground and the other half imprisoned" (Chronaki, interview). New and remaining students were immersed in an entirely claustrophobic environment. Extensive surveillance inside and outside the university was guaranteed by the widespread use of undercover "student" agents of the regime. Suspicion among students grew to the point that any new acquaintance was considered to be a trap. In order to control the universities and the acting teaching body more effectively, the authorities established mechanisms of persecution, repression, and reward. No act of dissent escaped unrecorded, unregistered, or unpunished. A British journalist reported at the time: "I heard this week of a young student … who was sentenced to two years for 'insulting the police.' His crime consisted of asking a girl, privately, why she hung around with informers."[47]

In due course, the Junta issued several decrees defining the "rights and obligations" of students, the most serious of which was to be 93/1969, which excluded any right of free expression. Furthermore, higher institutions lost their independent character altogether.[48] The Junta appointed retired generals as "governmental commissioners" in the universities, in higher positions in the central administration of the Ministry of Education, and in educational institutions, putting them in charge of the "appropriate functioning" of educational units.[49]

Moreover, universities soon became heralds and propagators of the dominant ideology as the Junta created a legal arsenal to control professors. The organization of political control within the universities included dramatic modifications of the composition of the academic staff.[50] Dimitris Fatouros, a professor of architecture at the University of Salonica at the time, dubbed by US reports a "liberal who favors avant-garde teaching,"[51] wrote later on:

> Professors were not allowed to leave the country, their offices were bugged, their meetings observed, the whole administrative system was modified, in order to allow the military authorities to choose and decide for the dean and all university authorities. It arbitrarily change[d] the schedules of lessons and the lessons themselves. It impose[d] appointments of assistants, it appoint[ed] relatives of the personnel of secret security agencies. The decision of each school, each university, about the most minor of topics depend[ed] on the central administration of the Ministry of Education in Athens.[52]

The majority of the remaining professors did not oppose the implementation of illiberal and unconstitutional laws, however, and in fact a good number of them took their own measures to curtail potential student initiatives.[53] Exemplifying the regime's philosophy and discourse for higher education is the speech of the *primus inter pares* of the Junta, Colonel Papadopoulos, at the University in Salonica: "The Greek students have to think that to have a letter sent by the principal to their village to be read by the priest from the pulpit would be a much graver penalty for them than to be expelled from university."[54] The professors enthusiastically applauded Papadopoulos's oration. Although some may have done so out of conviction, Alexander Solzhenitsyn's question, "What sort of an education can you get from a professor who's scared stiff of losing his job?"[55] seems appropriate.

It is noteworthy that the Colonels abolished the Educational Reform and its main mouthpiece, the Educational Institute, and reintroduced the neoclassical purist language *katharevousa* as the official lingo of state and university. They also reintroduced the certificate of social convictions, not as a prerequisite for entering university but as a necessary condition for receiving a scholarship.[56] Before a student could receive a certificate, the minister of public order had to guarantee to the university authorities that he/she was inspired by "national ideals." When certificates were not issued, the parents' political stance was often a major reason. One typical report reads that a certain student was "influenced ideologically by the communist beliefs of his father."[57] On the opposite side of the spectrum, 10 percent of Greek students entered university on the army's recommendation, and some entered without having to take exams on the grounds of their exemplary "nation-loving character" and "moral education."[58]

The strategy that the Greek dictators implemented in the university is characteristic of the populist character of the regime as a whole. Alongside an increase in wages, tax reductions, and the canceling of debts, the number of teaching positions for new professors holding "healthy social values" increased, and student grants were doubled. Books were offered at no cost.[59] In this spirit, one can read propagandistic messages claiming "limitless opportunities to study" in the newspapers of the time.[60] In addition, the inauguration of the University of Patras, the construction of the Athens campus, and the project of building a new university in Crete were placed in the context of the regime's efforts to build up necessary infrastructure for education.

The shock that followed the abrupt change in the country and in university life after 21 April 1967 left many shattered, but most students were indifferent. Even those who were most politically conscious were uncertain how to react. The majority of students felt disoriented. Their fear, confusion, and displacement, both in temporal and in spatial terms, is rendered powerfully by Rena Theologidou, a humanities student in Salonica at the time and present-day journalist:

> The picture that I see within the Humanities Faculty ... is [that] ... we have realized nothing, that is we don't know where we are, in which epoch, in which country. Kids from the countryside mainly, but also the kids from Salonica, are either a small category of bourgeois families, rich and maybe right-wing, and a very small minority of kids who come from left-wing families and look, they are scared; the families are scared, everybody is scared. (Theologidou, interview)

Another female student in Salonica admitted that "we were bowing down our heads," trying to remember the state of mind that led them to this point: "We were not indifferent, but scared. We were worn down. I don't know how we were, what we were thinking of" (*Georgia, interview).

In *Youths of Sidon* (1970), the left-wing poet Manolis Anagnostakis points the finger at the young and their passive stance. Anagnostakis evokes in his title the decadent youths of Greek poet Constantine Cavafy's universe ("The Youths of Sidon, 400 AD"). Just like Cavafy, he accuses the younger generation of historical amnesia and vain radicalism, and he indirectly hints that dictatorship means nothing to them. The poem's conclusion is a bitter acceptance that the older generation was running out of energy, invalidated by circumstances and unable to be a source of inspiration for the younger generation, who supposedly looked at them with hidden contempt:

> Fresh young girls—stout-bodied lads
> All passion and love for life and action.
> And your songs too, good, with meaning and substance
> So very human, so moving,
> About infants that die in other continents
> About heroes killed in former times,
> About revolutionaries, Black, Green and Yellow ones,
> About Man's grief in his overall suffering.
> It's especially to your credit that you involve yourselves
> In the issues and struggles of our age
> You directly and actively make your presence felt—in view of which
> I think you more than deserve
> In twos, in threes, to play, to fall in love,
> And unwind, for sure pal, after such exertion.
> (They've aged us prematurely Yorgos, do you realise?)[61]

Anagnostakis was a prominent exponent of the so-called forties generation and the so-called poetry of defeat. Himself a communist combatant in the civil strife, he uses passivity as a rhetorical feature, in contrast to the epic and heroic model of the Resistance, the civil war, and even the Lambrakides. Anagnostakis also makes a bitter commentary on the internationalism of this generation, ironically remarking on the solidarity songs of the younger generation, whom he understands and to whom he condescends. His poem also expresses a generational anxiety of the old intellectuals concerning the newcomers.[62]

In fact, "passivity" became a discursive element in the rhetorical canon of the Left's supporters that described their feeling of defeat. Giorgos Karambelias, a member of the proto-Maoist group PPSP, stressed the feeling of frustration resulting from the fact that none of the predictatorship political entities managed to undertake initiatives to resist the Junta: "The tragic thing was that there was no other organization, since Anagennisi collapsed, PPSP didn't do a thing, EDA did nothing whatsoever as Rigas and PAM started being created after the winter of '67 to '68. In the beginning everything collapsed, everyone got caught, and so on; few people managed to survive" (Karambelias, interview).

Despite the reigning atmosphere of defeat and fear, as well as the impossibility of mobility in the universities, a small number of students embarked on desperate and nonsystematic attempts to take clandestine action through the few resistance organizations that remained. Secrecy limited the membership of these groups: students without a political background had little chance of making contact with them, since approaching them was extremely dangerous. As was the case in Spain at the time, in Greece comparatively privileged channels of contact with politics reinforced the peculiarity of radical students and their isolation within the general student population.[63]

A few militant students attempted to operate in small, tight cells called Democratic Committees of Resistance (DEA), part of the Fourth International, the main core of which was Trotskyist.[64] According to one of their manifestos, the DEA were created in reaction to the helplessness of parties and other organized entities. They were committed to having no leaders and to the "great advantage" that each member knew only what was necessary so that the organization would be protected in case of interrogation.[65] Following a pattern of political participation connected to a certain left-wing ethos, the imposition of the dictatorship led to a limited number of women students joining clandestine organizations. Christina Vervenioti, along with her sister, became part of this resistance group. She recalled:

> We were working day and night, we were working, printing, distributing, printing, distributing, this was one part of the organization that was under our control, we were printing the paper and the

leaflets and all that. There was another part which probably had, as was probably proved, some connection with bombs, to plant bombs and that sort of thing. We were doing this until we got caught. They arrested us very quickly. They took us in on 3 September 1967; we had worked in April, May, June; as little as that. (Vervenioti, interview)

Vervenioti's final phrase, "as little as that," expresses her regret that she, like the majority of people involved in clandestine action, did not manage to stay undercover for long. Most managed only a few weeks of action followed by many years in prison. Her careful formulation concerning the group's use of violence reflects the divisions of the time, but also the cautiousness of ex-militants when they talk about their experiences in the present day.

In February 1968, almost a year after the coup occurred, moderates who expressed criticism of the official line were expelled from the Central Committee during the Twelfth Plenary Session of the exiled Greek Communist Party in Budapest. They, in turn, created the "Interior" faction, which supposedly had closer ties and connections to the actual situation in Greece.[66] This move came as a shock. Not only had the communist leadership not managed to put forward a precise project of resistance, it had suffered a dramatic schism at a time when unity was vital for keeping a left-wing front against the regime alive. The lack of good information about the causes of this division reinforced the uncertainty already present in Greece. The disoriented communists in Greece soon felt compelled to choose between the two lines.

'68 as a Point of Reference

Until 1967, the social agitation in Greece, including the students' and workers' movement, had developed in parallel with the 1960s protests in industrialized countries, including the United States, the Federal Republic of Germany, and France. The fact that Western countries were starting to experience a crisis of parliamentarianism at the same time that Greece's "limb" had been placed in a "plaster cast" (according to dictator Papadopoulos's favorite metaphor) was a factor that highlighted the disparities between subsequent events in Greece and abroad. As the "world was burning," with the great uprisings in Western Europe, the Prague Spring, and the US antiwar movement at its height, Greek trade unionism on all levels was forcibly silenced by the violent Greek Junta, which was reintroducing the basic conservative values of "patria, religion, family." Still, news of what was happening abroad traveled to Greece, sometimes exaggerated and sometimes understated. The

Figure 2.4. Propaganda sign of the regime reading "Always walk to the Right, 21 April Avenue," demonstrating its extreme communistophobia. (Source: ELIA, Greek Literary and Historical Archive)

regime chose to demonstrate the peace and quiet reigning in Greece by disseminating distorted accounts of events occurring elsewhere. Propaganda through the press was thus a major part of the Colonel's reeducation process: a deliberate, systematic attempt to shape perceptions, manipulate cognitions, and direct people's behavior away from what was deemed to be antinational and anti-Greek.

The Junta's response to the counterculture also highlighted the differences between Greece and other Western nations. At the same time that the Summer of Love and the Monterey Pop Festival were marking the apogee of the American hippie scene, the directives of the Colonels' Ministry of the Interior instructed that "Beatles and beatniks, the products of 'teddy-boyism,' have no place in Greece."[67] According to the notorious secretary general of the Ministry of Public Order, Ioannis Ladas, these tendencies were just "pretend[ing] to have a social content": "The unwashed long-haired hippie [culture] provided a refuge for the useless and the lazy.... Watch the rotten foreign youth, who has sunk in the mud of drugs, of pansexualism, decadence and degeneration, wander around in the streets of the big cities without dreams, without ideals, without hopes, without a future."[68] Similarly, Georgios Georgalas, the main theoretician of the regime, published a book called *The Crisis of Consumerist Society* where he diagnosed the West as currently suffering from materialism, nihilism, sadness, and despair.[69]

In spring 1968, the rector of the University of Salonica, in his address to the assembly of the students, juxtaposed the international student unrest with the tranquility reigning in Greek institutions:

> The European youth is suffering, nowadays, from a moral and mental disease, which has grown so much, as to tear down values, tradi-

tions, and habits.... Fortunately, these signs have not come to our country. Our youth is healthy.... Of course there are some students who are miserably trying to imitate foreign models, disregarding the breadth of splendid ideals of the Hellenic civilization. Even so, they are not outrageous "yé-yés" like those abroad who talk nonsense and keep shouting, who put metal sticks in their boots, razorblades in their clothes, take drugs, and carry out robberies.

He added:

You must have been informed by the newspapers about the wave of violence and the turbulence that took place recently in several European universities, including the burning of institutional buildings and other antiacademic activities which were committed by your colleagues abroad. Those students have been "used" by others in whose interest it is to create unrest.... You, on the contrary, should be grateful because thanks to the national government and the prevailing order you can focus on your studies without being distracted by anything.[70]

As is often the case, this use of foreign patterns of youthful delinquency and of 1968 as a negative point of reference often backfired. Instead of causing a "moral panic," to use Stan Cohen's famous term,[71] the message that the authorities actually transmitted was that there was something happening abroad that was worth mentioning and that was contrary to the value system established by the Junta itself. In one interesting example, the paper *Ta Nea,* of centrist leanings but highly distorted by censorship, made an extensive anonymous report in which it compared pictures taken from the unprecedented student strikes and the clashes with police and protesters in May 1968 in Paris to photos of the events of July 1965 in Athens. The report argued that a similar anarchist attack ravaged both cities and put the existing social order in grave danger. According to the commentary:

The events repeat themselves. The goals are the same. The means are identical. It is difficult to discern which photos depict the deeds of the Greek communists and which ones those of the French. It is, however, easy to establish that Greece, on the one hand, was definitively freed after the 21st of April from the same danger that has reigned today in France. These parallel pictures demonstrate two parallel mortal dangers. One of them has been avoided. We wish that the other one be prevented too.[72]

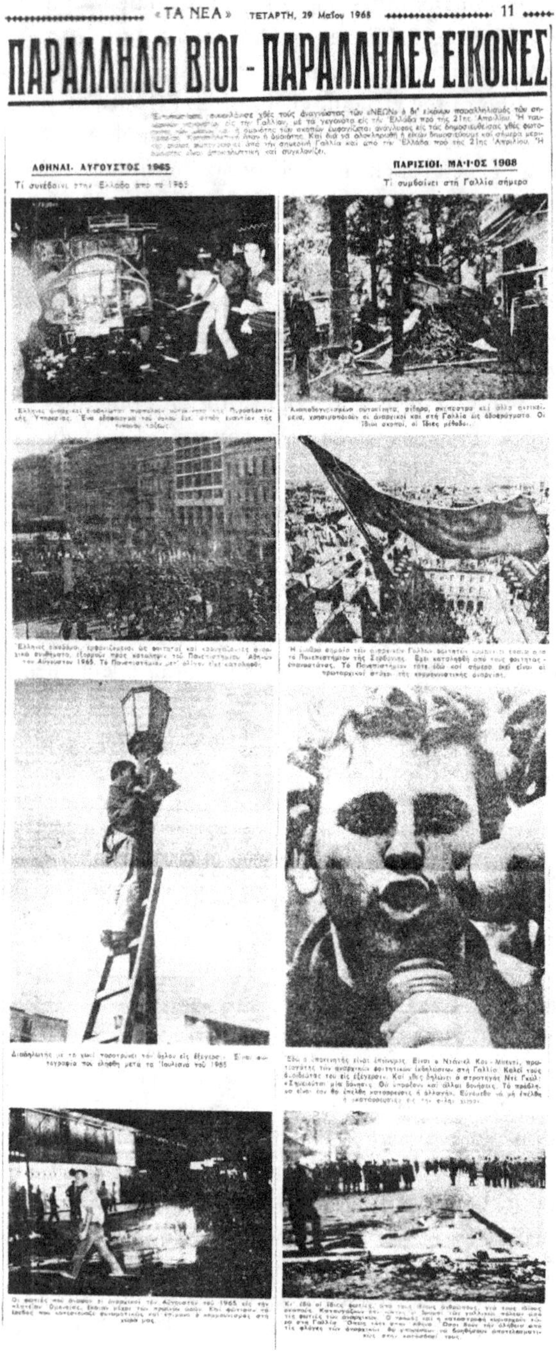

«ΤΑ ΝΕΑ» ΤΕΤΑΡΤΗ, 29 Μαΐου 1968 11

ΠΑΡΑΛΛΗΛΟΙ ΒΙΟΙ - ΠΑΡΑΛΛΗΛΕΣ ΕΙΚΟΝΕΣ

ΑΘΗΝΑΙ. ΑΥΓΟΥΣΤΟΣ 1965

Τί συνέβαινε στην Ελλάδα από το 1965

ΠΑΡΙΣΙΟΙ. ΜΑΪΟΣ 1968

Τί συμβαίνει στη Γαλλία σήμερα

Figure 2.5. "Parallel Lives, Parallel Images." Caption of the centrist newspaper *Ta Nea* comparing the events of May 1968 in France to the events of July 1965 in Greece on the basis of "moral panic," 29 May 1968. Notice the images of the occupied Sorbonne and of Daniel Cohn Bendit in the right column. (Source: *Ta Nea* newspaper, Lambrakis Press Group)

There followed pictures from the July events of fires, ravaged street signs, barricades, and buses with broken windows. At the same time, the French May events were presented as an ensemble of overthrown cars and ruined pavements. It is interesting how the two narratives were constructed and the way in which the images were juxtaposed: two parallel columns, one on the July events on the left and one on May '68 on the right, focused on the chaos, havoc, and destruction induced by the "anarchists" respectively. The captions beneath each one of the photographs used words such as "mob" and "revolt" and the fact that the rebels used the "same objectives, same methods." Jean-Luc Godard and Jean-Pierre Gorin's conclusion that photographs often "talk through the mouth of the text written beneath [them]" and that therefore words often override the visual evidence, is particularly pertinent here.[73] Both pictures and text tried almost obsessively to show the common goals, the same tactics, and the identical ideologies behind the "extremists," trying to capitalize on the contemporaneous French chaos and disregarding the largely different political contexts and the asynchronic nature of the events. The evident conclusion drawn was that the Greeks should feel relieved about the social order brought about by the revolution of 21 April.

The abundance of information that one can find in the journals of the time was coupled with that of the foreign press, which circulated without restrictions in the urban centers and was therefore available to those fluent in foreign languages. When Agis Tsaras, an engineering student and a Maoist, argues that nothing was written in the papers, then, he merely reproduces a topos: "We learned about May from listening to people who had been there, from the radio or ... Nothing was ever published by the newspapers" (Tsaras, interview). The fact that Tsaras's mistake concerning this matter is a recurrent one in most life stories has to do with the actors' state of mind at the time, with their relation to subsequent historical developments, and with the dynamic processes of memory and imagination. Panos Theodoridis, an architecture student and co-publisher of the avant-garde literary journal *Tram*, paints a different picture:

> What had happened to us toward late '67, early '68, was a transformation. In the meantime all the messages from the people of Czechoslovakia were coming to us from the riots, the Prague Spring, all the stories about what was going on in Germany with Rudie Dutschke, what was going on with May '68 in France, and certainly by watching photos, because, I remind you, there was no television, there were only some magazines from which we gathered some information. Oh, and some letters from friends who were already abroad. And at this point we started to throw away our jackets,

to throw away our suits, we started avoiding the clubs ... and we reached the point that we put on a greatcoat, hobnailed boots, we remembered that we had to have a shower once a month ... and to start growing our hair as long as it gets.[74]

The meaning conveyed is that media manipulation was not total and that news of the insurrections abroad was not entirely silenced. Instead, the processes of information gathering were much more dynamic despite the overtly repressive context.

In a way, however, the 1968 rebellions called many of the Greek students' primary preoccupations into question: their consumerism, material goods, the myth of the affluent lifestyle, and the guarantee of a technocratic professional career. As Triantafyllos Mitafidis, a militant Greek Trotskyist student of this generation, points out, "We did not grow up as the children of Coca-Cola or Marx and of the critique that the universities produce technocratic experts. For us this was the demand. The things about the 'affluent society' and 'consumer society,' these were unknown to us" (Mitafidis, interview). Mitafidis, the president of the humanities student committee in Salonica in 1966 and currently a teacher and trade unionist, makes a double reference to both John Galbraith's bestseller of the time, *The Affluent Society*, and a key phrase taken from Jean-Luc Godard's film *Masculin Féminin* (1966).[75] "The children of Marx and Coca-Cola" is a recurrent theme in the self-representation of this generation. For instance, the critic Aris Marangopoulos said: "This phrase corresponded to the French May but to us over here it seemed out of place, unfamiliar, even insulting. ... Even if some of us were Marx's children, we definitely did not understand the allusion about this 'unholy' marriage with the American brand."[76] The repetition that a specific generation did not belong to a mass cultural trend raises doubts as to whether this strict negation constitutes an affirmation in Freudian terms—something that can be observed in the life-stories of the generation of Spanish activists of about the same time.[77] Historian Antonis Liakos, in contrast, who used to be in the same clandestine organization with Mitafidis, maintains that his generation "eagerly identified [itself] as the 'Children of Marx and Coca-Cola.'"[78] Though it is true that in Greece there was no real affection for the United States and capitalist culture, there was an indirect flirtation with many of its by-products, such as music, clothing, and cinema, and most Greek students at the time were attracted to material culture.

Coca-Cola—this powerful symbol of US capitalism and "Americanization" in the post-WWII era—arrived as a product in Greece as late as in 1969, that is, during the Junta. Panos Theodoridis gives an interesting account of the exultation that he and his friends felt when they first came in contact with it some years earlier in London: "In 1965, to photograph yourself with a Coca-Cola bottle was quite a big thing ..., because these little products, Coca-Cola, or a pair of white fabric shoes meant for us something more than a cult item, they were for us part of a uniform, which we 'digged' very much."[79] Tasos Darveris, a student militant who was arrested for underground activities and imprisoned in the early years of the Junta, makes an interesting, albeit ironic, association between freedom and consumerism. He describes his memory of being transferred from one jail to another, the most striking sights being a woman and a Coca-Cola advertisement: "A young woman was coming down a muddy earth-road ... : the most beautiful image of their life! And on the pound the advertisement of Coca Cola, 'Coca Cola: Lust for life, LUST FOR LIFE!'"[80] "Coca-Colonization" and the Greek dictatorship went hand-in-hand.

The sort of pop politics that appeared in Western Europe did not make their way to Greece, however, not least because of the political situation. Accordingly, the students of this generation did not have a chance to absorb the paradigm offered by international events, such as the protest movements and their countercultural features. Mitafidis remarked: "Of course the movements of the '60s and so on, Che Guevara and so forth, we missed them all, this is very important.... We grew up in such conditions that we were deprived of all this" (Mitafidis, interview). In a similar tone, the music critic Giorgos Notaras notes: "From '67 to '69 there was hullabaloo out there. With Woodstock, May '68, long hair, peace movements, *we missed these things.*"[81] Although these statements do not seem to convey the complete picture, at least concerning rock music and new modes of behavior, they do express these individuals' genuine regret to have missed the evolution of their counterparts abroad.

This generation of students experienced the toughest years of the Junta's austerity and restrictions (1967–71), with martial law and preventive censorship in full operation. A large number of them, already on file with the police as politicized individuals, were tried on the basis of the Anti-Espionage Law 375 of 1936 and imprisoned immediately after the coup. Therefore, those belonging to this generation tend to represent the early period of the Dictatorship as the protraction of the civil war and the repression that followed. Overall, student organizations mirrored the disarray of the political parties themselves. According to theorist Giannis Papatheodorou, the dictatorship burdened this generation by calling off its revolutionary youth.[82] Its imposition clearly marked a traumatic moment, which acted as a "generational" or "unifying" event. Those who were already students when the coup took place or who entered university in the first few years were inevitably conditioned by the past, as most of them had already participated in the events of the early 1960s and experienced continuity in discourse and action. It was hard for those students to adapt to the new conditions created by the Junta and to switch to successful forms of defiance, as they had already exhausted their creativity in previous years. The Lambrakides were dispersed and did not leave any considerable organizational legacy, despite their excellent networks.

A good number of students went abroad immediately after the coup took place. As a result, a significant portion of the antidictatorial movement built its headquarters overseas, connecting with Greeks who already resided outside the country. This included some of the most radical organizations, and it was often from there that activities in Greece were coordinated. In fact, the Hellenic Student Societies in France, Italy, and West Germany considered themselves to be an integral part of the Greek student movement. Most of these students were both inspired and perplexed by their contact with the '68 revolts.

Life Is Elsewhere: Greek Students Abroad

"The First Square Meters of Free Greek Soil"

The laboratory par excellence of revolutionary aspirations was Paris, the "Mecca of the Revolution."[83] Tasos Darveris's description in his roman à clef *A Night's Story* reflects the Marx and Coca-Cola generation as he describes the city as an "ideological supermarket" where one could buy "theories for all tastes and measures, solutions for all problems of the revolutionary movement, people who are ready to pick out of their pockets this or that type of revolution, wrapped up in the ideological paper of your choice." Darveris's account further presents Paris as a major place for the formation of radical intellectual elites, who embraced radicalism as a political habitus alongside their higher studies: "Student Cafés, where one imagines that Marx, Lenin, Trotsky, and Che are walking around, next to Tupamaros, Vietcong, and Palestinian commandos. If someone were to judge just from the Latin Quarter, one would conclude that all those haunted, hungry, and barefoot revolutionaries had at least one doctorate from the Sorbonne."[84]

Paris had long been established as a destination for Greek students wanting to pursue postgraduate studies. On the eve of the outbreak of the civil war in late 1945, thanks to a series of scholarships provided by the French Ministry of Education in connection with the Institut Français of Athens, the legendary ship *Mataroa* brought some of the most promising young intellectuals and artists out of Greece. Their arrival signaled the creation of a predominantly left-wing Greek émigré intellectual elite.[85] The Association des Etudiants Hellénes à Paris (EPES), which had coordinated various political and cultural initiatives since the 1930s, had as its headquarters the Greek Pavilion of the Cité Universitaire. Soon, inner political divisions, predominantly between Trotskyists and Stalinists, split this small Greek Parisian community. Greek émigrés, however, briefly rediscovered a sense of unity in the spring of 1967 in response to the coup. One of the vehicles for coordinating common activities within the Greek community was the student union, which quickly took up a series of initiatives, including raising funds, publishing the journal *Poreia* [March], and organizing open discussions, film screenings, street marches to the embassy, and other ventures.

The year 1968 was crucial for shaping the diverse militant identities among Greek students. The dramatic rift in the Greek Communist Party that appeared during the winter and resulted in the creation of the interior and exterior factions proved influential. As expected, when the *événements* of May 1968 started, the orthodox communists, like the PCF, regarded them as the result of the irresponsibility of "politically inexperienced student masses," who in any case could not be the avant-garde of a popular uprising. Leading communist cadre Grigoris Farakos accused the students of inexperience, opportunism, and overt anticommunism. He also rejected the rival faction of KKE-Esoterikou [Interior], which by and large endorsed the '68 uprisings through the journal *Enotita* [Unity] and declared the Sorbonne to be a "new Smolny." Farakos equally criticized renowned political theorist Herbert Marcuse for leftist opportunism that undermined the "revolutionary capacities of the working classes." He concluded that Marcuse's attempt to "reconcile" Marx with Freud was an unscientific venture aimed at incorporating revolutionary theories within bourgeois ideology.[86] For the KKE, the discourses and actions of May '68 constituted a deviation from the official revolutionary process and were therefore sheer opportunism.

In general, the émigré students' stance was not a clear one. Few took direct part in the May events, and for a large part of them the libertarian attitude of the protests seemed an incomprehensible luxury at a time when things were so serious in Greece. Vasia Karkagianni-Karambelia, an art history student and a leftist militant, belongs to those students who felt a connection with the French movement and was convinced that its liberating potential could even affect Greece. Her words delineate the distance between imaginary projections and reality: "We were saying that if this thing is possible, then it might also be the beginning of the Junta's downfall, while in reality it was very early for anything to fall. We experienced it as a double liberation, many of us. It was spring, we were young, and all that jazz" (Karkagianni-Karambelia, interview). In general, however, as Greek students abroad regarded themselves as crusaders in the mission of liberating Greece, they tended to reject '68's libertarianism and lack of direction. As the president of EPES, art historian Nikos Hatzinikolaou remembers, "We felt somewhat awkward in the middle of this fiesta (πανηγύρι)."[87] The word "fiesta" recurs frequently in students' recollections of the period—especially the ones belonging to the two communist parties, who tended to be the most dismissive.

Eleni Varikas, a Trotskyist activist and present-day historian, was one of the few Greeks to gain organic relations with French political organizations in the après-'68 era. She remembers that "the Greeks, in general, a great part of them, did not have any relation to the French movement whatsoever.... And they were saying, "Oh, well, the French." ... But who was giving them passports? Who was giving them money? The French. Who was getting beaten up in demonstrations? Who was there? No one talks about this" (Varikas, interview). It is a fact, that both the French Socialist Party and Communist Party, trade unions such as CGT and CFDT, and leftist organizations such as La Cause du Peuple, Ligne Rouge, and Révolution offered moral and financial support to the Greek émigrés.[88]

Former leftist activist and present day scholar Kostas Vergopoulos remembers that most Greek students were rather hesitant to join the French movement, as they grew suspicious of what was happening—at times falling prey to a standard anti-Semitic conspiracy theory that linked De Gaulle's pro-Arab policies and the avalanche of French-Jewish leaders on the top of the movement to a supposed Israeli involvement: "For the ones who expressed the party lines, from KKE to KKE Int. up to the Maoists and the Marxists-Leninists, the May movement was a provocation: it was Jewish-American meddling which mobilized the rich kids in order to get rid of General De Gaulle. At a certain point a comrade from KKE stood up and said: 'Colleagues, we say yes to the red banner, but at the right moment and in the right place.'"[89]

A number of Greek students who resided in France at the time currently attribute their cautious relations with the ongoing French movement to two causes: the fear of losing their residence permit—even though the French authorities proved to be extremely lenient, even to the most radical cases[90]—and, more significantly, their focus on what was going on in Greece. For example, Anna Frangoudaki, a sociology student, says, "We had the Junta in our minds," and talks about a realist stance vis-à-vis the events, for which she feels justified at present. "The weight of the dictatorship on our shoulders made us see clearly that May '68 was not going anywhere," she argues (Frangoudaki, interview). For others, even sporadic participation in the French movement was interpreted as a way of contributing to the cause at home through the circulation of placards, leaflets, and journals in a campaign to promote the case of resistance. Nikos Hatzinikolaou notes: "We were considering the events of May from our own point of view. We were wondering in what ways all these things that were happening could contribute to our cause in Greece. This was the only thing that mattered to us."⁹¹

Despite some people's reservations, May '68 would become a catalyst for Greek students of that period in Paris.⁹² The film director Nikos Koundouros writes:

> We were carrying with us the shame that we were defeated without resisting; we were envious of the French who were carrying out their revolution against an autocratic but lawful and democratic government. So, we stood there, on the pavements of Paris, witnesses of foreign affairs and we were staring with a lump in our throat at the way in which the enraged French were going down the streets like human waves, floating from everywhere like a rough river, seizing the pavements, the squares, the universities, the schools, the factories.⁹³

The May events acted as an excuse for triggering what was to become the Greek students' most visible act of protest: on 22 May, a number of them occupied the Greek Pavilion inside the Cité Universitaire, clearly capitalizing on the subversive climate of those days and mimicking the French forms of protest, which were based on a series of occupations. The *maison hellénique* was declared to be "the first square meters of free Greek soil."⁹⁴ Greek students regarded this both as an act of resistance against the Colonels and as their way of participating in the May events. According to the manifesto issued by the *comité d'action* that took responsibility for the occupation, "The occupation is simultaneously an act of resistance against Greek fascism and an act of participation in the popular French movement."⁹⁵

According to philosopher and novelist Mimika Kranaki, a banner outside the gate of the pavilion announced that "here the imagination has conquered power," paraphrasing May '68's most famous situationist slogan.⁹⁶ The students also stressed the interconnection between different parts of the world and the unity forged by oppression and revolt. Their communiqué read: "The struggle of French youth is equivalent to the struggle of all people. If the establishment of fascism in Greece is a threat to Europe, the battles in the streets of Paris are hope for the whole world. ... We will try to use the experience of this struggle, its problematization, its enthusiasm, its inspirations, for our popular resistance against the Junta."⁹⁷

The occupation lasted for about a month and brought about the implementation of some of the French protesters' radical demands, such as the famous "autogestion."⁹⁸ This experiment, however, soon degenerated into quarrels and endless discussions among the various political factions. Film student Teos Romvos recalled the introverted attitude of the Greek revolutionaries: "Only some miles away from the Sorbonne and the uprising of the French students, the street battles which continued in the central boulevards seemed too far away. The whole climate at the Greek Pavilion was one of theory and introversion."[99]

This, however, was not always the case. May '68 and the occupation of the Greek Pavilion acted as a springboard for the creation of several Paris-based clandestine organizations with the aim of pursuing "dynamic resistance" in Greece. Nikos Hatzinikolaou, in his capacity as the president of EPES, had famously declared regarding the Greek dictatorship only ten days after the coup "to violence ... we are forced to respond with violence. And we shall use it wherever it is efficient."[100] Greek students showed signs of increasing radicalism, partly due to their physical distance from the events in Greece but mainly because of their constant mobilization and direct or indirect contact with international militancy. A whole new sect of "ultras" was bred in this period, reinforcing the Trotskyists and effecting the spectacular rise of Maoists. The latter would soon be designated by the derogatory term "leftists" (αριστεριστές)—a direct translation of *gauchistes*—and treated as a separate category by the left-wingers of the time.

The antiauthoritarian messages of '68 were among the inspirations for the creation of two Paris-based organizations, which did not, however, come into contact with the *tiersmondiste* or any other organization in France. These were the October 20th movement and the May 29th movement (K29M). Greek organizations took their names from the day on which they were formed, following the model of Daniel Cohn-Bendit's March 22nd movement in Paris. K29M was also a powerful reference to the "national" past—the date that Constantinople fell to the Ottomans in 1453—which reflected the organization's mingling of left-wing symbolism with romantic nationalism, typical among Greeks at the time. What is more, in the epic-heroic code as it was conceived by these militants, to conceive a date as the starting point of the whole enterprise signaled the beginning of a long process destined to bring revolution or at least a radical change.

The October 20th movement, whose main cadres were followers of the Center Union Party before becoming radicalized, carried out some extraordinary bomb attacks, one of which destroyed a statue of US President Truman in November 1970. The group also distributed the clandestine journal *Synergasia* [Cooperation], speaking to the need for closer cooperation between antidictatorial forces. Members of the organization were arrested in autumn of 1971. As an American report of the time sarcastically pointed out, the arrests, "fittingly perhaps, took place on October 20."[101] The May 29th movement covered a wider range of leftists, including a large group of Maoists in

Berlin known as the Berliners. It followed a stricter path of revolutionary politics, with its cadres being trained for city and mountain guerrilla warfare in Cuba. Inner divisions led to a separation of its German component in 1969, which later became the Revolutionary Communist Movement of Greece (EKKE), and to the transformation of the original organization into a different entity called Popular Revolutionary Resistance (LEA). In October 1970 LEA firebombed two US military vehicles in order to protest against the state visit of Vice-President Spyro Agnew (actually of Greek descent); in April 1971 it "celebrated the five years of military dictatorship" by bombing a statue erected by the Junta in Athens of General Ioannis Metaxas, a military dictator in the years 1936–1941.[102]

Those organizations, formed solely to pursue "dynamic forms of action," were mainly inspired by the urban guerilla theories and methods of Che Guevara and the Tupamaros in Uruguay in the 1960s. These focused on the role of small, fast-moving paramilitary groups that would act as revolutionary vanguards and would provide a focus for popular discontent against a sitting regime; later on and to a lesser extent, they also drew inspiration from the antiauthoritarian messages of May '68 in France.[103] Both organizations managed to gain the moral and financial support of prominent European intellectuals such as Jean-Paul Sartre and "professional revolutionaries" such as the Greek Trotskyist leader Michalis Raptis, alias Pablo, one of the prominent figures of the Fourth International.[104] One important feature that distinguished groups originating abroad from those based in Greece was the increasingly radical rhetoric of the former, whose members hinted that they would bring about not only the downfall of the dictatorship but also radical social change. According to a K29M member, Victor Anagnostopoulos, the constant discussion among the organizations' militants concentrated on "issues which were not of that time, such as how one imagined socialism, what peoples' power would be like."[105] The October 20th movement talked about an "anticapitalist, anti-imperialist, antibureaucratic socialist democracy of workers,"[106] while the K29M and later LEA foresaw that the "tough and long armed struggle of our people" was the only way to obtain "real national independence" and "popular sovereignty."[107] The dictatorship provided the context and the opportunity for a revolutionary uprising, which would be brought about by ongoing militant action that, in turn, would gradually enlighten and guide the people. For this purpose, the organizations were "determined to use the experience of the revolutionary struggles of other people, taking into account the special conditions of Greece."[108] The Castroist notion of action prior to consciousness was among their guiding principles.

The Greek Carbonari

Another Greek student community formed in Italy in the late 1950s and grew impressively during the Junta years. To the students who traditionally considered Italy a favorite study destination were added those guided by a "repulsive cause" who were searching for better living conditions and more liberty.[109] Most Greeks idolized Italy as a paradise of individual freedom in the form of both political expression and limitless consumption. A Greek student interviewed in the 1980s remembered his brother, who was studying in Italy, telling him, "In Italy life is beautiful, comfortable. You can have what you want, a car, entertainment, and on top of that you are free, something that in Greece you can forget about."[110] Three latter-day leading figures of the Greek student movement remembered how striking the open political radicalism that was common in Italy was to them. Dionysis Mavrogenis spent some time as a pharmacy student in Bologna in 1971 and experienced the Italian national celebration of 25 April, which contrasted with the black anniversary of the Greek 21 April. In a private conversation he recalled that this was the first time in his life that he saw "a red flag waving." The ecstatic feeling of seeing communist and antiauthority symbols being overtly and proudly exposed en masse is manifest in most life stories of Greek students who happened to travel or study in Italy. Vera Damofli recalls how Italy evoked memories of predictatorship Greece and its continuous political struggles: "I remember I went to Venice, I was still a student, and I saw slogans written on the walls, you know, I had missed that so much" (Damofli, interview). Angeliki Xydi's recollection focuses on the commercialization of the symbols of transgression: "I went to Padova for a year.... I came back with the symbol of anarchy. There they were selling them in the supermarkets" (Xydi, interview).

Greek students formed a number of committees in Italy, organizing demonstrations and exhibitions and denouncing the use of torture in Greek prisons.[111] Journals such as *Grecia Libera* contributed to the campaign by disseminating information on human rights violations in Greece. Efforts were made in the direction of consciousness raising; a telling example is a leaflet circulating at the time that asked, "What did you do against the dictatorship in Greece?" In 1971 at the Piazza Matteotti in Genova, the young student Kostas Georgakis set himself ablaze in protest against the Colonels, copying the Czech Jan Palach, who had done the same three years earlier after the Soviet troops invaded Prague.[112] Alkis Rigos, a Panteios student and present-day political scientist, recalls how he suffered when Georgakis died, being inspired by his action, appalled by his own indecisiveness, and thrilled by the general excitement of those times: "I had written poems for Georgakis, for

Palach, I stayed awake overnight. It was partly out of jealousy, that I hadn't done it, that I hadn't gotten as far, these are vivid things, they are a … You live in your entirety, you live in your entirety, and every moment is unique. It is something that cannot be copied" (Rigos, interview).

Public interventions by the members of a number of intellectual circles abroad gave a boost to the protest movement against the Colonels' regime. Exponents of the world of the arts such as Bernardo Bertolucci publicly supported groups involved in the armed struggle against the Junta. A number of first-rank Italian intellectuals participated in an event organized in support of the October 20th movement, giving legitimacy to its cause and practices.[113] In late 1968, on the eve of the imminent execution of Alekos Panagoulis, who had tried to assassinate dictator Georgios Papadopoulos, Pier Paolo Pasolini wondered in his column of the journal *Tempo* whether Italian students, "who by shouting are spreading panic," would demonstrate in favor of Panagoulis as well.[114] Andreas Papandreou's PAK enjoyed financial support from the Italian Socialist Party, and Italian politicians of the caliber of Pietro Nenni and Sandro Pertini supported that organization with articles in Italian newspapers.[115]

Theories on the armed struggle found fertile ground among Greek students, who were becoming increasingly radicalized due to their extensive contact with the Italian New Left. Interestingly, many Italians participated in the various attempts to transfer arms to Greece. Most commonly, the transfer of weapons took place through "cruises" in the Aegean. In a famous November 1968 case, an airplane was hijacked and redirected to France by Umberto Giovine, a young Italian journalist and a member of the International Commandos for Greece, who demanded democratic reform in Greece. Adriano Sofri, then leader of the autonomist extraparliamentary group Lotta Continua, even argues that, for many Italians, supporting the Greek resistance-in-exile was the immediate precedent to the armed struggle in Italy in the following years:

> This common militancy makes you better understand the drama of our comrades who were involved in the so-called Italian terrorism (some are dead), after having played an important role in the movement of a concrete solidarity with the Greek resistance. I remember, in particular, one lady, Maria Elena Angeloni, who was distributing arms and explosives and ended up exploding in front of the American Embassy in Athens. In the backyard of our house we thought that these dear friends were not just justified, but in fact ennobled by the fact that they took up arms against a fascist regime, which was violent and a product of a coup d' état.[116]

Sofri stresses the reciprocal impact between militants of the two countries but especially the influence that Greeks exercised over militant Italians. In this context, the Greek students who were committed to the resistance against the dictatorship were seen as blessed with the heroic aura of political exiles, which shaped their self-representation. On an institutional level, the Italian state endowed them with a series of benefits and privileges, including university scholarships offered by the Ministry of Public Instruction. Often, Greeks in both Italy and France could count on the tolerance of the police and the solidarity of university teachers.[117] In order to understand this wave of sympathy, one has to bear in mind the fact that a right-wing coup was thought to be imminent in Italy as well, especially after the Piazza Fontana bombing of 1969.[118] The Italian Left saw the Greek case, and later the Chilean one, as precedents in a domino effect of authoritarianism that could affect their own country, too.

At this point, protest material was diffused across national boundaries by means of personal contacts. It was common at the time for "subversive" music to be imported from abroad, mainly via students who studied in Italy and France. Those who managed to dwell in Greece without major problems brought with them banned music (especially Mikis Theodorakis records), Marxist books, leaflets, and sometimes explosives.[119] Latter-day student leader Nikitas Lionarakis recalled his admiration for Paki Kyriopoulou, a female student who organized in Italy: "Paki was one of the most heroic figures; in Rigas in Italy, she was going in and out of the country, very brave woman, very much so, with leaflets, with duplicators, with machines, some little bombs at a certain point" (Lionarakis, interview). Greek students also brought with them the ideas and the spirit of the Italian '68. Literature student Maria Mavragani vividly remembers an Italian antifascist song and points out the almost metaphysical capacity of Greek students to sense the content of the album without understanding the words: "We were singing Italian songs from the *Bella Ciao* cycle, I remember the vinyl, I miss it now. ... The cops could not understand what we were singing. For example, the famous one ... [she sings] "Bandiera nera la vogliamo? NO!," all together. Without knowing Italian ... But we knew what we were saying" (Mavragani, interview).

Students who traveled abroad were looked upon as a window on the world. Damofli remembers regarding them as carrying along the aura of '68: "They were bringing with them a sort of fresh air. They were coming back to Greece in the summers and they were describing their experiences to us, you know, after '68, and we were jealous" (Damofli, interview). Actor Giorgos Kotanidis similarly notes in his memoirs: "The world was in turmoil, news was coming from everywhere and we were upset that we couldn't even speak, as the fascist Colonels hindered us under the threat of arms."[120] For those in Greece, '68 came to symbolize the desired insurrection, while their counterparts abroad acquired a legendary status. This view contrasted with that of many Greek émigrés, who regarded features of the '68 movements as bizarre, grotesque, and definitively less militant and serious than their ideal. A female student in Munich who left the movement in Greece to pursue postgraduate studies and found herself demonstrating in her adoptive country conveys the feeling that her German counterparts had far too many rights. In a letter in February 1972, she wrote: "I felt an immense shame ... participating in the demonstrations of the students here—who struggle in order to acquire even more rights, along with their many already established ones."[121] Law student radical and latter-day publisher Myrsini Zorba's view on the '68 revolutionaries illustrates this issue further: "I too believed that they were just thugs, who, okay, made a painless revolt, you know, while ... while the issue down here was a dictatorship" (Zorba, interview).

Later on, the seriousness of the Greek "revolutionaries" in France and Italy made them suspicious of any sort of mass protest; they envisioned instead armed struggle. In his autobiographical book on émigré students in Italy, Giorgos Vavizos notes with evident self-irony the prevailing hyperrevolutionism and the majority endorsement of the use of radical tactics in Greece: "We all thought that the creation of a guerrilla war in Greece was necessary, in order to overthrow the Junta. Our major concern was whether the armed struggle should start from the mountains, so that the guerrilla army would occupy the cities later on, or whether the cities should rise up first, so that from there the guerrilla warfare would be spread to the mountains."[122]

The legitimacy of violence as a means of resistance was one of the main points of friction among the Greek émigré organizations. The traditional left-wing leadership not only opposed so-called dynamic action, meaning armed resistance, but tended to stigmatize those who deployed it as agents provocateurs of the Junta, an accusation that had been a favorite topos of the Left from the 1930s onward. It is no coincidence that when Alekos Panagoulis attempted to assassinate the dictator Papadopoulos in summer 1968—later on immortalized by his companion Oriana Fallaci in her widely read biography "A Man"[123]—the reaction of most left-wing leaders was one of distrust. Myrsini Zorba encapsulated the popular feeling: "If he doesn't belong to our organization, if one cannot check who he is, we don't trust him" (Zorba, interview). The violent groupings, on the other hand, regarded this attitude as reformist and rejected it as a lack of revolutionary commitment.

As a result, a number of students who were members of both the Communist Party and some clandestine circles were expelled from the former due to their one-dimensional insistence on the armed struggle, which was attributed to an alleged flirting with *gauchisme*.¹²⁴ For the expelled, the Communist Party had lost its revolutionary spirit and had become a "reformist" entity, remaining passive and unprepared for the Colonels' dictatorship. The only way to challenge the Colonels was to create organized nuclei of city guerrillas, they maintained. The K29M described the situation in these terms: "If you deal with an opponent who is basically relying on the use of force, there can be no other reply by the people fighting against it than force. The armed struggle is the basic form of our political battle."¹²⁵

Belief in the appropriateness of the use of force as a carrier of social change was not always shared by the organizations that were not programmatically against it. One of them was headed by Giorgos Karambelias, who recalls arguing with Alexandros Giotopoulos, K29M's controversial leader, during the student meetings in Paris: "The argument we had with the K29M and Giotopoulos—I remember quarrelling with him—was that they were of the opinion that city guerrilla could be the main feature [of resistance]. We were saying that there were no conditions for urban guerrilla; the whole thing was just symbolic armed acts, which we supported" (Karambelias, interview).

Since symbolic acts of violence were directed against "US imperialism, oppression, and the financial supports of the system,"¹²⁶ the most frequent targets were government buildings, banks, enterprises (Andreadis/Esso Pappas), and, frequently, US buildings and sites. The United States and NATO were largely understood in the left-wing popular mind as the dictators' major abettors, which fitted perfectly with the anti-imperialistic and *tiermondiste* discourse of the time, thus placing the Greek example alongside the Vietnamese one. In the trial of the alleged members of the terrorist organization 17N in 2003, Vasia Karkagianni-Karambelia remembered:

> The armed struggle in that period was a common topos for all of us. When we had tanks facing us and a dictatorship which was supported by a huge power, and you know it, the power of the United States, it was not possible to think about anything else than the armed struggle. But this was on a symbolic level. We never identified a human target, not even in our imagination, saying it's this person, that person. This dimension didn't exist. ...
>
> I, myself, designed posters ... which used this iconography, people with guns. Despite the fact that none of us had ever touched a piece of wood in our hands. This was on the symbolic level, that given that the dictatorship was continuing in Greece all the people should take up arms. But there were no targets, this was entirely on the

imaginary and symbolic level, but this was our decision then, to fight with all means.[127]

Although bombs were often put in streets, squares, parks, cars, and state buildings, even the most violent groupings conceived of this as a means of enacting essentially bloodless protest.

Home-Grown Revolutionaries

A group that propagated the necessity of armed resistance as part of a wider international class struggle was the Trotskyist organization called Spoudastiki Pali [Student Struggle]—soon to be renamed Laiki Pali [Popular Struggle]—in Salonica. A leaflet circulated in spring 1968 described the group's position: "The 'democratic' fronts beyond parties from above and the parliamentary pressures are unable to overthrow the dictatorships. Young workers and students move on like brothers. The only right way is the way of class struggle."[128] Numbering about ten persons as its leading nucleus and not more than fifty in total, this group made resisting the Junta an ideological prerogative. Triantafyllos Mitafidis, one of the group's leading members, recalls: "Ideologically we were in favor of a revolution, we talked about a workers' democracy—we also said these things in the court martial. We were in favor of the violent overthrow of the dictatorship, of the regime, all of that. Of course, we translated that to bombs, with that logic. Others did that as well, even without having the same principles" (Mitafidis, interview). Tasos Darveris, another leading member of the organization, novelistically re-created a discussion among its members in which they quarrel about whether violence could act as the catalyst for history's revolutionary process. At a certain point, one of the characters muses, "In other words you want us to put our finger in History's asshole."[129] Here, revolution, the "asshole" of history, and violence's "finger" ironically describe the precarious expectation of historical recourse in a Bakhtinian inversion that renders the whole process ridiculous.

The actions of Laiki Pali, which began with the circulation of leaflets and the unfolding of large anti-Junta banners from the tops of central buildings, turned to the planting of explosives in key areas. Members' clandestine lives were twofold, since these actions were covered with a gloss of legality, including regular class attendance. The organization's members were arrested after one and a half years of underground activity just before executing an ambitious, organized plan to plant a bomb in the military pavilion of Salonica's International Fair in autumn 1969 during Papadopoulos's speech. Its members were court-martialed and received severe sentences, including life imprisonment.[130] Interestingly, in their pleas, both leading members of the organization rejected "dynamic action." Antonis Liakos, a leader of Laiki Pali and now a historian, declared that "Our credo is that the mobilizing force of History is the class struggle, and we don't believe in dynamites and terrorism," while Mitafidis stated bluntly that as Greece was not Latin America, the armed struggle in Greece had no chance of succeeding.[131] However, the pleas of the leading members of Laiki Pali are starkly distinguished from Darveris's own literary depiction and can hardly qualify as reliable evidence of what their true beliefs were.

According to the recollections of former Laiki Pali members, the inherent contradiction between putting people's lives in danger and aiding the cause created a traumatic dilemma. Mitafidis recalls the risks of being involved in this sort of action and stresses the biographical rupture between past and present: "And of course the great danger was to get killed. And not only to get killed but also to get the people of the whole building block blown up with the dynamite.... Those were great risks, but we had different minds back then" (Mitafidis, interview). At the same time, this was the moment in which the euphoria of finally being active and efficient replaced the agony of wondering whether people read the brochures, breaking the wider societal inertia. As theorist Giannis Papatheodorou argues, "It [wa]s the bombs and not the leaflets that br[oke] the inertia of the society under surveillance."[132]

At the other end of the spectrum, journalist Klearchos Tsaousidis remained a member of Laiki Pali up until the organization decided to take up arms. Looking at his past choices now, he views his decision to distance himself from Laiki Pali as an equal result of individual consciousness and the instinct of self-preservation: "When the moment of the more aggressive tactics arrived, at that point I distanced myself, probably because of fear. That is, one has to look oneself very carefully in the mirror in order to know whether it is because one doubts the necessity of wasting human lives or is it because one is scared. Or both?" In his retrospective analysis, Tsaousidis blames his disillusionment with the organization on a rejection and condemnation of violence as he reflects on the humanity of the policemen of the time: "No matter what you do, no matter how many precautions you take, with the explosives there is always the danger of making the innocent pay the price. Now that I think about it, I say, isn't the average gendarme, the one whose mind is filled with crap about the mean communists and the enemies of the nation and religion, innocent?" (Tsaousidis, interview). Mitafidis also evokes the fear factor, but he presents it as a source of adrenaline. For him, fear reinforced the determination to continue the struggle despite the awareness of being trapped in an impossible situation: "When an organization got hit, you felt a shivering in your neck. How can I put it now? It was a situation in which you were living under suspension.... We were facing great dangers. There was no way that they would take pity on us" (Mitafidis, interview).

Films lent their images to the resistance fighters' fantasies of taking up arms. The idea of resorting to violence was already based on reenacting cinematic prototypes, such as seeing oneself from a distance as an action hero. Lindsay Anderson's emblematic movie *If....* (1968), which tells the story of rebel British students who take up arms against the oppressive establishment and execute the entire staff of their reactionary college, was briefly screened in Greece after an initial ban. Militants hoped to imitate this, and thus real life mimicked cinema rather than the other way around. Former militant and present-day playwright Andreas Staikos, a K29M member, comments on the training of the members of the organization by saying, "It has remained in my mind as a very cinematographic experience."[133] Cinematic images and titles are also evoked in self-representations in what Liakos calls "cinema as a way of conceptualization and comparison with lived experience."[134] Comparison, however, often reveals a great distance from the idealized images. Mitafidis's assertion, "We were not the children of Marx and Coca-Cola," falls into this category. Even more so, at a key point in Darveris's autobiographical novel, one of his imprisoned heroes comments on the failure of one of the members of Laiki Pali to escape when he had the chance. A traumatic gap emerges between fiction and reality as the latter is recast as a poorly-written script: "'This is something that would never take place in cinema,' Labros said. 'In cinema everybody escapes.'"[135]

In other cases, there is a striking similarity between fictional narrative and lived experience, at least as it is represented in the present. Liakos's own conceptualization of clandestine struggle included *L'Armata Brancaleone* (1966), Mario Monicelli's parody of a knights' quest in the Middle Ages. His projected identification with Brancaleone, the antihero of Don Quixotesque qualities, points to considerable self-irony in his organization's conceptualization of militantism. In his *ego-histoire* Liakos stresses the fact that this is not an ex-post invention but an actual occurrence, as the film functioned as a driving force of militancy: "This film belonged in some way to the micromythology of our resistance group. Those of us who founded this group had our first discussion after we had seen this film in a Thessaloniki cinema in the summer of 1967. Often sarcastic towards ourselves and our activities, we likened ourselves to the comic heroes of Brancaleone. Great words, poor results. An ineffectiveness, somehow comic and ironic at the same time."[136] Liakos's comrade Darveris also used tragicomic elements and bouleversement of registers in his description of how the four leading members of the organization burst out laughing after the absurd sentence of life imprisonment was announced by the military court during their trial.

In contrast to antiheroes, however, certain heroic icons of wartime resistance were very present in the imagination of most young people involved in underground activities. These included Aris Velouchiotis, the most famous communist guerrilla leader during the German occupation and a Guevarist figure *avant la lettre*. Obviously Che Guevara himself was another. Aris, the *supremo* of the partisan army ELAS, had decided to carry on the armed struggle after liberation, contrary to the party's wishes. This decision, his expulsion from the Greek Communist Party (KKE), and his early death led to his canonization by party dissidents as a figure of uncompromising and relentless struggle. To the imaginary link with war-time resistance one should also add the connection between underground activity and the construction of masculinity. Historian Polymeris Voglis notes, regarding people who made use of political violence against the Junta: "when the interviewees speak about the bombs they prepared and planted, they talk about temper, pride, 'guts,' being active, inventive and audacious—qualities assigned to male identity and performance."[137]

Most female members of the resistance did not acquire high positions within clandestine organizations. Still, law student Anna Mandelou (connected for a while to Spoudastiki Pali) maintains that, given the shared tough conditions, her male comrades regarded her as an equal. She further represents her action within the group as an indirect form of feminism: "When you come into conflict with such a tough regime, you look at things in a profound way, you know what I mean? You get to the essence of things, you cannot say, 'I am a woman, I won't speak.' … By rebelling, you also challenge the role of women in patriarchal society" (Mandelou, interview). Vervenioti argues, however, that basic inequalities continued to hold sway; in contrast to men, female students were more prevented from resistance action because they were more strictly controlled by their families. They could not spend the night out printing leaflets, for instance. Naturally those who studied away from home enjoyed a greater freedom of movement.

An average of twenty-seven bombs were planted every year during the seven years of the dictatorship, reaching a peak in 1969. A number of unexploded bombs were discovered, and in most cases the bombs did not cause any physical damage. According to theorist Nikos Serdedakis, this was due to the organizations' lack of experience and expertise.[138] It is no coincidence that the overwhelming majority of the students involved in violent activity were either Centrists or members of the Lambrakis Youth in the early 1960s. Resorting to dynamic action was a dramatic about-face from the peaceful methods of protest they had used prior to the Junta. This could be seen as the "return of the repressed," to use Stuart Hall's term, that is, a way of fighting against the passive, defeatist, painful past.[139] People who joined the underground organizations made the choice to finally "do something" and do it radically. As Tasos Darveris argues, however, "No one was convinced that the Lambrakides were transformed from peaceful legalists into city guerrillas in just three months, no matter how much they got involved in explosions at that time."[140] Stergios Katsaros's confession is equally telling and contrasts sharply with his ardent support of political violence, his fascination with Che's voluntarism, and his training in Cuba. Although his organization decided to shoot stool pigeons, who he said were "easy targets," it did not accomplish this aim in the end, as "[Their] hands were still trembling": "In order for the revolutionary to shoot a person, he himself is bound to have lost a part of his humanity. But back then there was no continuity. From lawful citizens of a parliamentary—even if conservative—democracy, we were called from one moment to the next to be transformed into executioners."[141]

What was the effect and reception of the "dynamic acts," and how effective was this sort of "armed propaganda"? There is no doubt that for many the acts served as proof of actual resistance to the regime. One British journalist quoted a man saying that under conditions of impotent and bitter silence, "The general reaction to the wave of bombings by the resistance in 1969 was enthusiastic."[142] In another account published in Britain, the diplomat and writer Rodis Roufos Kanakaris wrote under the nickname "the Athenian," "People, greatly encouraged, went to sleep and woke up with the hope of hearing of further attempts; their morale shot upwards."[143]

Petros Efthymiou, a student leader at the University of Ioannina at the time and an education minister in a Center-Left government about twenty years later (2000–2004), shares this view. He wrote in praise of Dimitris Psychogios, a leading member of the October 20th movement, who in May 1972 placed a bomb inside the General Confederation of Greek Workers (GSEE), which was controlled by the regime: "I will never forget the wild joy that I owe him when on a night in May 1970 the explosion of a bomb that Dimitris had planted in GSEE came to possess me, while I was mixing in a pot the 'materials' for the production of home-made TNT, just like a little magician." The emotional way in which Efthymiou recalls this incident captures the moral weight that acts of resistance acquired in the general stalemate and passivity that reigned in the Colonels' Greece. He uses humor—"like a little magician"—to draw attention away from the fact that he, too, was involved in the preparation of explosives. This narrative choice suggests the difficulty in addressing a past that involved preparing and planting bombs, regardless of how "just" the cause was. Yet Efthymiou goes so far as to praise the value of bombs by comparing them to a sort of heavenly music, a reminder of the more relative moral statements regarding violence at that time, which contrast with present attitudes: "If at present bombs are associated with crime and the blood of innocent people, back then they were the most beautiful music, the most spontaneous song of freedom against oppression."[144]

The larger picture suggests, however, that for most people the "dynamic acts" under the Junta remained isolated events, since at least until the beginning of the great trials, it was difficult to relate their shadowy actors with real people. There is no substantiation for social psychologist Anna Mantoglou's claim that the Greek people's lack of condemnation of these acts as terrorism constituted a general silent approval.[145] On the contrary, it seems that several people did consider the bombings to be the acts of extremists. As a foreign correspondent commented at the time, most Greeks regarded bombs as threatening, since "very few of them can bear to contemplate the fear of another Civil War."[146]

What is true, is that bombs, as well as the members of resistance groups, received a great deal of publicity in the regime's papers, both in order to demonstrate that violent elements were still lurking inside Greek society and to showcase the regime's efficiency. Accordingly, there is a significant asymmetry between the organizations and the few acts that they managed to inflict before getting caught, on the one hand, and the amount of notoriety that they acquired through the media, on the other. Usually on the front page of the papers, the antiregime "criminals," "lunatics," and "terrorists," as they were routinely described, were becoming a sort of popular myth for those inclined to sympathize. Inverting Liakos's description of his "Brancaleonic" resistance's failure to match great words with grand deeds, the regime gave these acts of resistance far more importance than they deserved in any pragmatic sense. From 1970 onward, the antiregime press would use the same strategy for opposite ends, taking advantage of the relaxation of censorship legislation to publish the defendants' defense pleas. One result of this tactic was that resistance actors became highly recognizable; another was that antiregime propaganda was more widely disseminated. These defendants, who had no possibility of appealing the verdicts in their trials, became models for younger students. The media's sensationalized image was a larger-than-life version of the real deeds, and it often struck younger people's imaginations. Pharmacy student and present-day journalist Stelios Kouloglou remembered that descriptions of torture in the published accounts of the clandestine organization Rigas Feraios trials played a major role in his politicization (Kouloglou, interview). In theatrical terms, the resistance organizations' performance had a disproportionate impact on the audience. In this sense, there was a twofold amplification: that of the media and that of the readers' own fantasies. But in addition to the idealization of the resistance organizations themselves was the equally important appropriation of the revolutionary past.

The Terrible Solitude of Rigas Feraios

Rigas Feraios was founded by former Lambrakides in December 1967 in Athens. The choice to adopt the name of the man who was probably the most prominent intellectual figure behind the 1821 Greek War of Independence against the Ottomans appealed to the iconography of the national revolutionary past and was a powerful reference to the relentless struggle against tyranny. As Karl Marx famously noted referring to Louis Bonaparte's farcical appropriation of France's revolutionary past, "[The living] anxiously conjure up the spirits of the past to their service and borrow from them names, battle cries and costumes."[147] Thanasis Athanasiou, one of the organization's founders, stresses, "Of course, the name Rigas Feraios was not incidental ... since it compressed this sense of struggle, democracy, unity" (Athanasiou, interview). The organization's founding manifesto concludes with his famous oath: "As long as I live, my only aim shall be to eliminate [the tyrants]." To quote literary theorist Stathis Gourgouris, "The invocation of the ghost of [Rigas], given especially his image as a revolutionary and a man of the people, simultaneously sanctifies his figure and declares ownership of his *logos*."[148]

Though the Junta used and abused the 1821 fighters in its ultranationalist propaganda, they continued to symbolize pure, patriotic fighting for young people in Greece, as the generation of the wartime resistance did as well. Placing oneself in a longstanding revolutionary tradition has been a typical feature in leftwing social movements ever since the *ur*-historical uprising of the modern era, the French Revolution. This is what Isabelle Sommier calls the "resurgence of the revolutionary myth in order to give meaning to one's engagement,"[149] an apparently timeless strategy. It was precisely this imaginary link with previous generations that Rigas Feraios tried to achieve through its choice of name and its manifesto.

Any open student activity within the grounds of the university was ruled out as unrealistic and too dangerous. Therefore, Rigas mainly focused on actions of attrition and on reminding the regime of its presence, with a repertoire including the distribution of leaflets and anti-Junta graffiti (despite Brigadier-General Pattakos's warning that political graffiti makers would be shot).[150] Michalis Spyridakis, one of the organization's members in Salonica, remembers "the brush, the paint, the leaflet from hand to hand" (Spyridakis, interview). The leaflets urged people to join the battle. One read: "Colleagues, all of you should join the struggle against the fascist dictatorship; let us never become slaves of the tyrants; long live proud Greek Youth." Another chastised: "Colleague, your fellow-students are in exile or prisons, being tortured ruthlessly. It is the duty of all of us to fight for their liberation."[151] Vera

Damofli remembers that one day as she walked with her mother, she noticed leaflets on the ground: "I remember taking them with care, like a sort of a wounded bird. Then we took them home, but didn't really know what to do with them [laughter]."[152] Darveris notes in his *A Night's Story* that people were mostly scared to read those leaflets, and even if they did they were an unsuccessful means of instigation. This is a valid point. As one of his novelized protagonists wonders in agony, "How can you work with the masses when people are afraid to talk to each other?"[153]

Rigas did not limit its activities to leaflets and graffiti, however. In an anti-Junta journal published abroad in March 1968, a Rigas member is quoted as saying, "The organization's aim is the resistance against fascism with every means until the final overthrow of the Junta." When the journal's collaborator asked if "every means" included armed action, the member answered: "It must be the final form of the movement's struggle. It is a fact, if we want to be realistic, that one has to work very hard, and all possibilities must be exhausted before that. Greek youth do not seek to cause bloodshed in the country. But if all other forms of struggle are excluded, what else remains? People want to live freely and peacefully. But if war is imposed on them, they fight it and they win it."[154] Reflecting the fear of being accused of causing civil strife, Rigas was indeed involved in nonsystematic actions of limited violence. It also published the clandestine journal *Thourios* [War-Song], a bulletin on resistance activities. The organization was helplessly alone in trying to mobilize the students, however, as Spyridakis recalls: "There was no one else [in the university]. It was us. No one else. We were the only ones who were mobilized" (Spyridakis, interview).

By 18 September 1968, a large number of Rigas Feraios's main cadres had been arrested, and on 29 October its leadership was put on trial and given severe sentences ranging from five to twenty-one years in prison. Speaking in their defense, the Rigas Feraios members declared proudly that they had been members of the Lambrakis Youth.[155] In fact, all of Rigas's founding members had been leading figures in the Lambrakis Youth, and they experienced and stressed the "continuity" between the pre-1967 Lambrakides and student action under the Junta, despite the fact that none of the earlier patterns carried over into the dictatorship era: "The Greek students have not forgotten for a moment the ideals which led to the great student struggles for the democratization of Education and National Independence.... We don't recognize any EFEE other than that in whose name all those great struggles took place for the Renaissance of Education and 114. As followers of this struggle we announce the rising up against the dictatorship."[156]

In its founding manifesto, Rigas Feraios employed a discourse with mixed references to the "heroic traditions of Greek Youth and the student movement" and destructive "foreign manipulation." It drew analogies between the Colonels and Ioannis Metaxas, Benito Mussolini and Adolf Hitler, calling the latter pair Papadopoulos's "teachers." The manifesto deliberately used a vocabulary that resembles EAM's discourse during the German occupation, aiming at evoking the spirit of resistance: "No student should become a quisling, collaborator of the tyrants." Since the majority of the people who participated in the Resistance under the communist-led EAM/ELAS were defeated and demonized after the civil war, there could be no reaction against this "heroic generation," which still had a legendary stature and was very prominent in the left-wing political imagination. Instead, this heroic past was appropriated: "The fighters of Rigas Feraios struggle using every means, following the democratic tradition of the generation of the '40s."[157]

Many Rigas members had parents who had participated in the Resistance. In his book, ex-militant and present-day writer Thanasis Skroumbelos makes many references to the heroic fathers of the group's members, who acted as models for their children, as did Athanasiou's father.[158] This is a direct and painful evocation of the Greek Civil War, in which the strife acts as a "skin-felt experience," not a vague and abstract evocation. At the time of her trial, Maria Kallergi, a student and Rigas Feraios member, gave a report to foreign correspondents in which she described the conditions of her arrest. In a recollection of the eighteen days of continuous torture that preceded her transfer to Averoff Prison, Kallergi referred to the painful visit of her father, a man who had participated in the Resistance: "My father started crying. My father is a courageous man, he is an old freedom fighter. He was arrested by the Germans in Crete, while he was working for an English commando. He knows what it means to believe in an idea. I have always been proud of him."[159]

Rigas's manifesto also proposed a continuum of vanguard student action in all national struggles, referring to 1821 war hero General Makrigiannis and the March 1844 constitution that was granted by the Bavarian King Otto, Greece's first monarch: "We shall continue the great traditions of students who fought in order to bring down Otto's monarchy, who alongside Makrigiannis fought for the consolidation of the Constitution."[160] It mentioned workers as part of a tradition of "heroic struggles ... of the pioneering workers' movement," describing them as "a volcano which boils quietly" in a struggle parallel to that of the students.[161] Lastly, the manifesto accused the Junta of "obeying foreign bosses" [ξενόδουλη], meaning the "imperialistic" United States. In the same spirit, a later issue of *Thourios* declares that "the country is further sold to foreign interests, thus cementing our dependence on foreign capital,"[162] echoing this well-known topos of the Greek Left throughout the postwar period: "[The people] understood well by now who is hidden behind [the dictatorship]: American imperialism, NATO, the monopolies.... [The Resistance] guarantees the continuation of the struggle until the substantial victory, the breaking of the bonds with foreign dependency which is directly responsible for the tragedy of the people."[163]

After the 1968 split within the exiled Greek Communist Party (KKE), Rigas gradually came to be identified with the moderate KKE-Esoterikou. Its attempt to be less dogmatic was more often than not interpreted as evidence of the group's reformism and lack of revolutionary fervor, however. Accordingly, and in contrast to the "negative" party line, *Thourios* referred in its December 1968 issue to the growing importance of the role of students in social struggles, pointing to student unrest worldwide: "[The Greek student youth] believes that the student struggles in other countries are part of the same struggle for the overthrow of reactionary forces on an international level. It observes with great interest those struggles and is reinforced and strengthened in its own antidictatorship, antifascist struggle."[164] In this spirit, *Thourios* introduced a column to document the international student scene and to inform Greek students of its struggles. So while the first issues of the journal expressed old-fashioned appeals to students' patriotism, by 1970 its tone had changed significantly, taking on a more open and internationalist approach with a clear anticapitalist and anti-imperialist character. A 1970 issue reads: "The struggles of the youth of Vietnam are leading us, the struggles of the youth of America and of Europe are moving our souls. We speak the same language. We fight against a common enemy." Despite this renewal, only three issues of *Thourios* were printed from late 1969 to 1971.

In terms of organizational structure, Rigas's contribution from mid-1969 onward was an appeal for the creation of student committees, small and flexible groups for a more dynamic and interactive participation. Parallel to that, the leadership of KKE-Esoterikou was hesitantly trying to organize an operational section in order to begin a limited armed action. The result was the creation of Aris–Rigas Feraios (ARF), the name a bellicose reference both to the ancient Greek God of War and to wartime resistance leader Aris Velouchiotis. ARF was led by the student Kostas Agapiou, who travelled around Europe in order to gather money and arms. The whole affair resulted in a grand fiasco, mainly because of the infamous "hundred and eighth" bomb, which killed two ARF members. The Greek-Cypriot student Giorgos Tsikouris and his Milanese companion Maria Elena Angeloni died on 2 September 1970 when the car bomb they were attempting to leave outside the US embassy detonated prematurely. In a recent interview granted to historian Polymeris Voglis, Giorgos Romaios, an ARF member who participated in this fatal operation, distances himself from the standardized narrative of martyrdom and heroic sacrifice. His testimony reveals that the memory of the incident was so traumatic for the ones involved, that for years they chose to deal with it through negation:

> It didn't happen. Neither did we discuss thoroughly the issue, and nor did we exchange experiences, views, memories etc. It didn't happen. And you know what? We didn't want to talk about these things. Because from many points of view it was … To begin with, it was a burden, let's say. For many years I had this inside me … that I was responsible for their deaths. You understand now … maybe K. felt the same way. We didn't want to talk about the incident. Looking back, I see that it wasn't the case, but you can't explain everything rationally. When you see the others a hundred meters away, when you see the smoke and the flame, say, it is not the best thing that can happen to you.[165]

Apart from the fact that Romaios and his comrades had to deal with feelings of guilt, grief, and regret for the years to come, the deaths of Tsikouris and Angeloni led to a number of significant arrests. But the incident at the American Embassy also caused a radicalization of some of Rigas's members who were involved in the operation and who distanced themselves from the party,

Figure 2.6. A tragic conclusion to the "armed struggle." The car in which Maria Elena Angeloni and Giorgos Tsikouris died on 2 September 1970, when the bomb they attempted to leave outside the US embassy detonated prematurely. (Source: ASKI, Archives of Social and Cultural History)

seeking new means of armed struggle.[166] ARF started collaborating with the Parisian LEA. In a joint leaflet distributed after the explosion on the night of 8 July 1971 of five bombs in different parts of Athens and Piraeus, the two groupings declared their determination to "combine right theory with right action," targeted the United States as the cause of all evils in Greece, and expressed the common aim to give "power to the people."[167] The fact that underground organizations concentrated so much on the US embassy and US vehicles (or President Truman's statue, earlier on), denotes the exclusively symbolic nature of such action and underlines people's conviction that the Americans were almost solely to blame for the Junta.

About a year later, on 29 August 1972, LEA paid homage to ARF, placing a bomb in the basement of the US embassy in order to honor the memory of the two members who had died at the same spot two years earlier, declaring: "Our anti-imperialist action today is dedicated to the memory of the fighters Tsikouri and Angeloni who lost their lives two years ago at the same place during a similar action."[168] The bomb caused material damage and no human casualties,[169] but it would become a cause célèbre several decades later: in 2003, as LEA's member Alexandros Giotopoulos was accused of being the leader of the terrorist group "Revolutionary Organization November 17th" (17N), a well-known journalist caused a sensation by insisting that this particular incident actually never happened.[170]

It has to be noted here that at the time when the research for this book was conducted Giotopoulos and Agapiou were both being tried for their involvement in 17N and ELA [Revolutionary People's Struggle] respectively, that is, leftist terrorist organizations that operated *after* the consolidation of democracy in 1974. Their arrests in the summer of 2002 gave rise to a media-generated hysteria that stopped just short of demonizing the entire clandestine resistance under the Junta. The so-called armed struggle against the Colonels was revisited in light of recent terrorism-related events, and the legitimacy of violence under any circumstances was brought into question. Former militants maintained a climate of silence and mistrust, because anyone with a solid history of antidictatorial clandestine action was potentially suspicious; this rendered fieldwork extremely difficult.

This shift also caused a disparity between people's self-images in the 1960s and those in the present. Dionysis Savvopoulos, the foremost songwriter of the late 1960s and early 1970s in Greece, likened the darkness and rage of his past persona to Dimitris Koufondinas, the main gunner of 17N: "The other day Kornilios, my older son, took me out and he put on a tape with the 'Black Sea' song from the *Dirty Bread* album. I listened to myself, with that darkest of voices in '72, singing alongside the distortions of the electric guitar, 'I do not have a sound, I do not have material,' and I thought

I was listening to Koufondinas!"¹⁷¹ Savvopoulos's conclusion provides an interesting example of how the present dictates the categories through which people tend to read the (cumbersome) past; in such a light the latter often resembles a foreign country.

The Historical Generation Retires

By 1971, Rigas's first generation had been detected and dispersed. Members of this "historical" generation of the student movement were the first to go to prison and thus acquire symbolic status. Two female members of Rigas were tortured and acquired legendary status through their courageous pleas during their trial. Nikitas Lionarakis recalled with emotion having "fallen in love" with both: "For Margarita Gerali and Tsembelikou I had cried bitterly, I had fallen in love with them out of their plea in the court. Even now if you want I can tell you their pleas by heart.... They were mythical figures" (Lionarakis, interview).

These students sparked a sense of admiration in the younger generation. Christina Vervenioti, a former DEA member, was married as soon as she left prison, and she recalls this moment with an evident sense of pride: "In the

Figure 2.7. Athens Military Tribunal. Members of a clandestine organization—probably Rigas Feraios—are transferred handcuffed from the court back to prison, 1968–1969. By 1971 underground resistance had been wiped out. (Photographer: Aristotelis Sarrikostas)

church it was not just the whole Panteios, my School, that was present, there was everyone.... This marriage was a sort of a rally. Everyone had come to honor me" (Vervenioti, interview). Mitafidis and his comrades came out of jail briefly when Papadopoulos granted an amnesty in 1973, whereupon they were immediately sent to the army. He remembers being struck by the differences five years in prison had brought about: "When we came out of prison we had a small problem of communication with the new generation.... We went [to a meeting] bald, with white hair.... But the new generation saw in us the people who could teach them. They did not have the usual rejecting stance. That generation was eager to learn. And of course it had us as its models" (Mitafidis, interview).

In his fictionalized autobiography, Tasos Darveris's surrogate is stunned by the extent of the changes that had occurred during those four years: "Deportations had ceased years ago, censorship had been abolished; the bookshops were full of Marxist books and Theodorakis' songs were often heard at the *boîtes*. In the taverns which were frequented by circles of students, the political songs were dominant, as were the jackets, blue jeans and beards."[172]

Accordingly, the imposition of the dictatorship had defined the first generation's student life, while those of the younger generation had still been teenagers. Those teenagers would come of age *under* the regime and for that reason would better understand its logic, exploiting the political opportunities that the dictatorship unwillingly allowed, in order to develop political disruption and everyday creativity. By that time, people of the first cohort, who had experienced the toughest years of the Junta's austerity, restrictions, martial law, and full-blown preventive censorship, and who had been more prone to clandestine networks and armed resistance, were already imprisoned or exiled.

Younger students' recollections encompass a broad spectrum: some emphasize the expertise and the intergenerational transfer of ideas that the so-called grandfathers of the movement had bequeathed them, while others lament the often patronizing stance that older students adopted toward them. Thodoros Vourekas, a Mathematics student at the time, recalls:

> The ones who were granted amnesty were some members of the previous student movement who had been expelled from the universities in '67, and they got back into the schools. One of them was a very important person, Thomas Vassiliadis in Salonica, he made a massive organization out of Rigas Feraios, KKE-Esoterikou.... He was a very intense personality. And others came from the extraparliamentary Left.... So, there are chains which transmit an experience. (Vourekas, interview)

Maria Mavragani appears more critical: "KKE Esoterikou had some 'ancient' students ..., meaning people who had already graduated or who were still registered.... For example comrade K., he was like the father, with us being the kids" (Mavragani, interview). In contrast, Angeliki Xydi remembered that her organization, A-EFEE, did not benefit at all from the experience of the earlier generation, a fact that she deeply regretted:

> It is significant too that many of these people were in jail, in exile, but I really felt, you know, this gap that exists between the first antidictatorship people and the student movement. I believe it had a negative effect on us because no struggle experiences were transmitted to us, but also on the level of political experience, because we had to find out about many things by ourselves, and this took us some time and marked us and our lives. (Xydi, interview)

In contrast to that picture comes Tasos Darveris's emphatic view that "there was no intention on the part of the elderly to 'educate' the younger ones with the aim of maintaining the movement." He argues that the dictatorship gave this older generation, which in the early 1960s had enthusiastically dedicated itself to nonstop political activism, the chance to take a rest and "live its life."[173] This idea was echoed by the singer-songwriter Dionysis Savvopoulos in a 1969 song that speaks of "the best of the kids" who "got tired and went back home." Another song by Savvopoulos from the same period refers to the "kids who were lost in the magic forests," those of this same generation who were consumed by drugs—a taboo subject of discussion for most people even today.[174] This verse could also be applied, however, to those who got involved in political action that ended in an impasse.[175]

For the majority of students involved in clandestine activities, activism during the Junta years ended there, but they were marked and altered by the events. They did not fulfill the political goal of their battle, and they spent years in jail during their early twenties. This was to be a source of melancholy for most of them, as they could hardly relate to the new generation and the exigencies of life under entirely new political conditions during the short-lived Markezinis government (8 October–25 November 1973— see chapter 5). Most of them were suspicious of the course to mass action that the antidictatorship student movement had taken. "The return from the lonely exaltation of violence and clandestinity to the everyday life of mass struggles is an unbearable normality," literary critic Zoumboulakis argues.[176] Ex-militant Stergios Katsaros claims that Papadopoulos's general amnesty in the summer of 1973 included the bombers in order to demonstrate that the regime had nothing to fear; this was a very clever psychological move. In that period an Athenian theater was staging a play with the comic title *Manolakis, the Bomber.*[177] Remembering this, Katsaros bitterly concludes: "This is what Papadopoulos succeeded in doing. To transform the city guerrillas into picturesque Manolakis."[178]

In his memoirs Katsaros solidifies the real and psychological distinction between his generation and that which followed in mythological terms. For the former, clandestine resistance had required the Promethean qualifications of laboriousness, self-discipline, and self-sacrifice. In contrast, he argues, the subsequent generation espoused Herbet Marcuse's critique of such self-effacing attributes. Instead, they admired Orpheus and Narcissus, who stand for liberation and hedonism: "If we take into account that the tactics of armed action entail planning, method, conspiracy and strict discipline it is very easy to understand the feelings of this rebelling half-anarchist youth."[179] Despite the somewhat overreaching nature of his argument, which seriously overstates the Dionysian element in the following generation's conduct, the analytical virtues of his categorization cannot be ignored—including the fact that Marcuse did indeed become one of the latter's solid intellectual points of reference (see chapter 4).

Historian Heinz Bude has written, "One of the paradoxes of historical procedure is that there is no necessary connection between the motives for an action and its outcome."[180] Surely the former Lambrakides had thought that by involving themselves in clandestine protest actions they would eventually raise people's consciousness and cause a massive resistance. Nevertheless, this generation's entire cycle of clandestine and violent actions eventually proved fruitless. Moreover, according to the definition by Friedhelm Neidhardt and Dieter Rucht, a social movement is "an organized and sustained effort of a collectivity of inter-related individuals, groups and organizations to promote or resist social change with the use of public protest activities."[181] As clandestine resistance did not manage to mobilize any significant sector of society, the student body included, it did not go public and therefore did not evolve into a movement.

Tasos Darveris quotes Jean-Paul Sartre's famous saying that World War II marked the most liberating years of his life, in order to retrospectively defend and justify the drive to live that dictated his life choices. In his half-fictional cathartic novel, Darveris represents resistance as the definite raison d'être of his generation. Vervenioti as well concludes that despite all the hardship, "those were very beautiful years, maybe the best years of our lives" (Vervenioti, interview). However, this resistance turned out to be symbolic, despite its enormous effects on the lives of the individuals who were involved. This contrasts starkly with resistance organizations in other repressive contexts such as the separatist Basque organization ETA, which operated simultaneously against Franco in Spain and ultimately crippled his succession. In Greece by the end of 1972, and with a mass student movement that generated an entirely different repertoire of action, it was clear that "vanguard organizations" were becoming increasingly obsolete.

Notes

1. Ioannis Tzortzis, "The *Metapolitefsi* That Never Was: A Re-evaluation of the 1973 'Markezinis Experiment,'" paper presented at the First LSE Symposium on Social Science Research in Greece, London, June 2003, 1.
2. The Junta's use of the term *revolution* was probably inspired by Nasser's movement—Papadopoulos was a great admirer—but it also referred to the Revolution of 1821, namely, the War of Independence against the Ottomans.
3. University of Warwick Committee for the Restoration of Democracy in Greece, *Dictatorship in Greece: A Preliminary Report,* 1967, (4), 3, Info file VI, League for Democracy in Greece Archive.
4. *Le Monde,* 2 June, cited in ibid., 3; John Warrack, "Greeks and the Arts," *Sunday Telegraph,* 1 August 1967.
5. Bermeo, "Classification and Consolidation."
6. O'Donnell, *Modernization.* Also see O'Donnell, "Tensions."
7. See Georgios Georgalas, Η Ιδεολογία της Επαναστάσεως. Όχι δόγματα, αλλά ιδεώδη [The Ideology of the Revolution. No Doctrines, Only Ideals]. Athens, undated.
8. Stockton, *Phoenix with a Bayonet.*
9. Papadopoulos, *Our Creed,* vol. 1, 11–12. Here I am using Kouloumbis's translation. "The Greek Junta Phenomenon," 355.
10. "Μέτρα δια την νεολαίαν. Κοσμία θα είναι η όλη εμφάνισις των μαθητριών." [Measures for the Youth. The Overall Appearance of Female Students Will Be Proper], *Vradyni,* 25 April 1967.
11. See Clogg, "The Ideology of the 'Revolution of 21 April 1967,'" 40.
12. According to Kouloumbis, "The old political establishment [became] synonymous with old parties, political feudalism, political families, old mentality, old relations, and old organizations. Hence, the slogan 'the old political world is dead'." In "The Greek Junta Phenomenon," 354. Also see Papadimitriou, "George Papadopoulos and the Dictatorship of the Greek Colonels 1967–1974."
13. Bermeo, "Classification and Consolidation," 441.
14. Liakos, "Το χαμένο ραντεβού" [The Missed Date], 48.
15. See Papathanasiou, "The Parliament Is Shut Down. The Putsch Has Been Carried Out. ..."
16. See, for example, L. Alexiou, N. Antonopoulos, M. Papazoglou, and K. Papaioannou, "Ετσι ο λαός πολέμησε τη χούντα" [This Is How the People Fought the Junta], *Ta Nea,* 11 December 1975, or the prologue by Stratis Tsirkas to the KKE Int. publication *Clandestine Resistance Journals* where he reproduces the common sentiment "[Our people] resisted with indomitable spirit."
17. Fakinou, *Eros, Summer, War.* Quoted in Gris, *The Ink Screams,* 267.
18. Chakkas, "Fish Bowl," 166.

19. John Gale, "Melina: What Those Colonels Told Me," *Observer*, 14 April 1968.
20. Dafermos, *Students and Dictatorship*, 26–27.
21. Gagnon, "Life Accounts," 54.
22. See Passerini's analysis of the role of laughter in everyday life under Italian Fascism, *Fascism in Popular Memory*, 86.
23. Passerini, *Autobiography of a Generation*, 65.
24. One could talk here of "hidden transcripts" of dissent, to use James C. Scott's famous phrase. See Scott, *Hidden Transcripts*.
25. Dimaras, *Toward the X Paved by Y*, 30.
26. Theodorakis's speech in Canada, 27 November 1973, quoted in a bulletin of the Historical Archive of the Fondation Hellénique.
27. Dafermos, *Students and Dictatorship*, 27.
28. Bermeo, "Classification and Consolidation."
29. See Charalambis, *Army and Political Authority*, 272. See also Grigoriadis, *History of the Dictatorship*, 1:261, 2:276.
30. With the Junta boosting growth in industry, construction, and small and medium enterprises, by 1969 the country had achieved the highest growth rate of the entire decade 1965–1975 at 11.6 percent, with inflation rates around 2.5 percent and per capita income around $1,135. See Kazakos, *State and the Market*, 267. The economic boom lasted until 1972.
31. "The Colonel Abolishes the Monarchy", *Time*, 11 June 1973. As the article concludes "[Greeks] have come to accept the Junta with a compliance that is surprising in a people noted for their volatile temperament."
32. Vlachou, *House Arrest*, 34.
33. Quoted in Meletopoulos, *Colonels' Dictatorship*, 110.
34. Doumanis, *Una faccia, una razza*, 165.
35. Herzfeld, "Mediterranean Dilemma," 441.
36. Quoted in Mantoglou, *Polytechnic*, 158.
37. Gerasimos Notaras, "Dictatorship," 188.
38. See the thorough account of one of its leading members, the sociology professor Vassilis Filias, *The Unforgettable and the Forgotten*. Another interesting personal account can be found in the prison diaries of the prominent Salonicean intellectual Pavlos A. Zannas, *Prison Notebooks*.
39. "Ο Αγώνας είναι εθνικοαπελευθερωτικός" [The Struggle Is One of National Liberation], *Agonas*, 22 September 1973.
40. Nikos Papandreou, *Andreas Papandreou*, 46. Andreas Papandreou habitually referred to the "US occupation of Greece." Ibid., 56.
41. For a thorough discussion of these resistance organizations, see Nikolinakos, *Resistance and Opposition*.
42. For a biased but interesting view of how Andreas Papandreou's behavior undermined the unity of antiregime organizations, see Murtagh, *Rape of Greece*, 207, 225.
43. A total of 280 student societies, associations, and organizations were banned, and their property was destroyed or confiscated. See Lazos, *Greek Student Movement*, 354–55.
44. "Greek Education Facing Revisions," *Sunday Times*, 11 June 1967.

45. Confidential, American Embassy Athens to Department of State, "Georgalas again Discusses the Future of the Revolution," 9 December 1970, POL 23, USNA.
46. Papazoglou, *Student Movement*, 14–16.
47. *New Statesman*, 18 August 1967.
48. Papazoglou, *Student Movement*, 14.
49. Giannaris, *EPON to the Polytechnic*, 325. See also Konofagos, *Polytechnic Uprising*, 26.
50. Altogether, 56 professors were sacked when the Junta took power, while 9 were suspended. By 1968, the regime had gotten rid of 167 professors. Even so, the view of the British embassy in Athens was that the regime had moved "with considerable circumspections, presumably to avoid either massive resignation from among the teaching staff or student demonstrations on their behalf." Restricted, British Embassy Athens to the Foreign Office, B. Hitch to J.E.C. Macrae, "University Dismissals," 2 February 1968, FCO9/196, PRO.
51. American Consul Thessaloniki to Department of State, "Follow Up on Rightist Student Demonstration, University of Thessaloniki, December 8, 1970," 14 January 1971, XR POL 13–2 Greece, USNA.
52. Fatouros, *Change and Reality*, 101–2.
53. The valedictory orations of Professors Mangakis in Athens and Maronitis and Manesis in Salonica that became occasions of student unrest were an exception.
54. "Ομιλών εις Θεσσαλονίκην ο Πρόεδρος της Εθνικής Κυβερνήσεως κ. Γεώργιος Παπαδόπουλος ετόνισε. Το Πανεπιστήμιο πρέπει να γίνη η εκκλησία πνευματικής αναπτύξεως του Ελληνικού έθνους" [Speaking from Salonica, the President of the National Government Stressed That the University Has to Become the Church of the Intellectual Development of the Greek Nation], *To Vima*, 6 January 1968, 1.
55. Solzhenitsyn, *First Circle*, 231.
56. "Μεταβάλλεται ριζικά το σύστημα εξετάσεων δι' Ανωτάτας Σχολάς. Δεν θα απαιτείται πλέον πιστοποιητικόν φρονημάτων" [The Exam System for Entering Higher Education Is Being Radically Transformed. No Certificate of National Beliefs Will Be Needed], *Ta Nea*, 1 April 1968.
57. Ministry of Public Order to the National Granting Institution, Confidential, "Μπαλαμπάσης Ευάγγελος, υιός του Γεωργίου και της Δέσποινας" [Balabasis Evangelos, son of Georgios and Despoina], 27 March 1970, private archive of Minas Kokkinos.
58. Decree 45/1967 of 25 and 26 August 1967.
59. See Krimbas, "Higher Education," 141.
60. *To Vima*, 5 May 1968.
61. Manolis Anagnostakis, "Νέοι της Σιδώνος" [Young People of Sidon], from the group of poems "Ο Στόχος" [The Target], originally in the *Eighteen Texts*, 128. Translated by David Conolly, http://www.lsa.umich.edu/UMICH/modgreek/Home/Window%20to%20Greek%20Culture/Literature/LIT_Anagnostakis_Manolis_Poems.pdf, accessed August 2013.
62. See also Zannas's *Prison Notebooks*, in which this film critic and translator of Marcel Proust into Greek expresses the same fear: "Is there going to be anything left for us?" (158).

63. Maravall, *Dictatorship and Political Dissent*, 105.
64. Katsaros, *I the Provocateur*, 102.
65. "Το κλειδί της δημοκρατίας. Εφημερίδα στην υπηρεσία των δημοκρατικών επιτροπών αντιστάσεως" [The Key of Democracy: Journal in the Service of the Democratic Committees of Resistance], no. 7, Leaflet Archive, Antidictatorship Organizations, Contemporary Social History Archives, Athens.
66. For documentation of this issue as seen from the point of view of the "reformists," see Dimitriou, *Split within the KKE*.
67. *Sunday Times*, 11 June 1967.
68. Ladas, *Speeches*, 9–24.
69. Georgalas, *The Crisis of Consumerist Society*. Also see Kouloumbis, "The Greek Junta Phenomenon," 357.
70. "Ο χαιρετισμός του Πρυτάνεως κου Γκανιάτσα προς τους φοιτητές του Πανεπιστημίου Θεσσαλονίκης" [The Greeting of the Rector, Mr. Ganiatsas, to the Students of the University of Salonica], *Makedonia*, 15 May 1968.
71. Cohen, *Folk Devils and Moral Panics*.
72. "Παράλληλοι βίοι—παράλληλες εικόνες" [Parallel Lives, Parallel Images], *Ta Nea*, 29 May 1968.
73. Sontag, *On Photography*, 78.
74. Theodoridis, *Macedonian Rock*, 240.
75. The original phrase, which appeared as an intertitle in the movie, went "This film could have been called 'The Children of Marx and Coca-Cola.'" The film recorded the uneasiness of a new generation in France against the background of the recently ended Algerian War and the ongoing one in Vietnam. Two different but complementary youth worlds are portrayed through the encounter of a consumerist woman and an idealist man.
76. Marangopoulos, "Children of Marx," 24.
77. See Kornetis, "¿Un 68 periférico?"
78. Darveris, *Night's Story*, 22.
79. Theodoridis, *Macedonian Rock*, 254.
80. Darveris, *Night's Story*, 202.
81. Giorgos Notaras, "Greeks Did Not Care," 136, emphasis mine.
82. Introduction to Darveris, *Night's Story*, 24.
83. This description echoes Karl Marx's labeling of Paris as the "Babel of Revolution." See Triantafyllos Mitafidis, "Ένα άγνωστο ντοκουμέντο από τον αντιδικτατορικό αγώνα" [An Unknown Document from the Antidictatorship Struggle], *Makedonia*, special section *Epiloges*, May 1998.
84. Darveris, *Night's Story*, 319.
85. For a detailed account, see Manitakis, "Struggling from Abroad." An excellent account in the form of a roman à clef is offered by Kranaki, *Philhellenes*. Two prominent members of *les boursiers* were philosophers Cornelius Castoriadis and Kostas Axelos, supposedly among the intellectual fathers of '68.
86. Farakos, "International Context."
87. "Ομολογουμένως αισθανόμασταν λίγο παράξενα σ' αυτό το πανηγύρι": Nikos Hatzinikolaou quoted in Afentouli, *May '68*, 197.

88. Kilekli, "Aspects of the French Policy vis-à-vis the Installation of Greeks in France and the Antidictatorship Struggle," 66.
89. Anna Chatzigiannaki, "Παρίσι Μάης '68. Κλίκες και ελληνικός χαβαλές ..." [Paris, May '68: Cliques and Greeks Hanging Out], *Epsilon/Eleftherotypia,* 3 May 1992.
90. One exception was the president of EPES, Nikos Hatzinikolaou, who after speaking in an occupied amphitheater at the Sorbonne during the events, was deported to Clermont-Ferrand. This was due to the authorities' interpretation of his move as a direct involvement in French affairs. See Hatzinikolaou, "Our Own May '68," in Afentouli, *May '68,* 98–99.
91. Afentouli, *May '68,* 198.
92. On this see Kostis Kornetis, "Les premiers mètres carrés de territoire grec libre."
93. Nikos Koundouros, "Μνήμες του '68" [Memories of '68], *I Lexi* 63–64 (Apr.–May 1987): 387.
94. The censored Greek press reported that "this action by the Greek students confirms their full alignment with the international anarchist movement, which at this moment is disturbing the whole of Europe." "Και Έλληνες αναρχικοί!" [Greek Anarchists Too!], *To Vima,* 23 May 1968.
95. Occupation of the Hellenic Residence of the Cité of Paris, ASKI, Collection Gogolou-Elefanti, box 4, EPES, 22 May 1968.
96. Kranaki, *The Philhellenes,* 317.
97. Occupation of the Hellenic Residence. Ibid.
98. For a comprehensive analysis of the occupation see Kornetis, "Les premiers mètres carrés."
99. Teos Romvos, "Η Φωνή της Αλήθειας" [The Voice of Truth], in *Μάης του '68. Οι προκηρύξεις* [May '68: The Leaflets], ed. Nikos Theodosiou, in *Makedonia,* special section *Epiloges,* May 1998.
100. *Poreia,* 1 May 1967.
101. American Embassy, Athens, to Secretary of State, 22 October 1971, 5765 Confidential, POL 21, DS, USNA.
102. See Ios, "Η βόμβα Πρετεντέρη" [The Pretenderis' Bomb], *Eleftherotypia,* 8 March 2003.
103. Giannis Floros, "Αντιστασιακές Οργανώσεις στη Δικτατορία. Στοιχεία για την εμφάνιση, τη δράση και την πορεία τους" [Resistance Organizations and Dictatorship: Elements for the Appearance, the Action and Their Itinerary], *Anti* 344 (17–23 Apr. 1987), 51.
104. Giannopoulos, "Resistance Forces," 283.
105. Interview with Anagnostopoulos, as cited in Papachelas and Telloglou, *17 November File,* 26.
106. Extract taken from the speeches of members of the organization in court, published in a leaflet dated 7 October 1972.
107. Common leaflet of LEA and Makrigiannis, a small clandestine organization that was united with it in October 1971.
108. See K29M's organ *Το Κίνημα. Για τη λαϊκή εξουσία στην Ελλάδα* [The Movement: For People's Power in Greece], Paris, 4–5 June 1968, 56.

109. Francovich, "Le migrazioni intellettuali," 634. For the tendency to migrate to Italy to study, see Kornetis, "Una diaspora adriatica."
110. Interview quoted in Papoutsis, *The Freshman*, 26.
111. For an analysis of Greek student activity in Italy through the lens of the Italian Ministry of the Interior see Raftopoulos, "Students and Dictatorship in Italy."
112. For a detailed reconstruction of this event, see Papoutsis, *The Great "Yes."*
113. Andreadis, *The Resistance of Memory.*
114. Pasolini, "Diario," 77. Some years later, Pasolini wrote the foreword to the Italian edition of poems that Panagoulis had written in prison.
115. Raftopoulos, "Between Italy and Greece: Resistance, Dictatorship and the Unfreezing Cold War, 1967–74," unpublished paper presented at the Second Ph.D. Symposium on Modern Greece, London School of Economics, 10 June 2005, 8.
116. Dimitris Deliolanis, "Η Lotta Continua μιλάει για τη 17Ν" [Lotta Continua Talks about 17N], *Krama* 9 (Dec. 2003).
117. See Cammelli, *Studiare da Stranieri*, 37; Papoutsis, *The Freshman*, 46.
118. Italian paramilitary elements were working closely with the Greek Junta for this scope. See Kleitsikas, *Greek Student Movement*. The pro-Junta Greek students in Italy were organized in the National Society of Hellenic Students of Italy (ESESI).
119. Being involved in antiregime activities abroad was not without dangers. Many Greek students were spotted by informers and reported to the consulates, embassies, and the representatives of the Orthodox Church.
120. Kotanidis, *All Together, Now!*, 109.
121. Papachristos, *He Lived Life*, 85.
122. Vavizos, *How Carbonara Was Tempered*, 67–68.
123. Fallaci, *Un Uomo.*
124. Papachelas and Telloglou, *17 November File*, 21.
125. *To Kinima*, 55.
126. Papachelas and Telloglou, *17 November File.*
127. 8 July 2003. In http://athens.indymedia.org/local/17N/praktika.php?day=81. Last access date 2 July 2011.
128. "Η διεθνής επαναστατική νεολαία καλεί στον αγώνα" [International Revolutionary Youth Calls for a Struggle], leaflet issued together with the International Workers' Union.
129. Darveris, *Night's Story*, 177.
130. Yiannopoulos, "Resistance Forces," 283.
131. "Η δίκη των εννιά" [The Trial of the Nine], *Thessaloniki*, 4 February 1970.
132. Giannis Papatheodorou, introduction to Darveris, *Night's Story*, 21.
133. Papachelas and Telloglou, *17 November File*, 24.
134. Antonis Liakos, preface to Darveris, *Night's Story*, 23.
135. Darveris, *Night's Story*, 204. See also 318: "He once again thought how different cinema was from reality."
136. Liakos, "History Writing," 53.
137. Voglis, "The Junta Came to Power by the Force of Arms," 565.
138. Nikos Serdedakis, "Political Violence in Post-War Greece: The Origins of Greek Terrorism," unpublished paper, September 2003.

139. Hall, "Rediscovering Ideology."
140. Darveris, *Night's story*, 111.
141. Katsaros, "We, the Guevarists," *Eleftherotypia*, 9 October 1997.
142. Mervyn Jones, "Witness in Athens," *New Statesman*, 3 March 1972.
143. Kanakaris, *Truth about Greece*.
144. Efthymiou, *For All Those*, 57.
145. Mantoglou, *Polytechnic*, 56.
146. David Holden, "The Revolution of Supergreek," *Guardian*, 15 February 1970.
147. Karl Marx, *The Eighteenth Brumaire of Louis Bonaparte*, 10.
148. Gourgouris, *Dream Nation*, 181.
149. Sommier, *La violence politique*, 35.
150. Pattakos's jocular remarks in the *New York Times*, 20 May 1967.
151. Pamphlets 1 and 2, 7.1.43, Dafermos Archive, EDIA.
152. Damofli interviewed for Stelios Kouloglou's television program *The Real 17 November*, 17 November 2002.
153. Darveris, *Night's Story*, 175.
154. Achilleas Kapageridis, "Ελληνική Πανσπουδαστική Αντιφασιστική Οργάνωση ΡΗΓΑΣ ΦΕΡΑΙΟΣ" [Greek All-Student Antifascist Organization Rigas Feraios], *Antistasi '68*, March 1968.
155. Nicole Dreyfus provides a picture of their trials from the point of view of an observer in *Les étudiants grecs accusent*.
156. *Thourios*, October 1968. Similarly, the December issue declares that "From the very beginning in the Rigas lines, students are present who fought for the ideals which have been forged in older struggles."
157. Founding manifesto of Rigas Feraios, Athens, December 1967. *Rigas Feraios Album*, 52–53.
158. Skroumbelos, *My Red Friends*.
159. Quoted in Minuzzo, *Quando arrivano i Colonnelli*, 108.
160. Rigas Feraios, *Rigas Feraios Album*, 52–53.
161. *Thourios*, 10, April 1969.
162. Ibid., 3, September 1968.
163. Ibid., 10, April 1969.
164. Ibid., 6, December 1968.
165. Voglis, "The Junta Came to Power by the Force of Arms," 562.
166. Papachelas and Telloglou, *17 November File*, 36. According to the authors, the smaller dynamic groups profited from the fact that the large ones (PAM and DA) were wiped out in 1969 and 1970.
167. Ibid., 37.
168. American Embassy Athens, "Popular Revolutionary Resistance Claims Responsibility for Explosion in Embassy August 29," 8 September 1972, POL 23–0, USNA.
169. See the front page of *Apogevmatini*, 30 August 1972.
170. See Giannis Pretenderis, "Η βόμβα Γιωτόπουλου" [The Giotopoulos' Bomb], *To Vima*, 5 March 2003 and Ios, "Η βόμβα Πρετεντέρη" [The Pretenderis' Bomb], *Eleftherotypia*, 8 March 2003.

171. Interview with Savvopoulos, *Epsilon*, 27/10/2002, 16.
172. Darveris, *Night's Story*, 283.
173. Ibid., 155.
174. For an interesting exception to this rule see Kotanidis, *All Together, Now!*, 100–101. It has to be noted here that the members of the rock band *Bourboulia* who collaborated closely with Savvopoulos were heavily involved in drugs and psychedelia, in particular its leader, bass player Vasilis Dallas (see chapter 4).
175. Savvopoulos, interview, 8 January 2004, Salonica.
176. Zoumboulakis, "One Night to the Next."
177. "Μανωλάκης ο βομβιστής" [Manolakis, the Bomber], *Eleftheros Kosmos*, 11 May 1973.
178. Katsaros, "We, the Guevarists," *Eleftherotypia*, 9 October 1997.
179. Katsaros, *I the Provocateur*, 213.
180. Bude, "German Kriegskinder," 290.
181. Neidhardt and Rucht, "Analysis of Social Movements," 450.

Chapter 3

A Mosquito on a Bull

Chapter 3 begins with an overview of the various student cultures, briefly analyzing the priorities and standpoints of the ones who supported the regime. Furthermore, the chapter concentrates on the students' mobilizing structures, mainly the so-called regional societies and the Euro-Hellenic Youth Movement, which was created by a circle of upper-class students. It concludes with an overview of the various student organizations, which reflected different ideological currents, and the relationships that grew up between them. The chapter further analyses the image of the "other" within the student groups and the "hardening" of subjectivity that the various rivalries brought about. Finally, through a narrative analysis of patterns it provides insights into individual subjectivity by considering the processes of conserving and innovating identities, attitudes, and behaviors.

Competing Youth Cultures

In February 1973 the *New York Times* correspondent in Athens commented on the university situation as follows: "[In 1970], a group of students told a visitor that, while campuses elsewhere in the world were alive with agitation, Greek students were in no position to act." According to the *Times*, Greek students expressed their desire to receive diplomas, their fear of the police and the army, and their inability to find more than a few dozen colleagues interested in open defiance.[1] Less than a year earlier, the American embassy in Athens created a useful classification of the state of affairs among Greek students by identifying four groups within the student population. The first and largest category was composed of apparently apolitical and nonactivist students. The report pointed out: "This group, for various reasons, [was] uninterested or unwilling to take risks of involvement in student activities which might threaten continuation of their education." Family and economic pressures to obtain a university degree had deterred their involvement in organized student activities, the report concluded.[2] This is probably why, as the rector of the Athens Polytechnic noted, the majority of Greek students after April 1967 "remained passive in regard of what was happening in our country," an "apathy" that he found surprising.[3]

The Junta offered various forms of entertainment as alternatives to student activism, among them excursions to the countryside, music festivals, and above all football. When in early 1971 *Protoporia* [Avant-garde], a student journal with antiregime leanings, carried out a survey on student conditions at Athens University, most students complained about the fact that there was no coherence in the student community and drew a very bleak picture of student life. One student told the interviewer: "We are definitely not united. There is no student community." A group of female students complained that male interests at the university were quite one-sided, as they talked only about sex and sports. More significantly, one student declared that there were no student societies, adding, "The students in their majority are rather bored with the student condition. They start out being bored and they end up being even more bored."[4]

Theodoros Kouloumbis, a Greek-American academic who visited Greece in the spring of 1972, noted that "most of the students seemed to be older in age and bored." "I felt pity for the Greek students," Kouloumbis concluded.[5] Similarly, an article in the *New York Times* called Greek students "for years the most passive in the West."[6] While a tiny minority of radicals took part in clandestine actions, the majority of students remained unresponsive to the authoritarianism imposed on the country and on the university system, continuing to attend their lectures peacefully in a highly policed university system.

A second group, according to the American report, comprised students whose orientation was pro-regime, mainly because they had benefited from the regime's actions. This small group centered on the leaders of the student organizations appointed by the Junta in April 1967, after previous groups had been dissolved. In addition to spreading propaganda in favor of the regime, these students often bullied with impunity those whom they considered its adversaries, including professors. In a telling incident, one group of them belonging to the appointed rightist Student Union of the Aristotelian University entered Professor Dimitris Fatouros's class in interior decoration at the School of Architecture in Salonica in December 1970, disrupted the lecture, threatened him and his students, smashed classroom objects, and wrote slogans on the blackboard. Despite the fact that an enraged Fatouros made a formal request that the students responsible be given the severest possible punishment, they went unpunished, and the university considered taking action against the professor himself, citing his "liberal" teaching methods.[7]

These were the same students who cheered the dictator Papadopoulos on every occasion. The most radical among them were members of the right-wing National Social Student Union. Michalis Skyrianos recalls being approached in order to participate in this group's activities:

That year a fellow student of mine from school happened to enter the same faculty. One whose family ... had embraced the Junta. So, within the first week that I went to Athens he came, he welcomed me, telling me, "How nice, we entered together, we're gonna do this and that." And within a week he suggested to me that we go and become members and participate and help the Student Society, the appointed one of course. Junta's society. (Tzortzopoulou and Skyrianos, interview)

The pro-regime societies' task was to organize talks and open discussions on student issues, excursions to the countryside, entertainment, and celebrations of national holidays, including the Day of the Student, a holiday established by the Junta alongside the Day of the Peasant and the Day of the Worker. Their statutes were modified to ensure effective control of their functioning by the Junta, and their constitution forbade discussion of nonuniversity and non-national issues at their meetings.[8]

Outside of the university, the dictators organized a Boy Scout and Girl Guide movement, the Alkimoi. Starting off with a thousand members, these organizations grew to twenty thousand by 1972. Alkimoi youths assisted in celebrations of Greek "polemic virtue," which the regime habitually organized in the Panathenaic Stadium and which were characterized by a delirium of kitsch nationalism, with reenactments of the glorious military battles of Hellenism that ranged from 480 BC and Thermopylae to the 1949 defeat of the Greek communists in Grammos and Vitsi.[9] Schools were often brought to watch the spectacle; on one such celebration the dictator Papadopoulos was prevented from speaking by cheering pupils in what constituted an effective but probably unintended act of protest.

Despite the "innovations" introduced by the regime, a letter sent by the regime's appointed Youth Directory to Papadopoulos in 1970 admitted to the "full inertia of the student societies, nonexistent contact between societies and the mass of students, and lots of university problems of the students."[10] Even though the regime envisioned the use of right-wing student societies for the "enlightenment" and guidance of other students, the societies never managed to gain significant momentum among students, not least because of their outdated and deeply reactionary character. Thus for freshmen, the societies' program included "general mass attending, screenings of films with a moral content, [and] musical breakfasts."[11] The activities aimed at boosting the youths' alliance to the Colonels' active promotion of the Hellenic-Christian credo that intended to "yoke these mutually hostile strands of the national heritage together," in anthropologist Michael Herzfeld's words.[12]

The societies offered free tickets for football matches and often sponsored excursions abroad, in which students already "stigmatized" as left-wing could not participate. Football in this period came to be identified with the regime, which systematically promoted sporting activities as part of the national revival. In particular, Panathinaikos's so-called epic course to Wembley for the European Cup finals became one of the highlights of 1970. A foreign account reported:

> The extraordinary demonstrations throughout the country when the team beat Red Star of Belgrade were an entirely new phenomenon for Greece. In part it was a chance to let off bottled-up steam, and at first the security forces were worried as hundreds of thousands poured into the cities' streets. But they were sharp enough to tie the football victory to the regime by infiltrating the crowds with men shouting 'Long live the revolution!' In the soldiers' view it is healthier to have people shouting in the streets about football than about politics.[13]

Gradually, any student interested in football came to be identified as pro-regime. Giannis Kourmoulakis was one nonpoliticized student who, up to a certain point, coexisted with students appointed by the regime in the pro-Junta societies, enjoying the benefits of this association. His is an exceptional case, as in his narrative he refuses to demonize those students, who were usually looked upon with distaste by the rest:

> I am an Olympiakos fan. In that period I used to have friends with whom I went to the matches, the Junta had formed some student societies in the faculties. They gave us tickets, the teams gave tickets, the societies went to the teams and picked up tickets and distributed them to us. We used to pay 10 drachmas then. There were some people who were chosen and appointed as administrative councils—without elections, they were appointed. I used to have contact with those kids, we talked, we had an opinion about what was happening and so forth, and with those kids we talked about what could be done, "We should do something in order to improve the situation," and those kids had the same agonies, the same problems about what should be done, that things were not going well, why not get better books, and so on. Up to the point at which the signatures started being collected in order to have elections in the societies.... At that point you had to take a position, to go either this way or the other. (Kourmoulakis, interview)

Kourmoulakis suggests that the appointed students supported the regime in part because they were ignorant: "It was a bit like a trench war, where, however, the differences were informal ones, namely, [that] not even the kids themselves, I imagine, that were on the other side knew why they were there." From 1971 onward, the right-wing student organizations indeed changed tactics and began attempting to win over students with an "alternative" taste by organizing rock concerts with French yé-yé icons Johnny Hallyday and Silvie Vartan, and Greek rock star Demis Roussos and by publishing student journals, such as *Foititikos Palmos* [Student Pulse] in Athens and *O Foititis* [The Student] in Salonica. These journals, which published editorials waxing lyrical about the Greek dictators, also tried to tackle issues such as the student condition, sexuality, and youth culture—without, however, abandoning either moralist discourse or attempts at ideological indoctrination.

Finally, a core of politically thinking pro-regime students participated in the National Movement of Young Scientists (founded 1969). Numbering five hundred members, all young technocrats, this group had ethnocracy [*ethnokratia*] as its main motto, an idealized reference to "the political regime whose every action results from the spirit of a bonding between generations and which will have as a prerogative the interests of the nation."[14] At the organization's first congress, its president argued that its leadership would "teach manliness to the leaders of the Western world," and others suggested that "Hellenic-Christian" civilization was a panacea that would cure the "ill societies of the West." A female student at the congress accused the older generation of being responsible for the decadence and dissoluteness of the young, and a female lawyer rejected feminism, since "a woman has to recognize the fact that she is a woman in order to remain such."[15]

A Rebellious Subjectivity

By the end of 1971, two other categories of students had made their appearance. The first of these consisted of students exasperated, according to the US Embassy report, with the "unsatisfactory conditions in the universities, including [the] extreme conservatism of the university administration and faculty, lack of student-professor contact, extremely over-crowded classes and others." Members of this category appeared willing to organize and participate in free elections of the representatives of various student organizations. The second, roughly described as political activists of the center but with primarily left-wing convictions, was antiregime and sought to "embarrass the government over academic issues and 'radicalize' the main body of their colleagues." This second category emerged at a point when the student movement's "historical generation" was out of action.

In recalling what it felt like to be part of this fourth, most radical group of students, Myrsini Zorba declared, "The dictatorship deprived me of those social and personal possibilities, the air, my oxygen, that is" (Zorba, interview). Stelios Kouloglou remembered that "after years of introversion, this new category emerged shouting and claiming its right to live/experience freedom without boundaries." Ioanna Karystiani similarly recalled: "When the time came to enter university, I didn't seek out all that really interested me, and no one helped me in that, whereas I would have liked to study literature abroad somewhere, I was getting all my kicks from going to university, coming to Athens and entering an organization fighting against the dictatorship. That was all. Nothing else interested me" (Karystiani, interview). It is noteworthy that Karystiani uses a word with strong sexual connotations (καύλα) in order to describe her drive to enter university and begin resisting the regime, denoting what was almost a sexual need, a physical necessity that was bound to bring her pleasure.

The majority of student activists of this new generation did not have a political pedigree and, unlike their predecessors, had not experienced the Second World War, the Greek Civil War, and their associated deprivations either directly or indirectly. Instead, they tended to "count the dictatorship as their formative experience."[16] For the previous generation's collective representation the assassinated Lambrakis was a key figure, which underscores the climate of permanent fear and repression. In contrast, this second cohort distances itself to a certain extent from the Civil War and does not seem to feel shaped by the experience of its aftermath. A typical statement from a female student born in 1951 reads: "I don't have memories from the post–Civil War years, none, meaning that I didn't experience that hideous anticommunism, or I don't remember it, so, I don't have these images in my mind of communists with knives in the mouth and so forth as personal images" (Alavanou, interview). Such students are referred to by one contemporary as "the new generation [that] is not very much influenced by events that it has not experienced itself."[17]

The writer Rea Galanaki sums up this generation's attitude with the seemingly inconsequential line, "I am not speaking about the pre-dictatorship situation, which I do not know."[18] In many ways, this attitude reflects a need on the part of the students to "kill" their predecessors and affirm their dynamic presence as a self-sustained entity, not the clone of the students of the post–Civil War period. The scarcity of references to earlier generations in student activist documents accords with their self-representation and gives the impression that the students of the movement almost deliberately represented their generation as distinct and refused to transmit their demands along preexisting channels.

As the quotations above indicate, a number of the students of this generation had felt pressure to rebel since their high school years, during which they were obligated to keep their hair short, to learn about Greek heritage in an old-fashioned manner, and to study religion, as well as to accept a ban on vernacular in the curriculum. These students had experienced the fruits of the 1964 Educational Reform under the Center Union in their earlier days, a period they remembered as a benevolent interlude. Vera Damofli said of the reform, "And then came old Papandreou and brought new books, new language, we could read whatever we wanted" (Damofli, interview). Law student and present-day economist Chrysafis Iordanoglou explained that the reform had a disproportionately great impact on his student generation. Iordanoglou's testimony is of particular interest here, as his own father belonged to the opposite political camp and had served as a minister in Karamanlis's right-wing governments up to 1963: "We grew up, in our teenage years, with Papanoutsos's reform, which changed the situation completely after '61. Things were turned upside down. For us the difference was much greater than for others" (Iordanoglou, interview). By contrast, schooling under the Junta was "a continuous bombardment of naiveties, inaccuracies and dangerous chauvinism."[19]

Most benefits of the Educational Reform for schools were short lived even prior to the coup. The short-lived governments that followed George Papandreou's sacking by the king between the summer of 1965 and the spring of 1967, though of nominal centrist inclinations, were quite reactionary, and they nullified parts of the reform, often with the backing of considerable parts of the academic establishment. The Educational Institute was attacked, its budget was reduced, and the curricula, which students of the era remembered as the most striking feature of educational democratization, was altered, banned, or simply abolished. The leap that people make in their memories from 1965 straight to 1967 disregards two years of regression that were crucial for creating the conditions for the coup itself.

Student radicals' recollections of the period of the dictatorship tend to describe life under the Junta in gloomy colors, in terms of its sensory feel. Vasia Karkagianni-Karambelia remembers that the coup felt in sensorial terms as a corporal abuse: "When the dictatorship took place in Greece we felt it, really, as if we had been betrayed. Betrayal was not only on your mind, you know, it was on your body" (Karkagianni-Karambelia, interview). According to Damofli, the dictatorship period was full of darkness: "I think that it was always cloudy." Indeed, for her, the political climate was stifling, leaving no space to breathe—a very common way of describing the frustration that characterized the affect of the time:

> [Y]ou had to put up with [these people] every day, with their yelling, with their dressing habits, with their horror. Every day.... It was

something that, since we were young, man, it was a burden. A tomb. Very bad. And you were saying, "Man, I have to make cracks over there, make some cracks in order to breathe." This was very powerful. It is a very heavy thing to live in a dictatorship. (Damofli, interview)

According to Giorgos Gavriil, a pharmaceutical sciences student in Athens, these were years of exclusion and obscurity, in which one felt a continuous sense of guilt, even for falling in love.[20]

Many politicized students of this generation speak of the vulgarity of the dictatorship's taste, including its ludicrous symbol, the phoenix emerging from the ashes, mockingly referred to as *the bird*, which was exhibited in all sizes and places. *Katerina, an architecture student in Athens, was firm in her assertion that her generation felt the preposterous aspects of the Junta more deeply than anything else: "We felt the ridicule of the dictatorship much more than its violence" (*Katerina, interview). Dictator Papadopoulos's almost paranoid appearance and manner of talking were also a major reason for disgust: "That voice of Papadopoulos, how can I put it, sounded like a pneumatic drill inside my nerves," writes Vera Damofli.[21]

The immobility of student life under the Junta may have caused these individuals and others to feel stifled by the dictatorship, since under normal conditions the university was a privileged site of freedom of expression. Tension fed a tendency to tear down the old world in order to escape from its sick atmosphere; one student remembered, "'Something is rotten in the state of Denmark,' we used to say."[22] This conceptualization of the situation in literary terms is also echoed in Dionysis Savvopoulos's opening lyrics, "Something in this town is making me sick," from his popular song of the time, "Elsa, You Scare Me" [Elsa, Se Fovamai] (1972), which subversively reappropriated Papadopoulos's favorite medical metaphor of Greece as a sick patient (while at the same time playing with the words Elsa and ESA, the military police). Students' everyday mantra was that "Something has to be done,"[23] according to a testimony. Some of these "teenagers" saw no other solution than to protest—thus claiming their right to experience freedom with no boundaries—against a collar that was tightening more and more, threatening to deprive them of the possibility of dreaming and living as they longed to. The archetypical teenager ontology of a rift with society functioned then in Greece not as a psychological necessity so much as an incarnated collective demand that had already taken over the Western world: the dream of the radical overthrow of hypocritical bourgeois values. The advent of the Junta was quite dramatic for young people who were coming into contact with an international protest movement that struggled "for a new way of living rather than for a new politics," as former activist Dimitris Marangopoulos puts it.²⁴ There was an alternative way, summarized by Damofli who mentions the most popular music producer of the period, Nikos Mastorakis, who systematically promoted a nonpolitical style of music entertainment through his television show: "Either you became part of the golden youth of this period with Mastorakis, the clubs and the quick degree, or you were looking for something else."²⁵

Some students started to be sensitized by reports on the trials, the torture, and the exile of resistance fighters.²⁶ Nikitas Lionarakis, a law student of solid right-wing background, claims that he was entirely unaware of the regime's cruelty until he happened to attend a trial. Soon thereafter, this young intellectual began to adopt an increasingly moral stance toward politics; the analogy to West German law students experiencing a rude political awakening during the Auschwitz trials in Frankfurt in the early 1960s is inescapable:²⁷

> During the first year in Salonica the great trials of PAM and Rigas took place, with Chalkidis, Spyridakis, Papalexis, and the rest. The trials took place right across from my house, within the International Fair.... As a law student I decided to go.... And there I had a great shock, because for the first time I heard about torture. There was a lady called Parthena Kerameida, I have no idea what happened to her since, and a certain Aristeidis Baras, who stated that they had been tortured and so forth. I went berserk, these were unheard of things for me, that they could take place. So, I followed the trial and started, on a rational level now, to realize that this was a regime that was a bit authoritarian. (Lionarakis, interview)

Like Lionarakis, other students lacking any ideological pedigree started analyzing the political situation with a certain open-mindedness due to the fact that they were not conditioned by the past, as was the generation before them, and lacked the political cautiousness of their elders. Michalis Sabatakakis explains: "The students who entered university from the dictatorship onward did not generally have organized contact with politics, did not consist therefore of members of groups and mainly of the Democratic Lambrakis Youth, as did the previous ones. So, they almost started from scratch, their relationship to politics starts from scratch" (Sabatakakis, interview).

According to one testimony, those sensitized students immediately formed strong bonds and constituted a sort of commune based on their common rejection of the Junta. Even so, students in general were divided into those who approved of the current state of affairs and those who disapproved. In an interview conducted in the late 1990s, a former student militant remembers: "The students did not have a life outside that of a common experience in this period. Namely, their personal life, the professional quests, the mentalities, the discussions, everything was turning around the issue of the Junta. ... The main issue was how to overthrow the Junta. And this defined their behavior."[28]

Sabatakakis describes the everyday contact between students in gatherings that signaled the creation of the first solid and extended circles of socialization, distinguishing between his generation and those that had gone before and came after: "My circle of friends, and not only mine, proceeded in an organized way to discussions in homes, of a philosophical nature, something that most probably did not happen in previous periods, it did not happen prior to '67, and does not happen after '74, that is, organized groups that are systematically discussing ... in an organized manner" (Sabatakakis, interview). Some of these groups of students chose to take their protest into the open and defy the risks this entailed. But for most students, participating in a large-scale protest was often accidental, more a decision made by intuition than as a result of the application of political criteria and judgment. Maria Tzortzopoulou, a Panteios student, tended to avoid the campus as an unpleasant place. Although she confesses that she was not one of the most politically sophisticated students, she nevertheless knew what was going on:

> I didn't want to enter this sort of environment, nor did I wish to attend courses. Even I understood what was going on. Anyway. Somebody approached me, it was Marinos, and he tells me, "We are collecting signatures for a paper." Now, why did this guy say this to me, what attracted him to me, [when] I had nothing to do with these things? "We are collecting signatures in order to improve the condition in the student domain and so on. Are you going to sign?" "I'll sign," I told him. ... Why he trusted me and why I trusted him, I don't know. (Tzortzopoulou and Skyrianos, interview)

Tzortzopoulou's testimony underlines the contingency of the recruitment process. Giannis Kourmoulakis also mentions the role of intuition in decisions of this sort. As a politically nonaffiliated student, he differentiates himself from his "organized" colleagues, who once in a group were guided by a collective body that made most decisions. In this respect, he presents himself as a loner, someone who was guided only by his "instinct": "We knew why we were here, but we didn't have ... instruction or anything like that. I was instructed by my instinct" (Kourmoulakis, interview). Still, politically active students remained small in number—what could be called a "strict minority."[29]

Heirs and Defectors

There was a gradual shift in the first category of students according to the aforementioned US Embassy classification, whose background did not "permit" them to take part in any antiregime activity. The very existence of the oppressive dictators transformed them into a politicized entity, reinforcing their need to "do something" and gradually to become associated with the Left. Kourmoulakis recalls: "We were not politicized up to that point. We hadn't read anything. They made us, through the beatings, through their stance, they turned us and made us, say, communists. We hadn't read a thing, we weren't communists, I was just a twenty-two-year-old lad, I was against the Junta because, you know, they were repressing us" (Kourmoulakis, interview). Similarly, Nikos Alivizatos, a law student of solid bourgeois background, writes that one did not need to be left-wing in order to rebel:

> You became left-wing through the indignation that a barbarous regime created in you, which condensed the most reactionary features of postwar Greek society: cheap patriotism, Greek Orthodox hypocrisy and servility vis-à-vis the foreign 'protectors.' … So you became left-wing by being antiregime in the first place. Readings, political thinking and ideological consciousness did not precede, they followed. In this sense—at least as far as I am concerned—freedom, democracy and human rights were the first issue, the fundamental right of political belonging. Revolution followed.[30]

In his index of the members of the "Polytechnic Generation," writer Dimitris Fyssas similarly argues that the Colonels' arbitrariness prompted youth of all backgrounds to embrace the left-wing paradigm and shape their oppositional tactics around its theoretical frame:

> We were the suppressed kids of the dictatorship, brought up with Papadopoulos's *kalamatianos* dances and Pattakos's trowel [used to inaugurate public works], fed up with the military marches and the "birds" of the regime of 21 April, enraged that they didn't let us listen to and read whatever we wanted, we were oriented, of course, toward the outlawed and sympathetic to the haunted ones: that is the Left and the left-wingers. The Junta made us left-wing without knowing it. That's why we come from all social classes, that's why we are children of right-wing and pro-Junta families as well.[31]

Fyssas disregards the influence of the international protest movement cycle of 1968, which would have radicalized the students with or without the

Junta. Still, he is right in pointing out that the very characteristics of this generation of rebels were defined by the Junta's vulgarity and its antimodernist stance. In this sense these were "children of the dictatorship."

Students of both this generation and the previous one refer frequently in their recollections to family traditions, particularly to left-wing political families. Luisa Passerini's observation that socialism or communism are conceptualized as quasibiological predestinations is particularly valid in this context. Passerini argues that there are key points in self-representation in which "personal and collective memory meet and the individual mythology becomes a tradition shared by a family, a circle of friends, a political group."[32] In this vein, Christina Vervenioti comments on Marxism: "Yes, it came as a natural continuation, [my father] was constantly talking to us, there was no way that in the evenings at dinner, on Sunday afternoons say, he would not talk to us about Lenin, Marx, Engels. Those people were part of our lives" (Vervenioti, interview). Myrsini Zorba remarks, "Of course it was clear that I would be oriented [toward the Left], as Resistance had a mythical dimension inside me, resistance to the Germans, the Left after the civil war" (Zorba, interview). "I consider that I was a communist straightaway," Kleopatra Papageorgiou remarks, "that is, from back then [laughter], since I was very little, as soon as I started to understand the world" (Papageorgiou, interview).

Such claims of continuity in politics are usually associated with the family's place of origin. "We were naturally left-wing, as we were refugees," Damofli remarks (Damofli, interview). Triantafyllos Mitafidis makes a similar point at greater length:

> We grew up within the atmosphere of poverty and suppression, of the, how can I put it now, of refugee life, we had the consciousness of the refugee. And of course the fact that we were the very history of multiethnic Salonica, all this had a, how can I put it, I found it very natural. Namely, I didn't have any inhibitions in getting involved in a movement with internationalist characteristics. (Mitafidis, interview)

Kourmoulakis acknowledges that a certain political pedigree naturally endowed certain people with a greater political awareness, in contrast to those with a more politically neutral home environment: "From one point of view we were quite ignorant, I and some other people. Others were smart, the ones who had a family background with some history, some past, an uncle who had experienced some deportation. Those knew some things about what to do" (Kourmoulakis, interview).

Some people from left-wing family traditions (who were therefore on the side of the defeated in the civil war) also indicate, however, that their parents' experiences made them cautious. The continuous persecutions of the postwar years and their parents' constant fear of being purged made it imperative to them that their children not get involved in politics: "What was coming out was ... the urge to be very careful," Thodoros Vourekas remembers. "Things were still very recent. My father had been persecuted up to '53, [when] I had already been born" (Vourekas, interview). "Our parents, even the left-wing ones, rarely talked about their past," says former student activist Kostas Kalimeris. Just like in post–civil war Spain, silence and repeated parental admonitions "not to meddle in politics" colored these young people's upbringing, heightening the effect of claustrophobia in post-1949 Greece.

As youths tend to internalize collective values, some chose to reinforce the bond with their families, whereas others opted to break with it. Accordingly, family traditions could act in a double-edged and random way, and individual agency played the primary role in political socialization. Robert Lane's classic "Mendelian law of politics," which insists on ideological consistency and political continuity over generations, does not seem to apply.[33] At times family orientation had a boomerang effect on the parents, as it brought about a generational clash, and the parents' attempt at extreme indoctrination often led to undesired results. Parents who fell strongly in the orthodox communist tradition, for example, often produced children who chose more radical communist paths. This was the case in the life histories of both Kleopatra Papageorgiou and Anna Mandelou, a Maoist and a Trotskyist, respectively. Mandelou explains her critical stance toward party orthodoxy as a logical outcome of the fact that she came from a communist family:

> Indeed I met kids, for instance the son of a general ... who of course would look at the left-wingers with awe, since they had been persecuted all those years.... I couldn't have such a stance, because I knew the civil war better, meaning the history of the Left in Greece. I had experienced it deep inside me. So I had a more critical stance. And I was not the only one. (Mandelou, interview)

Christina Vervenioti reacted against her socialist father's rejection of the Communist Party's dogmatism by embracing the KKE. She evokes with distress her father's endless repetition of a particular personal misfortune, aiming to reinforce his argument, which in the end had the opposite effect:

> In general my father would tell me not to get involved with the KKE.... And this of course made me at some point embrace it with

all my might [laughter]. Because my father would tell me about all those mistakes committed by the party, about Zachariadis [KKE's controversial historical leader], about all those things. He told me that once there was a gathering at my aunt's place and my father disagreed on certain issues, and when he left someone shot them, because my father was with someone else and they had a disagreement concerning that particular line, and on their way out they fired at them. And he kept on telling me this over and over again. (Vervenioti, interview)

Olympios Dafermos argues that in that epoch, class could be a major deterrent to activism, because risking a university degree was a dangerous possibility for people from the lower classes: "When someone entered whichever faculty in the university coming from a rural, petit-bourgeois, working-class background, one changed class, one could change class.... One was guaranteed a decent life, changes were radical. This was an impediment to action against the regime, because one was risking one's degree. But the ones coming from higher strata in terms of income, what did they have to lose?" (Dafermos, interview). To this one could add the relative social isolation that students with solid working-class backgrounds might experience at the universities. However, the class origins of the students who became politically involved varied, suggesting that material conditions cannot entirely account for students' decisions to engage in antiregime activity. Commenting on this phenomenon, economics student and present-day writer Dimitris Papachristos sounds categorical:

> I dare say that it was no one's hereditary right to enter the struggle or the student movement because he or she was from a left-wing family background, or like that, a priori. The processes themselves were such that they put into the game kids and students who were going against the family background of their parents or their political history. And we have many examples like that. (Papachristos, interview)

Similarly, Thanasis Skamnakis, a law student belonging to the young communists league KNE says: "It was of course a conflict with the parents as well, meaning that half of the kids of Varvakeios, which used to be a model high school and an experimental one, were in the Communist Youth ... beyond any suspicion" (Skamnakis, interview). Heterodoxy apparently confused the authorities, who could no longer classify their opponents according to their family status, as had been the case until then. These students, offspring of "well-to-do families," with no record of political deviance, and in some cases even sons of conservative ministers in the cabinets prior to 1967, like Chrysafis Iordanoglou, were hard to suspect of dissident action. In the words of Vourekas they also brought "a culture of their own to the movement " (Vourekas, interview). After all, a certain milieu could contribute considerably to the shaping of one's consciousness due to an access to specific resources that was guaranteed by a solid social and cultural capital. According to *Katerina, that was the case with the major student leaders in her school, architecture, which was traditionally one of the most politically active:

> The kids that were—we could use the word "avant-garde" in scare quotes—the kids who dedicated their time to the antidictatorship struggle were not peasants. They were city kids, and they were kids who had some political and intellectual stimuli, from home, in other words. They were not from the poorest, more suppressed, more tormented strata. These were few. They existed, but they were, I believe, the exception. I cannot speak in percentages, but ... As I saw them, they were kids who had the luxury, if not to make a trip abroad, at least to buy books, to read books, speak a foreign language or two and eventually to have contact with what was going on abroad. (*Katerina, interview)

To her final point, regarding a privileged access to the outside world by students with means, one should add travel as another way to come into contact with militant ideologies.[34] Similarly, Kaiti Saketa, the owner of a left-wing bookshop in Salonica, argues that her student friends belonging to the Stalinist-Maoist organization EKKE were all bourgeois, a fact that accounted in her opinion for their sophistication. Saketa argues that this was a well-known reality: "The EKKE kids first and foremost, as we all know, came from bourgeois families. All EKKE kids, we knew them.... The most intellectual, the most well-read of all" (Saketa, interview). Coming from a higher social status also meant being less scared to express one's views, at least during the initial stages of the movement.[35] In contrast to the previous generation, middle- and upper-middle-class students of solid right-wing family backgrounds started to become radicalized and to turn against their background, embracing the dominant left-wing paradigm of the time. This quasi-Oedipal tendency of "killing the father" was a common trend in the '68 movements in the rest of Europe, in which, to quote Robert Lumley, "the phenomenon of 'defection' by the sons and daughters of the wealthy and influential [had taken] on scandalous proportions."[36] One interesting example of such a defector is the daughter of Nikolaos Efesios, the Junta's Minister of Defense during the 1973 events; as a member of Rigas she was inside the Polytechnic shouting "Freedom!" and "Democracy!" while the tanks were crushing the gate (see chapter 5).[37]

In addition, the students who first inspired and participated in the Hellenic European Youth Movement (EKIN), one of the main cultural platforms created in late 1970 in an attempt to use legal channels to pressure the regime to democratize, were all of well-known bourgeois Athenian families. Nikitas Lionarakis, one of EKIN's leading members, stresses that they were sons and daughters of army generals and ship owners, who first socialized with each other at parties and soirées organized by the Rotary Club "in order to reproduce the bourgeois establishment in Greece" (Lionarakis, interview). Similarly, the American College of Athens, arguably the most prestigious private high school in the country, was a PAM and Rigas hotbed. As Nikos Bistis, a law student at the time and present-day politician writes, "The Junta could not imagine that for months the leaflets of PAM were being printed by a mimeograph of the American College. Same with the leadership of KKE in Bucharest."[38] All of the above demonstrates some kind of *Gemeinschaft* feeling or esprit de corps among youngsters who went to the same schools and underwent similar patterns of socialization.

Architecture student and present-day writer Panos Theodoridis writes that his way of thinking at the time concerning people of a conservative background was that youth was a defining factor that rendered continuous political "progress" inevitable:

> We believed that progress was a rather mechanistic thing, namely, it was enough to be young in order to be oriented toward progress, and as the years go by you become even more progressive, this is why when we were students we had among our cadres, in those small left-wing groupuscules, sons of right-wingers, whatever you can imagine, we believed that there was no way that the change experienced by these youths, these colleagues of ours, was not organic, was not internal.[39]

There are elements of intergenerational conflict in these remarks, whereby the young articulate their distinct political and social views in contrast to conservative family values. Lacking in these testimonies of past and present, however, are angry references to parents as "compromised" and "conformist"—a verbal element of violent generational clashes typical of the global '68. Rather, many children of right-wing parents—people who were least tolerant of the coup in their youth, including Nikitas Lionarakis and Angeliki Xydi—expressed tender views of their parents. Xydi commented that her father "used to help the people," that "he had a good reputation" as "an honest right-winger" who would "rush sometimes to the police" to effect the release of someone who had been imprisoned unjustly (Xydi, interview). In addition, politicized students from right-wing families tend to claim that their parents were surprised by the Junta's mistreatment of the people and that they ultimately opposed it.

Tale of Two Cities

Despite the severe intergenerational clashes, Greek students were not a generation that "chose to be orphans," to quote the demand of the Italian Sessantotto.[40] Interestingly, it was the passing away of two prominent "father figures" that served as an opportunity to stage massive demonstrations against the regime during the first period of its rule (1967–1971). This was the period of "clandestinity," with martial law in force in Athens and Salonica, open-air rallies and demonstrations being banned, and offenders risking court-martial. The public funerals of the liberal politician George Papandreou and the Nobel Prize–winning poet George Seferis triggered the only recorded incidents of open protest in a time in which power was not openly contested and public space was devoid of exchange.[41]

Figure 3.1. Funeral of former prime minister George Papandreou, 3 November 1968. Alongside poet George Seferis's funeral in 1971, it was one of the few recorded incidents of mass protest during the first years of the dictatorship. (Source: ELIA, Greek Literary and Historical Archive)

An estimated quarter of a million demonstrators attended George Papandreou's funeral (3 November 1968). The fact that the octogenarian former Prime Minister, nicknamed the "Old Man of Democracy," had died in house confinement that was imposed by the regime only heightened the emotion. In this first instance of public protest, slogans played an important role. These included "Democracy," "This is our referendum," "You are our father," "Elections," "The army to the barracks," "114," "Stand up Old Man to see us," and "Hail to the heroes"—the latter referring to Alekos Panagoulis's group, which some months earlier had attempted to assassinate dictator Papadopoulos. Slogans were interspersed with the singing of the National Anthem, which is an early nineteenth century hymn to freedom, and of songs associated with the Resistance. The US Embassy reported: "One remarkable aspect of the demonstration was that party youth groups, which were disbanded after the April 21 occupation, appear to have retained cohesiveness and organization, for they appeared to be out in force, well led and disciplined and with a prepared action plan."[42] This comment seems likely to be a gross exaggeration, however, given that, according to participants, massive attendance was largely spontaneous, and all that remained of the party youths were rudimentary groupings.

Poet George Seferis's funeral (22 September 1971) was the culmination of his role as a sort of symbolic leader of the resistance (see chapter 4). According to Modern Greek scholar Karen Van Dyck, it resembled the funeral of Kostis Palamas, another "national" poet, who died in 1943 under German occupation and whose funeral was "attended by thousands who came to protest and mourn the death of a country as well as that of a man who had fought for its survival."[43] The Seferis funeral gave the ten thousand people who reportedly attended the opportunity to sing the banned songs of the self-exiled communist composer Mikis Theodorakis, a good number of which featured the verses of Seferis's poems.[44]

Just like in Francoist Spain a decade earlier, when the funerals of emblematic writers José Ortega y Gasset and Pio Baroja provided the occasion for the show of liberal dissent, these symbolic moments offered a safety valve for political expression in Greece as well.[45] To paraphrase political theorist Doug McAdam, framing a march as an act of public mourning involves the appropriation of long-standing cultural symbols in the service of protest: "The cultural legitimacy that [is] attached to the march encourage[s] participation while constraining official efforts at social control."[46] Student activist Katerina Detsika, who was present at both funerals, recalls: "I think that we wanted that. We expected, how can I put it, what I'm saying is macabre, someone of such stature to die in order to express ourselves, to express this blatant anti-Junta feeling. So, we were given those two opportunities which were unique" (Detsika, interview). As the people were denied a

Figure 3.2. Police arresting a protester during Papandreou's funeral. In the background one can discern advertisements for one of the anticommunist military films that were financed by the regime. (Source: ELIA, Greek Literary and Historical Archive)

private space to gather—any indoors assembly of three or more people was prohibited—public spaces such as squares and avenues inevitably became territory for open confrontation in both of these occasions, and later on in Papandreou's five-year memorial service (see chapter 5). The theater of the streets confronted the grandiosity of state power. By 1973 "liberated spaces" in the occupation of various schools became a "territory for dissidence,"[47] resonating with Henri Lefebvre's idea of vindicating the "right to the city" in an openly repressive context.[48]

The most important student activities were coordinated in Athens and Salonica. The youth of Athens played the dominant role and had a vanguard position in terms of student action, not least because of their numeric superiority (44,880 students to Salonica's 25,838).[49] In the summer of 1971, the *Economist* commented on changes in these urban centers: "Athens [and] Salonica … are sophisticated cities. The best hotels are as good as any in Europe and their service is probably better; boutiques and supermarkets have arrived; the traditional, exclusively male coffee-houses have given way to smart cafés to cater, not just for the tourists, but for the rapidly changing pattern of Greek life."[50] These evolving cities can be differentiated in terms of student activities, philosophies, and action, all of which were shaped by the different urban traditions, spaces, and experiences that influenced their student movements. The pace and style of youth movements are directly related to the character and distinct features of the city in which they evolve and the physical space of instruction.[51]

Cultural historian Carl E. Schorske has argued that cities "symbolic[ally] condense … socio-cultural values."[52] In the case of Salonica, these values are reflected in the city's stark post–civil war social alienation and its "tradition" of underground networks of extreme right-wingers, the so-called para-statals. The latter earned the city the title "mother of all bullies." As the modern city is the classic locus of collective memory, vestiges of earlier times are strongly imprinted on people's memories.[53] Thodoros Vourekas describes the remnants of political violence in Salonica: "The Lambrakis case … the more intense para-state … Nikiforidis, who was killed because he was gathering signatures for peace. Yes, there was a tougher political climate in Salonica. This is also proven by the later suppression through terrorizing, bullying student groups" (Vourekas, interview).

Architecture student Andrianos Vanos agreed and noted how this urban environment affected student politicization: "Here in Salonica there was a very strong politicization because [of] two very intense political events that had taken place. One was the assassination of Lambrakis, and the other one was that the farmers had entered Salonica. And in relation to the whole political climate, the youth of that period had been very strongly politicized" (Vanos, interview). Another striking feature was the powerful presence of the extreme right-wing student organization EKOF. In episodes that took place on campus a month prior to the coup, its members became involved in violent clashes with left-wing students, leaving many of them seriously injured.

Again, the fact that these confrontations took place in Salonica rather than Athens draws a dividing line between the two cities.

Those who were involved as students in the Salonica movement are much more likely to stress the post–civil war terrorization of defeated left-wingers than are those from Athens. Comments like the following one from Vourekas characterize Salonica's limited space as an ideal ground for the "hide-and-seek" between police and students: "The police had experience, the student branch of the police had organized this network of repression in Salonica very well. They could do it because the space was, as I said, limited. This was good for us, but it was also good for the police, they could intervene everywhere" (Vourekas, interview). Nikos Kaplanis, a dentistry student and member of the clandestine mechanism of KNE in Salonica, argues similarly: "Salonica, don't forget, was a very tough city for those in clandestinity, first of all the geographical way the city is structured, you cannot hide in too many places, it's not like Athens.... There were many para-statals, it was like this, the people were not that positive. Right? We shouldn't forget this. It wasn't like Athens, where the university professors or the intellectuals opened their doors" (Kaplanis, interview). Kaplanis's assertion that Athenian professors were more supportive of antiregime action lacks further substantiation, however, and seems to be an idealized version of reality in the capital.

Salonica and Athens do not seem to fit with architect Dimitris Fatouros's view that "the university is the city itself and vice versa."[54] Salonica's reactionary character was supposed to be balanced by the liberal character of its university. Traditionally, the city's university was known for its progressive positions, mainly on the so-called language question. It is telling that twice as many professors were sacked from Salonica than were dismissed from other institutions.[55] The opposite is true for Athens, as its university's reactionary reputation and perceived old-fashioned character stood in stark contrast to the liberal tendencies of vast segments of its population. Sociologist Lynn Anderson notes that these perceptions concerning the nature of the universities were shared by students in the early 1970s: "The 'image' students have of the University of Salonica is more 'modern' or liberal than the 'image' they have of the University of Athens."[56]

Political Opportunities

By February 1972, Greek campuses all around the country were so quiet that Colonel C. M. Woodhouse, a renowned connoisseur of Greek politics since the time of the German occupation, stated in an article in the *Observer* that "hard as it is ... to detect a spark of revolt among older Greeks, it is harder still among the young."⁵⁷ Some weeks later, the student movement took off with a series of organized actions aimed at winning free elections.⁵⁸

What were the underlying dynamics that allowed the Greek student movement to explode onto the scene after appearing so negligible for so long? A major contributing factor was the new phase in the Colonels' politics that began already in 1969–1970 but picked up steam in 1971, the period of "controlled liberalization." This attempt at normalization aimed to win public support for the regime and ensure a long-lasting authoritarianism with a democratic façade. It also intended to silence criticism abroad and break the international isolation of the regime.⁵⁹ In this phase, the Junta removed martial law in most parts of the country, softened censorship, and allowed for more social interaction.⁶⁰ By autumn 1971, it had abolished the infamous certificate of civic mindedness. At the same time, the verdicts of the martial courts were becoming less ferocious. Later, the state granted a general amnesty to all political prisoners and scheduled parliamentary elections.

Regardless of his motivations, Papadopoulos's maneuvers and his decision to proceed toward the gradual normalization of political life opened a space for the reactions of counterelites and civil society in general. This included the students, whose mobilization potential was gradually reinforced. The regime's liberalization offered a clear opportunity structure,⁶¹ namely, room for the student body to maneuver and "carve up public space"⁶² and thus to develop into a more robust entity.⁶³ The opening of the regime, which reduced policing of the public sphere and offered more occasions for the diffusion of "subversive" material, provided the student body with the cohesion and optimism it had previously lacked. The repertoire of student protest changed significantly after 1972 as conditions changed: mass struggle replaced clandestinity, and the closed nature of the clandestine groups became redundant.⁶⁴ This represented "a transition of the antidictatorship struggle from a personal individual stance to collective action," as former student radical and present-day scholar Alkis Rigos has remarked.⁶⁵

Incubator Chambers

Theda Skocpol argues that people cannot engage in political action unless they are "part of at least minimally organized groups with access to some resources."⁶⁶ There were two Greek initiatives that would comply with this rule and that would, as sites of dissent, prove instrumental in enhancing the organizational capacities of students: the reopened regional societies, and EKIN, namely the Hellenic-European Youth Movement. The regional societies used the legitimate façade of a cultural club to act as headquarters for "theoretical reflections and discussions during the day or up to the morning light" (Karystiani, interview), and these discussions included the delineation of student strategies. Following the regime's decision to reinstitute the right of association, regional societies became legal entities with their own offices, which allowed them to avoid the authorities' direct control or harassment. One Athens Polytechnic student from Patras notes that apart from anything else, these societies acted as a first point of reference for newcomers: "A kid who was coming from the countryside and did not know anyone, mainly in the big faculties, the massive ones, could find someone there. If not people with the same ideology, some people who were on the same wavelength" (*Katerina, interview).

The Cretan Society of Athens was one of the most active, featuring among its ranks some of the students who would become the most prominent members of the movement. In late March 1972, the Cretan Society became the first to elect its own council, and it demanded permission for all other societies to do the same.[67] The president-elect of the society was Ioanna Karystiani, a law student known for her charisma in inspiring student crowds. Her election was a breakthrough without precedent in gender politics. Karystiani took over leadership of an entity that had been representative of a traditionally male-dominated and macho Cretan microcosm. For a time, the society's journal, *Xasteria* [Starry Nights], became a standard point of reference for antiregime students alongside the regional societies. Societies also organized discussions and concerts that did not always take place due to police interference. A concert organized by the Cretans in May 1972 ended in a demonstration of three thousand people, the first of such proportions during the Junta period.[68]

Regional societies attempted to reverse and employ two of the regime's main propagandistic materials: tradition and folklore. They mobilized folk culture as a form of resistance, following the American model, which included Pete Seeger and for a while at least Bob Dylan's music. Students also assimilated elements of traditional dress, such as headscarfs, hand-woven bags, and knitted skullcaps. Panos Theodoridis describes this retro fashion thus: "We suddenly wanted to decorate our student rooms, and we suddenly went to antiquarian shops, we discovered barbers' chairs, old mirrors ... then *sarakatsanika* clothes appeared: whatever was folk culture began to attract us."[69] Kleopatra Papageorgiou depicts the folkloric localism displayed by members of the Cretan society with a somewhat critical tone:

> These kids also had an intense localist, not nationalist, feeling. In a good sense of course, because maybe through this localism, and through cultivating it, [they got] the chance to express themselves

against the Junta. For example, imagine, some of them didn't miss the chance to even wear the headscarf, the one that Cretans wear [laughter]. Or boots, or they were showing off their Cretan accent. They showed that they were Cretans, though they could also speak without an accent. They did it on purpose. (Papageorgiou, interview)

Local societies promoted active subversion, appropriating the local and traditional as innovative and as a means of protest that always referred to the pure demotic psyche. Not surprisingly, this unsubdued revolutionary spirit was often connected to the archetype of the 1821 War of Independence against the Ottomans. The societies' engagement with local tradition related to a general *problematique* that goes back to the writers of the so-called Generation of the 1930s who dealt with the necessity of retaining the "living" parts of tradition, thus redefining and consolidating the very concept of "Greekness."

The second initiative that revealed an opportunity for potential action to forge student cohesion was the Hellenic-European Youth Movement, alias EKIN, which began as a platform made up of children of wealthy, conservative, well-respected families. Some of its most illustrious members were young members of the Rotary Club, and the early members were students with "clean" records who generally came from well-to-do circles. EKIN's choice of name was symbolically important, linking Greece with Europe, extending its hand to the outside world, stressing their similarities. One of the society's founding members, the law student Giorgos Vernikos, was a ship owner's son and a nonaffiliated student throughout the dictatorship. Now a businessman, Vernikos argues in recent writings that the group's name was chosen "because in that period the European Union [European Economic Community, EEC] opposed the Junta and forced it to leave the Council of Europe." He explains: "We also thought that the European Union presented the only hope in terms of opposing the arrogance of the United States and overthrowing the dictatorship."[70] EKIN co-founder, Xenofon Giataganas, notes that this act, alongside the EEC's suspension of the Treaty of Association with Greece, endowed the *institutions communautaires* with a "dimension of resistance."[71] The fact was, however, that the EEC, apart from individual member states such as the Netherlands, was not actively involved in the so-called Greek Case, that is, Greece's forced withdrawal from the Council of Europe on 12 December 1969 on grounds of the systematic use of torture. Rather, it was the three Scandinavian countries—not EEC members at the time—that brought the motion forward.[72]

Little by little, EKIN became a public arena for discussion and the exchange of ideas. It focused on culture as the key to acquiring political consciousness and became involved in publishing, including the printing of basic texts on education by Greek intellectuals[73] and classical texts examining questions of knowledge, such as Plato's "Sophist." The first article of the society's bulletin pointed out that though "youth all over the world has become one of the privileged fields of reflection and protest," Greek higher institutions had turned "from spaces of intellectual restlessness and conflict of ideas" to "places of relaxation or, in the best of cases, of coffee-time small talk."[74] In a communiqué issued on the occasion of the avant-garde theater group Elefthero Theatro's staging of John Gay's *Beggar's Opera* in 1971, EKIN remarked harshly on the "guilty silence" of the majority of youths and declared itself to be conscious of young people's enthusiasm and romantic combativeness. It concluded that its members were determined to struggle in order to win all they could through "truth and honesty" against the awful and inexpressible things happening to the country. On this occasion, EKIN, based on a core of nonaffiliated, noncommunist individuals, launched an appeal for the unity of all youth with reforming tendencies, appealing clearly to the communist faction. Interestingly, the society's members maintained that the "development of folk culture," which "suffered under the coordinated attack of the technocratic pseudo-civilization of Athens," was a precondition for any progress.[75] Antitechnocratic rage and folk revival are two recurrent features in the student discourse of the time.

Alongside EKIN, the Society for the Study of Greek Problems, alias EMEP, was a parallel organization with similar function and aims. It was founded and run by the old guard of democratic politicians headed by John Pesmazoglou, former deputy director of the Bank of Greece; Rodis Roufos, a diplomat and writer; Anastasios Peponis, a former Center Union minister; and Virginia Tsouderou, a liberal female politician. Despite professing respect for this group's actions, Nikitas Lionarakis confesses that to the younger generation, EMEP's outlook seemed too conservative. Ridiculing its lack of revolutionary zeal, EKIN's members dubbed EMEP "PEPON," paraphrasing the name of the wartime Communist Youth (EPON) and linking it with the surname of one of EMEP's leading members, Anastasios Peponis, which resembles the sound of the word "canteloupe" in Greek: "We used to make jokes about them because we were very revolutionary. We used to call them PEPON, from Peponis" (Lionarakis, interview).

Nevertheless, many regarded these two groups as the most effective of the Greek resistance organizations and as "incubator chambers for the development of new political forces."[76] Both hosted speakers, escaping the ban on political parties by performing an active political function. The most successful events were the heavily attended public meetings addressed by Cambridge economist Joan Robinson and West German writer Günter Grass in 1972, both of whom were quite outspoken in their criticism of the Colonels' regime. Grass's talk, in particular, became a cause célèbre, since he made direct references to the reigning oppression in Greece, paralleling the US aid to the Colonels with the Soviet invasion of Czechoslovakia; this comparison infuriated the authorities.[77] Dissident academic D. N. Maronitis wrote in a feuilleton in the liberal daily *To Vima* [Tribune], "The purpose of [Grass's] brief presence and concise talk was (as he himself confessed) to break the loneliness of the ones who—skillfully or clumsily, complacently or desperately—still defend the case of democracy in our land."[78]

"Treading with the utmost caution, and stretching to the limit the tight margins which the regime allowed for the expression of open dissent," wrote British journalist Leslie Finer in 1972, these two societies, under "innocuous names, ha[d] become the focal point for the desire of Greece's intellectual leaders to engage in active opposition."[79] Participating in them gave students an opportunity to exploit the contradictions of the regime by collectively coming out in the open, thus challenging the traditional conspiratorial practices of the Greek Left.

According to an internal circular by leading member Nikos Alivizatos, EKIN's "intellectualism" was only reproduced within its tiny ranks in the beginning, and members "worked, published, and read" their texts among themselves.[80] Soon, however, going to the EKIN meetings—which took place in a basement in the center of Athens—became a fashion of sorts that extended to other students too. "It became trendy to be there," remembers Lionarakis. Myrsini Zorba stresses the importance of this place, which satisfied a strong need for an alternative public sphere and for social interaction. She distances herself from the general tendency of ex-militants to speak seriously of the organization by pointing out that one good-looking woman—Olga Tremi, a famous television news anchor at present—acted as a magnet for other students to join the meetings:

> From the very outset, Olga Tremi would come with her fur and her little dog.... I remember I was with some friends, and someone came and told us, "Hey, it is nice out there, there are also some gorgeous chicks with furs." [laughter] And all the boys from my group of friends really went there because of this. Look, the social space was missing, what is self-evident was that there was no social space. You were confined, in fact you felt suffocated. How to communicate with other people, what could one say? This was a social space. (Zorba, interview)

EKIN's president, Panagiotis Kanellakis, is one of the few to have commented explicitly on the amorous aspect of the society: "These were nice times. Rich in experiences and emotions. And we experienced them fully. And one should think that the other story of EKIN, the erotic one, has not been written yet, though it wasn't negligible."[81]

While remarks like Kanellakis's cast light on an important dimension of EKIN, its political dimension was no less dangerous and risky. Showing one's ID to the policemen at EKIN's door and later on being "invited" to the police station in order to be disciplined served as a rite of passage. Taking one's first beating or finding one's way to the police station for the first time were symbolic events that signified the journey to a definite radicalism. In this way, the major psychological impact of the dictatorship's relaxation was the normalization of oppression. Another fundamental issue was that bourgeois students, because they did not fear being characterized as subversives, confronted the police, at least in this phase, with a certain naiveté. Their decision to break with their social identity helped others go along and contributed to the multidimensional character of the movement. Accordingly, upper-class, working-class, highly ideological, and nonaffiliated students all co-existed.

Antiregime students had significant success with legal action, winning most of their battles with the Junta. The wisdom of engaging in such action became the subject of great contention among the emerging student organizations, however. "Reformist" communists, who emerged among student circles in early 1972, supported legal action from the beginning and managed to execute it, whereas the revolutionary "leftists" viewed it as a way to legitimize the regime, a de facto recognition of its legal authority. In any case, the regime only tolerated the two cultural organizations for two years, during which time they were allowed to operate despite constant punitive threats. Both were banned in mid-1972 on the grounds of pursuing antiregime activities, and many of their leading members were placed in detention.

The president of the last Greek parliament before the coup, Dimitrios Papaspyrou, stated that the regime would never be able to alienate the young from the struggle for freedom, nor "stupefy them with football, pool, the racecourse, the casino of Mont Parnes, and the dictatorship's literature." In this way, he expressed his admiration for the protest actions of the youth that took place despite the Junta's attempts to distract them from activism. The conclusion to Papaspyrou's appeal encompasses the grief of all antiregime figures for the loss of the rare opportunity for dialogue that the two societies had represented: "The recent upsurge of cultural activity among the young has illuminated our epoch. It has proved that the sense of liberty has now withered in the new generation.... The dictatorship, panic-stricken, resorted to old methods of persecution and deportation. Security police cells are crowded with brave and proud students … and there is much concern about their fate."[82] As social psychologist Bert Klandermans has argued, existing organizations and networks lay the groundwork for the formation of social movements, as they not only "increase the chance that persons will be confronted with a mobilizational attempt, but also make 'bloc recruitment' possible."[83] The existence of the two societies was of paramount importance for the process of student mobilization in the following period.

The first small demonstration, numbering some fifty students, took place at the propylaea of the old Athens University on the fifth anniversary of the institution of the dictatorship on 21 April 1972 and was followed by a number of arrests. Lionarakis remembered this day, stressing the grassroots character of the mobilization and minimizing the role of leadership:

> [We] realized that we had enormous strength in our hands and that we should do something. If you ask me now where this thing came from and if it was organized I wouldn't know, but I imagine that there was no need for it to be organized. Some rumor was urging "everyone to the propylaea." Alright, I spread it too, and everybody spread it. Then we got caught, four people, as the ringleaders. Honestly, I don't know if we were leaders. We were all leaders. Everyone was a leader. (Lionarakis, interview)

Michalis Sabatakakis remembers the gathering: "We sang the slogan-song of the period, which was 'When will the skies clear,' we sang the National Anthem, which is a hymn to freedom, you know, and the funny thing happened that a soldier passed by then, a soldier in uniform, and he stood still and saluted [laughter], the guy knew that this is what one does when one hears the National Anthem" (Sabatakakis, interview).

A second gathering took place outside the Archaeological Museum a few days later, where students demanded the release of their arrested peers. Another major protest in the courtyard of the Polytechnic on 1 May 1972, numbering about four hundred students, was directed against the appointed faculty council's refusal to meet in the presence of students. At the same time, some Athens University students attempted to demonstrate at Kotzia Square, a central point in the city. Mass arrests of students followed these protests.

According to the interviews conducted by the Greek-American professor Theodoros Kouloumbis in 1972, "respectable" figures (such as professors and retired generals) with antiregime leanings thought that it was about time that some mass events take place in the central Syntagma Square in Athens, but they did not know how to make this happen. One idea was to bring back the self-exiled former prime minister, Constantine Karamanlis, to provoke an instant popular reaction. Intellectual and political circles thus envisioned action initiated from the top rather than from below.[84] Foreign observers, such as the *Economist*, expressed great astonishment when students began to lead the movement: "Surprisingly enough, the demonstrations were organized and led by Greek university students, who have until recently been considered the most passive and timid in Europe." The title of the article referred to a statement made by a higher official of the Junta that the students were to the regime just like a "mosquito on a bull."[85]

The catalyst for spreading the "protest virus," as US officials called it, which transformed Greek students from a passive entity into a major obstacle for the military regime,[86] was the students' initiation of a legal battle with the authorities over their right to elect their own representative student councils. As the students struggled against their exclusion from structures of university representation, they became inspired for further protest.[87] In late March 1972, forty-two students from the Athens Law School, followed by several of their colleagues in Salonica, appealed to the courts in the first instance against the hitherto government-appointed student councils, demanding the right to hold free elections. Lionarakis, who was one of them, described the limitations of this venture in the existing conditions: "We started collecting signatures, semilegally by that point. In a faculty of six thousand people, forty-two individuals were found [who would sign]. We could not hope for anything better.... Two and a half months in order to collect forty-two signatures" (Lionarakis, interview). As collecting the signatures itself became trendy, however, the number tripled after only a week, and the police did not interfere—a fact that Lionarakis attributes to the right-wing family credentials of most students.

Due to its youthful composition, the part of the student body that became active did not carry the weight of the Left's past experiences and therefore did not have preconceived notions of what had to be done in terms of political action. There was an attempt to bring the students together outside of strict ideological affiliations, following a model of independent student action that was new and had been partially imported from abroad. In fact, the post-1971 student movement embodies a relatively successful attempt to go beyond party orthodoxy. Because the Junta outlawed political parties, party control was looser in Greece than elsewhere, giving students greater ideological autonomy when they began organizing. According to one testimony, "the fact that the student movements abroad did not seem to be guided [by the communist parties]" reinforced this tendency.[88]

In terms of organizational structures, the students were coordinated by the Student Committees of Struggle (FEA), which were founded in December 1971 by students with no strict political affiliation.[89] Although they started off as circles of friends who shared an antiregime spirit, the FEA soon began to operate separately in each faculty and were coordinated by an "interfaculty" organization. The committees' structure functioned in an open form and included assemblies, gatherings, and meetings with participation on equal terms, with discussions and voting. In his detailed analysis of the antidictatorship student movement, Olympios Dafermos, himself a protagonist, argues that these committees never acquired a clear theoretical line, since their members were devoted exclusively to the overthrow of the Junta.[90] In his view, this was instrumental in the development of the movement into a more robust entity, as its mobilizing structures were reinforced by the committees' independence from political stewardship. This situation was short lived, however, as gradual politicization led to the committees' dissolution.

Students transferred the battle with the state to the university. Their right to vote, denied by a dictatorial regime, was vindicated in the university microcosm; although the regime initially declined to grant this right, it ultimately agreed to allow students to hold general assemblies that would eventually lead to elections later in the same year. In this interplay between state power and student unionism, the dilemma was how far the students could exploit the possibilities opened by the regime's own contradictions. Lionarakis discusses the students' strategy of infiltration by combining a serious contemporary Leninist argument with a much lighter tone that results from his present-day perspective: "We were going to ensure just one thing, that the committee which would result from the assembly would have a 100 percent majority, that's what we thought, and then even if they won the elections this would be 'dual power,' as Lenin said. It was a nice little trick; we did it in the Law School" (Lionarakis, interview).

October 1972 signaled the final break with the old state of affairs as twenty student societies gathered together and demanded to vote for a supervising committee, modifying the existing appointed constitutional charters (ND795/69) and simultaneously rejecting the omnipresence of the so-called student branch of the police. In Salonica, things were tougher, as regular and general assemblies took place while marines carried out exercises outside the university building, and the electoral offices for voter registration were closed. The large demonstration that took place in protest resulted in numerous arrests. In its usual fashion, the regime conceded a number of rights to the students in order to defuse this explosive situation (14 November);[91] meanwhile it validated the notorious decree 720/70, which allowed the state to cancel the military deferment of male students in cases of failure to demonstrate "national behavior" (15 November). This measure was systematically implemented only some months later.

In late November 1972, when the student electoral procedures were rigged once again, two hundred students signed a petition urging their peers to abstain from voting. In the end, only 15 percent of the student body participated in the elections; the rest boycotted them, occupying the electoral premises and denouncing the misconduct. Following the intervention of the police, Byron Stamatopoulos, the spokesman of the regime, announced that a student minority of "terrorists" wanted to revive the chaos that existed prior to the Junta by "mimicking the methods of Mussolini," thus drawing a parallel between them and Fascist squadrists. He also tried to demonstrate that older student circles were still active and disruptive by quoting the case of an arrested student born in 1943. Stamatopoulos insisted that the minority of "modern stick carriers" numbered no more than a few hundred. They were anarchists, communists, and people guided by the "old parties" that had fallen prey to the former. His explanation was that they were "kids of rich families, who [had] lost their privileges because of the revolution and envied the great majority of Greek youth who could now study for free and have equal career opportunities."[92] The representation of antiregime student activists as children of privilege who were bitter for losing their monopoly on education and career opportunities thanks to the "revolution" became a recurrent theme in government propaganda throughout this period.[93]

Similarly, the government-appointed National Student Union (EFEE) issued a statement condemning the purportedly communist-led minority and threatening legal action.[94] A leaflet had been circulated during the events by the Society of National-Minded Students of the Polytechnic (EMP); it argued that the anarchist "zealots" wanted to create another May '68 and condemned their appeal to the students to abstain from voting in protest:

Dear Colleagues,

The Struggle is ideological. . . . It is not we who have rendered it political. It is these neoleftists, zealots of new Mays ['68] who wish for polarization. Isolate them. The legal order irritates the anarchists and the outflanking infuriates the "irresponsibles." They react spasmodically, and having no purpose in their action, they abandon the battle. They propose abstention. Colleagues, abstention means weakness, negation, cowardice.[95]

The epithet "a small anarchist minority," used both by government officials and pro-regime students, would stick to the actors in the antidictatorship student movement throughout the course of subsequent events. Still, the violence, fraud, and mass abstention in the electoral procedures and the electoral fiasco proved to be defining factors for the evolution of the movement headed by this minority and for the amplification of its repertoire. Lionarakis argues that electoral irregularities made government-appointed candidates lose momentum, and they were utterly discredited: "Those who got appointed were pointed out with a finger because they were exposed in front of the people by that time; people knew them. There was, say, Giorgos, whom you saw in the street and you would spit on him. These people couldn't find a girlfriend, such was their problem" (Lionarakis, interview).

By that time, student combativeness had increased, not least due to everyday clashes between the police and students supporting the regime. Giannis Kourmoulakis recalls that at Panteios, "fascists used to gather and we used to beat each other.... Hard beatings, punches, blows, kicks, with wooden sticks, flying desks—we're talking about real beatings" (Kourmoulakis, interview). A Maoist leaflet that circulated at the time reflects the atmosphere of aggression behind these confrontations: "One impudent fascist who dared to sustain the proclamations made over the previous days by another arch-fascist student who had said that as soon as he was elected president he would ... [a vulgar word] them all, was bravely beaten black and blue by a combative anti-fascist, with the support of the attendant students."[96]

Law School student leader Ioanna Karystiani underlines a major reason for the sudden explosion in student activity, drawing a line between the lower and higher points of the movement. The movement itself was an explosion in people's lives, and participation in it was far too exciting an activity to allow people to remain absorbed with everyday trivialities:

> There was nothing else in our lives. And the simple everyday things that mattered to us were not, you know, to clean our house, the floor, you know, to wipe up and buy yogurt for the fridge. It was how to organize the food problem inside the Polytechnic during the occupation. It was how to collect money for people who needed it, how to learn about more political prisoners, how to obtain information necessary for the one and only thing that mattered to us back then: the movement. (Karystiani, interview)

Angeliki Xydi shares this view and emphasizes that as a result, the students experienced politics in their purest form: "The politics that we were experiencing were not as the people seem to understand it in recent years, just a dry thing, an arid function, for the very reason, I believe, that it was a matter of life" (Xydi, interview). *Katerina remarks that these initial activities were above all else "a great political education, lessons in political conduct" (*Katerina, interview).

Technocracy and Its Discontents

For the first time in Greece, young, privileged, affluent children saw themselves as an oppressed group. Medicine, law, and Polytechnic students, most of them from the middle class, were the most combative of all faculties, which prevents one from drawing the Marxist conclusion that the Junta triggered a working-class revolutionary response. On the contrary, sociologist Nikos Serdedakis argues for the purposeful incentives of the students in joining the movement, namely, their interiorized aspirations "concerning their future role as intellectuals who were destined for higher positions in the distribution of labor." This incentive, he maintains, "guided the confrontation with the anachronistic, antimeritocracy and antimodernist regime of the militaries."[97] In other words, these students needed to "secure a new corporate identity within society or a new role in politics,"[98] and they feared that the regime would hamper their future in more ways than one.

This insight corresponds to a point made by Jürgen Habermas in 1968. Until that time he had been convinced that students did not play a political role in developed industrialized societies; however, he was nevertheless sure that "in countries in which revolutionary nationalist groups, usually army officers, have come to power, students exercise a permanent political pressure." In Venezuela, Indonesia, and South Vietnam, where governments had been overthrown by students, Habermas explained, students had a more politicized consciousness because they understood themselves as future elites with responsibility for the modernization process, and they regretted that "their studies were not organized according to well-…defined and socially normative models." He further argued that the structures of the old society, organized according to kinship relations, were the same as those that defined the lives of the students' families. Thus, Habermas concluded, "there is a singular parallel between the socialization process of the individual student and the overall process of social change." In this way, the student "links his private destiny with political destiny."[99]

And indeed, a series of purely student affairs concerning future occupational guarantees were in some cases a catalyst for student action in the Greek case. In March 1972, the subengineers, graduate technicians who handled minor construction projects, absented themselves from university lectures in both Athens and Salonica in order to criticize the regime's decision to downgrade their status in relation to fully matriculated engineers.[100] Soon after the student elections, although the students at some other schools (Humanities and the Higher Commercial School of Athens) expressed their support for the striking students, the engineers stayed away from classes to protest the subengineers' demands. At a later point, the students would channel their actions against the English-speaking Technological Institute that was operating in Athens, which they saw as a threat, hence establishing a die-hard trend in Greek education.[101]

At a different point, however, the ideological prerogatives of the students came first, suggesting a divided value system in which students' concern for their professional futures clashed with their ideology. This happened when the US-trained education minister Gerasimos Frangatos began promoting the technocratic reorganization of the university (August 1971–June 1972), clashing also with the feudal establishment of Greek academic bureaucracy on the issue of teaching and research assistants. The introduction of assistants would have rendered the academic environment more impersonal and would also have enabled the creation of large educational centers. Frangatos further planned to appoint professors he had chosen from the United States.

From the perspective of left-wing students the intensification of studies that the Junta's education minister proposed would transform the university into a knowledge factory catering to corporate interests. They associated this reform with the image of uniform, machine-like experts in the service of US-driven capitalist production, and they fiercely rejected it as "technocratization." They also argued that the imposition of the reform would mean the exclusion of fellow students who worked either part time or full time, as they would inevitably drop out due to time restrictions.[102] As a result of the protests, Frangatos had to resign, and the reform was postponed. Yet Frangatos proved to be instrumental in the changes that took place within the institutional framework of Greek higher education, and teaching assistants were indeed institutionalized.

Similarly, the Constitutional Charter for Education was considered a threat to the university administration and a prelude to the intensification of studies. Through the charter, the Junta attempted to intensify the rhythm of studies, reducing both the exam periods from three to two, abolishing the possibility to transfer a course from one year to the next, and making class and lab attendance obligatory. In hindsight, reflecting on student rage against Frangatos's reform, leftist leader and present-day journalist Stavros Lygeros suggests that it was an unjust reaction: "How could they [Frangatos and his supporters] have proved to be right? They were opposed by a student movement which allowed no room for change in that period. They were right, I'm telling you, that they wanted this, but how could they manage? We had a different logic then. That is, the climate didn't allow this" (Lygeros, interview).

Despite these corporate problems and demands, however, it must be noted that students in Greece did not yet have any realistic reason to fear unemployment, as students in other industrialized countries did. *Katerina explains:

Degrees were not yet discredited. Students, apart from the shine that they had because they participated in the antidictatorship movement, were not necessarily the future unemployed. That is, one did not say, "Poor kids, what are they going to do in the future?" ... In one way or another they would find a place in the job market, and in that sense they were receiving in advance the prestige that they would have in society in the future. They were the "blue-eyed boys" of society for that reason too.

In one way or another, and despite everything, students—especially of the Polytechnic, Law, and Medicine—were aware of the fact that they would be part of the future ruling elite, just like their counterparts abroad who had acted in the '68 movements.[103]

Marx's Children

Apart from the common goal of struggling against the authoritarian regime for greater liberties, Marxist tradition and its variants constituted the common theoretical underpinning of young militants' strategies and utopias. Giorgos Kotanidis, a young militant actor at the time, opens his autobiographical section about his political militancy by quoting these verses from Vladimir Mayakovsky's 1930 poem "At the Top of My Voice": "We opened each volume of Marx / as we would open the shutters in our own house / but we did not have to read / to make up our minds which side to join, which side to fight on."[104] "I could hardly find a text that could better express our beliefs and our wishes during that period," Kotanidis explains.[105] Indeed Marxism was the antiregime students' "master protest frame."[106] However, the formation of specific political subcultures also reflected local and international communist dichotomies. By late 1972, Greek student activists were already split in their ideological affiliations and in their ideas about achieving the overthrow of the Junta. Their new collective identities all involved different political rituals and were characterized by diversity in both discourse and performance.

Apart from the coordinating role of the FEA, the students' organizational structures were the clandestine political organizations. These organizations all operated within the same context but made different political choices. By 1973, for example, the two splinter communist parties had established their respective stances on the issue of a potential change to controlled parliamentarism, and the ideological rift between them deepened. Fierce debates raged between orthodox and reformist communists, Trotskyists, Maoists, and those who were nonaffiliated, because the groups assigned paramount importance to their particular theoretical conceptualizations of dissidence. By that time, the radical split within the Greek Communist Party of 1968, as well as the Soviet invasion of Czechoslovakia in the summer of the same year, had already had a considerable impact on students, making them either more critical of the traditional Left or more proud of its "clear" and "adamant" line. At times, the splinter groups were also aligned with different cultural politics.

The strict hierarchical structure of the clandestine organizations came as a stark contrast to the basically antihierarchical and decentralized ways in which student societies had functioned. Despite the open nature of the student movement, the covert organizations respected Leninist principles regarding clandestinity and reproduced the communist approach, including instructors and cells. The first students to join took more prominent positions in the hierarchical structure of each group, positions that everyone could theoretically achieve in due time as dynamic processes took place within the groups, "reproducing the instructing ranks from bottom to top."[107] Each organization was split into two subgroups: one was the ideological head, the so-called clandestine mechanism, which acted underground, and the other was the public face, which had acted openly in the universities since the early 1970s, when political organizations decided to focus their politics on unionist activities and on the professional grievances of the students.

Moralistic tone and extreme seriousness characterized the organizations and their writings. The resistance journals, alternative circuits of information, were tied to the interests of the respective communist factions and acted to propagate their views. Though most of these journals sought to report all resistance activities in Greece and abroad, and though they shared anti-American and "antifascist" principles, their political discourse otherwise had little in common with each other. These writings were rather old-fashioned in their expression of militantism, reproducing the post-1949 communist writing style. The radicalism the leftists voiced was one new element, but it was often too extreme in its ideological reading of the Greek political situation.

It remains doubtful how representative these texts were and how widely they were shared among members of a group. The texts were usually written by members higher in the hierarchy who were either in a state of "deep clandestinity" or abroad. Moreover, the journals' distribution could not be very extensive, due to the restrictions imposed by limited printing facilities and the fact that they were illegal material. Usually, journals were passed from one student to another in an endless chain.[108]

The Reformists

The 1968 split in the Greek Communist Party in Budapest had a considerable impact on a great number of students in Greece, making them more critical of the Old Left. Rigas gradually embraced a sort of "New Left" attitude, with a clear anticapitalist and anti-imperialist character but "Euro-Communist" overtones. By 1971, the old Rigas had ceased to exist, as a significant number of its most important cadres had been arrested. New conditions, including the Junta's liberalization experiment, led to a reformulation of Rigas's objectives. Gradually, the organization became willing to defend a democratic and antihegemonic way of conducting politics. According to historian David Close, its members were induced to make this shift by "the KKE's traditional and continuing devotion to Soviet policies and interests, a stance which was out of tune with the strongly patriotic and libertarian views of much of the left-wing public" during this period.[109]

The attempts by Rigas and KOS—KKE-Esoterikou's youth section—to be less dogmatic were more often than not interpreted as "revisionism" that had led to "reformism," that is, as evidence of the organizations' lack of revolutionary fervor.[110] For example, Papadopoulos proposed a schedule for guided parliamentary elections in the summer of 1973, and it was embraced by KKE-Esoterikou and consequently adopted by Rigas and KOS; it subsequently became the focus of widespread accusations that their members practiced wishy-washy left-wing politics. Still, these organizations were, to quote historian Thanasis Sfikas, "the best in sowing the seeds of New Left, believing in the possibility of the creation of viable models of socialism that, instead of conforming to the emerging Stalinist straitjacket, would be flexible enough to fit indigenous conditions and needs."[111] The attention to indigenous conditions and needs did not imply introversion; in its manifesto in 1972 KOS declared its "solidarity with the people of Indochina and above all the heroic people of Vietnam, the Arab people, the people of Spain, Portugal and Turkey, and all people who struggle for their freedom."[112] Lastly, these organizations had a more direct connection to culture, a fact that was often used to label them—as will be explained later—with the derogatory term *koultouriarides* [artsy fartsies].

KNE, the youth organization of the Communist Party, was created in August 1968 by old party members in prison or in exile. Sticking closer to party orthodoxy, it soon attracted the smaller branch of the Lambrakis Youth, but it lacked a strong following until the early 1970s. By 1972, it was the second largest clandestine political student organization, competing and eventually surpassing Rigas numerically. KNE's student branch, Anti-EFEE, founded in autumn 1971, propagated its action through the clandestine journal *Panspoudastiki*. The organization's name referred to the National Student Union (EFEE), which had been disbanded in 1967 but was reappointed from 1971 on. The name of the Anti-EFEE was often interpreted as an attempt to place the entire student resistance movement under its control, since the EFEE was a union that—at least nominally—encompassed all students. A-EFEE was often accused of authoritarianism within student circles and of bullying individuals from rival groups.

A-EFEE tried to launch itself as an all-inclusive trade-unionist organization fighting for more academic freedom. It did not openly express only one line, stressing that "it was formed by students regardless of ideology and their social position, by students who struggled in parallel with antidictatorship organizations."[113] In reality, A-EFEE was strongly political. It expressed its orthodox dimension, had an admittedly hegemonic vision of the student movement, and possessed a clear organizational hierarchy according to "democratic centralization," to borrow the contemporary term for higher party control. A-EFEE became very efficient in recruiting students, as its small and strictly clandestine nuclei of action succeeded in attracting even the indecisive. Stelios Kouloglou, a latter-day AASPE leader, collaborated with the group without realizing that he was thus becoming a member:

> I was an independent, a trade-unionist. Then, there was a period in which some KNE people approached me through A-EFEE, and they asked me whether I would like to enter the group and so on, and I said, "Alright, I will collaborate," but they tricked me. They presented it in such a way, because A-EFEE was recruiting people very discreetly, namely, they were saying, "We are having discussions about the movement," and I accepted. (Kouloglou, interview)

In A-EFEE's founding manifesto, as in the Rigas manifesto, tradition is a major point of reference, although in this case the reference is clearly to the workers' movement: "We are guided by our rich fighting traditions." The manifesto lists nineteen unionist demands, ranging from better teaching and grading approaches to more sports facilities, increased scholarships, aid for working students, and the reduction of military service. It also calls for the liberation of imprisoned and exiled colleagues and the bans on decree 180/69 concerning the "governmental commissioners"; decree 93/69, which endangered asylum; disciplinary committees; and the student section of the police. Finally the text asks for the appointed student councils to be ousted and for free student elections and greater student participation, even in university administration. Only at the end of the text does the organization clearly label its initiative as part of the "struggle against tyranny," concluding:

"Three cheers for our unruly student youth, our never enslaved Greek Youth, our proud people!"[114]

A-EFEE stood in stark contrast not only to its rival communist organizations Rigas and KOS but even more so to the so-called leftist groupings. Its age-old clashes with the Trotskyists—traditionally accused of being police agents—were extended to the Maoists. KNE's organ *Odigitis* often condemned "leftist opportunism," claiming it led people to neglect students' real problems.[115] Leftists were consequently labeled "irresponsible." Vera Damofli, an A-EFEE member at the time, remarks with contempt: "The self-defined hyper-revolutionaries were calling [us] mass reformist groups of the traditional Communist Left."[116]

The official KKE strongly criticized the Dubcek experiment in Prague and saw no merits in the '68 movements, which were described as the result of the irresponsible "masses of politically inexperienced students." The latter, according to their Marxist analysis, could not be the avant-garde of a popular rising. Grigoris Farakos, the theoretical head of KKE then, and subsequently responsible for youth matters, argued that it was wrong to consider the youth as a separate social group with its own political demands. Young peoples' input could be great in social revolutions, he added, provided that they received the necessary guidance by the "great party of the proletariat."[117]

The Robespierres

There was a long tradition of "Robespierrism" in Greece. Leftists reappeared in the political scene of the 1970s with a new face, bred from the international protest movement and constantly trying to outdo each other with intransigence and maximalist rhetoric. Following Che Guevara's maxim that "the duty of a revolutionary is to bring about the revolution," these people viewed the use of violence, at least on a theoretical level, as a way of measuring collective revolutionary engagement.[118] The "new Robespierres" articulated ideas about patriotic resistance, always in connection with the "grandfathers" of the revolutionary Left. They defined themselves as "revolutionary Marxists" or "Communist internationalists," and their discourse carried a romantic revolutionary tone, with the desire to "blackmail history" and accelerate the arrival of the revolution.[119]

Even today Stergios Katsaros, who was mainly influenced by Guevarism, is among the most fervent supporters of the violent route to revolution. In his memoir, Katsaros argues that the inspiration for this militancy lies in third-worldism. Disillusionment with the "reformist" tactics of the traditional Left nurtured his belief that a left-wing offense would eventually replace the passive "martyr" stance that Greek communists had adopted ever since the end of the civil war. Once again, Katsaros locates the starting date of that new radicalism in 1965 and the death of Petroulas: "Cuba exercised considerable charm on all of us. It was the metropolis of world revolution. Castro and Guevara were known to the Greek movement. But our discovery starts with the death of Petroulas. Then, for the first time, the ineffectiveness of the methods of the traditional Left became evident. For the first time we said that we should not just be martyrs calling for mercy, but fighters who would generate fear in our adversaries. Guevara's aggressiveness inspired us."[120]

A number of heterogeneous internationalist groups were labeled "leftists," a new category born as *gauchistes* in May 1968. Cohn-Bendit's *Leftism, A Remedy for the Senile Disorder of Communism* (1969), a response to Lenin's pamphlet *Leftism: Communism's Infantile Disorder*, appeared in Greek in the early 1970s and became one of the best sellers of the time. It analyzed how leftism promoted petit bourgeois thinking through dangerous "deviations" from straightforward Marxism. Therefore, for the orthodox-minded, the term *leftism* bore pejorative connotations and became synonymous with opportunism. In terms of whether the time was ripe for revolution, leftists went against the Old Left's theory of the necessary steps forward and questioned the classic Marxist presupposition, which claimed that the revolt was subordinated to the unquestionable supremacy of the workers' movement and the class struggle.[121] Leftists were accused of being obsessed with what Alain Krivine has called "burning off the stages" and a need "to analyze a political situation not for what it is but for what [they] would like it to be."[122] In order to bring about the revolution, they attempted to eliminate the negative influence of the "revisionism" of the old parties of the Left. In a holistic approach to militancy, moreover, they (re)introduced the notion of the austere revolutionary: the "professional" whose whole existence was dedicated to the cause. In fact, leftist militants, more than other left-wingers, rejected the idea of parliamentary democracy succeeding a potential downfall of the Junta, since they considered parliamentary democracy a petit bourgeois political system.[123]

Leftists were also preoccupied with "revolutionary violence." Their use of such phrases as "political power comes out of the barrel of a gun" never translated into concrete action, however. According to Katsaros, "Armed struggle was a declaration of faith, rather than a conscious and elaborated tactic."[124] This observation fits well with Pier Paolo Pasolini's acute description of the Italian leftists' methodology of "oratory struggle," namely, of making rhetorical declarations of their violent intentions.[125]

The Trotskyist tendency had a long history in Greek politics, including a powerful presence in the interwar period[126] and some leading members in the Fourth International and its various branches, including Dimitris Giotopoulos, Cornelius Castoriadis, and Michalis Raptis. Trotskyists were usually dubbed "traitors" and "stool pigeons" by their Stalinist counterparts, with whom they had waged a constant war since the 1930s. During the Resistance period and the December 1944 events in Athens, a number of Trotskyists were liquidated by OPLA, the notorious secret police of the communist-led EAM. Historian Eleni Varikas, herself a Trotskyist at the time, notes how remarkable it is that the "orthodox" Greek communists had no designation for deviation even up to the 1960s, other than that of Trotskyism. They thus often dubbed "Trotskyists" people who had no connection whatsoever to the Fourth International: "It made a huge impression on me because I knew the Trotskyists, because my father was a Trotskyist, and I knew them. I knew both the old and the young ones. And I was saying "but this one is not a Trotskyist, guys" (Varikas, interview).

In the postwar years, their few but faithful followers practiced the strategy of "subversive infiltration" within the official left-wing entities. The idea was to ideologically redirect them toward "correct" revolutionary positions, according to the 1917 model. Old Trotskyists, such as Agis Stinas, Christos Anastasiadis, and Sotiris Goudelis, remained points of reference and were consulted in how the movement should orient itself throughout the 1960s and 1970s. These people—mainly old tobacco workers, shoemakers, tailors, and printers—famously resided in basements and became some of the first to open tiny publishing houses that printed left-wing literature during the early 1970s.[127]

The main Trotskyist organizations were SEP (Socialist Revolutionary Struggle), members of which became connected with the latter-day terrorist organization 17th November, and EDE (Revolutionary Internationalist Union), which was part of the International Committee of the Fourth International in London. Other groups, such as Spartacus, were more peripheral. Interestingly, shortly after the coup, Spartacus's homonymous journal condemned "Yankee imperialism"; warned youths to stay away from the communist-led PAM's (Pan-Hellenic Anti-Dictatorship Front) "national unity," which it considered the utmost expression of reformism; and urged people to stop attending cinemas, theaters, and football matches and participating in gambling pools. The journal claimed that if, in addition, people could considerably reduce smoking, indirect taxation and state revenues would fall to zero, and the regime would consequently collapse.[128]

The Trotskyist groups never really acquired a mass following and were characterized by constant quarrels and schisms that reflected the divisions within the international Trotskyist movement. Daniel Bensaid's pejorative portrayal of Trotskyist environments as a "secret, grupusculous and conspiratory universe"[129] is nonetheless a faithful description of some of the unconstructive aspects of these groups. An illustration is a leaflet circulated by EDE within the Polytechnic in November 1973, in which it proclaimed itself the only genuine Trotskyist organization in Greece, "fighting to give power to the working classes." It labeled all the others Stalinists, "centrists," or "Pablists," the latter described as a dangerous deviation from the true spirit of Trotskyism.[130]

Right after the Soviet-Chinese split, old revolutionaries who had been historically affiliated with the former Stalinist leadership of the Communist Party became the point of reference for those who flirted with the Chinese model.[131] The OMLE (Organization of Marxist-Leninists of Greece) and its frontal student group, the PPSP (Progressive Student Unionist Party) were formed in the mid-1960s in order to express this tendency, and they won a short-lived following in student circles. Panos Theodoridis remembers that the "Chinese," as they were called, were quite fashionable and almost exotic in their aesthetic preferences and combative spirit: "The 'Chinese' of the Architecture School, who were famous for the way they used to dress, for the way they used to challenge everything and the way they used to worship Mao's experiments, his swim in the Yangtze River, all those things, they were the majority, the only majority in the Polytechnic School."[132]

During and after the Junta years, these Marxist-Leninist groups continued to theorize their political affiliations, speculating on China's "revisionist" turn and flirting for a while with the Albanian model. Their dynamism, however, was mainly channeled abroad; in Greece, they did not have a consistent and uninterrupted antidictatorial presence.[133] As conditions were supposedly "immature" for a popular uprising, they opted instead for "passive combativeness."[134] Followers of this line were advised to wait. Tasos Darveris, himself a member of the predictatorship OMLE, echoes in his novel the analysis promoted by this organization: "The Revolution would arrive later, when the proletariat, freed from revisionism, would build those conditions which would allow it to launch a campaign in order to crash the cancerous fascist cells and their origins, namely capitalism—or at least monopoly capitalism, to use the 'Chinese' terminology—and bring the bloc of 'anti-imperialist' classes to power."[135] Agis Tsaras, a PPSP member prior to 1967 who later moved to the rival group EKKE, argues similarly: "They said let's get organized, let's get together, let's become many, let's do this, let's do that. [laughter] They did not fight. They did not issue even one pamphlet" (Tsaras, interview). In fact, the groups were issuing two journals in which they characterized themselves as the "consistent Left," a much repeated, all-encompassing phrase among organizations of the extreme Left.[136] Still, PPSP's journal gave the following explanation for its absence during those years in an issue published some months after the fall of the Junta:

"PPSP was an organizational form that corresponded to particular needs. It was created under the conditions of 1966, and for the same reasons it is reconstructed at present."[137]

Nevertheless, the Marxist-Leninists launched themselves as the continuation of a long tradition. Ideologically, they came to favor the "Albanian" model, closer to China but also to the Soviet ideal until Stalin's death. Vourekas argues that their ideological rigidity was a positive aspect of their image as "relentless fighters," which in his view paid off psychologically when they were caught: "Absolute dogmatism, they were listening to Tirana radio station and were copying what it was saying. [laughter] Yes, this line of thought was terrible. But they also had a certain heroism, a personal one, being the 'unwavering' ones. And this gave them prestige, you know, to be severe, to be able to confront the police, suppression, to look ahead, you know, is an important element" (Vourekas, interview). Lionarakis, who belonged to EKIN, did not see OMLE as heroic, however. He notes that OMLE members accused the students participating in EKIN of "legalism," while OMLE proposed instead a future "armed struggle," making them "pseudo-revolutionaries," to use his own term. His discourse reveals the great fragmentation within the ranks of antiregime students:

> A great part of the Maoist Left ..., OMLE, was getting on our nerves. They might see someone who for some reason had spent ten days in jail or had been exiled, because a few had been to exile and a few had gotten caught, and they would say, "You know, you shouldn't do this kind of thing because we are ready to carry out the armed struggle." And we would say, "Wait a minute guys, you sit at home doing your stint, your studies, reading, while we're taking great risks and you're telling us these things?" (Lionarakis, interview)

PPSP defensively charged EKKE (the Revolutionary Communist Movement of Greece), its main Maoist rival, with not being very active during the Junta either. Instead of waging a "consistent" political battle, the PPSP accused, EKKE members were immersed in Herbert Marcuse, whom PPSP circles regarded as a degenerate intellectual. A *Neoi Stochoi* [New Aims] article read: "Trotskyism, anarcho-syndicalism, and of course ... Marcusism [are] carriers of capitulation and compromise that disorient and disorganize the progressive movement, be it student movement or not."[138] Far from being influenced by Marcuse, EKKE had been the main group behind Maoism's reappearance in Greece in the early 1970s. An idiosyncratic body, it presented itself as a mixed revolutionary organization of workers and students aiming at "the radical overthrow of the capitalist system and the dominance of the bourgeois classes, and at the creation of the dictatorship of the proletariat, the construction of socialism and classless society."[139] All this would be "imported" from West Germany, as the organization was created in West Berlin in spring 1970.

In the case of EKKE, too, the choice of name was not accidental: it contained the acronym of the historical Greek Communist Party (KKE) with the addition of a revolutionary prefix. Accordingly, EKKE presented itself as "antirevisionist" and defended the authenticity of its revolutionary aims as those of the "real" Communist Party. Already in its founding manifesto, the organization pursued hegemony of the revolutionary movement, attacking rival Maoists for being an "antiproletarian stream within the antirevisionist movement" and for suggesting examples taken from the Chinese model, which could not be applied to Greek conditions.[140]

In November 1972, EKKE started circulating pamphlets and the clandestine journal *Kommounistis*. This Maoist bloc was fascinated with the idea of permanent mobilization and idealized the notion of "cultural revolution."[141] Maoists believed that cultural revolution was a method of avoiding Soviet-like bureaucracy (though the EKKE did admire Stalin's achievements) and of keeping the masses in constant motion. It did not have serious reservations, at least in theory, against the use of violence, as according to Chairman Mao, "Revolution is not a banquet." EKKE's founding manifesto read: "A precondition for the development of the class struggle in Greece at present is to break down the climate of terrorization that the fascist Junta implements, and as the attainment of power by the proletariat and its allies cannot but be carried out through armed popular violence, EKKE is preparing concretely and since its founding for the armed struggle."[142] As the armed struggle never materialized, however, one can conclude that the group's talk about armed violence functioned as a ritual invocation.

The EKKE became influential within student circles through its front student group, the Anti-Fascist, Anti-Imperialistic Student Front of Greece (AASPE), whose name reflected its anti-imperialist, anti-US prerogatives. Its clandestine cells infiltrated the Greek universities and declared "the need to link the corporate with the political struggle, the student movement with the people's one and the struggle against the dictatorship with the struggle against imperialism."[143] AASPE's first pamphlet, circulated at the time of the electoral imbroglio at the universities, clearly identified the student movement as the spearhead of the entire people's movement. Still, it purported that the student struggle would "acquire perspective only when ... tied to the struggles of working-class popular strata."[144] The pamphlet attributes the increasing class division in Greece not to the politics of the Junta so much as to the nature of imperialist dependency.

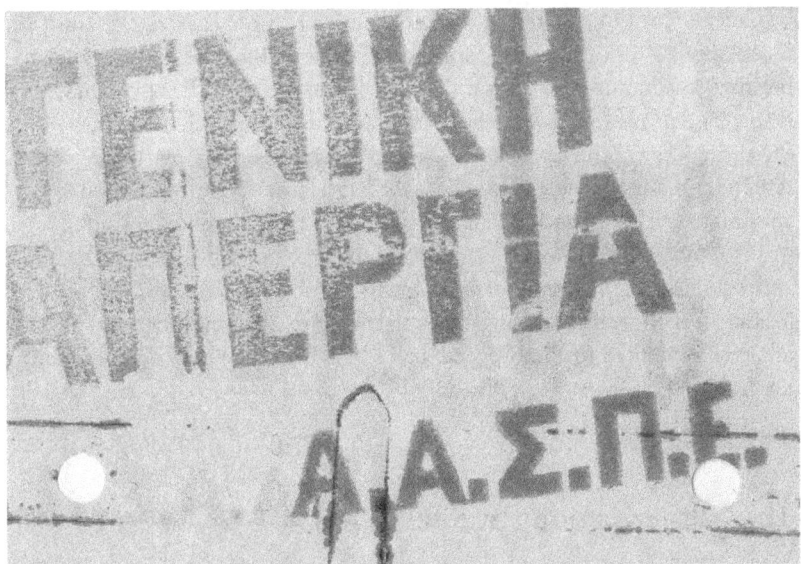

Figure 3.3. Leaflet distributed by the Maoist-Stalinist student organization AASPE (Anti-Fascist, Anti-Imperialistic Student Front of Greece) calling for a "general strike." (Source: ASKI, Archives of Social and Cultural History)

Though AASPE expressed its faith in the possibilities of exploiting the legal loopholes allowed by the regime, it recommended refraining from student elections; in its view, student participation would do nothing but legitimize the regime.[145] The group reckoned that student elections were of strategic importance to the Junta, as they were part of the gradual implementation of the 1968 constitution and the country's false democratization.[146] It expressed its support for a vaguely defined mass struggle, at the same time disclosing its attraction to the dynamic solutions of the past. Apart from their contempt for other organizations of similar or different leanings, EKKE and AASPE also expressed deep distrust of the cast of "bourgeois politicians."[147]

Lastly, there was the PAK (Pan-Hellenic Resistance Movement), a leftist organization with no roots in the past. This hybrid of social democrats, old Center Union members, and aspiring revolutionaries had limited representation among young people. Andreas Papandreou, its charismatic leader abroad, also asserted that armed struggle was the only way forward, as "the country [found] itself in a belligerent situation and a prerevolutionary period."[148] PAK professed revolutionary action, hinting at a struggle not only against the Junta but for general social change, including liberation of the Greek nation from US imperialism: "Our country is a land under occupation. And that occupation is American … We will not have democracy in Greece without the real, substantial, unconditional liberation from the shackles of American imperialism in the framework of the Atlantic Alliance. For that reason our struggle is for national liberation."[149] This exuberant *tiersmondisme* proved to be purely rhetorical and performative. By early 1971 Papandreou gave the signal to the group to enter the mass struggle instead, rather than remain aloof from it. PAK's activities were reinforced by the cultural youth organization Panarmonia, which was mainly involved in organizing concerts of antiregime composers that became a point of reference for antiregime students. Some of its student members were strategically placed inside the Polytechnic during the crucial events of November 1973. Most of these students acquired several political positions when, after the fall of the Junta, PASOK, PAK's political reincarnation, formed successive socialist governments.

The "Other" among Student Groups

Incorporation in one of these groups played a significant role in the creation of a social identity and a sense of belonging.[150] Being part of a group and entering into collective action meant a fundamental shift in the individual experience of the world; it was a "state of birth," to use sociologist Francesco Alberoni's term.[151] In turn, the groups required compliance with their rules and conventions. The relationship between instructors and the instructed corresponded essentially with the rapport between the initiator and the uninitiated. Initiation required, among other things, putting on a particular face, a certain "uniform," in a process of homogenization. It is no coincidence that former activists tend to delineate their differentiation in aesthetic terms and to insist that members of various groups could be told apart through the semiology of appearance. The militant, nonaffiliated Maoist Kleopatra Papageorgiou uses theatrical terms when talking about EKKE's "colorfulness" and attributes this to the fact that one of the organization's leaders, Christos Bistis, was a director in Berlin and therefore knew how to stage a performance:

> If somebody told you that he was a Maoist, you could tell from the face, the clothes, the style if he was with PPSP or with EKKE.... PPSP people were a bit like religious people, their face and their way of dressing were more austere. [laughter] EKKE people were more liberal, more colorful we could say, they didn't have this homogeneity of PPSP. Those were all shaved with the military jacket, you know.... They were more military in style, but a religious kind of

military [laughter], whereas the EKKE people were cuter. After all, Bistis was a [theater] director, he studied at the Berliner Ensemble and he knew how to put up nice scenery. (Papageorgiou, interview)

In most cases affiliation was accidental, rather than the result of rational choice; it was largely a question of which group first approached a student for recruitment. Giannis Kourmoulakis recalls this procedure as being quite crude:

We went inside [the apartment]. There was no furniture; we sat down and he had some boxes with the *Epitheorisi Technis,* a journal of the time, and he took it out and started to read Mayakofsky to me: the guy started reciting poems. And in the morning he tells me, "I'm going to have you enrolled into *Panspoudastiki.*" "Come on," I told him. "No, I will have you enrolled. In any case, someone will approach you; your code name is Robinson Crusoe." "Oh, c'mon," I told him. This was the first attempt to proselytize me. (Kourmoulakis, interview)

Angeliki Xydi, on the other hand, describes the recruitment process as an endless chain resembling a rosary: "Alekos Alavanos must have been organized first of all, and Alekos organized Ariadni and Ariadni very quickly, in a matter of days in any case, organized me. And this went on like a *komboloi* [chaplet], yes, you know, round and round" (Xydi, interview).

As political scientist Donatella della Porta notes, within a social movement, rational processes, such as identification, are placed next to more instinctive mechanisms.[152] In this sense, emotional and psychological motivations often tended to overtake rational ones, and thus students' reasons for joining a particular group were not strictly ideological. This makes it difficult for former student revolutionaries to reconstruct the sequence of their lives in narratives of linear, coherent choice.[153] It is often hard for people to remember what they believed once if—a frequent phenomenon—their later experiences have led them to the revise their former opinions, or if they do not consider a certain point of the narrative worth remembering.[154] A female activist of the Communist A-EFEE, when asked about the rationale behind her choice to join the organization, commented that "these details are a bit too personal" before arguing unpersuasively and after a long hesitation that the decision was motivated by strict political considerations. A male activist, on the other hand, frankly highlighted the clearly nonpolitical stimulus that drew him to the group: "I was ready to get enrolled into Rigas. Though it may sound strange and demonstrate a lack of seriousness, it was the relationship with a woman that was crucial in making me go to A-EFEE [laughter]" (Kalimeris, interview).

When searching for meaning, however, it is necessary to clarify "the symbolic universe of actors, their organized system of representations, their attitudes, the affectively connoted norms that filtered their definition of the situation and oriented their behavior."[155] There is no doubt, for instance, that certain groups had a greater impact on students' imaginary than others. Nikos Bistis, one of A-EFEE's leading members, attributes the fact that his organization attracted the largest numbers of people, not to KKE's clandestine expertise, but because of the awe that the party's history produced and all kinds of imaginary assumptions that this inspired:

> We realized that in reality we were the party machines. That is, there was no great party machine behind us. But there was History. The sense of it, many times the illusion of it. But suddenly you became part of a great tradition and this gave you a greater self-esteem.... So, there was a new batch of people that took this whole story into their hands. Without knowing it. Thinking that there were regiments behind them. But behind, there was mainly History.... It had a symbolic weight.... This is why, you see, all those references were always made to the Generation of the Resistance, to the EPON. (Bistis, interview)

A-EFEE inherited KKE's culture, which included subjugation to the leadership and the party, and the "glorious past" became a context for the construction of identity. This sense of belonging to a certain tradition was "great equipment" and "something that one needed in order to confront the difficulties of the struggle" (Bistis, interview). At the same time, however, "it was a limit in terms of opening up one's mind to certain things." Bistis benefits from hindsight when he concludes that despite being blessed by history, A-EFEE's attachment to the Communist Party limited its members' capacity to judge without restraint.

Rigas, by contrast, attracted a vast number of well-to-do "progressive" kids, as its line was less rigid. Rigas was not inflammatory in its declarations, and there were no serious discrepancies between its theory and action, nor was it dogmatically attached to any given "truth." Its members, however, were accused of being so moderate that they were ready to negotiate and make concessions on anything, simply in order to prevent direct confrontation. Kleopatra Papageorgiou charged the well-known leaders of Rigas in Salonica with purposely postponing the universally desired clash with the regime because "the time was not ripe" (Papageorgiou, interview).

The creation and diffusion of protest involved imitation and competition between rival groups.[156] The process of choosing one group or another, based as it was on exclusion, suggests that difference was a key notion. Identity only exists in relation to others: it is in conflict with the "other" that the sense of the self is constantly renegotiated. As identity is defined by poles of similarity and difference, otherness is an inherent component in its constitution.[157] Going beyond the initial level of differentiation between those who tolerated or supported the regime and those who were keen to change things, there also was a gradual demarcation between "ourselves" and "others" within the rank-and-file of the student movement itself. Ideological differences ended up cutting across divides of class, age, and gender. Even though the real enemy was supposed to be the Junta, distinctions and behaviors based on "otherness" were rampant within student circles. Ioanna Karystiani describes how nonradical left-wing students were treated differently from those belonging to one particular clique, for example:

> There is something from that period that burdens me. When the medical student Vassilis Pendaris got caught, as he did not belong to our group, in the wider sense of the word—the group of progressive left-wingers, let's put it that way—we did not immediately issue an announcement. In retrospect, I find this thing terrible. I think I realized this only later. I don't remember how I felt back then, but if they had caught Nikos Bistis or Vernikos, Alekos Alavanos, one of our buddies of this period, we would have been mobilized in a second. (Karystiani, interview)

Karystiani's recollection reveals the difficulty of dealing with past events through the perspective of the present, because it masks one's former motivations. She is troubled by her explicit juxtaposition of past and present attitudes, in which what seemed normal then sounds entirely outrageous at present; but her story also presents a truthful indication of the atmosphere of the period in question.[158] Each organization, and to a broader extent each faction, became obsessed with proving that it differed from its supposed "other": the leftists tried to differentiate themselves from the politics of the two KKEs and vice versa.[159]

The most dramatic example of the discrimination this produced among students was the accusation of being a stool pigeon or an *agent provocateur*, a tendency with long-standing roots in the Greek Left. Agis Tsaras describes how this accusation was often part of the organizations' tactics to handle students who refused to collaborate with them or decided to change political affiliations: "While I was hiding I was in contact with some Anagennisi people, fellow students of mine, that is. After two to three years, some of them tried to … find me and have me enrolled again in the same "club."… I declined. I was already in contact with EKKE. And they called me a stool-pigeon, just like that, immediately" (Tsaras, interview). Lionarakis recalls a similar incident involving the pro-Moscow faction, and his experience reminds him of the historical smear campaigns of the Communist Party, such as the one against communist leader Nikos Ploumbidis in the early 1950s:

> I had a very traumatic experience: these were probably the worst days of my life, because coming out of prison there was a whisper, which was a very bad one, nothing precise, I hadn't even been beaten so that one could say that I turned in someone. Nothing, there was nothing, they almost didn't interrogate me. I didn't know any clandestine things either, we were doing everything lawfully. But there was a whisper: "Isolate him." Which after a long, long investigation and so forth I understood that it all originated from the KNE section, from A-EFEE. To come out of prison, to feel that "something" and to have your own friends saying it, was very traumatic. I was shocked. (Lionarakis, interview)

Other life stories describe the rejection of the "other" in caustic or ironic terms. According to an A-EFEE member, "People's Courts used to function in AASPE" (Kalimeris, interview), whereas an AASPE member noted, "A-EFEE was a really dark organization" (Papageorgiou, interview). Even people belonging to ideologically related groups demonstrated equal or greater hostility. A-EFEE members clearly despised Rigas members as conservative copies of them ("right-wing revisionists"),[160] whereas Rigas criticized the former's authoritarianism. EKKE rejected PPSP's apathy, and PPSP castigated EKKE for its self-proclaimed leadership of the Maoist movement in Greece. The "reformists" tended to reject the Maoists as somehow grotesque people. Leftist *tiersmondiste* internationalism was often ridiculed by the rest of the students, such as the unaffiliated student leader Giorgos Vernikos, whose caustic comment about their incomprehensible and "picturesque speculations" on the "rural question in China" was quite characteristic.[161] These moral interpretations, characterized by bitterness and resentment, reveal a lasting pathos and an age-old fracture in the communal ethos.

Despite the fact that there is no stable concept of identity, certain "hard" elements of past identities seem to survive. Patterns emerge from interviews with former militants, which demonstrate common attitudes resulting from the interviewees' prior organizational affiliations. This resonates with oral historian Luisa Passerini's notion of a "hardening of subjectivity" and Ronald Fraser's concept of "frozen memory," but also Raymond Williams's classic "structure of feeling."[162] According to these theories, people demonstrate deeply entrenched patterns of behavior, despite the time lag between past and present: it makes sense for those who used to belong to Maoist groups, for example, to share a common conspiratorial code in the present. People moreover tend to adopt the analytical and hermeneutical categories of the time, such as the polarity between "organization" and "spontaneity;" thus past rifts between "reformists" and "leftists" remain strongly reflected in the interviews. As oral historian Riki Van Boeschoten notes, these elements deriving from individual positions in the past tend to survive and come to the surface, and they often create a contrast to the present attitudes and beliefs of the interviewees.[163]

Still, the same people also stress moments of solidarity and allegiance with their ideological rivals and a present bond that springs out of common action. This tension between rivalry and solidarity seems to have been part of the polarity between identity and otherness, which can also be seen in the '68 movements. It is manifest in several recollections, noticeable despite the respondents' use of self-presentation strategies that adopt a holistic approach to militant life, including elements of self-justification and self-knowledge.[164] As clinical psychologist Ruthellen Josselson argues, "We must cease [regarding] people as finished entities and, somewhat paradoxically, we must find those places within narrative where the self is most clearly in dialogue with itself."[165] This dialogue is evident when, in reviewing their lives, several "orthodox" female cadres distanced themselves from the KKE's dogmatism and party discipline and sought to render an image of themselves as more anarchist at heart. Katerina Detsika commented with a laugh, "As my instructors used to tell me, I was much more a person, as they told me, with a leftist psychology than with a typical KKE one" (Detsika, interview). Angeliki Xydi, one of A-EFEE's leading members, said: "I was reading Bakunin and other anarchists, I used to like them very much. And I think they influenced me very much, that is, later on as well. Although I remained many years within KKE, I always had this libertarian attitude, I had it as a person, I had it, it seems, as regards my influences, and I still have it" (Xydi, interview). Accordingly, apart from mechanisms of cohesion within group identity, one can also discern conflicts within them. Xydi adopted a rather apologetic stance:

> And I did things which I have regretted very much. In any case, things that I would have preferred not to have done. Both back then and later on. That is, a certain political stance vis-à-vis, say, the other members of the movement. And then, inside the Polytechnic and

later on, things that I said from a position of power, through imposition, a certain authoritarianism in political behavior. It would have been better to have avoided them, but ... (Xydi, interview)

On the opposite end of the spectrum, Kleopatra Papageorgiou, a Maoist of radical inclinations, admits the depth of her own loyalty to the Communist Party at the time, which kept her from fully accepting criticism of the Soviet regime:

The policemen in jail were telling us, "Aren't you ashamed? In the Soviet Union and the countries over there, women sell themselves for a pair of nylon stockings." And we were thinking, look at what these filthy, miserable perverts are telling us. We didn't believe this. Although we were antirevisionists and although we indeed accepted that the regime that ruled over there was a form of state capitalism and that, alright, there is a nomenclature that oppresses the masses and the workers, we could not grasp that the collapse that had taken place there was really that great. We didn't believe it, we thought [they were saying this] just in order to disturb us, to accuse us. And of course, despite our critical stance and despite our disagreement with what the KKE did, namely, that it reacted and that it sought to control the masses, we had deep in our souls a respect for the party. The Communist Party was a notion that was sacred for us. (Papageorgiou, interview)

Others, like Bistis, fall into contradiction: he initially admits that A-EFEE tended to put other groups "into its pocket" but then turns this argument on its head by saying that this was never put in practice, as unity was of paramount importance. Bistis further blames the rifts among the organizations on the *Metapolitefsi*, the transition to democracy that followed the Junta, thus understating the tensions that were an integral part of the predictatorship movement:

We in the Law School occupation had the upper hand. We were the best-known trade-unionists that existed, that is. Nevertheless, we had natural and good relations with the rest. No, there were no attempts to put the others into our pocket and so forth. The conditions we experienced inside the Law School, which was the epicenter, were so important that an organization could not control things on its own even if it wanted to. You were forced to communicate with the rest. We could not afford not to coordinate with the Rigas people, for example.... This is why the fanaticism and the confrontations took place only after the regime change. (Bistis, interview)

Other student group members similarly stress that prior to November 1973 differences were lurking but never directly affected relations among groups. Ariadni Alavanou and Giannis Kourmoulakis remark that as the dictatorship was the main issue at stake, differences were of lesser importance. When the dictatorship ceased to exist, however, the "age of innocence," in Kourmoulakis's words, ended abruptly. In fact, the void and friction that follows the achievement of a given movement's goals (be it protest against the war in Vietnam or against an authoritarian regime) is a recurrent element in most student uprisings in the "long 1960s" worldwide.

> During the first period of *Metapolitefsi* [there were] many clashes, this is where the ideological distinction became very clear. That is, while there were differences [between us] during the dictatorship, I have the impression, at least for myself, that I had no knowledge of the differences, which was the difference between Interior, Exterior, the leftist groups, Anagennisi, all these were ... How can I put it to you? ... Byzantinisms. The main thing was to be all united against the dictatorship, that element was dominant. Very much so. (Alavanou, interview)

> I remember the get-togethers, taverns until late, wine, sexual relationships within this space, these were developed on a very tender and very friendly level. Even today, even though relationships have matured or ended, some have been maintained, in a very nice and tender way; we meet each other, we talk and laugh and remember. It's nice, these were beautiful years from this point of view, because we were connected with a common element in that period. After the *Metapolitefsi*, this thing broke because we got organized into parties and the thing turned bad, but at that period, it was still the age of innocence for the student movement in Greece, because we were still united, not yet split, we had a common target, a common enemy. And it was still very early to take different directions. (Kourmoulakis, interview)

As all these elements in people's memories and writings from the time or the present indicate, tracing the clashes among the different organizations of the time can be of great interest; all the more so since they tended to be fierce before the fall of the dictators as well, even if not as violent. Here I tend to disagree with historian Jeffrey N. Wasserstrom's conclusion that in the study of student movements one should put "less emphasis upon tracing the relationship between student protesters … or upon analyzing the attraction of specific ideologies and much more upon locating student protests within the context of their social milieu and the dynamic … political culture of which they were part."[166]

Because the students' memories were mediated by time and experience, however, they tend to be distorted in two distinct ways. Some apply the rancor created during the *Metapolitefsi* to the past immediately prior to it; it stiffened affiliations and broadened divisions. Rather than a hardening of subjectivity, this looks like an anachronistic judgment. In other cases, one can discern nostalgia and a sort of idealization of the remote past and the steely solidarity of the dictatorship years, as opposed to the postdictatorship fratricide. So while some remember continuity from the Junta years to the *Metapolitefsi* divisions, others recall a dramatic rupture.

Libidinal Politics

Sexuality was suppressed in Greek society at the time of the dictatorship, following the rigid social attitudes of the postwar period. Repressed desire makes itself apparent in the magazines of the period, which were filled with nude pictures and spicy comments. Kiosk owners, by contrast, commonly "hid" the graphic parts of erotic magazines by blacking them out with magic markers.[167] It is telling that although Bernardo Bertolucci's *Last Tango in Paris* was banned by the puritanical censors in 1972, the entire script of the film was published by the daily *Thessaloniki,* attracting a wide readership, full of a voyeuristic desire for its salacious details.[168] A year later, the avant-garde theater group Eleṟthero Theatro (see chapter 4) made some satirical allusions to the film in its performance of *…And You're Combing Your Hair* and the notorious "butter" scene, demonstrating an extraordinary familiarity with the subject matter. The cue for a song called "Last Tango in Kurdistan" was: "With a little butter and some marmalade/ your bum puts everyone in a whirl/ and when there's no butter left/ you can all put Vaseline on your bread," whereby the play of words between *psomi* (bread) and *psoli* (prick) is more than obvious.[169]

Despite a certain liberalization of mores within the student movement, another limitation on sexual freedom was the real or perceived restriction imposed by political organization on the private life of cadres. Comments on sexual restrictions within rival organizations echo the stereotypes of the time concerning interpersonal relations and can be found in most of the former militants' life stories. A common allegation is that the Maoists were the tightest and most disciplined concerning sexual life. A Rigas member comments, "There was an incredible social conservatism. Mainly among those EKKE people, they were marrying each other. A sect" (Mavragani, interview). An A-EFEE member similarly notes, "We were making fun then of a leftist organization, PPSP, which had issued an announcement: it was very characteristic; it was written in their paper too, stating how many times in the week the fighter should make love. [laughter] Yes, decision of the central instructional organ" (Alavanou, interview).

The same argument is also used in the opposite direction, as Agis Tsaras, a member of Maoist group EKKE, argues that in the Communist KNE it was not permissible to have sex with someone from a different organization ("A KNE guy should go out with a KNE girl"), and that, on top of that, sexual relations should lead to marriage (Tsaras, interview). Similarly, the fierce animosity between the two Maoist organizations, EKKE and PPSP, is clearly recorded by the student actor Giorgos Kotanidis, one of EKKE's leading members. His comment makes clear that allegations of orgies and open relationships were considered stigmas rather than praise for those militants of the Left: "[PPSP] hated us more than anyone else.... They were saying that we were libertarian, followers of Marcuse, having orgies. And we blamed them for being ... conservative, prudish, supporting organizational orthodoxy." Kotanidis goes so far as to maintain that PPSP members were so prudish they were "fucking with their underpants on" (Kotanidis, interview). Such mocking descriptions of rivals as potentially castrated by their organization reveal, in addition to a deep animus, a macho attitude among the politicized male students. Still, Kotanidis admits that sexual policing existed in EKKE as well—in some way echoing the age-old puritanism of the Communist Party itself. In his memoirs he remembers how Dimitris Kamberidis, a fellow actor and member of the organization, was expelled, partly for sleeping with someone other than his partner: "On top of everything, he had fucked a comrade and he went through a people's court, being accused of opportunism and such things. They even turned him in to Lena, his partner, who tried to cover for him, but they put pressure on her to separate from him, following the standard practice of KKE, whose methods we were supposed to have denounced."[170]

It should be noted that discipline was indeed imposed on Maoist cadres, following the dictum that the revolutionary should not consume energy on physical pleasure, a behavior that "the workers" would neither understand nor sympathize with. As Eric Hobsbawm ironically pointed out in around the same period, "[Sex] consumes time and energy and is hardly compatible with organization and efficiency."[171] The only organization that is not accused of trying to impose rigid sexual control is Rigas. In fact, respondents often stressed that Rigas had the reputation of having the most open-minded members in terms of sexual conduct.[172] The fact that Rigas female cadres, in particular, were sexually free became a common topos in postdictatorship left-wing circles and led to considerable controversies even in recent years.[173]

All of these continuities and discontinuities in history and discourse are part of what Pierre Bourdieu calls "*l'illusion biographique,*" a narrative organized according to intelligible relations on the basis of the idea of a sense of existence.[174] In either case, memory both distorts and reveals interesting phenomena, due to an interchange between the present and several layers of the past that intermingle. And even in spite of this distortion, the life stories provide authentic elements of subjective representation, often of a collective character.

What is certain, and beyond the fallacies of memory, is that the common denominator between all these heterogeneous student groups was the Junta itself. It provided the common enemy, just like Franco in Spain, De Gaulle in France, and Nixon in the United States. Fragmentation was already present among the groups, but collaboration was desperately needed, at least on a tactical level, as protest was widely spreading. Still, if political affiliations could generate serious disputes even in terms of libidinal economy, cultural politics seemed to provide much more of a common ground among dissident students—even though the two spheres cannot be entirely isolated from one another.

Notes

1. Alvin Shuster, "Greek Students, Long Passive, Now Challenge Regime," *New York Times,* 28 February 1973.
2. American Embassy in Athens to Department of State, "Student Discontent: An Analysis," 6 May 1972, POL, USNA.
3. Konofagos, *Polytechnic Uprising,* 24.
4. *Protoporia* 2 (Jan. 1972).
5. Kouloumbis, *Notes of an Academic,* 157.
6. Shuster, "Greek Students," *New York Times,* 28 February 1973.
7. American Consul Thessaloniki to Department of State, "Follow Up on Rightist Student Demonstration, University of Thessaloniki, December 8, 1970," 14 January 1971, XR POL 13–2 Greece, USNA.
8. Papazoglou, *Student Movement,* 26.
9. For a comprehensive analysis of those spectacles see Gonda Van Steen, "Rallying the Nation: Sport and Spectacle Serving the Greek Dictatorships."
10. Lendakis, "Επιτελείο για τη φασιστικοποίηση της νεολαίας" [Directory for the Fascistization of the Youth], *Anti* 18, cited in Dafermos, *Students and Dictatorship,* 45.
11. Ibid., 46.

12. Herzfeld, "Towards an Ethnographic Phenomenology of the Greek Spirit," 17. Pagan Hellenism and Orthodox Christianity had already been "reconciled" by nineteenth-century nationalist historians such as Konstantinos Paparrigopoulos and Spyridon Zambelios and their supposed organic link actively promoted by the dictatorship of Ioannis Metaxas in the late 1930s.
13. "Football Yes, Politics No," *Economist,* 31 July 1971.
14. EKNE. *First Congress.*
15. Ibid.
16. Van Dyck, *Kassandra and the Censors,* 65.
17. Yiannopoulos, "Resistance Forces," 289.
18. Quoted in Van Dyck, ibid. The literary exponents of this generation were summarized as the "generation of the '70s."
19. Metaxas, *Political Socialization,* 104. For a survey of school books and teaching methods under the Junta, see Polichronopoulos, *Education and Politics,* esp. 423–654.
20. In *The 'Real' 17 November,* by Stelios Kouloglou NET, 17/11/2003.
21. Damofli, "The Assemblies," 199.
22. Dimitris Marangopoulos, "Unknown Soldiers," 51.
23. Ibid., 53.
24. Ibid.
25. Damofli, "The Assemblies," 199.
26. For a detailed analysis and contemporary reports of the torture that took place from 1967 to 1969 see Giourgos et al., *The Terrace.*
27. See Marcuse, "The Revival of Holocaust Awareness," 424.
28. Interview quoted in Mantoglou, *Polytechnic,* 181.
29. For the use of the term see Theodore Roszak, *Making of a Counter Culture.*
30. Alivizatos, *Does the Journey Go On,* 11.
31. Fyssas, *Polytechnic Generation,* 19.
32. Passerini, *Torino Operaia,* 6–8.
33. Lane, *Political Life: Why People Get Involved in Politics.*
34. For the importance of traveling in the development of the European youth cultures in the "long 1960s" see Schildt and Siegfried, "Youth Consumption, and Politics in the Age of Radical Change," 25–27.
35. See Maravall, *Dictatorship and Political Dissent.*
36. Lumley, *States of Emergency,* 40.
37. Karatzaferis, *Polytechnic Slaughter,* 321.
38. Bistis, *Moving On and Revising,* 105
39. Theodoridis, *Macedonian Rock,* 225.
40. Passerini, *Autobiography of a Generation,* 22–36.
41. Lefort, *L'invention democratique.* The situation changed in 1972, when the student movement went public.
42. Confidential, Department of State telegram, 7658 Athens, "Papandreou funeral turned into first political demonstration in eighteen months," 4 November 1968, POL 6 Greece, USNA.
43. Van Dyck, *Kassandra and the Censors,* 27.
44. For a US report of the funeral see Confidential, Department of State telegram, Athens 5050, "Seferis Funeral Singing Theodorakis songs could draw charges of 'carry-

ing out propaganda against the established social order,'" 23 September 1971, POL 6 Greece, USNA. For a very detailed description of young people's reactions, see Andrews, *Greece in the Dark*, 41–58.
45. See Maravall, *Dictatorship and Political Dissent*, 103.
46. McAdam, "Culture and Social Movements," 38. In this context, Clifford Geertz's observation that symbolic performances can be understood as "social dramas" is particularly valid. See Geertz, *Local Knowledge: Further Essays in Interpretive Anthropology*.
47. Diouf, "Urban Youth," 43, 64.
48. Lefebvre, *Le droit à la ville*.
49. *Statistical Yearbook of Higher Education for the Academic Year 1968–69*, ESIE.
50. "Two Headed Phoenix," *Economist*, 31 July 1971.
51. Swanson, "Memory," 123.
52. Schorske, *Thinking with History*, 6.
53. Boyer, *City of Collective Memory*, 16.
54. Fatouros, *Change and Reality*, 75.
55. American Consul Thessaloniki, "University of Thessaloniki: The Former Rector Speaks Out," 12 March 1969, EDU 4–3, Greece, USNA.
56. Anderson, *Personality and Stance*, 101.
57. C. M. Woodhouse, "What Greeks Think about Greece," *Observer*, 13 February 1972.
58. This comment about the absence of potential student revolts bears striking similarities to the famous *Le Monde* article that concluded that France was feeling "bored" some weeks prior to the events of May 1968. See Pierre Viansson-Ponté, "Quand la France s'ennuie," *Le Monde*, 15 March 1968.
59. Nikolinakos, *Resistance and Opposition*, 267.
60. Martial law, in operation since 21 April 1967, was removed from the whole country except the two big cities on 31 December 1971. This was extended to Salonica on 12 December 1972 and Athens on 20 August 1973. The Law about the Press of November 1969 removed preventive censorship, and the responsibility passed over to the publishers. Decrees issued by the National Revolutionary Government in November 1968, April 1969, and April 1970 restored several major constitutional rights, including the right of association and cooperation, the inviolability of the home, and the right to personal safety. Alivizatos, *Political Institutions*, 286; "Επαναφέρονται εις ισχύν τα άρθρα 10 και 11 του Συντάγματος. Το δικαίωμα του συνέρχεσθαι και συνεταιρίζεσθαι" [Articles 10 and 11 of the Constitution Are Back in Force: The Right of Assembly and of Association], *To Vima*, 29 May 1972.
61. For a theory on the importance of the structure of political opportunity for the successful outcome of a social movement, see in particular Tilly, *From Mobilization to Revolution;* Kitschelt, "Political Opportunity Structures"; and Tarrow, *Power in the Movement*. To look at the role of political opportunities not in terms of their eventual potential but as the only and absolute drive behind social movements often leads to a "structural" or "objectivist bias," however. As McAdam notes, "mediating between opportunity and action are people and the subjective meanings they attach to their situation," *Political Process*, 48.
62. For an elaboration of this notion of carving up public space, see Eyerman and Jamison, *Social Movements*, 104.

63. This development reflects McAdam, McCarthy, and Zald's point that a movement only emerges out of the combination of political opportunities and mobilizing structures, which afford groups a certain structural potential for action. In order to mobilize, people must be not only aggrieved but also optimistic that by acting collectively they can redress a problem. See McAdam, McCarthy, and Zald, introduction to *Comparative Perspectives*, 5.
64. Notaras, *Dictatorship and Organized Resistance*, 197.
65. Alkis Rigos, "Φοιτητικό Κίνημα και Δικτατορία" [Student Movement and Dictatorship], *Anti* 344 (17–23 April 1987): 54–55.
66. Skocpol, *States and Social Revolutions*, 10.
67. Vernikos, *Antidictatorship Student Movement*, 20.
68. Dafermos, *Students and Dictatorship*, 61.
69. Theodoridis, *Macedonian Rock*, 323.
70. Vernikos, "Personal testimony," in *Antidictatorship Student Movement*, 144.
71. Giataganas, "Dynamic Acts," 61.
72. For a detailed review of Greece's expulsion from the Council of Europe, see Constas, *Greek Case*; Becket, *Barbarism in Greece*; and Council of Europe and European Commission on Human Rights, *The Greek Case*.
73. See, for example, Alexandros Delmouzos's Δημοτικισμός και Παιδεία [Demoticism and Education] and Giorgos Koumandos's Ανώτατη Παιδεία [Higher Education].
74. "1° ενημερωτικό δελτίο" [First Bulletin], in Vernikos, *Antidictatorship Student Movement*, 226.
75. "Συμμετοχή στο Διάλογο' [Participation in the Dialogue], in ibid., 223.
76. Kouloumbis, "The Greek Junta Phenomenon," 368.
77. Byron Stamatopoulos, the regime's porte-parole, used Grass's talk as a proof that there was freedom of expression in Greece. Joan Robinson's talk in Athens prompted the authorities' reaction and banning of her programmed follow-up talk in Salonica. For a detailed description of EMEP's activities, see the autobiographical account by Anastasis Peponis, *1961–1981*, 270–80.
78. D. N. Maronitis, Ανεμόσκαλα και Σημαδούρες [Rope-Ladder and Buoys], Athens 1975, 31. See Papanikolaou, "Making Some Strange Gestures," 186.
79. Leslie Finer, "A Gleam in the Greek Dark," *New Statesman*, 21 April 1972.
80. "Προτάσεις Αλιβιζάτου' [Alivizatos's Proposals], in Vernikos, *Antidictatorship Student Movement*, 217–19.
81. Kanellakis, "In Those Years."
82. Quoted by Mario Modiano, "Greek Jails Crowded with Brave Students Says Former Politician," *New York Times*, 12 May 1972.
83. Klandermans, "New Social Movements," 24.
84. Kouloumbis, *Notes of an Academic*, 186.
85. "A Mosquito on a Bull," *Economist*, 12 March 1973, 12.
86. One telegram read, "A protest virus has affected students since last spring." American Embassy Athens to Secretary of State, "Initial Reactions Subdued Following Student Elections," 24 November 1972, POL 13–2 Greece, USNA. Interestingly, US reports talk about a growing student "cynicism" that undermined government initiatives and attempts to demonstrate normalization.

87. For Alessandro Pizzorno, the combativeness that springs from collective action directed toward the constitution of a group's identity, such as its right to representation, tends to be more intense than average trade-unionist demands and therefore assumes a new type of content. From this point onward, conflict did not depend on the negotiation process, as the real aim of student interaction with the regime was the constitution of a new collective identity—a fact that became the precondition of any negotiation. See Pizzorno, "Le due logiche," 13.
88. Testimony in Kyparisis, *Antidictatorship Student Movement*, 36.
89. Dafermos, *Students and Dictatorship*, 52, 70b.
90. Ibid.
91. These included an increase in the fund allocated to the refectory, grants for all, full medical care, a third exam period, a third transferable unit, free tickets for cinema and theater, timely circulation of curricula, and continuous teaching schedules.
92. "Αι δηλώσεις του υφυπουργού κ. Σταματόπουλου" [The Statements of the Deputy Minister Mr. Stamatopoulos], *To Vima*, 21 November 1972.
93. This brings to mind Cyril Levitt's controversial argument that the rebelling students in the West during the 1960s were talking about egalitarianism in order to camouflage their injured elitism. See Levitt, *Children of Privilege*.
94. "Αι χθεσιναί φοιτητικαί εκλογαί" [Yesterday's Student Elections], *To Vima*, 21 November 1972.
95. Ibid.
96. Pimblis, *Student Movement*, 27. The comment in brackets is part of the original text.
97. Serdedakis, *Social Movement Production*, 185. Also see Wilson, *Political Organizations*.
98. Wasserstrom, *Student Protest*.
99. Habermas, *Toward a Rational Society*, 13.
100. See Serdedakis, *Social Movement Production*, and Giannaris, *Student Movements*, 448.
101. See Lygeros, *Student Movement*, 79–81, and Krimbas, "Higher Education," 143.
102. See the leaflet circulated by KOS, the student organization of KKE-Esoterikou, which talks of a "capitalist modernization of education" and the "rationalized submission to the needs of the monopolies." "Για την ανάπτυξη του αντιδικτατορικού δημοκρατικού φοιτητικού κινήματος. Θέσεις της Κομμουνιστικής Οργάνωσης Σπουδαστών του ΚΚΕ (Εσωτερικού)" [For the Development of the Antidictatorship Democratic Student Movement. Positions of the Communist Organization of Students of KKE-Esoterikou], October 1972, 11.
103. Siegfried, "Understanding 1968," 61.
104. Mayakovsky, *The Bedbug and Selected Poetry*, 221.
105. Kotanidis, *All Together, Now!*, 234.
106. For a definition see McAdam, "Culture and Social Movements," 42. It also brought Greek militants close to what Philip Altbach defined as "an association of students inspired by aims set forth in a specific ideological doctrine, ... political in nature." See Altbach, "Students and Politics," 82.
107. Liakos, *Appearance of Youth Organizations*, 73.

108. For the clandestine press under the Junta see *Dictatorship 1967 1974. Resistance in Print.*
109. Close, "Road to Reconciliation."
110. See Dafermos, *Students and Dictatorship*, 76.
111. Sfikas, Review of *New Voices in the Nation.*
112. "Για την ανάπτυξη του αντιδικτατορικού δημοκρατικού φοιτητικού κινήματος. Θέσεις της Κομμουνιστικής Οργάνωσης Σπουδαστών του ΚΚΕ (Εσωτερικού)" [For the Development of the Antidictatorship Democratic Student Movement. Positions of the Communist Organization of Students of KKE-Esoterikou], October 1972, 18.
113. See Filippou, *The KNE Kids.*
114. A-EFEE's founding manifesto, published in *Eleftheri Patrida*, London, 28 August 1972.
115. *Odigitis*, 154.
116. Damofli, "The Assemblies," 201.
117. Farakos, "The International Context of the Ideological Struggle of Our Party," 15–31 and Farakos, "The Youth and the Worker's Movement," 12.
118. Sommier, *La violence politique*, 33. Although Sommier's point refers to the French and Italian cases, it could also be applied to the Greek case.
119. Papatheodorou, introduction to Darveris, *Night's Story*, 19.
120. Stergios Katsaros, "Εμείς οι γκεβαριστές" [We, the Guevarists], quoted in Ios Press, *30 Years Che: Tribute to Che Guevara*, no. 4, *Eleftherotypia*, 9 October 1997.
121. Junco, *Movimientos Sociales en España.*
122. Sommier, *La violence politique*, 42.
123. Quoted in *Neoi Stochoi* 4, 2nd ser. (Jan. 1972): 48.
124. Katsaros, *I the Provocateur*, 212.
125. Pasolini, "Il cerimoniale della violenza," 127.
126. See Paloukis, *Left-Wing Opposition.*
127. See Emanouilidis, *Heretical Routes.*
128. *Spartakos*, n.d., around April–May 1967.
129. Bensaid, *Les Trotskysmes*, 6.
130. "Σεχταρισμός, ο δίδυμος αδελφός του οπορτουνισμού" [Sectarianism, Opportunism's Twin Brother], *Neoi Stochoi*, 1975, 52. The Organization Socialist Revolution (OSE), which published the journal *Mami* in Paris, was an anarchist-Trotskyist group. The neo-Trotskyist KO Machitis was a miniscule group that appeared in November 1973, as did the organization Bolsheviks, based in Paris.
131. The tendency of the so-called Chinaphiles, or simply "Chinese," found its expression in the avant-garde journal *Anagennisi*, later on *Laikos Dromos* [People's Path], and *Istorikes Ekdoseis* [Historical Publications]. These, coupled with other antiparty and *tiersmondiste* entities, such as PANDIK and the Friends of New Countries, succeeded in creating a rift within the ranks of the Lambrakis Youth. Petroulas, the student symbol of the mid-1960s, was affiliated with these groups.
132. Theodoridis, *Macedonian Rock*, 177.
133. Nevertheless, five OMLE members were tried in Salonica in the summer of 1971, receiving stiff sentences. See Yiannopoulos, "Resistance Forces," 283.

134. Darveris, *Night's Story,* 69.
135. Ibid., 153.
136. The journals were *Proletariaki Simaia* [Proletarian Flag] and *Protoporia* [Avant-Garde].
137. "Απάντηση της ΠΠΣΠ σε μια επιστολή της ΑΑΣΠΕ" [PPSP's Reply to a Letter by AASPE], *Spoudastikos Kosmos* 2nd ser., 1 (Nov. 1974): 54.
138. "Η εξέγερση του Νοέμβρη" [The November Insurrection], *Neoi Stochoi* 52 (1975): 55.
139. "Προγραμματική Διακήρυξη του Επαναστατικού Κομμουνιστικού Κινήματος Ελλάδας (Ε.Κ.Κ.Ε.)" [Founding Manifesto of the Revolutionary Communist Movement of Greece], 1970, published in *Kommounistis* 1 (March 1972).
140. *Kommounistis* 1 (May 1972): 18.
141. Sommier, *La violence politique,* 37.
142. Founding manifesto of EKKE, ASKI.
143. Ibid.
144. Pamphlet, 21 November 1972, reproduced in *Two Years of Struggles,* 8.
145. Pamphlet, 16 November 1972, in ibid., 10.
146. The fierce Marxist-Leninist reply to this was that AASPE did not respect Lenin's maxim concerning tiny little victories as preparatory stages for something greater.
147. EKKE criticized the orthodox KKE and its branches as highly revisionist, while at the same time it castigated KKE-Esoterikou for aspiring to a radical revision of the implementation of the Dictatorship of the Proletariat as it adopted "the bourgeois principles of a multiparty system." In "Founding Manifesto of the Revolutionary Communist Movement of Greece," op.cit.
148. *Documents of PAK.*
149. "Ο Αγώνας είναι εθνικοαπελευθερωτικός" [The struggle is one of national liberation], *Agonas,* 22 September 1973.
150. Fischler, "Food, Self and Identity."
151. Alberoni, *Genesi.* Also see Sommier, *La violence politique,* 37.
152. Della Porta, "1968," 131.
153. On this problem, see Linde, *Life Stories.*
154. Van Boeschoten, *Troubled Years,* 221.
155. Sommier, *La violence politique,* 25.
156. Della Porta, "1968." Also see Tarrow, *Democracy and Disorder,* for a description of a similar process in Italy in the 1960s.
157. Venturas, "Identité féminine," 813–14.
158. Also see oral historian Van Boeschoten, *Troubled Years,* 222. Van Boeschoten argues that these "perverse" situations are recorded and recollected much more easily than "normal" ones.
159. Dafermos, *Students and Dictatorship,* 205.
160. KNE 1968–74, brochure issued by KNE, 1974.
161. Vernikos, *Antidictatorship Student Movement,* 150.
162. Passerini, *Storie di donne;* Fraser, *Blood of Spain;* Williams, *Long Revolution,* 64–88. Oral historian Riki Van Boeschoten talks about "parts of collective memory which remain unchanged." See Van Boeschoten, *Troubled Years,* 215, 223.
163. Ibid., 221.

164. Rosenthal, *Erlebte und erzaehlte Lebensgeschichte*, 85.
165. Josselson, "Imagining the Real," 37.
166. Wasserstrom, *Student Protest*, 9.
167. Van Dyck, *Kassandra and the Censors*.
168. In a different authoritarian context, in Franco's Spain, thousands of curious and sexually excited people passed the borders to Perpignan, in the eastern part of the Pyrenees in France, in order to watch Bertolucci's banned cult movie. See Sánchez Vidal, *El cine español*, 89.
169. See Mackridge, "Theater in the Colonels' Greece," 15–16. I am using his translation here.
170. Kotanidis, *All Together, Now!*, 487.
171. Hobsbawm, "Revolution and Sex," 260.
172. The poet Manolis Anagnostakis wrote under the nom de plume Manousos Fasis some humorous ballads, whereby he sang the praises of three fictional female cadres of KNE, Rigas, and PPSP, reproducing the main topoi regarding the outlook, discourse, and action of the respective organizations.
173. The most interesting controversy in as late as 1995 included journalist and later-day publisher Themos Anastasiadis who published an article in his extremely popular satirical column in the daily *Eleftherotypia* attacking Rigas members for pseudo-revolutionism and cowardice but praising its "girls" for being the prettiest. Anastasiadis, a former "orthodox" communist, implied that even though Rigas women were hot-to-trot they preferred men from other organizations who were more "virile." The extreme sexism emanating from this article and the author's contempt for Rigas in general led former members of the organization to protest directly to the publisher of the newspaper. Three former female members of Rigas threw yogurt at Anastasiadis in protest. See "Μαύρη Τρύπα" [Black Hole], *Eleftherotypia*, 10 May 1995.
174. Bourdieu, "L'illusion biographique," 69.

Chapter 4

Cultural Warfare

Chapter 4 engages with the dialectical relationship between culture and politics. As ideological reasons alone do not account for the creation of the Greek student movement, the chapter explores the roots of its cultural background, as well as the ways in which the latter in turn reinforced student combativeness. It examines new trends in cinema, theater, music, aesthetics, and everyday life in an attempt to explain how new cultural identities were shaped. It turns to alternative forms of culture that were created in juxtaposition to the Junta with an interest in how several countercultural elements acquired political significance over time. This section also addresses the role of female students in both the student body in general and in the movement in particular, in an attempt to account for continuities and ruptures with the past. Lastly, references are made to the contested issue of a belated "sexual revolution" and private going public.

Media and Publishing Strategies

Just like any other authoritarian regime the Colonels tried to achieve near complete control of the mass media in order to ensure an informational monopoly. Preventive censorship was in operation up to 1969, and no printed document could circulate without the authorization of the Censorship Office. This created a vacuum of alternative information and intellectual cultivation, as the heavy weight of voicing opposition fell on clandestine papers. Inevitably, the very moment the regime allowed relative freedom of expression, parts of the press began to express a mild critique of its governance, breaking its "information monopoly."[1]

Since 1967, Greek writers had refused to publish anything as a means of demonstrating passive resistance through silence. "Refusing to submit your writings to be examined by the police authorities and the censorship office is after all an issue of self-respect and self-dignity," said writer Spyros Plaskovitis in talking about this period.[2] This proved to be a controversial decision that contributed to the lack of the circulation of any alternative and heterodox ideas during the first years of the dictatorship. In fact, Filippos Vlachos, the founder and director of the publishing house Keimena [Texts], appeared extremely critical of this tactic years later concluding that "silence was also convenient ... an escape, not resistance."[3]

Whereas antiregime artists continued to protest by refusing to write, publish, or exhibit, some journalists devised a range of strategies to counter the effects of censorship. Integral to their creativity in resistance was the fact that repression helps to create new sorts of knowledge and different ways to communicate a message. According to Michel Foucault, "Censorship not only cuts off or blocks communication, it also acts as an incitement to discourse, with silence as an integral part of this discursive activity."[4] In this sense, erasure can be enabling as well as delimiting. Comic strip artists, such as Bost, Kyr, and Kostas Mitropoulos, who collaborated with the major dailies of the time, were among those who managed to undermine censorship most successfully through references, allegories, and innuendos that were confusing to the uninitiated but easily discernible to the ones looking for a hidden message.[5] American writer and Athens resident at the time, Kevin Andrews argued that people who were hastily reading these cartoons in the papers "almost had the sense of participating at the cost of a couple of drachmas, in resistance activity."[6]

The press was a major factor in the dissemination of information and the development of the awareness of the political situation in Greece under the Junta. In so far as the press fully covered the court-martial trials and published complete trial transcripts, it provided an opportunity for students to learn about resistance efforts. The pleas of the accused offered them the opportunity to defend their actions while condemning the regime and reporting having been tortured. The press also offered detailed, often provocative full coverage of student mobilizations. The Athenian and Salonicean dailies *Ta Nea* and *Thessaloniki* dedicated a daily column to student issues (both using as their logos images associated with May '68), which served as means of constant update on student mobilizations. Minas Papazoglou's column in *Ta Nea*, titled "Youth and Its Problems," promoted the antiregime students' demands and criticized the appointed student councils during the spring and summer of 1972. The column also published letters of protest by antiregime students. A series of journalists writing for *Thessaloniki* followed the same pattern in their regular feature "The Students' Column." According to a US report, *Thessaloniki* was an "anti-American [and] anti-regime" publication with "strong influence among younger leftists and students."[7] Chrysafis Iordanoglou, a law student in Salonica, emphasizes, "If this communication medium with the journalism it represented had not existed, it is doubtful that the student movement of Salonica would have survived."[8] Another typical pattern of *Thessaloniki* was to present the student unrest in

Figure 4.1. Headline of the antiregime daily *Thessaloniki* reading "Freedom ... Freedom," and with small letters in the subtitle "in Spain." This was a typical strategy of the newspapers during the Junta, testing the boundaries of censorship. (Source: *Thessaloniki* newspaper)

other countries with large headlines, extensive photographic material, and direct allusions to the Greek situation. Typically, a large headline would read "The Militaries Are Panicking" or "The Student Revolt Is Spreading," and with tiny letters underneath one would read "in Italy" or "in Spain."[9] It is not at all surprising that *Thessaloniki*'s director, Antonis Kourtis, was constantly warned and fined by the regime.[10]

As was the case with students elsewhere, Greek students read the papers voraciously in order to find out what was going on in the world in a period of dramatic events, from the Vietnam War to the Middle East crisis, and also to read accounts of events in which they themselves had participated, resulting in a rather self-reflexive position. Giannis Kourmoulakis observes: "Messages were coming, even if curtailed, but they found fertile ground and they touched us. And somehow we started as well little by little also to get revolutionized" (Kourmoulakis, interview).

As we have seen, the dictatorship's liberalization experiment proved to be crucial for the development of the student movement, contributing to a significant change in the political and social climate of the country. One major reason for this shift was the production and circulation of books, a defining factor for the enhancement of antiregime consciousness among students. The critical silence-breaking moment in publishing was the publication of the *Dekaochto Keimena* [Eighteen Texts] (1970), which followed a 1969 dramatic statement by the Nobel Prize–winning poet George Seferis condemning the Junta at the BBC—the first public condemnation from within Greece made by a respected, noncommunist intellectual.[11] These eighteen allusive literary texts were written by well-known intellectuals who avoided naming the Greek Junta outright but used, in the words of one of the contributors, "innuendo, transposition and ... metaphors which the reader could easily understand, but for which it would be difficult for the authorities to prosecute."[12] Four short stories, for example, referred to a fictitious Latin American country under dictatorship called "Boliguay." The experiment was followed by the publication of *Nea Keimena* [New Texts] and *Nea Keimena 2* and the journal *I Synecheia* [Continuity] by the same circle of intellectuals, including a number of left-wing writers.[13] In April 1973 one of the contributors to this symbolic rupture, the poet Manolis Anagnostakis, appeared self-critical about the years of artistic silence:

> What could be ... the picture—if any—that today's twenty-year-old youths, who were 14 *then*, might have of the condition of our cultural and political landscape before the April coup? If we talk to them ... about the Spring that was about to bloom on our intellectual horizon, what mechanisms of representation do they have to follow us? With what depot of nonexisting experiences would they grasp what the three-year relentless silence meant, and how would they be convinced about the necessity of the intellectual transition to a specific moment in time from speechlessness to direct discourse?[14]

The publication of *Eighteen Texts* coincided with the regime's decision to open itself up, suspending preventive censorship and abolishing the last blacklist of books in 1970. Up to 1969, the only publishing houses that had been established and whose books became points of reference (*Keimena, Kalvos, Stochastis*) focused on classical political thought and literature. The softening of censorship led to a spectacular increase in domestic cultural output, however, and publishers found a way out of the previous stagnation.

From late 1970 to late 1971, 150 new publishing houses were opened, and 2,000 new titles were printed in inexpensive paperback editions.[15] This overproduction of publications aimed to encourage critical thinking in young readers, which could help them to understand existing realities. Books were needed that would provide a "practical perspective" or a way out of the political impasse. Publishers believed that through books, they could "ideologically awaken the people against the dictatorial regime," as they believed that books would be food for the intellectually starving Greeks and a direct means of political acculturation.[16] Some publishers were oriented toward the publication of left-wing books (Odysseas, Praxi) with a program that "covered the range of Marxist and Leninist books" (Synchroni Epochi), the "renewal of official Marxist thought" (Odysseas), the "ideological armament of young people" (Neoi Stochoi), and the "creation of an antiauthoritarian movement in Greece" (Diethnis Vivliothiki).[17]

Books like Jean-Jacques Servan-Schreiber's *The American Challenge*, John Kenneth Galbraith's *The New Industrial State*, and Paul Baran and Paul Sweezy's *Monopoly Capital* soon became bestsellers, just as they had abroad.[18] Vladimir Ilyich Lenin and Karl Marx, as well as Mikhail Bakunin, Rosa Luxemburg, and Gyorg Lúkacs appeared in bookshop windows. American writer Kevin Andrews observed that "after 1970 some foreigners wondered how Greece could be a dictatorship when the kiosks around Athens University were filled with the works of … Marxists of the Twenties and Thirties, all in paperback."[19]

Other publishing projects aimed to satisfy readers' need to reexamine phenomena and problems from within the tradition of contemporary Greek philosophical and sociological standard works. Those books introduced a new closer theoretical scrutiny. Publishing was limited at the beginning (1970–1971) but more extensive later on. Andrianos Vanos explained how the slow trickle of books in 1970 and 1971 acted as a catalyst for the dissemination of ideas:

> There was something that was very much of help, apart from the illegal books that circulated, which in a way helped everybody: That just before this political explosion took place, political publications started coming out, like those of *Kalvos*, or others, but which were coming out little by little, since up to that point no books were published. So, everyone read the same books.… A book would come out, and since there was no other, everybody was talking about it. So, we were analyzing from all sides. Same thing when another book would come out. So, in a way we were following some common steps. There was no chaos in information. (Vanos, interview)

The Arrival of the 3 M's in the Colonels' Greece

Within the '68 movements the expression "3 M's" was a quite common way to refer to the fashionable theoretical triangle between Marx, Mao, and Marcuse. The (re)appearance and large-scale diffusion of a series of basic Marxist texts by Greek and foreign authors through Themelio [Foundation], a traditional left-wing publishing house that had been closed down immediately after the coup spread this expression among Greek students.[20] *Neoi Stochoi* [New Aims] was a Trotskyist publishing house that exercised even greater influence through a series of publications, as well as an eponymous journal. With articles from a whole range of Marxist revolutionaries and writers, *Neoi Stochoi* made the first attempt to defy the barrier of censorship and test its limits by openly adopting Marxist terminology. Its publications appeared in a pocket-sized format in order to reach a wide readership, rendering so-called alternative Marxist analysis an extremely popular and common point of reference. Nikitas Lionarakis offers a comment on the influence of *Neoi Stochoi*: "I have studied Marxism through the *Neoi Stochoi*. My entire generation, that is … This approach of the publishing houses 'Marxified' our generation very much. That is, it turned [the] insurrection into a Marxist one" (Lionarakis, interview).

Among the most fashionable topics diffused in these "unorthodox" publications featured so-called center-periphery and third-worldist theories of a global class struggle that would supposedly result from the student periphery, joined by the working classes, closing in on the imperialist pole. As might be expected, the Greek political stalemate was another favorite topic, framing the imposition and maintenance of the dictatorship as a token of US imperialism. The "foreign factor theory" became a permanent element in Greek conceptualizations of politics.

It is noteworthy that some students at the time attributed the re-appearance of Themelio and the circulation of *Neoi Stochoi* to the police. A common pro-Moscow communist trope held that the police allowed *Neoi Stochoi* to be published in the hope that the journal's Trotskyist line would divide and disorient left-wing students. Interestingly, however, followers of the Communist Party were among *Neoi Stochoi*'s fanatic readers, despite the fact that "instructors" warned the students that it might be a governmental provocation.

These publications spurred on the diffusion of sociological works and the rediscovery of the classics of socialism (Marx, Lenin), as well as social theory (the Frankfurt School, Louis Althusser) and psychosexual theory (Wilhelm Reich). Antonio Gramsci and Regis Debray, "heretical" writers according to the standards of the Old Left, were among the most translated authors. Their works, which challenged Marxist orthodoxy, became fashionable among the New Left and were intellectual landmarks for many students. They tapped into the students' desire to oppose authoritarianism, revealing a growing demand for revolutionary and subversive texts. Marcuse's *One-Dimensional Man*, "the gospel of '68" according to student Ilias Triantafyllopoulos, became a guiding book that familiarized the Greek radical readership with the idea that students and disenfranchised social outcasts would be the future carriers of social change, instead of the "compromised" working class. Marcuse's motto, "The only hope lies with the hopeless," became a slogan. As Triantafyllopoulos explains: "Through Marcuse I started rather to realize, to rationalize or to interpret the world. Marx came afterward, then came all the other things, but we started with those everyday situations, the elements of lived experience" (Triantafyllopoulos, interview).

The need to be up-to-date with the latest trends in critical theory became part of socialization among student groups. Law student during the Junta years and present-day constitutionalist Nikos Alivizatos notes the impact of the radical French *maîtres a penser*, stressing that those students who did not possess some basic knowledge of theories, such as structuralism and poststructuralism, were considered uncool: "In terms of readings, France was, of course, the center of the universe and the whole Marxist structuralism with Althusser, Poulantzas, and all the things you can imagine. To put it bluntly, in the post-'68 climate you could not date a woman if you hadn't read Althusser" (Alivizatos, interview).

Less influential were the Soviet books, such as *Leninism and Modern Times*, published by Synchroni Epochi [Modern Times], the publishing house affiliated with the Communist Party. Though widely read, these were often perceived as passé. "Books of the Soviet school of thought did not endure over time," former communist student leader Nikos Bistis remarks, citing as an example "a book on Czechoslovakia, which had come out right after, which justified the invasion with puerile arguments" (Bistis, interview). Nikos Kaplanis, a dentistry student in Salonica and head of the clandestine KNE, argues the opposite, "In terms of Prague, I personally was fooled by KKE's myth that whatever thing is not ours cannot be revolutionary either" (Kaplanis, interview). The leftist *Pavlos recalls that he and others like him became obsessed with books on Marxism-Leninism in order to address their theoretical deficits, since they did not come from left-wing families. Still, the vast bulk of students joined the orthodox communists, reserving their heretical training for future occasions, as Bistis points out: "It is impressive that although the first books that were circulated were 'heretical' books of the Left or the American Left, Marcuse and so on, the great majority of the youth joined the KKE in the end" (Bistis, interview).

Marxist indoctrination was so widespread that even conservative professors who had outlived the purges of the Junta were aware of it. Angeliki Xydi goes so far as to maintain that these professors even adopted an apologetic stance toward the Marxist students:

I remember that we had a philosophy professor at the university, Mr. Moutsopoulos, who entered at the second year of the department where I was, and he knew that the things he would say would seem to us rubbish, even if we wouldn't tell him that they were rubbish. And he would tell us, "Alright, I apologize to the Marxists." Yes, and these things right in the middle of the Junta. (Xydi, interview)

Alkis Rigos, meanwhile, reconstructs students' tendency to use their theoretical arsenal to confront the Junta's professors:

We had many Junta professors in the university, namely, ministers of the Junta. Our professor of sociology was Tsakonas, who was minister of the presidency, that is, of propaganda of the dictatorship, and who was offering some supposedly free seminars, and, after we argued with each other on whether to take them or not, we decided that we should participate, but in order to tear them apart. We would show off how left-wing we were, but with arguments. One couldn't use the empty political rhetoric that we had right after the *Metapolitefsi*. One talked about the substance. (Rigos, interview)

The distinction that Rigos draws between the fruitfulness of discourses and theoretical explorations, both during the time of the Junta and the period of the democratic transition, is present in most recollections.

In the first years of the 1970s, the publication of any book of critical thinking, including literary works, could be assessed as political resistance against the authoritarian regime, and almost every book could be considered political.[21] Dissident figures such as the Turkish poet Nazim Hikmet and Chilean poet Pablo Neruda were translated repeatedly during the dictatorship and read in a heroic light. Ioanna Karystiani stresses the importance of poetry in the training of the students. In her view, poetry's contribution was literal rather than ideological, though for her own part she argues for a self-sacrificial romantic determination: "This is how I tuned in, by reading poems, having read Ritsos, Dostoyevsky, by reciting Mayakovsky, and these were ... ideological equipment in the full sense" (Karystiani, interview).

It seems that publishers who sympathized with the student movement often exploited young people's eagerness for new ideas. An article that appeared in 1973 in the literary journal *I Synecheia* condemned the fashion of "transferring the foreign problematization which emerge[d] from a different reality [and] translating it into Greek without any introduction or even warning about the different conditions."[22] In many cases, the introductory sections of the books seem entirely out of place, trying to establish connections with the Greek case no matter how different the paradigm was, while the quality of the translations was often very poor.[23] In another issue of *I Synecheia,* a literary critic concluded, "We had forgotten that enlightenment needs enlightened people."[24] Others felt, however, that the uncontextualized appearance of such literature in Greek could serve as a useful intellectual exercise. Myrsini Zorba remarks: "I fell onto Gramsci and there I started having more complex thoughts, but this is how you realized that you could interpret any text and any thought on the basis of your own needs and your own experience. Radicalize it, orient it toward a different direction" (Zorba, interview). Michalis Sabatakakis, on the other hand, is firm in his conviction that publishers paid too little attention to Italian and French Euro-Communism:

> There was a suffocating absence of books about the stream of thought which in that period was blossoming in Europe within the environment of the communist Left and was called Euro-Communism.... In reality, we did not systematically follow all this stream of thought, whether this was the Italian Euro-Communist school around the PCI, the Italian Communist Party, or the French one, let's say, with the characteristic case of Poulantzas. Only too occasionally. This was our contact with the political book" (Sabatakakis, interview).

Andrianos Vanos stressed the fact that readings created cohesiveness, due to the pressing need to put new ideas into action. In his view, this process produced people with a firm theoretical background: "People with a solid theoretical training emerged, who had read, who had discussed, who had exchanged conflicting views, without a theoretical aim, an exercise on paper, but with the intention of applying all this" (Vanos, interview). Panos Theodoridis, on the other hand, points out that all these heterogeneous and fragmented readings often created intellectual chaos: "We were reading chunks from Marx, Lenin, Trotsky, the anarchists, all the time; our education was full of things like that. We were continuously reading French intellectuals and monopoly capitalisms ..., things that we half understood, but half of which we didn't understand a word."[25]

Books on the history of the Greek Left focusing on the 1940s, the resistance, and the civil war were another point of reference for students. These were very popular at the time, since students liked to think of their own struggle as the continuation of the mythical, albeit defeated, Greek Left, just as the dictatorship was the natural outcome of decades of arbitrary right-wing rule. In contrast to Italy and the critique of the *Resistenza* by the '68ers, student activists in Greece in the 1970s did not attack this sacred shibboleth of the Left. Instead, they idealized the wartime communist resistance and its revolutionary tradition. *Les Kapetanios* (Paris, 1970), a book by the French author Dominique Eudes, provided a romanticized version of the Greek partisans and became a best-selling vehicle of instruction, as for Greek students up to that point "there was a gap, a void, a black page" concerning this period (Tsaras, interview). The old partisan songs likewise reemerged as an emotional form of entertainment and a "transfer" of the revolutionary spirit of history. In terms of aesthetics, the "wild bearded men" of Greece in the early 1970s were strongly reminiscent of the communist guerrillas. Giorgos Kotanidis recalls fantasizing about "the revolutionaries with the red flags going down Alexandras Avenue," an inescapable reference to EAM/ELAS; "My dreams were deep red," he reminisces, stressing the revolutionary color of his imaginary projections.[26]

In addition, the publication of a series of protest magazines promoting "critical thinking" (*Prosanatolismoi, Protoporia, Politika Themata, Anti*) and a series of underground magazines that focused on avant-garde art (*Lotos, Tram, Kouros, Panderma*)[27] caused a considerable stir with the authorities.[28] There followed a series of translations of basic texts on student uprisings abroad, which provided the theoretical toolkit for student revolt. The collective volume *Student Power* is a major example (1973). According to its introduction, "Just as the liberation movements of the Third World have long ago decided not to wait for the liberation of their countries as a consequence of the socialist revolution in the imperial metropolis, so students today refuse to wait for some external deliverance from their condition."[29] Fred Halliday's chapter from the volume had been published separately a year earlier under the title *The History of Student Movements Worldwide* (thus modifying the original title "Students of the World Unite"). According to Trotskyist militant Giannis Felekis, this little booklet on Argentina, Vietnam, and Palestine, was priceless as it introduced multiple revolts from which one could draw valuable conclusions (Felekis, interview).

All these readings were a precious resource for the circulation of information on theoretical matters connected to the movement, as well as on international developments. In the foreword to *Student Power*, the Greek editor issues the warning that although "the assimilation of the experience of others is necessary, at the same time the mechanistic transfer of models of thought and action which were shaped under entirely different conditions would be unrealistic." Nonetheless, that book would provide Greek readers a chance "to approach the questioning, the demands and the methods of students beyond Greece."[30] Often, the Spanish model was evoked as one to emulate, as in Fred Halliday's remarks, reproduced in the student journal

Protoporia: "The Spanish students succeeded. They created reaction in the illiberal regime of the Caudillo, proving that student forces can act under conditions of fierce repression."[31]

The ritual whereby left-wing books were acquired is also worthy of consideration: they could be purchased at left-wing bookshops or at street vendors. Some of the bookshops became meeting places for discussions, such as Manolis Anagnostakis's and Kaiti Saketa's bookshops in Salonica and Manolis Glezos's bookshop in Athens, which were attacked by extreme right-wingers on more than one occasion. Saketa remembers that when a new book was published and ordered from Athens, her shop would put its cover in the bookshop window for students to see. "Such was the longing of the people" (Saketa, interview). One student bookshop in Athens with a fanatic readership was called The Clockwork Orange, a classic reference to a film that had acquired a cult status despite its being banned. The bookshops also became meeting points where hard-core political analysis took place. As sociologist Hank Johnston argues, "When political opportunities are severely constricted, much of the *doing* of contentious politics is *talking* about it."[32] Paraphrasing Primo Moroni and Bruna Miorelli, one could say that in 1970s Greece the old eighteenth-century idea of the bookshop as a place of culture was combined with the modern one of the market opening onto the street.[33] Rena Theologidou's recollections are evocative of the depth and fervor of the students' dialogue at their bookshop meetings:

> We were going to Kaiti Saketa's [bookshop] and we gathered there, she was KKE-Esoterikou. She had a basement down there. And we were saying, "What is the revolution like?" "Is it this way?" "Is it that way?" "Should we publish *Avgi* clandestinely?" "Should we not?" (Theologidou, interview)

Many students immersed themselves fully in this climate of intellectual overproduction and became manic consumers of the printed word. The *Guardian* pointed out in 1972, "The security authorities have long been worried about the effect these [books] might have among students as, with the news media comparatively muzzled, they are making increasing use of the wave of left-wing books which have been appearing."[34] Thereafter, the new list of "discouraged books" included books by Marcuse, Garaudy, Sartre, and Brecht, which were, however, already sold and circulating in massive numbers. As publisher Loukas Axelos suggests, "Regardless of the quality of the responses [these books] gave to the present and the future, they were literally sucked in by the already awaiting, and at this point reading, public ... mainly by the students which were its basic body."[35]

Political books undoubtedly contributed to the creation of a critical stance and to the shaping of an alternative political position on behalf of the students. Book consumption and the circulation of journals helped create a common style and transmit a universal and direct message by the encouragement of creative reading.

Cinema as a Gun

Jean-Luc Godard has famously argued that film is "a gun that can shoot twenty-four frames per second." It was precisely this capacity of cinema to impregnate people's minds with ideas and to radicalize its spectators that was internalized by the militant student audiences of the time. The large-scale diffusion of the journal *Synchronos Kinimatografos* [Contemporary Cinema], which became a standard point of reference, encouraged the generally enthusiastic reception of the French and American avant-gardes and the trend in Greek political cinema known as "New Greek Cinema." The journal—the Greek equivalent of the French *Cahiers du Cinéma*—was concerned not only with cinema but also with general theoretical discussions and debates, usually seeking connections to politics.[36] It was the successor to the influential *Ellinikos Kinimatografos* [Greek Cinema], which had published five issues before the coup, including articles by the French critic André Bazin on "how film as a medium was difficult to read for clear cut messages."[37] Beginning in the late 1960s, New Greek Cinema followed this rule by adopting indirect codes of expression in order to communicate sociopolitical messages. In the face of strict censorship, the filmmakers of New Greek Cinema began using a cryptic visual language that could elude the censor's eye. This was done through metaphors, allusions, and elliptic filmic language. In Pandelis Voulgaris's movie *The Matchmaking of Anna* [To Proxenio tis Annas] (1972), for example, the restriction on female subjectivity, personalized by a thirty-year-old domestic servant working for a middle-class family in a world dominated by male power relations,[38] offers a strong critique of social relations in early 1970s Greece while it also seems to refer to the country's suppression under the domination of the Colonels or the United States. This kind of cinema was occasionally rejected by young politicized spectators, however, and in 1971 there was already criticism of the "students and liberals who fill the cinema Alkyonis and all at once praise often insignificant films, just because they were 'transmitting a message.'"[39]

The New Greek Cinema also sought a return to an authentic Greek rural spirit, symbolized in *The Matchmaking of Anna* by the maid from the provinces and the "real," "authentic" culture that she represents, which comes across as a liberating force. In a similar manner, Theo Angelopoulos's *Reconstruction* [Anaparastasi] (1970), about a murder in the Greek countryside, was filmed in a remote village that led him to "discover" the traditional rural spirit: "This was the image that was representative for me. I, a man of asphalt, pollution, Athens, suddenly came to know a part of Greece, I came to know Greece, the middle Greece, the unknown Greece."[40] This rediscovery of Greek "roots" and of rural tradition also became conceptualized as a pole of resistance in terms of music, as will be shown later. However, *Katerina remembers a discussion at EKIN following a screening of *Reconstruction*, in which she was irritated by Angelopoulos's "folklorist mannerisms" (*Katerina, interview).

More than *Reconstruction*, Angelopoulos's direct indictment of the Junta came in 1972 with his film *Days of '36* [Meres tou '36]. This was a film that chronicled the coming of the dictatorship of General Metaxas in 1936: clearly speaking about one military regime in the context of another was too direct a message to be missed. As for the film's cryptic mode of expression, the filmmaker himself is quite revealing: "The dictatorship is embodied in the formal structure of the film. Imposed silence was one of the conditions under which we worked. The film is made in such a way that the spectator realizes that censorship is involved."[41]

The new manner of filmmaking led to a rift with mainstream Greek cinema productions, which consisted of farces, war epics, and melodramas—formulas that had proven commercially successful. Because mainstream Greek cinema was endorsed by the dictators, they were viewed as a major cultural weapon aimed at imposing a "stupefying sentimentalism," according to film critic Giannis Soldatos.[42] The New Greek Cinema film productions, by contrast, were characterized by social sensibility and a direct and unsentimentalized approach to everyday stories with neo-realist and Brechtian characteristics.[43] Even films with no blatant political characteristics, such as Giorgos Stamboulopoulos's *Open Letter* [Anoichti Epistoli] (1968), a film about a disoriented young man and his constant mental references to the Occupation period (which was nevertheless butchered by censorship), or Angelopoulos's *Reconstruction*, were consumed and received by antiregime actors as purely political. In other words, spectators of a general antiregime disposition were reading the political into everything.

Cinema became extremely significant not only in terms of its form, content, symbolism, and reception but also as a point of meeting and recognition. The discussions that necessarily followed the screenings were of vital importance: "[I remember] the terrible explosions in the discussion of *Alkyonis* following the movies," Myrsini Zorba recalls, "where the hard-core ideological confrontation lurked once again as soon as the lights were turned on" (Zorba, interview). In Salonica, a law student, Vangelis Kargoudis, took the initiative to organize a cinema club, which ended up having four thousand registered members. The club soon became an important meeting point, attempting to bring students closer to the spirit of the movies of the time. Political cinema was the most popular genre, including films such as Bernardo Bertolucci's *The Spider's Stratagem* and *The Conformist* (1970), both about the rise of Italian Fascism. Such screenings were often linked to political provocation: "We searched and found Melville's movie, *The Stool Pigeon,* and we put big posters around the city, 'The Stool Pigeon!,' 'The Stool Pigeon!'" (laughter) (Kargoudis, interview).

In the cinema club, too, the movies were followed by a three-hour discussion directed by Kargoudis himself. This practice focused on the dynamic aspects of collective viewing and the communal experience of watching and debating about a film, juxtaposed with the solitary practice of reading books and the "passive" viewing of television. The debates following the screenings, which were also attended by policemen in civilian clothes, reinforced the quite popular idea of the active and reflexive spectator. Students soon became real film buffs. Vourekas remarks:

> The cinema club was in reality a forum for political discussion. It was a context which legalized politics, ideological discussions, and confrontations within the Left and its streams. So it happened. We all got registered of course in the cinema club, with ID cards and everything. Naturally, the police watched [the movies] too, and there were screenings of Italian neorealism but also more recent movies, for example Godard—hermetic, difficult, but it looked as if he was trying to say something. (Vourekas, interview)

The club's organizer, Kargoudis, was the one to pay the price for any sort of revolutionary exaltation during the discussions: "I got beaten black and blue for any nonsense that the PPSP and EKKE people said. This had become standard; screening on Sunday, on Monday I was arrested at home" (Kargoudis, interview). Kargoudis recalls with emotion the cinema club's last session:

> At some point we realized that this was the last Sunday and that they were going to hit us.... Around 9, 9:30 in the morning there came two riot vehicles, which were brand new, they were received in '72. And they blocked Pallas cinema in a vertical fashion, one from here

and one from there, and there was a big gathering, according to the more modest calculations 700 to 800 persons. And the whole thing turned into a demonstration, and the respective beatings took place too. (Kargoudis, interview)

Although the Maoist organizations were, alongside a handful of anarchists, the most faithful carriers of the spirit of the '68 uprisings, they often opposed culture of all sorts. This attitude was probably inspired by the general destructive mania of the Chinese Cultural Revolution, which rejected all artifacts as products of bourgeois decadence. Greek Maoists' rejection of the aesthetics of most '68 movements as "bourgeois" was reinforced by the conviction that art could only be engaged with, since its main task was to generate an oppositional political consciousness. Panos Theodoridis recalls that in 1973, at the invitation of the appointed student council, the composer Manos Hadjidakis came to Salonica with the filmmaker Pandelis Voulgaris in order to present *Magnus Eroticus* [O Megalos Erotikos] (1973) at the city's Film Festival. Voulgaris's film was inspired by and based on Hadjidakis's eponymous LP. Left-wingers were furious, Theodoridis says, though "deep inside we were all Hadjidakean." Similarly, Vourekas explains that to young people like him it seemed utterly inappropriate to produce an artistic creation that disregarded the political situation:

> It seemed to me quite extreme to release *Magnus Eroticus* during the Junta. It broke my nerve, I couldn't … this thing seemed unbearable to me. … I was an enemy of his music precisely because he could not express what all the rest were feeling. Expression for us was action, political struggle, anti-Junta, antidictatorship action, what could the *Magnus Eroticus* say to us? We considered it an irony at least. A man, a petit bourgeois, closed inside his world, "Here the world is falling apart and the whore is washing her hair." Precisely this, this was the sensation. And we snubbed him and despised him. (Vourekas, interview)

Panos Theodoridis still regrets this attitude today: "To have in the midst of the years of the Junta and all this turmoil … two sensitive persons talking about erotic discourse was for us the most insulting thing, so we went into the dress circle and booed *Magnus Eroticus*. This is one of the deeds of which I will be ashamed for the rest of my life."[44] His sentence clearly represents the abyss of temporal and semantic distance between past and present self.

Similarly, in a characteristic discussion following the projection of Theo Angelopoulos's *Reconstruction,* at which he was present, a hard-core group of Maoists attacked the up-and-coming filmmaker and the most charismatic exponent of New Cinema in Greece, as petit-bourgeois. Andrianos Vanos, a Maoist student himself, vividly remembered Angelopoulos's screening, though in a very different way. In his recollection, these screenings were the point at which the conflict went public:

> Clashes took place, no matter which movie was coming to the cinema club. But the people in charge brought Angelopoulos, they brought him and he made a speech. Another hundred policemen gathered, and we couldn't get in anymore, and a conflict started in the city. In the open. Not introverted, within a cinema. So, everything was going outdoors. (Vanos, interview)

Even though Vanos mentions the cinema club, in reality his description is of the screening of *Reconstruction* at the State Theater during the Film Festival, where it won the award for best film of the year (1970). Angelopoulos himself recalled that a demonstration started immediately after the ceremony, with students cheering at him in exaltation since "at any opportunity that was given there was an attempt to do something against the dictatorship." He described a screening of the film at the University of Patras that same year, 1970, as a poignant moment that characterized the cryptic communication between artists of the time and their audiences. During the discussion that followed the film because policemen were present in civilian dress, Angelopoulos recalled that students asked questions in a hidden manner, and he gave affirmative answers. Angelopoulos characterized such peculiar communication "between the lines" as a form of magic, as it was denser than any detailed explanation.[45]

In its attempt to censor movies, the dictatorial regime constricted itself to a naive handling of film topics, searching for messages only on the surface (slogans, songs, and labels), so that movies with indirect social implications and political dimensions escaped the censor's eye. From the early 1970s onward, however, amid the softening of censorship and the rise of general radicalism, the politicization of Greek directors became blatant. This shift is apparent, for instance, in Thanasis Rentzis and Nikos Zervos's film *Black-White* [Mavro-Aspro] (1973), which contained direct references with footage of a "cinéma-verité" kind to the rising student movement and castigated social apathy. Even "conformist" directors chose to use words like "democracy" and "weapon" in their titles in order to attract an audience with vague references to politics and revolution.[46]

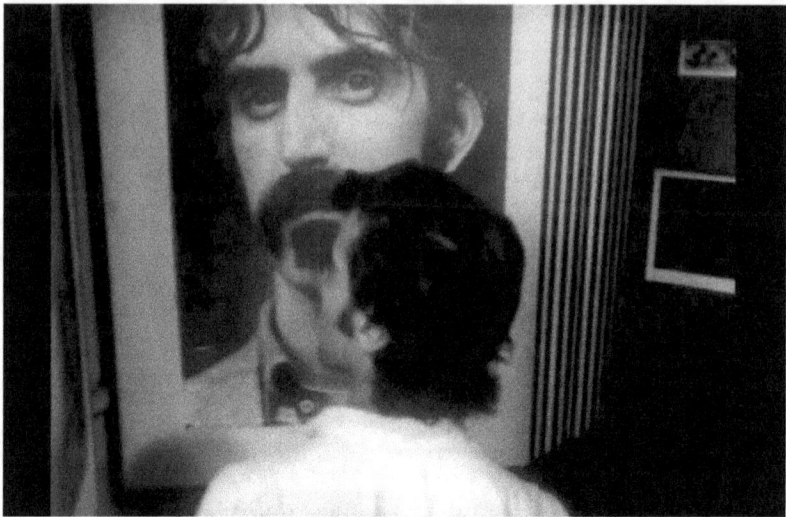

Figure 4.2. Scene from Thanasis Rentzis and Nikos Zervos's movie *Black-White*, 1973. The student protagonist enters a record store in Athens and stares at a poster of Frank Zappa, while in the background one can hear a song by Deep Purple. The film shows the extent of familiarization with Western pop culture, including progressive rock. It also contains direct references of a "cinéma-verité" kind to the rising student movement. (Courtesy Thanasis Rentzis)

A Window on the World

Greek students discovered Soviet and Eastern European cinema—first and foremost Sergei Eisenstein and the legendary Hungarian Milos Jancso—and were equally attracted to the innovations and experimentations of the French Nouvelle Vague; as Antonis Liakos aptly put it they were "the bastards of Hollywood, Eisenstein and nouvelle vague."[47] They were also seduced by the liberating energy of films such as Paul Williams's *Out of It*, which treated the subject of rebellious youth in the United States; angered by the injustice committed against Sacco and Vanzetti in Giuliano Montaldo's eponymous film; and blown away by the hippie hit *Easy Rider*.[48] The opening credits, which featured Steppenwolf's hymn "Born to Be Wild" and offered a positive depiction of hippie communal life and sexual freedom, were strongly imprinted on the minds of Greek youth. Michelangelo Antonioni's *Zabriskie Point* was another hit, with its different handling of the same topic and its aggressive depiction of youthful rebellion. The film's musical score familiarized the students with the sound of the Grateful Dead and the experimental rock of Pink Floyd.

In addition to being a means of drawing people closer together, films also encouraged reaching out to others. Cinema acted as a universal code and a means of "transmitting experiences"—the very experiences that Greek students were lacking. Angeliki Xydi remembers that the global repertoire of youthful defiance struck her through the documentary on the festival of Woodstock rather than through the reporting of the '68 events, which for some reason passed unnoticed for her:

> Various things that were taking place abroad reached me of course, but these too came through in strange ways, not very clearly. I do not remember, that is, being intrigued by May '68. I should not lie about that, I discovered it later on. But I remember that I was impressed by *Woodstock* and that I saw the movie three times and that once I also dragged my mother. I wanted to bring her to the cinema and make her watch as well and understand what incredible things were taking place outside Greece. (Xydi, interview)

As Xydi's remarks suggest, movies depicting the countercultural hippie scene of US youth and its political awareness incited an emotive response in the youthful Greek audience. In some instances, they generated instantaneous antiregime reflexes and were banned shortly after their release, thus acquiring legendary status. According to newspaper reports, screenings of American movies focusing on the rebellious youth were often followed by staged performances of the films' subject matter in the streets. Roger Miliex, the director of the French Institute in Greece, recalls in his diaries: "Yesterday [30 November 1970], on their way out of a screening of the film *Woodstock,* which presents American youth pop festivals, two thousand young Athenians demonstrated in the center of the capital, shouting slogans against the police, while engaging in a confrontation with them."[49] This was an interesting phenomenon of reenactment and mimesis, whereby imitation became active interpellation.[50]

Leonidas Kallivretakis, a lower-school student during this period, recalls that the police ordered the closing of the doors before the *Woodstock* screening started, when the cinema was still half-empty. The result was that three thousand youths broke the cinema's shutters and staged street battles with the police in the entire center of Athens, where many got beaten up, arrested, and had their hair cut.[51] Greek youths were effectively displacing their opposition to the dictatorship by adopting the countercultural energy of *Woodstock:* "They were thus *locating* their struggle in (the context of) the 60s and *dis-locating* the abusive topos of the Greek dictatorship," cultural theorist Dimitris Papanikolaou observes.[52]

These students were out of tune with the conservative Greek society's attitude toward protest and counterculture. In an article published in the liberal newspaper *Ta Nea* the playwright Dimitris Psathas observed with revulsion: "The whole story was that some people wanted to get inside [the cinema] and watch the hippies and listen to the hippie songs, and the police were so scared by the possibility that our youth would also be seduced during the screenings by the frenzied action, the hysteria, the madness and the maniac crises of foreign youth—especially American—that at some point it thought of prohibiting the movie." Later on in the article, Psathas continued in the same line:

> The hysterical yelling of youths with their hair pulled out and of singers wearing long moustaches and beards, dressed in rags, covers the greatest part of the hippie movie. The whirling dervishes of hippie music beat themselves, pull their hair out, faint while singing, bleat desperately or holler. Maybe there are a few kids here in this sick category as well, among whom were certainly those silly chits with or without long hair who created the fuss last Sunday. The greatest part of our youth, however, is not being seduced by such rubbish."[53]

Psathas's comments are reminiscent of the moral panic that Western pop music was causing to officials in the Communist Bloc countries in about the same period.[54]

The day after *Woodstock*'s failed screening, Deputy Minister Georgalas visited Panteios School and made a speech "analyzing the aims and ideology of the Revolution of April 21." Thereafter, a pro-regime medical student complained that "after three and a half years of efforts to detoxify the youth nothing ha[d] been achieved," since "the distancing of the youth from other activities ha[d] pushed them deeper into hippyism." Georgalas retorted that the youth was effectively detoxified, that the revolution had not yet used all its potential, and that the *Woodstock* incident was of no great importance. When the student mentioned the appearance of "three to five thousand anarchists," Georgalas responded that "they weren't anarchists but vivacious youths,"[55] as it was probably too hazardous to label them otherwise. The interchange between the two, which included frequent references to "detoxification"—Georgalas's favorite phrase to use when referring to the youth—and to anarchists and hippies, conveys the level of public debate on such matters and the negative charge with which these were loaded. It is noteworthy that at this time the Greek film comedies *My Aunt, the Hippie* [I Theia mou I Chipissa], *A Hippie with Tsarouchia* [Enas Chipis me Tsarouchia], and the theatrical play *Hippies and Dirladas* [Chipides kai Dirladades] enjoyed great success.[56] This suggests the almost obsessive treatment of the subject of "hippies," who were presented as grotesque, buffoonish, and as engaging in decadent cultural behavior. Equally interesting was the mainstream comedy *Marijuana Stop* (dir. Giannis Dalianidis, 1971), which adopted a strongly moralist tone in reference to the hippie counterculture, including drugs. Meanwhile, for dissident students hippieism connoted apolitical behavior, and drugs were identified with the underworld. They longed to be energetic rather than "stoned" and were getting their "fix" with adrenaline alone. "It seems that the [student] movement itself is like a drug," former student leader Giorgos Vernikos concludes.[57]

However, the fact that Greece was a stage for hippieism contributed to locals' being accustomed to freer habits, even if by 1971 the Holy Synod of the Greek Orthodox Church was calling all monks and nuns to pray for help because Greece was "scourged by the worldly touristic wave" and "contemporary western invaders."[58] The *Economist* further reported: "The Greeks, and not just the soldiers, don't much like to see unwashed, barefooted and shabby youth sitting on the pavements in the center of Athens; nor do they have any respect for the dropouts hitch-hiking their way to Istanbul, Kabul and Goa without a drachma in their pockets. But they tolerate them."[59] In contrast to this article's assertion, however, hippie attire gradually became fashionable in Greece; though drugs, yoga, and Zen Buddhism remained largely unknown, the spirit, the fashion, and the aesthetics of the hippies influenced everyday life, despite the fact that this was an otherwise authoritarian society and state. From the hippies came the trends of wearing bloomers and carrying handwoven bags. In addition, words and phrases like "flower power," "make love not war," "Twiggy," and "Carnaby" penetrated the Greek vocabulary, and a multicolor, dreamlike psychedelic aesthetic was promoted by commercials.[60]

Connected to US counterculture was also Stuart Hagmann's *The Strawberry Statement* (1970), which became the "cult" feature movie of the time. The film, based on a best-selling autobiographical account of a "college revolutionary," chronicled the uprising of Columbia University students in 1968, exalting student activism and free love and rejecting university authoritarianism and police brutality.[61] The most powerful point in the movie is its final scene, in which the barricaded students welcome the storming police while rhythmically chanting "Give peace a chance" before the action turns into brutal clashes and beatings. Myrsini Zorba remembers this as an explosion that the students "were internally ready for" (Zorba, interview). American Ambassador Henry J. Tasca reported in November 1970 about the screening of the film in Athens in a telegraphic fashion:

At several performances in at least two theaters, spectators in front rows stood up and shouted slogans. In one case groups shouted "1-1-4" which refers to article in former constitution promising equality to all citizens and was popular leftist street chant before coup. In another case disturbance was so great that police were called in to remove some of those causing disturbances, although as far as informant was aware no arrests were made.... Anti-regime slogans shouted during performance of feature film and accompanying newsreel, reported applause for episodes in which students beat up police and applause following glimpses of photographs of Robert Kennedy, Che Guevara and Mao Tse Tung.[62]

The enthusiastic responses that the film generated among students demonstrate their identification with the rebellious protagonists, confirming Laura Mulvey's analysis that spectators in cinema blatantly project their repressed desires onto the performers.[63]

Apart from offering a space for mimicking foreign student movements, cinema halls—especially Alkyonis and Studio in Athens and Thymeli in Salonica—served as sites for information exchange and recognition. "In the movies everyone participated—police spies and left-wingers. They all watched along," Thanasis Skamnakis remarks. "And you started getting to know faces, you saw them at the university, you saw them in the places where you hung out. And you started, you know, acquiring a visual connection to some people" (Skamnakis, interview). Thodoros Vourekas explains: "It became a nucleus; it became an agitational network between us, a very serious agitation, meaning that all the preparation was taking place there. Afterward I realized that most

Figure 4.3. Projecting the repressed desire for freedom onto the screen. This was the 1970 advertisement for the film *The Strawberry Statement,* which dealt with student uprisings on US campuses. The film caused a sensation and was subsequently banned.

people who were acting in the student movement were also there" (Vourekas, interview). "The only issue was how to break the ice. This was the big issue," Chrysafis Iordanoglou remembers. "How to break it, how to bring the people out, how to get to know each other." (Iordanoglou, interview)

Cinema was a major advocate of common consciousness and a vehicle for self-education—"a whole internal world," in the words of Iordanoglou. Greek students shared what media theorist Peppino Ortoleva has defined as the "eros of student movements for cinema" in the 1968 era.[64] In her life story Angeliki Xydi recalled a day associated in her memory with Alain Resnais, highlighting the fact that hers was a generation of serious film buffs:

> I remember that I saw *Last Year in Marienbad* the day in which I went for the first time to the Police Station for "a private matter." This terrible piece of paper had arrived home calling me to go in for "a private matter." It was 8 November 1972; I remember well because it was my name day.... They wanted to advise me of course in the way that they knew best. In any case, I was beaten black and blue that day, and I used to have very long hair back then, which I had just shampooed because it was my name day, it was beautiful. And they pulled it so hard [laughter] that it became like a wig and my head was aching terribly. But the evening was booked: in no case would we miss *Last Year in Marienbad*! [laughter]. (Xydi, interview)

This passage vividly depicts not only the repressive character of the regime even in the period of liberalization but also the strong connection between students and visual culture, with the latter offering a magical "window to the world," a tool that could reverse and smooth over existing harsh realities. Therefore, I strongly disagree with eyewitness Kevin Andrews's conclusion that "the result of these very few, uneasy and hesitant productions was that tired audiences could come away refreshed for yet one more tomorrow of boredom, anxiety, humiliation and eventually ... indifference because it's all too difficult."[65] Instead of acting as a two-edged sword, as Andrews suggests, art in general, and cinema in particular, proved to be a game-changer in the arena of protest. Film became the necessary companion of dissident students, facilitating the emergence of a militant social network and bringing culture and ideology together with artistic consumption and political agitation.

A place of recognition but also a *lieu par excellence* for voicing dissent was Salonica's annual Film Festival. The screenings offered opportunities to assemble and became the definite meeting point for students in late September each year. It was state policy to promote and reward war epics about Greek bravery against either the German or Bulgarian aggressors during the Second World War. Since these films supposedly promoted the military virtues of Greek people, students tended to mock them. The darkness and the relative anonymity in Salonica's large State Theater offered a perfect setting in which young people could vent their anger against the state-imposed movies and indirectly against the general political situation. According to filmmaker Grigoris Grigoriou "resistance ... started from the spectators. Within the dark theater, during the screening hours, people applauded any scene that they considered as a hint against the Junta and wildly booed any scenes of anticommunist hysteria."[66] The pro-regime newspaper *Eleftheros Kosmos* reported with annoyance in 1970:

> A group of immature youngsters during the screenings is booing whatever is not of their liking from an artistic or historical perspective. Hiding themselves within the darkness of the theater, these coward "revolutionaries" create a rude atmosphere that disturbs the other spectators who have gathered in order to take part in an artistic show and not a political meeting. Shouldn't the police be present at the balcony ... in order to bring the troublemakers back to order?[67]

Frequently, students opened a mock dialogue with the characters in the movies, asking them questions, responding to their lines, or just commenting. During one season, the Junta's main film producer, James Paris, provoked the angry disapproval of students who exited in protest ("Shame on you!") and the outburst of a young filmmaker who asked in a loud voice, "Is there no censorship for this?" Maria Mavragani remembers that it was an obligation to go to the theater balcony and shout. The students' reactions tended to be overtly subversive, using irony and references to television commercials. Another film presented at the same festival was called *Raging Youth* [Orgismeni Genia] (dir. Gerasimos Papadatos, 1972), hinting at young people's rebelliousness but clumsily presenting them as disoriented and vain. Students repeated slogans from television commercials in order to ridicule the dialogue, for example by starting to sing the tune of an advertisement called "Mr. Forte" when the film's male protagonist demonstrated his toughness to his female counterpart. When he was informed by his girlfriend that she was pregnant, young people sang yet another common television commercial called "Now you know." The reverberation of these commercials on behalf of dissident students points to the growing presence of a mass culture in Greece that was reinforced by a boost in mass consumerism by the regime.[68] It also indicates a "situationist" mode of inverting and subverting the commercials' initial meaning. During a moment of provocation, some youths shouted that they preferred watching the well-known porn star of the period, Kostas Gousgounis, to the film.[69]

During the screening of costume drama *Hippocrates and Democracy* [O Ippokratis kai I Dimokratia] (dir. Dimis Dadiras, 1972) at the thirteenth festival in September 1972, the character Hippocrates at one point said, "Then we have democracy," and a student from the gallery asked, "Come again?" When Aspasia, Pericles' wife, said, "There are greater sorrows awaiting us," someone replied, "Us too, us too!"[70] Here too, the "situationist" practice of mock dialoguing with the film undermined the spirit of official propaganda in which the movies were packaged, as well as the serious character and prestige of the festival as a whole. Historian Nikos Papadogiannis's conclusion that this was a typical case of the survival of the practice of "dialogue with the screen"—a practice that dates back to the early days of cinema—is particularly pertinent.[71]

The movies offered an opportunity to express anger and dissatisfaction with the cultural priorities and aesthetics of the pro-Junta artists, as well as space to branch out. More importantly, the students made subtle references to the political situation. Little by little, and especially in 1973, their reactions in the gallery of the theater tended to be dictated by exclusively political criteria. A contemporary film critic characteristically complained in the autumn of 1973: "We understand the hunger of the audience for politics but we should not abandon our aesthetic standards entirely; a bad movie should not be praised just because there are glimpses of the Vietnam War or snippets of revolutionary songs and political slogans."[72] The fact that this kind of critique was not voiced by an "indignant" pro-regime intellectual demonstrates the growing politicization of public discourse at the time and the rising fear of critics that qualitative criteria would be eventually entirely overshadowed by cheap militantism. In any case, the dissident subculture that was established in Salonica Film Festival's gallery during the Junta years was to be continued and even intensified in the years following the restoration of democracy in 1974.

"Tickets to Freedom": Theater

Another privileged site of student communication and interaction was theater. From April 1967 through November 1969, the Colonels exercised direct state-imposed censorship over theater productions, making it "virtually impossible," according to theater specialist Gonda Van Steen, "for stage companies to stage anything capable of being construed, or misconstrued, as a challenge to authoritarianism."[73] The initial ban on plays included a number of classical dramas deemed radical in their political ideas: *Prometheus Bound* by Aeschylus (revolutionary ideas and unbowed spirit of Prometheus), *The Phoenicians* (heretic in morality, nonbelief in religion, radical in politics), the subversive *The Suppliants* by Euripides, *Ajax* by Sophocles (lack of solidarity within the army), and above all *Antigone* (a standing incitement to civil disobedience to a military usurper who has taken over an enfeebled monarchy).[74]

Similarly, Aristophanes' comedies, which are characterized by a general distrust of authorities and intellectuals alike, were banned; *Lysistrata*, with its 'ithyphallic apparatus ... and thrasonical soldiers on stage" was the worst offender.[75] A foreign correspondent observed: "The censors consider that [these plays] contain ideas subversive to society, the King and religion, the three pillars of the regime instituted by the coup of April 21. They have substituted other plays regarded as 'less dangerous to the public mind.'"[76] The dictators treated Aristophanes as a nonconformist creator of irreverent artifacts, occasionally allowing his plays to be staged in an attempt to seem liberal and to offer "safety valves for venting dissent." This trick failed miserably, however: because modern opposition plays were banned, Aristophanes provided the raw material for criticizing the excesses of the ludicrous dictators. It was up to the audience to identify the resemblances.[77]

By the early 1970s, the theater, like the cinema and the publishing world, had been somewhat liberalized. The softening of censorship allowed certain plays to return to the stage, even if norms of production and reception remained distorted. As the classical actress Anna Synodinou maintained in late 1972, one of the main reasons for the reemergence of artists, including playwrights and actors, was a growing concern that the new generation should not suffer from a cultural void—a statement similar to that made by Manolis Anagnostakis concerning books.[78] In other words, artists like Synodinou wished that the previous generation of young people, which suffered the absence of any substantial cultural activity from 1967 to 1971, would be succeeded by one that would experience a renewed intellectual dynamism. In July 1972, Synodinou reemerged with Sophocles' *Elektra*, and in early 1973 she went overtly political with the staging of Bertolt Brecht's *Antigone*, in which she played the main role.

Soon, the subtext became more important than the apparent subject matter, and theater became a venue for dissent. The relationship between spectacle, text, music, and dance, and particularly the metatheatrical and extradramatic elements in the performances of politicized actors, contributed to that shift. By 1972, a number of directors, playwrights, actors, and actresses had devoted themselves to a theater that would reach the people and would communicate political messages. The journal *Anoichto Theatro* [Open

Theater] (Athens, 1971) outlined this new role in an editorial published in its first issue in 1971 that defined "political theater." The editorial concluded, in line with the reelaboration of tradition, that the correct knowledge of tradition "is always the starting point of every renewal."[79]

In Athens, Karolos Koun's Theatro Technis [Art Theater] basement performances were a focal point of the theater revival. The Theatro Technis's particular approach to Attic comedy followed an idealized quest for pure folk culture. There followed productions of plays by Harold Pinter, Luigi Pirandello, Samuel Beckett, Eugène Ionesco, Jean Genet, and a single production of a Shakespeare play, *Measure for Measure*, which, according to Modern Greek scholar Peter Mackridge, was "a symbolic choice of play, with its central themes of justice and mercy."[80] To paraphrase sociologist José María Maravall's conclusion about anti-Franco Spanish students at the same time, cultural deviance in the Colonels' Greece was equivalent to political deviance: Beckett or Genet were as subversive as Lenin.[81] For *Katerina, these performances contained "an allusory wink" that the trained student audiences of the time "could easily grasp" (*Katerina, interview). The Stoa Theater in Athens that was inaugurated in 1971 by Thanasis Papageorgiou and Eleni Karpeta also staged performances of political plays, such as Peter Weiss's *The Song of the Lusitanian Bogey*. Drama teams like Stefanos Linaios's Synchrono Elliniko Theatro [Contemporary Greek Theater] (Athens, 1970) performed plays that included political references, among them *Goodnight Margarita*, an adaptation of an old theatrical success based on a dramatic story during the German occupation. Nikos Bistis points out how this particular play helped to break down barriers and attract people to the student movement: "This was a classic performance of the bourgeois woman who passes over to the Left, she falls in love with a partisan.... All these spectacles helped people to be drawn to the Left" (Bistis, interview).

In Salonica, interest in theater blossomed tremendously under the Junta. The State Theater's productions managed to attract more than three hundred thousand spectators per year to their performances, a great number of whom were students. As the state-controlled theater did not make a serious effort at transcendence in its repertoire, the growth seems indicative of a new form of group socialization and exchange through the theatrical ritual. Gradually, young people became increasingly preoccupied with theater. It became a widespread phenomenon, giving the students an important and influential role as consumers of cultural artifacts. The general director of the State Theater of Salonica, Georgios Kitsopoulos, stated in an interview with the pro-regime student paper *O Foititis* in late 1972 that he was seriously considering asking the opinion of the students, whom he considered a "class" on their own, before deciding to stage future plays:

The attendance of all these students in theater, the get-together, this lively participation, the notes with opinions and comments, have created a community. We have the perspective of having a closer relation to the class of youth, so that you should not be surprised—this is the first time I say this—if in the future we invite representative groups of youth before staging a play, in order to read it to them and let them give their opinion on the reasons why that play should be staged or not.[82]

Theater journals containing quite radical standpoints began to appear and were readily consumed. The most influential was *Anoichto Theatro,* a "monthly review of political theater" that contained articles by renowned left-wing intellectuals like Gyorg Lúkacs and traced international innovative developments such as the Living Theater in the United States. In an interview with *Protoporia,* the director of *Anoichto Theatro,* Giorgos Michailidis, stated clearly that "for us political theater means, first of all, opposition to any form of power."[83] Similarly, the journal *Theatrika* [Theater Issues] had as its motto a phrase by Eugène Ionesco: "All people that have the tendency to dominate others are paranoid."

In late 1971, the theater scene started changing in Salonica as well, and interesting links were created between the literary scene and the Theatriko Ergastiri [Theatrical Workshop], which was run by students. A network of publishers, theater persons, and accommodating student groups was put into place. Bookseller and theater aficionado Kaiti Saketa recalls: "Filippos Vlachos of the *Keimena* publications came to Salonica. Salonica then was a distribution center for books, and we were in contact with all the publishers of Athens. So, where did he go when he came over here? Straight to the Theatriko Ergastiri." At the same time new creative spaces were developed around theater, which facilitated the creation of new meaning. For a long time there was no student society that could accommodate dissident students; thus Saketa argues, "It was as if [students] had theater as their base" (Saketa, interview).

When the Theatriko Ergastiri brought Bertolt Brecht's *Man Equals Man* in late 1972—a play full of references to everyday alienation, including the loss of innocence, the impossibility of communication, and the estrangement of the self ("You should forget about your opinions")—the first performances took place in half-empty theaters. The theater columnist for *Thessaloniki* wondered, "How many—if not everybody in the theater room—should leave the Amalia Theater skeptical every night? It is an obligation, it is an injunction to get to know ourselves, to judge ourselves."[84] His moralist tone condemns the passive attitude of those who did not join the spectacles and who did not question themselves about the restrictions that were imposed on them on a daily basis.

The students redeemed themselves, however, proving to be some of the most sensitive receivers of theater and establishing a direct dialogue with the art form and its content. Brecht's epic theater was much more influential on the young people of Greece than, for example, street theater, which did not manage to penetrate the country. The Theatriko Ergastiri turned to a more Greek-centered repertoire and in 1972 performed Greek playwright Mendis Bostantzoglou's (Bost) *Fafsta,* a satire of bourgeois life and its linguistic anarchy. The workshop's contributors articulated a desire to form a sort of "Greek Theater" by adopting a Greek repertoire and themes close to the Greek reality. The whole play is a sort of feast, in which the spectators themselves are involved in the end, in this way partaking in the spectacle in a dynamic way. The farce established a special relationship with the spectators by inviting them to interact—a practice that was about to become a standard feature in alternative theater performances over the following years.

Elefthero Theatro [Free Theater], the most remarkable of all of the theater groups of this period, was a collective created in 1970 by young actors and artists. With "living theater" features and a belief in Brechtean *Verfremdung,* the group decided to abolish the "director-dictator" in a symbolic antiauthoritarian move that resonated both with the repressive state of affairs in the country but also with a general radical tendency abroad: everything had to be the result of collective creation—in the tradition of Ariane Mnouschkine's Théâtre du Soleil.[85] Many of the Elefthero Theatro's actors were members of the Maoist EKKE, not least because one of them, Giorgos Kotanidis, belonged to the organization's leading group. As he notes in his memoirs, "In Europe a revolutionary ideology was being born and artists were in the vanguard. What better proof that theater, cinema and the revolution are part and parcel?"[86] The collective's political radicalism also inspired a stance critical of the "absolute spectacle" and a search for theater of contestation. Elefthero Theatro's manifesto declared, with extraordinary frankness in its Marxist wording, that it was a group comprised of people under twenty-eight who detested bourgeois theatrical values.[87] Just like with cinema, the idea here was that the spectators should be induced to think critically: "We oppose this passive attitude of the audience; its decline in front of a universe of heroes, divas, routine, lots of crying, lots of laughing. In contrast, we advocate a spectacle that keeps the audience alive, perceptive and happy."[88]

The group was composed of graduates of the National Theater, some of whom were also enrolled as students in the universities of Athens or Salonica in order to retain their student status. This link with the student world was intensified through their close collaboration with EKIN, which included the staging of plays in the latter's basement and the active role of some actors in its initiatives, and vice versa. The main contact was Elefthero Theatro's leading actor, Nikos Skylodimos, himself a graduate of the prestigious Leonteios School and therefore a fellow student of some of those well-to-do youths who comprised the main circle of EKIN.

Elefthero Theatro had a spectacular debut when it staged John Gay's *Beggar's Opera* on 3 September 1970, in Athens. Kaiti Saketa remembers the same performance when it was staged in Salonica the following year: "This was a revolutionary act for Salonica, to have a play similar to Brecht's *Threepenny Opera* staged at the Royal Theater, with innuendos, with pantomime against the dictatorship, things that were not stated clearly" (Saketa, interview).

Another breakthrough event for the Elefthero Theatro was its staging in 1971 and 1972 of Petros Markaris's *The Story of Ali Redjo* [I Istoria tou Ali Redjo]. Being a clear indictment of the socioeconomic exploitation of the powerless have-nots by the powerful haves, the play was a succinct but unambiguous statement of social protest. The play included, among other things, the projection of a film that involved images of a tractor intercepted by shots of a tank. When the still of the tank covered the screen in the end, it became clear that it "pointed to the colonels and their military semiotics."[89] Playwright Markaris argued in an autobiographical text years later that the Elefthero Theatro's staging of his play was the most collective and full-fledged resistance act in the field of the arts throughout the Junta years.[90]

In 1973, due to political differences the initial group of Elefthero Theatro broke up.[91] Nonetheless, in the summer of the same year, and with some of the founders of the group persecuted or imprisoned for subversive political action, Elefthero Theatro made a direct statement regarding the current affairs and especially the dictators' "controlled liberalization" experiment. With *…And You're Combing Your Hair* […Kai Sy Chtenizesai], a production in the tradition of the Athenian *epitheorisi* (revue genre) and co-written by the group members together with left-wing playwrights Kostas Mourselas, Giorgos Skourtis, and Bost, it advanced the idea of abstention from the 29 July 1973 referendum for the abolition of the monarchy. The revue's title ("You're combing your hair," meaning you are brushing your problems away) and the show's poster and program (a collage with a finger pointing at the reader/audience over bodiless dancing legs), were a clear indictment of the entire society of indifference and social apathy.[92] Since Elefthero Theatro members believed that the lifestyle and conformism of the Greek petty bourgeoisie were responsible for many of the country's ills, several of the revue's satirical numbers actually castigated issues such as the lower-middle-class

Figure 4.4. The avant-garde theater group Elefthero Theatro performing John Gay's *Beggar's Opera* in 1970. The group, which decided to abolish the *director-dictator* in a symbolic antiauthoritarian move, exemplified the fusion between politics and the arts. (Courtesy Giorgos Kotanidis)

obsession with socioeconomic mobility, its hypocritical stance regarding premarital sex, and its fascination with football and television.[93]

By this point, audiences interpreted Elefthero Theatro's productions as political commentary with great potential and impact.[94] Rena Theologidou remembers the performances of *…And You're Combing Your Hair* as "a revolution within the [Junta's] 'Revolution'—a real revolution": "We used to go to [the theater of] Alsos every night, I could go on stage and play it. We knew it by heart, the dialogues, everything" (Theologidou, interview). Even though magazines of the time attest to the fact that the greatest and most enthusiastic part of the audience was comprised of students, the massive numbers of people that flocked to watch the show reveal that performance theater with a political edge was becoming mainstream.

By 1973, even mainstream companies, such as that of popular actress Jenny Karezi, staged political plays. Karezi, with her husband and fellow actor Kostas Kazakos, commissioned Iakovos Kambanellis to write a play that was performed in the spring of 1973 and was about to become one of the most popular anti-Junta theatrical events of the entire dictatorship period: *Our Grand Circus* [To Megalo mas Tsirko]. Academic and antiregime activist Giorgos Koumandos claims that the performances of this particular play "became massive political demonstrations, the biggest ones during the seven-year dictatorship—before the events at the Polytechnic."⁹⁵ The play was based on a series of historical vignettes that were filled with allusions and references to the Greek people's suffering throughout the centuries from either foreign rule or domestic autocracy. In an alternative reading of Modern Greek history, *Our Grand Circus* paralleled authoritarian moments of the past to the rule of the Colonels and to US neocolonialism. Ostensibly in reference to the constitution granted by the first sovereign of Greece, the Bavarian King Otto, in 1844, characters in the play voiced the slogans "The people's voice equals God's rage" and "Constitution"—drawing an inescapable comparison to the savage violation of constitutional rule by the Colonels ever since 1967.

The play was highly charged emotionally, not least because of a very powerful music score by Stavros Xarhakos that was performed by dissident student idol Nikos Xylouris.⁹⁶ Through an unconventional stage and seating arrangement it granted multiple occasions for direct interaction between the performers and the members of the audience, who were mutually exposed.⁹⁷ As drama scholar Gonda Van Steen explains, "The majority of the spectators could ... observe other people's reactions which encouraged self-observation and self-reflection, especially when the actors fired difficult questions at them."⁹⁸ The fact that the audience, mainly composed of students, went off to demonstrate soon after the play's premiere, demonstrates the clear agitprop effect of the play and its metatheatrical elements. Playwright Kambanellis recalled with emotion that the popular response was so enthusiastic that youths at later performances did not simply ask for tickets, but for "tickets to freedom."⁹⁹ In November 1973, some of the play's slogans, written on huge placards, were taken up by student protesters, and right after the Polytechnic occupation, actress Jenny Karezi spent a month at the EAT/ESA and was subjected to psychological torture. When she resumed the play, the greatest part of the historical references that had been its major strength had been butchered by the censorship.

All in all, students were patrons of cultural creations and bearers of a new cultural radicalism, which again was facilitated by their predominantly middle-class background. They experienced and contributed to the radicalization of the entire cultural scene, a process in which theater played a fundamental role, partly due to the direct interaction between artists and audience. Theatrical journals openly questioned the boundaries between culture and politics, introducing a new, direct discourse that differed from the previous secrecy. The term *political theater* penetrated everyday jargon. By the winter of 1973 so many political plays were staged that critics started to doubt the solely artistic aspirations that their producers claimed. As had happened with political books and cinema, performances with an *engagé* content were often judged to be superfluous and cunningly misleading, as the political subject matter ensured success with audiences. An editorial by *Anoichto Theatro* was so harsh in its criticism that it dubbed extreme "politicization" demagogy: "The pseudo-resistance of big words, the people with their collars turned up, the blood-shedding students, the red cloaks, the iron bars of prisons, and, in general, the 'pornography of violence' do not render anybody emotional. Being a creation of the last few years, the theater of demagogic findings has tired and disappointed."[100]

It is important to note that this specific editorial placed "pseudo-resistance theater" alongside three more potential enemies of Art, which were either introduced or boosted by the military regime: television, football, and the Ford Foundation. The fact that the latter, in particular, was famously granting abundant grants to Greek intellectuals and artists during the Junta period was often interpreted by left-wingers as a sell-out to the Americans. In his memoirs, Elefthero Theatro actor Giorgos Kotanidis analyzes at length how tempted the group was to accept a lavish Ford grant which it ultimately rejected due largely to the fact that it was coming from the States, "the country which created and supported the dictatorship."[101]

Nevertheless, this whole discourse on the crisis of theater (a similar one was articulated by literary circles) seems to come from the future, and in particular the *Metapolitefsi* period. It is astonishing that in the midst of the Junta period critics would emphasize issues such as overpoliticization and commercialization. Despite all this, theater proved to be a privileged space for voicing dissent, just like cinema. It managed to go from "the margin to the mainstream," to quote theater specialist Philip Hager's term, and from "pocket theaters" to big outdoor productions in front of mass audiences.[102] Political, "engaged," or agitprop theater flourished during the last years of the dictatorship and turned out to be a major rallying point for students who opposed the regime and were eager not only to share their subversive artistic codes but to participate actively in the shows, demonstrating their direct complicity.

The Musical Culture Wars

"Revolutionary" music was another subversive artistic product that circulated in the early 1970s. Eclecticism, one of the landmarks of the international art scene during the 1960s, ruled. A mixture of Mikis Theodorakis's banned reworkings of poetry and Dionysis Savvopoulos's "paralogical" texts was coupled with the parallel discovery of the local *rembetika* and foreign imported Anglo-American music, resulting in a fusion of the old with the new. The mixture between traditional folklore and experimental rock created an explosive blend.

Rock music was becoming popular, and a form of rock culture infiltrated Greece and the antidictatorship student movement in different forms and colorations, both directly and indirectly, through the folk rock of Bob Dylan and Joan Baez, through movies such as *Woodstock,* and even through Greek artists like Savvopoulos. In addition to the Beatles, the Rolling Stones, and the Doors, Frank Zappa, Pink Floyd, Deep Purple, Led Zeppelin, and most of the artists who had played at Woodstock (Jimi Hendrix, Jefferson Airplane, the Grateful Dead, Janis Joplin) became points of reference. Militant student and present-day journalist Antonis Davanelos remembers that students differentiated between "politicized" and "apolitical" rockers: "I remember that in my school we were split in two, the nonpolitical rockers, that is, Led Zeppelin, to put it in a schematic way, and the politicized part that listened to Dylan; Crosby, Stills, Nash and Young; and these were like Gospels." He goes on to argue that the spirit of contestation was arriving via music: "The message that was coming from abroad, mainly from abroad, was the following, the wind of freedom that was unleashed after May '68. Since in Greece there was no political discussion, it was banned by the Junta, it's strange, but I think, without being sure, these are at least my memories, that the message was coming mainly from the States and mainly through music" (Davanelos, interview). Music from the *Dark Side of the Moon* by Pink Floyd comprises part of the soundtrack of the film *Black-White*—alongside tunes by the Greek songwriter Manos Loizos. At one point in the film, the student protagonist enters a music store in Athens and stares at a poster of Frank Zappa, while in the background one can hear a song by Deep Purple. This scene suggests the extent of young people's familiarization with Western pop culture, including progressive rock groups, at the time.[103]

A number of Greek rock bands gained popularity by referring to drugs and rebelliousness in their lyrics. The most significant were Socrates, Exadaktylos, and Damon and Fidias. Other bands perpetuated the 1960s trend of combining political and countercultural elements. The hippie message "Make love not war" was echoed in the Greek smash hit of 1972, "Make Love, Stop the Gunfire" [Anthrope Agapa] by the rather conventional rock group Poll, which referred directly to the Vietnam War.

As former militant and present-day historian Leonidas Kallivretakis recalls, however, this generation, despite its contact with the rock scene, clearly preferred the Greek political song.[104] Greek resistance music led the way, with Theodorakis's heroic tone encapsulating the spirit of the time and marking continuity with the past in the form of the eponymous Lambrakis movement. In the early 1960s, Theodorakis was the first to gather large crowds of people in big stadiums to hear his musical reworkings of poetry by George Seferis, Odysseus Elytis, and Giannis Ritsos, whose work he consciously attempted to popularize. Theodorakis's music had been persecuted by right-wing governments and ultra-right-wingers in the past, who tended to disrupt his concerts—events that were "widely reported, and contributed to the political reinvestment of [his music's] symbolic status before the dictatorship," as Dimitris Papanikolaou writes. "It was the Gramscian overtones of Theodorakis's rhetoric," however, "that rendered all popular culture described in his [work] potentially political."[105] Theodorakis invested much of his time trying to demonstrate that true popular art is political.

As one might expect, Theodorakis's music was banned in Greece after the Junta came to power in 1967, a situation that continued even after the regime lifted censorship of theater and literature, for the Colonels believed that the people "must be protected from any contagious disease, such as Left-wing views or Left-wing music, which could delay the day when [Greeks] will all become true Greeks, following truly Greek policies and principles" in a general process of reeducation.[106] Accordingly, the buying, selling, transmission, reproduction, or lending of Theodorakis's music became a court-martial offence.[107] Dissident students had his records smuggled to them by friends studying abroad (giving them new ways to escape discovery by the police); copying and reproducing them became a common clandestine activity.

Soon, not only his music but his entire Gestalt turned political, rendering Theodorakis a powerful icon of resistance, a status reinforced by his legendary escape from arrest for many months after the coup. His famous song cycles, such as *The Songs of the Struggle* [Ta Tragoudia tou Agona], which are mostly about freedom, prison, and lost dreams—many inspired by old partisan melodies—became the necessary companions of young people, who eagerly sang them in the tavernas. Many commentators have seen Theodorakis as the embodiment of the 1960s' spirit of liberty, the engagé artist *par excellence,* leading to his mythologization at home and his commodification abroad.[108] Vera Damofli remarks of Theodorakis's ubiquity and importance: "It was more revolutionary for us back then ... to receive the illegal songs of Theodorakis that arrived here in tapes, and we learned them by heart, no matter if they were nice or not. But in those days it meant something, that the tapes came from abroad, and this was spread out, the one told the song to the other, you know, we put them in our house and this was something [meaningful]" (Damofli, interview).

There was a strong divide between Theodorakis (who was committed to communist ideals, partisan traditions, and Generation Z) and another figure of the early 1960s, the *poète-chansonnier* Savvopoulos. Savvopoulos represented both a continuity with the avant-garde "New Wave" of the

Greek song of the early 1960s and also a break with it, in a Bob Dylan-esque way. Apart from Dylan, Savvopoulos's role model was Georges Brassens, the French anarchical "singing poet" who fused folk song elements canonized as "oral poetry" with identifiable popular song.[109] Similarly, the Greek troubadour took disparate strands of traditional music and wove them together with electric guitar into a form of "serious pop" with folk elements. In his shows—immensely popular among progressive students—Savvopoulos revisited regional variants of folk known as *dimotika*.[110] Members of his show were iconic folk singer Domna Samiou, shadow puppeteer Evgenios Spatharis, circus strong man Jimmy the Tiger, and experimental filmmaker Lakis Papastathis. Despite his often unorthodox, grotesque, and ironic reinterpretations, Savvopoulos was a central figure in the use of folkloric elements and traditional instruments as part of a new revolutionary spirit. In his words there existed an interesting tension between tradition and revolution: "Tradition with one hand was giving us shapes of life and with the other was reducing our revolutionary spirit. How can I be revolutionary and traditional at the same time? Revolution is a mute instrument without tradition. And

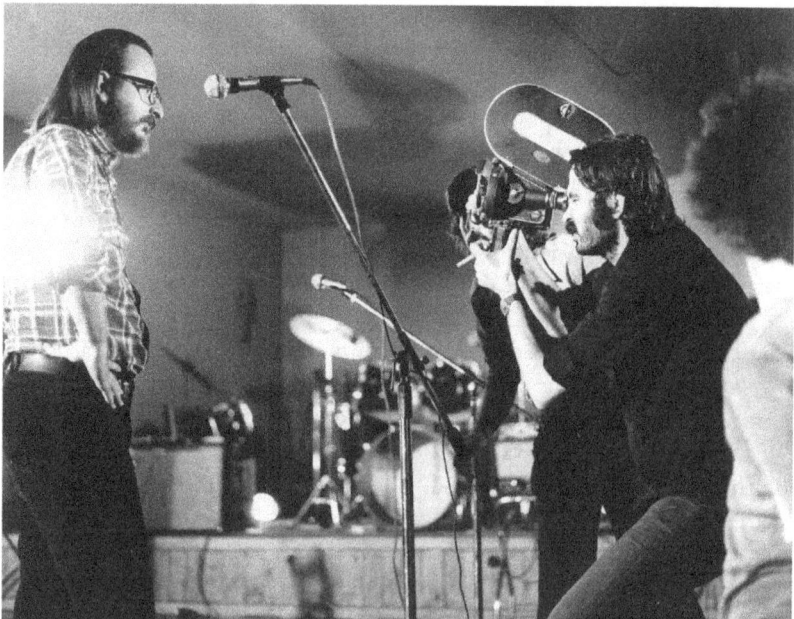

Figure 4.5. Dionysis Savvopoulos being filmed by one of his collaborators, director Lakis Papastathis, during the legendary sessions at the Kyttaro Club in 1973. Kyttaro was a meeting point of the political and the countercultural. (Courtesy Lakis Papastathis)

tradition without revolutionary spirit is a fossil."[111] It was precisely this gap that Savvopoulos was trying to bridge.

Savvopoulos's songs made constant reference to the youth of his time ("the lads with the long hair and the black clothes") and masterfully described the mass consumption that had arrived in Greece by the late 1960s. He referred to the destructive influence of the mass culture promoted by the hegemonic media as "tons of excrement" in his song "The Baby" [To Moro] (from the LP *Filthy Bread* [Vromiko Psomi], 1972), for example. In a 1970 interview, he described the rapid changes brought about in mass consumption after the Junta took power: "I haven't been to Salonica for seven years. ... Last time I went I was impressed by the change. Many things which were not accessible to the lower classes, now are everywhere to be found. You see them being sold on every corner: refrigerators, televisions, kitchens. Let alone the building blocks."[112] The rapid increase in mass consumption that Savvopoulos refers to was partly the result of the booming economy in the early years of the Junta and of the dictators' inclination to buy off political dissent through increases in state allowances and benefits. The electrical devices and elements of household modernization had made their way through to Greece in the 1960s, but they were consolidated on a grand scale throughout the country only in the early 1970s. While television was still a luxury in the late 1960s, it was a standard accessory in half of Greek households by the mid-1970s.[113] Artists and intellectuals tended to view television as "the new dictator," its invasion an epidemic that facilitated the consumption of cultural garbage at home.[114] As was the case in Franco's Spain, television became a major instrument of regime propaganda, but also of entertainment and a certain homogenization, not least because of the advertisements.[115] *Him and Him* [Ekeinos ki Ekeinos] by Kostas Mourselas was probably the only exception to this, being a show that had a subversive, albeit cryptic, script.

In a period in which direct political expression was banned, the kind of music Savvopoulos produced conveyed indirect messages and a general ethos.[116] As social scientists Ron Eyerman and Andrew Jamison have argued, some popular music in the 1960s through form and content "translated the political radicalism that was expressed by relatively small coteries of critical intellectuals and political activists into a much different and far more accessible idiom."[117] In this respect, Savvopoulos, like Phil Ochs and Bob Dylan in the United States, Lluís Llach in Spain, or Paolo Pietrangeli in Italy, was providing a new kind of political discourse: "a musical variant of critical social theory."[118]

In contrast to Theodorakis, however, Savvopoulos shaped and reflected on youth culture without feeling himself to be an enlightened instructor who would educate the masses. Accordingly, in the same 1970 interview cited above, he questioned: "Who are you? Is there a group around there with a common conscience, a different desire, needing a 'representative'? Because from your side I don't hear any sound! ... Ah, of course! Singers in London and New York can easily act as the 'representatives.' But down here?"[119] One cannot but note here the similarity between this and Bob Dylan's rejection of the role of the guru of the American New Left through his phrase "There really isn't a New Left";[120] this becomes even more pertinent since Savvopoulos very consciously mimicked Dylan, not only in terms of music.

His daily program at the Athens *boîtes,* namely the small music halls of the early 1960s, became an important meeting point for nonconformist students. These youths, critic Giorgos Notaras writes, "had no relation to tradition, no serious education, but were full of imagination and passion and a suppressed drive which at some point [was] about to come to the surface."[121] Former student militant Giorgos Karambelias argues that Savvopoulos expressed the "marginal element" of the period, "that element which was secondary to the central aims of modernization and democratization, but which was already mobilizing the most progressive section of youth."[122] Savvopoulos himself has criticized purely political music—implicitly that of Theodorakis—and argued that songs which went beyond party folklore, attacked ideological discipline, and were closer to everyday realities, were more appealing to students who thought critically: "It used to be fashionable and people wrote political songs, like 'We have to reinforce the struggle.' Some epic stuff ... The [song] "Assembly of EFEE" was more meaningful, as the guy fancies a chick who is not at the assembly. This became a symbol for students, you see. ... That is, if you were a bit more aware of the things that were going on, this is the kind of song you would seek out" (Savvopoulos, interview). In addition, what can be discerned in most life stories is the conclusion that Savvopoulos brought Greek society into contact with the spirit of international student protest.

Given the success of Savvopoulos's concerts, the creation of the Kyttaro Club in Athens in 1970, which could host up to four hundred people, partly accommodated his large audiences, which the seventy-seat *boîtes* could not do. In a way, the clubs Kyttaro and Rodeo (opened in 1967) in Athens were the equivalent to the legendary Fillmore Auditorium in the United States and the Marquee and UFO clubs in Great Britain at about the same time.[123] During his gigs, Savvopoulos performed next to dynamic representatives of the emerging rock scene, whose stated intent was not only to copy the foreign model but to initiate rock with Greek lyrics and explore the realities of the youth, as in the legendary live recording *Zontanoi sto Kyttaro* [Live at Kyttaro] (1971). This album documents a fusion of progressive, folklorist, and acutely political elements, both indigenous and foreign.

Savvopoulos's song "Black Sea" [Mavri Thalassa], an Epirote folk tune mixed with psychedelic flute solos, was followed by Exadaktylos's controversial pop and Socrates' imitation of Jimmy Hendrix's famous napalm bomb-like guitar solo at Woodstock. Socrates' guitarist Spathas describes his guitar effects as containing "the sense of protest" and remembers the young people who were at the concert as an audience full of energy, singing along and applauding with exhilaration.[124] Despoina Glezou, the singer of the popular band Nostradamus, recalled with pride in an interview that even experienced foreign artists were impressed by the countercultural energy exposed by the performers at Kyttaro. Once again, both in the case of Socrates and hers, Woodstock seems to be the absolute point of reference:

> Some amazing nights at the Kyttaro were a total confirmation of the beauty that emerged from inside this place. Mike Wadleigh, who directed the film "Woodstock" came, Cat Stevens came, Richie Havens, the black performer who sang "Freedom" at Woodstock, came, and they all were completely enchanted. I mean the nights were so powerful that these people with all their experience, who had experienced thousands of people when they performed at Woodstock and who made "Woodstock," were entranced by us![125]

The fact that as early as 1971, when the student movement was still low-key, a major event of such transgressive intensity took place, in which avant-garde musicians were "jamming" together with the underground rock scene of Athens, indicates the explosivity of the Greek counterculture.

In addition to becoming political, rock music also borrowed from the folk scene, creating a vibrant fusion of genres. Rock groups Damon and Feidias and Bourboulia played songs "based on folk music and classic rock," with lyrics in Greek and with "sociological sensitivities," according to the groups' own description.[126] One of the most promising rock producers of the time, Stelios Elliniadis was a member of the Maoist EKKE and a frequent habitué of the cult record shop Pop 11. Elliniadis plainly describes the hybridization of the cultural tastes of this generation: "Verses, characters, underground social streams, political environment, aesthetical tendencies, cinema and literature were shaping the rock scene together. Paul Butterfield, Electric Flag, the Grateful Dead and John Coltrane, instead of the treacly Baez and the childish Utopia of the flower children. And at the same time Vamvakaris and Hadjidakis and, of course Savvopoulos, in Rodeo. Light behind the dazzling façade."[127]

Music halls became a meeting place and a melting pot for both apolitical youth, who were still called yé-yés, and politicized students. Savvopoulos remembers: "The main audience at the *boîtes* were students. At Rodeo, in those clubs, there were students but not [an] unmixed [group] anymore. A youth was coming too that liked to listen to rock groups.... We called them 'yeyedes.' Different kinds of youth started meeting each other" (Savvopoulos, interview). This mixture, which led to the creation of a new youth culture combining political with countercultural features, was also apparent in the appearance of the youth. The militants started adopting the yé-yé style, wearing long hair and beards. The opposite was also true, as Panos Theodoridis, a student who considered himself a typical rocker of the time, explains: "So, whereas we were rockers and did not have responsibilities, being apolitical and cool, all of a sudden we got transformed into political creatures."[128] Whereas former student militant and present-day historian Leonidas Kallivretakis asserts that students left rock culture behind when they were organized into antiregime political groupings, in reality rock and politics coexisted.[129]

Reinventing Tradition

In one of his most emblematic songs of the period, "Ode to Georgios Karaiskakis" (1969), Dionysis Savvopoulos mixed traditional instruments and tunes and a ballad-like melody with political undertones. Though the song's title suggests that its subject is the nineteenth-century hero Karaiskakis, in fact it refers directly to Che Guevara. The mixture between politics, tradition, revolution, and electronic communications is striking:

> Where are you going brave man?
> Beautiful like a myth
> You are swimming straight to death.
> And all the antennae
> of a battered earth
> loudspeakers and wireless everywhere
> they sing you sweet lullabies
> and you rise
> high among the kings of the skies.[130]

Savvopoulos often performed together with Marisa Koch, a flamboyant singer—a 1973 article in *Thessaloniki* described her as "a mixture of the wildness of Janis Joplin, the endurance of Yoko Ono, and the sensitivity of Joan Baez"—who specialized in performing demotic songs. The *Thessaloniki* piece remarked, "Folk song and rock music become one in order to convey the new Greek musical 'color,'"[131] defying the regime's demand for cultural authenticity. In Koch's concerts acid rock, funk, garage, and country were mixed with famous folk songs and songs with clear antidictatorship connotations, such as Giannis Markopoulos's emblematic "Enemies" [Ochtroi] (1972), which pointed to the Colonels. Theodoridis remembers with emotion a combined concert of Savvopoulos and Koch in Salonica where they launched their own versions of folk songs: "In 1970, I think, Savvopoulos's 'Ode to Karaiskakis' came out, with those bagpipes at the end of the track—or was it a clarinet?—well, this thing came out and Savvopoulos came over with Marisa Koch, I think it was in 1970, to Palais des Sports Stadium, and Marisa Koch sang the 'She-Deer' [I Elafina], which was, a folk song, for 3,000 to 3,500 enraged students."[132] The fact that all those "enraged" Greek students got all fired up listening to a traditional folk song speaks volumes about the political electricity that this kind of music was generating.

Koch's own recollections highlight the manifest antagonism between old-style folk songs championed by the regime and new-style, reelaborated ones favored by its opponents:

> When I met Dionysis Savvopoulos in 1969 and we arranged the program for Rodeo, above all I didn't want to sing any song that had been submitted to the censorship committee.... So, it crossed my

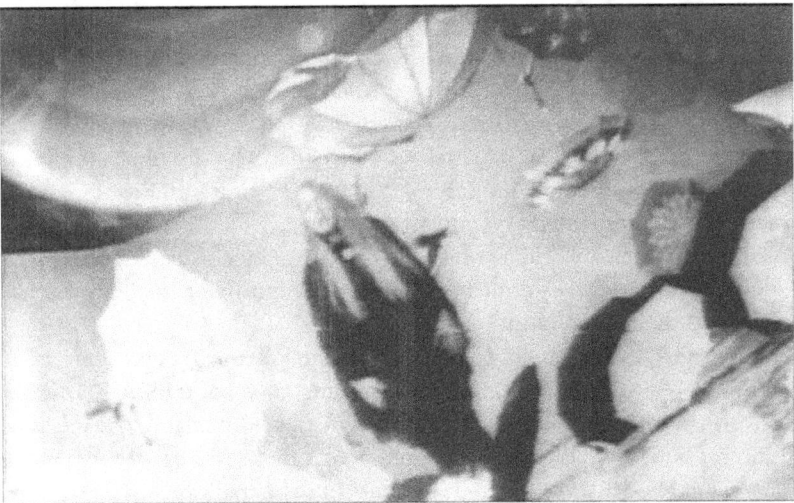

Figure 4.6. Marisa Koch performing in a video clip of the early television shows. The fusion between the traditional song ("Armenaki"), Koch's hippie attire, and the psychedelic background was part of a conscious strategy to "harm" tradition. (Courtesy Nikos Mastorakis)

> mind to sing old songs in a way in which I could express my inner drive but also the sounds that I had in my ears back then, listening to them day and night.... The issue was to not let anyone hinder the cry and the wildness in singing, in order to sing in a "traditional" way.... The songs had such an immediate success, as if the people were waiting for this. As a matter of fact, the people then, at least the ones who were coming to those places, were the same people that a bit later were inside the Polytechnic, and they wanted to do "harm" to the traditional songs, because every statement of the Colonels was accompanied by a traditional song.[133]

Koch's reference to censorship is important: the raw material of reinvented folk hardly attracted the censor's eye due to its national characteristics. Understanding this fact is crucial to interpreting the rediscovery of tradition in countries under an authoritarian regime, such as Greece, Spain, Portugal, Chile, and Brazil. Folk revivals never became an emblematic feature of the '68 movements in Western Europe like they did in Colonels' Greece because it was only in the authoritarian context that seemingly innocent music could be used as a weapon against the authorities. Tradition thus became a point of departure for fighting the regime's monolithic attempts to defend Hellenic civilization. The fact that the dictators were great proponents of folk songs and dances who never missed a chance to publicly promote them by demonstrating their skills in *kalamatianos, tsamikos* or *karagkouna,* prompted a number of dissident artists to explore folklore in a heterodox way.[134] Here, I share Modern Greek scholar Karen Van Dyck's conclusion that the paradoxical embrace of folk-culture by this alternative sphere was the equivalent of the physician's homeopathic cure, whereby "that which is threatening can be used to strengthen the immune system."[135] The clearest indication of this method was offered by Savvopoulos in an interview in 1972: "We conceptualize the material world as a piece of filthy bread which could, from filthy and unhealthy, be transformed into clean and healthy for the body and the blood, via the process of eating it."[136]

Dissident artists sought to explore genuine folklore in depth in order to generate opposition to the hegemonic culture's revival of tradition. This created two competing folk cultures: the dictators' favorite dances broadcasted and promoted by radio and television, versus the "subversive" folk culture represented by artists of the opposition. While the traditionalist use of folklore by the regime resisted the mixing or recombining of different genres, antiregime artists tended to undermine the supposed purity of folk culture by joining it with other varieties.[137] Their uses of folk music testify to the fact that popular practices, including festivities and music, can be interpreted

Figure 4.7. Regent General Georgios Zoitakis—with glasses—and Brigadier Dimitrios Ioannidis—the notorious Head of ESA and latter day "invisible dictator"—championing a folk dance during Orthodox Easter in 1971. Regime figures never missed a chance to demonstrate their skills in the folk dances *tsamikos* or *kalamatianos* in public. (Source: ELIA, Greek Literary and Historical Archive)

and used in the opposite ways of those initially intended by a given authority, challenging power from within.[138] Still, both sides were arguing for "authenticity," be it in form (the regime) or in content (the artists).

A Singing Movement

The most popular of the folk songs were from Western Crete, the *rizitika*, rediscovered by the composer Giannis Marcopoulos, who also crafted political songs with a surreal twist that created semantic confusion, such as the enormously popular "Tarzan" (1972) and the evocative "Papadop dop dop" (1973) whose concluding stanza was quite telling: "Whoever remains silent is going to wither away." *Rizitika* were usually sung by one of the students' idols, the Cretan singer and lyra player Nikos Xylouris. The songs, which dealt with the fictional struggles of local heroes with Death (Charos) and the historical Cretan uprisings against the Ottomans in the late nineteenth century, already belonged to the canon of resistance. Crete itself functioned as a place with symbolic value, condensing the traditional popular patriotic and neo-romantic sentiment: peripheral but proud. The absolute favorite from this tradition was the cortege song "Xasteria" whose refrain was, "When will the season of starry nights come round again?" Anthropologist Jane Cowan remarks that "this song was unmistakably a call to arms": "When will the skies clear? / When will February come, / so that I can take up my rifle?"[139] The song in reality declares in a celebratory manner a series of intended massacres: "I shall leave mothers without sons, women without men."[140]

Equally militant were the old left-wing guerrilla songs, the so-called *andartika*, which also underwent a revival. These were songs sung by the rural folk during the resistance period and the civil war in the 1940s. Their raw militancy created the illusion that the students were communicating with the romanticized heroes of wartime resistance. These songs contained a significant amount of communist propaganda, but it was always amalgamated with "the traditions of populist agrarianism and age-old peasant traditions."[141] Many of these songs were a call to arms, and their appropriation by the students in the 1970s can be described as "retro resistance." Art historian Elizabeth Guffey argues that "retro" should not be confused with "nostalgia," since nostalgia involves "a heavy dose of cynicism or detachment," demythologizing its subject.[142] I believe, however, that in the Greek case, and in particular concerning the resistance, "retro resistance" and nostalgia were hardly distinguishable from one another.

Often, the *andartika* were reelaborated versions of *kleftika* folk songs from the period of Ottoman rule. Similar to the partisans in the 1940s, antiregime students were attracted by the rich kleftic tradition and its semantics. Its songs fit well with the imaginary of the premodern, renegade, freedom-fighting figure, already exploited by the left-wing generation of the 1940s. The *kleftika* were altered, transformed, and modified in the process of their adoption by students. A well-known song containing the line "Bleak is the life we dark klefts are leading," for example, was rewritten as "Bleak is the life we students are leading."[143]

Dissident students also discovered and reappropriated the *rembetika*, songs imported from Asia Minor in the 1920s that both were strongly associated with the underworld and marked a form of social protest. The *rembetika* had a strong countercultural resonance because of their plentiful references to drugs, being "songs of love, sorrow and hashish."[144] They were banned in the interwar period and officially denounced by the Communist Party as lumpen, as they supposedly led working-class fighters to stupefaction and degeneration. During the first years of the Junta, the rigid moral code of the "Hellenic Christians" regarded the *rembetika* as offensive. To take one prominent example, the breakthrough study of Ilias Petropoulos *Rembetika Tragoudia* (1968) was banned, and he was imprisoned. The situation was not entirely restrictive, however, as old *rembetes* such as Vassilis Tsitsanis, Markos Vamvakaris, and Sotiria Bellou performed in dives in Athens and, to a lesser extent, in Salonica. Savvopoulos himself turned to *rembetika* to acquire raw material, as many a composer had done before him, including Hadjidakis and Theodorakis in the late 1940s and early 1960s, respectively.

The *rembetika* offered rich material evoking past epochs, a favorite tendency at that time. Apostolos Kaldaras's song "Night Has Fallen without a Moon" [Nychtose Choris Feggari], recorded in 1947 during the Civil War, goes: "A door opens, a door closes / but the key is turned twice; / what's the kid done / that they threw him in jail?" Jane Cowan rightly observes that "with the regime's prison cells full of young people brought in for interrogation and torture, the lyrics simply achieved too direct a hit."[145] A similar example is offered by Markos Vamvakaris's song "The Prisons Are Ringing Out" [Antilaloun oi Fylakes] (1936), a very popular tune dating from the time of General Metaxas' dictatorship. *Rembetika* songs, always sung collectively, fitted neatly with the formation of large groups of friends who met in tavernas or went to the basements where the old *rembetes* sang. Vera Damofli remembers that what counted was the allusion, that "one word within the song" (Damofli, interview). Ilias Triantafyllopoulos characterizes this as a joyful rediscovery of a long-lost socialization through music: "It's the rediscovery of Bellou, Tsitsanis, again the popular songs and the *rembetika* and of course Savvopoulos and the others and the international streams [too], rock and all the rest. But the tavernas start all over again, the songs restart, and this was what created the groups of friends" (Triantafyllopoulos, interview).

For politicized students, *rembetika* became part of the canon of resistance, acquiring signifiers that were not recognizable by others. Their use of *rembetika* evokes the notion of cultural practices as "maps of meaning" which are intelligible solely to the members of the group.[146] It is noteworthy that *rembetika* became a general fashion at the time: *rembetomania*. *Rembetika* venues became so popular that they ended up being publicized by the pro-regime student paper in Salonica, in this case stripped of their subversive nature.[147] Angeliki Xydi recapitulates this tendency of the politicized students to recast cultural trends for their own uses and highlights the ways in which they conceptualized *rembetika*, focusing on their social characteristics: "And of course we had the tavernas. Where we gave away our souls. Regularly, with *rembetiko* until the point of exhaustion. Which was in a way a fashion, but not only that. I think that it fit in well, it corresponded to this situation of social upheaval and discontent towards a suppressive regime" (Xydi, interview).

Although there was an association of the *rembetika* with drugs, it was unusual for the politically engaged students to partake. This did not apply to the rest of the society, however. When a hippie commune that used opium was discovered in Athens in October 1973, both the reportage and trial revealed the press's utmost contempt of drug use. When the defense questioned the hippies about the music they listened to and they answered "modern music," the defendant replied in astonishment: "This is the first time that I've heard of an 'opium dive' without *rembetika*." At another point of the trial, the defense commented that the authorities had mobilized to arrest the hippies under the false assumption that they were a large resistance organization. Instead, "they bumped into kids."[148] With this comment, the defense juxtaposed the "dangerous" and "mature" resistance fighters to the "harmless" and "childlike" drug-consuming hippies, who were often castigated and ridiculed by the press.

In the words of Eyerman and Jamison, "Many social movements bring older movements back to life by remembering the songs that were sung and the images that were drawn by giving them new meaning."[149] The same applies to the case of the antidictatorship student movement in Greece and the fact that *rizitika, kleftika, andartika,* and *rembetika* became the soundtrack to student action. The performance and multiple reappropriations of these older musical genres located the students firmly within a long-established, *longue-durée* tradition of protest.

A Collective Falling in Love

Singing banned songs in the tavernas at night was the first testing ground in defiance of the authorities, but it was also a means of nonconformist socialization. A favorite meeting place was the nightclub Lidra, where student idol Nikos Xylouris performed. It was temporarily closed by a police order in 1973 due to "serious disorder taking place" and the fact that it "constituted a definite danger for the public order and the safety of citizens." An *Observer* report called it the "Secret School," a name that referred to a well-known myth from Greece's past concerning underground schools teaching Greek language under Ottoman rule; a US newspaper referred to it as "250 square meters of freedom in Greece."[150] Such places became sites where the radicalized, rebellious identity of students could be freely and collectively manifested, and the students could express ideas forbidden in all other contexts.[151] Ioanna Karystiani stresses this point:

We used to go to the tavernas in order to let off steam by singing the banned songs, and in a provocative manner in fact, as if we were looking for trouble, for some cop passing by to ask us for our ID and bring us to the police station. You know, this thing that you have when you are eighteen or twenty years old and you want to be provocative. (Karystiani, interview)

Karystiani's description corresponds quite well with the image of renegade individuals who collectively defy the authorities. Groups of friends acted as a sort of collective subject, such that the context of their collectivity reinforced the individual will of defiance, braving fear and danger.

Tavernas became the meeting ground par excellence, where clashes among the students were temporarily suspended in a celebratory atmosphere. They functioned as a parallel, antithetical sphere to the existing authoritarian order and its institutions. The day's threatening reality gave way to its joyous flip side as those places of relaxation offered a therapeutic outlet to unwind. Damofli preserves in her memory moments of liberating laughter, which brings to mind Bakhtin's assertion about its subversive character: "And of course the nights we went to tavernas and we sang and laughed, and we laughed. We used to laugh a lot" (Damofli, interview)[152] Kleopatra Papageorgiou makes a similar comment, stressing the communal element in life and drawing the classic contrast with the present: "We had some great years back then in the tavernas. We were very lucky kids, because despite the sufferings inflicted by the Junta and stuff, we had a very intense social life, a great camaraderie, and we shared everything. Our thoughts, our desires, everything. We weren't closed in ourselves as today's students are, I suppose" (Papageorgiou, interview). The collective superseded the individual; the rise of individualism, a typical byproduct of the 1968 movements according to critics such as Eric Hobsbawm, seems entirely absent in the case of Greek protesters.[153]

Student communities and social interactions provided the necessary space for the development of strong bonds, both of friendship and sexuality. Francesco Alberoni has written that when a movement is about to be born, there is a collective falling in love,[154] and the Greek student movement confirms this truth. Participants in a collective movement acquire a dynamic and elevated self-image that differs substantially from their everyday selves. Falling in love or joining a collective movement, Alberoni maintains, may seem dissimilar, but nevertheless they are both experiences that lead to an exalted period of self-regeneration.[155] One of EKIN's leading members, Giorgos Kanellakis, encapsulates this feeling of exaltation in his description: "In the groups of friends, in the political quarrels, in the tavernas, in the excursions—with the banned songs—there was an excitement, euphoria, to the extent of ... libertarian paranoia."[156]

Gendered Militancy and "Sexual Revolution"

What was women's role in all this? Novelist and former activist Maro Douka's semiautobiographical novel *Fool's Gold* [I Archaia Skouria] (1979) is an interesting exposé of the difficulties, including family constraints, faced by young women coming of age during the dictatorship. It also faithfully reconstructs the rhetoric employed by the dictatorship as a step backward for public discourse on women, who were valued only for their capacity to biologically perpetuate the nation. This rhetoric bears a striking resemblance to fascist and national socialist ideologies. As dictator Papadopoulos put it in *Our Creed* [To Pistevo Mas], his manifesto, "The Revolution sees in the Greek woman her primary biological mission as the Mother. It honors her for this capacity with a deep consciousness of her importance."[157]

Nevertheless, by 1972–1973, Greek women represented 33.7 percent of all students and 38.5 percent of all graduates.[158] The shift of young women beginning to live away from home to study was a breakthrough for their place in Greek society and was regarded by the women in question as a liberating experience. Still, an American report of the time describing the infamous incident in which right-wing students disrupted the lecture of Professor Fatouros in Salonica's Architecture School in December 1970 provides insight into the moral standards that were shared by military authorities in the universities. The report quotes the wording of "Governmental Commissioner" General Polizopoulos in his correspondence with the Ministry of Education: "The General, arriving on the scene immediately after the incident, was shocked at finding ... one girl student who was seated on [a] table displaying herself in a most immodest manner,"[159] thus implying sexual provocation.

Long-established mentalities continued to define the student body as well. Most men were still in favor of separate socialization, and most female students remained largely intimidated and socially conservative. In a series of interviews conducted by the antiregime student journal *Protoporia* in 1972, several female students were asked vague questions on their views about university life, interpersonal relations, and established social practices.[160] Their replies reveal their social conservatism, eagerly condemning premarital sexual relations and defending the merits of the traditional "Greek way of life." They habitually refer to sexual intercourse as "that thing," discuss their parents with fear and awe, and express concern that they might be caught doing

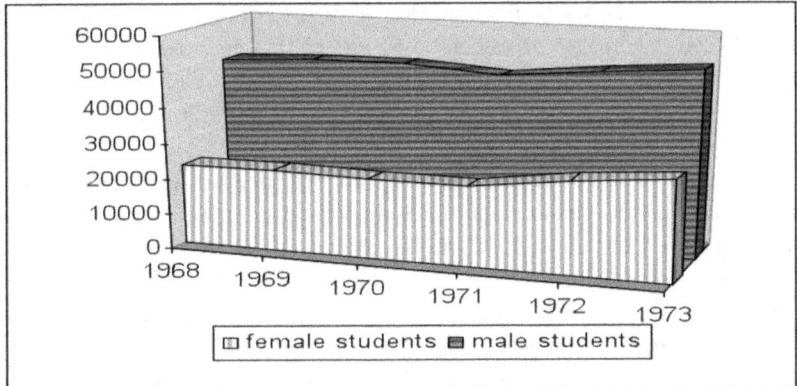

Figure 4.8. Change in Male and Female Student Numbers in Greek Institutions of Higher Education, 1968–1973. (Source: National Institute of Statistics, ESIE)

something "improper." Last but not least, the women complain about being treated by their male fellow students with scorn and arrogance:

– A guy would never start a serious discussion with a woman maybe because he would think that she's incompetent to follow.

– Yes, yes! You're right. Once it also happened to me that I intervened in a serious discussion and then they said surprised "Ah! So, you know something about these things too!" and then they started taking me for a ride![161]

Growing female participation in antiregime activities, such as the first student committees of action, finally facilitated a degree of parity. In her own account, Myrsini Zorba, a leading student nicknamed "Rosa Luxemburg" as she was, in her own playful words, "dogmatically radical," makes an interesting juxtaposition between the freedom of spirit that left-wing women acquired over the years and the female image of the happy housewife promoted by television commercials at the time: "Much later from commercials and images I realized too that [women] were very lowly placed, they didn't work, they stayed at home, they were very oppressed. Left-wing women, in contrast, went out of their homes, they ran out" (Zorba, interview). It is interesting to note, however, that at the beginning of the 1970s television commercials also embraced the "trendy" issue of female emancipation as a selling strategy. A washing machine commercial of the early 1970s reported: "The emancipation of the woman, working or not, starts from home. It begins when she gets rid of the stress of laundry, for example."[162] Other commercials embraced the sexual liberation model by promoting, for the first time, overtly sensual images or associational names that referred to the general climate of the period. The much-advertised shampoo "Eleftheri kai Oraia" [Free and Beautiful], for example, used words that corresponded fully to the feminist movements of the period.[163]

One important stage in the development of the student movement was a juncture for female students to acquire a pivotal role; this was when the Junta passed a decree in 1973 enforcing the military draft of eighty male students who had taken leading roles in organizing student unrest. This decision of the authorities to suspend military deferment was directed exclusively at men, leaving women aside as less harmful; it was sexist and misplaced in its conceptualization of the student movement as exclusively male driven. As a result, women students moved to the forefront of the movement across numerous faculties. Albert Coerant, a Dutch reporter in Athens, recalls that during the Law School occupation in winter 1973, many female students surrounded their male counterparts in order to protect them from being photographed and consequently sent to the barracks (see chapter 5).[164]

Women became leading figures inside the student movement in both Athens and Salonica. Kleopatra Papageorgiou and Ioanna Karystiani, in particular, are often referred to as inspirational figures, "Las Pasionarias" according to Vourekas – a powerful reference to the legendary Communist leader from the time of the Spanish Civil War, Dolores Ibárruri. Klearchos Tsaousidis argues that Papageorgiou was very well known, including to the police, as women leaders were few and far between and thus were immediately spotted: "She was also a girl that stood out: she was not some silent girl, she was a shouter, and she distinguished herself" (Tsaousidis, interview). Many former student activists speak of Karystiani as the "northern star" of the student movement, the most charismatic personality: "Given the situation, equality was imposed by reality. When you had Karystiani in the Law School, would anybody doubt her because she was a woman? Ioanna was a tornado. She would sweep everything. She was a personage.... Up to '73, before the Polytechnic, she was the point of reference for the whole movement" (Skamnakis, interview). Nikos Alivizatos remembers on the contrary, however, that in the immediate past Karystiani had been given secondary roles, as was the norm for women:

> I remember that in those first days Ioanna Karystiani had come to EKIN with a scared look. "I want to help," and things like that, and we didn't know who Ioanna Karystiani was, the future writer and leader of the student movement; she was a freshman; we put her to sweep the floor.

"Why don't you do a bit of mopping?"

"Guys, don't let me just do the mopping."

And we had those kinds of conversations. [laughter] (Alivizatos, interview)

In addition, Vervenioti recalls that, apart from a few cases, it was the men who led the way in leading the organizations, not least due to their greater experience in public speaking. Women remained far more intimidated: "We could possibly say better things than they did, but we didn't do it. Men did the talking. I remember that very well" (Vervenioti, interview). Zorba too claims that the role of women in the Left, though comparatively privileged, was still not one of leadership, as emancipation did not coincide with empowerment: "Despite the fact that within [the Left] women really do the 'dishwashing,' always the 'dishwashing,' they are nevertheless dynamic, responsible, and in the end equal" (Zorba, interview).

Women gradually developed a greater female consciousness. Traditionally male practices such as smoking and using offensive language were adopted by a new generation of left-wing women, not least because of their desire to emulate female prototypes abroad. International developments in fashion influenced their dressing habits too; in 1960s Greece, trousers were still considered a male trademark. Tasos Darveris's impression is that the transformation in women students' dress took place over a very limited timespan during the late 1960s. In his book, his literary surrogate, who is being transferred from one jail to another, takes notice of the shift, which he perceives as a huge transformation—an impression that was probably reinforced by the fact that he had spent eight months in isolation: "Several women wore trousers, which was something unprecedented in the history of Modern Greece."[165]

By 1973, moreover, one result of progressive female students' everyday interactions with their male colleagues in shared antiregime activities and socialization was a more uninhibited attitude toward sexuality. Student everyday habits became liberalized, despite the fact that Damofli argues that "it was the previous generation that started the sexual revolution and we the ones who consolidated it"—referring to liberal outbreaks as part of the 1965 "July events." In comparison to the previous student generation, the new one appeared more open in its attitude toward sexual conduct, not so much in seeking to transform the public sphere as in conquering the private one. Zorba remarks: "Sexual liberation was a trademark. We women became more liberated, we started finding jobs, anything you can imagine" (Zorba, interview). In early 1970s Greece, however, birth control remained taboo, abortion was "a crime under all circumstances," and female adultery was a serious offence. In addition, female contraception was still finding its way, as the selling and advertising of the birth control pill was prohibited and punished by criminal law.[166]

In these conditions, and with social conservatism being reinforced and rewarded by the regime, the enjoyment of open sexual relations was soon understood as a means not only of social emancipation but also of political resistance, and this despite the fact that the absence of the pill deprived Greek female students of a major emancipatory practice in terms of taking control over their sexual practices. Interestingly, the otherwise very open life stories of female students largely omit any mention of abortions, which remained underground and traumatic. Only Karystiani broke the barrier of silence when she mentioned coming together to pay for students' abortions as an example of collective bonding and solidarity (Karystiani, interview).

In former militants' life stories there is disagreement concerning the nature of sexual encounters among the politicized students, as some stress the arousing effects of tension under the stressful circumstances of the student struggle while others castigate the strict monogamy that reigned supreme. Maria Mavragani remembers that, at least in her environment, sexual experimentation was common: "We, that is in my group of friends, we discussed it, naively or not, but we discussed, 'Can I go out with others,' the couple, you see? It constituted a subject of conversation and speculation and many things happened, you know, sure, we had taken it seriously" (Mavragani, interview). Kleopatra Papageorgiou insists, however, that no "revolution" took place:

> We ate out together every night, in tavernas, in pizzerias, we talked, our life was collective, almost communal. Alright, we might not have slept in the same houses, but we ate together, we discussed much. Now, sexual relations were not that far out as in the United States or in Europe. Sexual revolution—no, this was a myth. In the end, there was conservatism, big time. And this was seen later on in the course of events; you see how these people evolved. They got married, they did all the usual stuff that the previous generations did. (Papageorgiou, interview)

There was no attack on the institution of marriage, nor was there any considerable sexual experimentation. Moreover, homosexuality and homoeroticism were taboo subjects that did not emerge as a transgressive demand in the student movement either, as they did in other countries. The celebrated translator and novelist Kostas Tachtsis, himself a homosexual, commented that when students shouted *"Eleftheria!"* (Freedom!), they only meant it in terms of political freedom, not including sexual emancipation: "If freedom was not to be uniform and indivisible, to hell with it!"[167] Drawing a connecting line between May '68 and the Greek student movement of the early 1970s, he added: "The struggle for freedom had to aim at the liberation of every kind of sexual desire too, namely that of the homosexual, and this would be realized only if one day all those who shouted 'Bread! Education! Freedom!' did not only mean political, but also sexual freedom, and in fact not just the right of some fuckers to come and go to the dormitories of women students at night, as happened in '68 in Nanterre."[168]

Despite the validity of his accusation, however, Tachtsis overlooks the revolutionary character of the demand that people of opposite sexes be allowed to sleep together without reproach, both in the Paris of 1968 and the Athens of 1973. The demand for sexual freedom was part of discovering the political side of every sphere, including the private one.[169] On a side note, and even though the Colonels' Greece was a macho society, a homosexual and "transvestite" liberation movement did spring up during the Junta years (though this movement was not at all connected to the parallel student activism), a phenomenon that Spain witnessed as well. Still, the Junta insisted that homosexuals no longer existed in the country.[170]

Anthropologist Alki Kyriakidou-Nestoros also argued that things were changing in female students' behavior. Kyriakidou-Nestoros was an associate professor at the University of Salonica, an uncommon position for a woman to occupy during this period in Greece. At an interview given to the pro-regime student journal in March 1972 she argued: "In contrast to the older female students, the new ones are not intimidated anymore, but are very active.... In general there is a big difference between the old and the new ones. The new female students are much more easy-going."[171] Shortly thereafter, Kyriakidou-Nestoros was expelled from the University as "non-law-abiding."[172]

Female provocation, a major trait of '68, was absent too. A possible exception is profanity. Damofli delineates the difference between women who cursed because they wanted to and those who were rather unwilling but did so because it was part of the package of a new transgressive identity:

> So, for example, they were calling a poofter "poofter," and they were saying many things, because the philology ... for me swearwords are part of a philology, there developed a philology. So, others were doing it—they didn't feel it but they were doing it—and others felt like it and talked this way. (Damofli, interview)

Interestingly, by using the more impersonal third person plural Damofli leaves herself out of this dualism. Taken in context, however, her story testifies to the radical change in the behavior of women at the time.

Women's limited emancipation was not necessarily greeted with enthusiasm by everyone inside the movement, especially by their male peers. Damofli continues:

> Probably some of them were shocked. Some girls were very loose-tongued. In our generation this became established. Or it was starting to be accepted that girls could use swearwords too. And for some of them it was also part of their style, others were exaggerating, you know, they were saying things that often shocked people. (Damofli, interview)

In the socially backward and politically reactionary Greece of the time, seemingly innocent gestures could be strongly symbolic for the movement's participants and authorities alike. Dimitris Papachristos writes in his memoirs that when he entered court to defend eleven colleagues of his in early 1973, the most striking feature he saw were his girlfriend's hippie trousers, which infuriated the policemen: "Above all, I will never forget the bellbottomed jeans that Olga wore, on which she had imprinted the peace symbol, and this provoked them, and it became the excuse for arresting her."[173] In that sense, there existed no provocation per se, but people were so sensitive to subtle nuances that such an act could be considered as a form of microprotest.

In contrast to Papachristos, Lionarakis reports being shocked by his own girlfriend's "provocative" way of dressing, which in his words consisted of a simple low neck and tights—thus revealing the puritanism that persisted even in the ethics of left-wing male militants:

> Melpo was a nice chick back then and very emancipated and all that jazz. I was containing myself, containing myself, containing myself, and one day, at 5 o'clock in the morning, after a night-long I don't know what, at Nea Philadelphia Square, I told her, "Look. I'm fed up. I'll tell you everything so that I can let myself go. I don't want us to be together any longer, because you are embarrassing me, you dress like a whore!" (Lionarakis, interview)

Historian Dagmar Herzog's conclusion regarding the German 1968 that "the longing for sexually free women and the fear of those free women came hand in hand," seems particularly pertinent here.[174] Dissident student Kostas

Kalimeris, on the other hand, expresses the conviction that equality was a fact, but that it was a negative outcome of extreme politicization: "Relations with the opposite sex were forcefully equal. Now, how can this function? It was the male comrade and the female comrade, it wasn't man and woman. There was no space to discuss such matters" (Kalimeris, interview). Contrary to Kalimeris's assertion about being gender-blind inside the movement, however, enforced equality did not abolish a protective male stance toward the so-called weaker sex. Tasos Darveris mentions in his autobiographical novel a deeply courteous posture toward women: "Despite all your efforts, you couldn't stop looking at women as creatures who were too delicate for prison cells and torture, even if they were comrades."[175] Even in the moments of panic during the evacuation of the November 1973 Polytechnic School (see chapter 5), gallant male behavior toward women was recorded. A later testimony noted that during the brief and abortive negotiation prior to the army's entrance, more time was requested on the ground that "there are women inside, small, delicate, how can they get out, they will be trampled."[176] Still, on an organizational level, the Polytechnic essentially signaled the institutionalization of female participation on equal terms. The presence

Figure 4.9. A female student is dragged by the hair by two policemen around the time of the Law School events in February 1973. Misogyny and a particularly harsh treatment of women protesters were part of the regime's repressive repertoire. (Photographer: N. A. Floros)

of quite a few women on the Coordinating Committee of the Polytechnic occupation and the crucial role of two women militants as speakers in the radio station are but two examples.

In ideological terms, women militants of Marxist inclinations often envisioned a socialist turn of society as the necessary precondition for an improvement in gender relations. In general, however, gender was and would continue to be an uncomfortable issue for the majority of left-wing organizations in Greece at the time; for them such matters were subordinate to the fundamental class conflict. It must be emphasized that despite the relative popularity of Simone de Beauvoir's seminal book *The Second Sex* among student circles, no early signs of feminist politics or a separate women's sector emerged in the Junta years—in contrast to Francoist Spain, where despite the oppression, protofeminist groupings emerged already in the late 1960s. In Greece, concerns about the oppression of women as the root of all oppression did not even become dominant after the breakdown of the Junta and the more vindicating period of the *Metapolitefsi*. Angeliki Xydi attributed the lack of any explicit feminist politics on the part of Greek women themselves or their organizations to the fact that this was too sophisticated a demand for the conditions of the time:

> I think that in general there was no such issue. Men, women, the feminist aspect, which I discovered only after the dictatorship was over, did not occur to us then. It is always like that in the great moments of struggles, both the resistance, the civil wars. I remember I read a nice phrase by Rossana Rossanda saying that after the resistance women went back to the kitchen. Yes, you know, as long as the struggle required it they inveighed against the male-dominated establishment, they put us in the first line. Afterward in the calm. … (Xydi, interview)

It can be concluded that although women militants acquired an important role in politics and more emancipation in everyday life, this never translated—with a few notable exceptions—into full equality, separate demands, or leadership. In the areas of affect and self-representation, one can observe a more self-assured attitude among women of the 1970s, even though their assertions about total equity are often contradicted by their bitterness about the male-controlled party hierarchy. Women's significant presence compared to earlier years, however, and their "alternative" socialization, including the free management of their private lives and their bodies, were among the most innovative elements in the movement, whose effect was the subversion of long-standing moral codes. In many ways, this shift went hand-in-hand with the exigencies brought forward by the movement's philosophy: the student movement was, after all, a powerful carrier of modernization, in the sense of redefining traditional perceptions of gender relations. And, in this sense, it was in keeping with the general wave of foreign female prototypes in the post-'68 cultural climate, which helped change the way people looked at women as a whole.

Revolutionizing Everyday Life

There is a clear relation between the personal, the everyday, and the political, which includes emotional expressions and symbolic meanings. It is in "everyday life practices" that the connection between conditions of life and subjectivity takes place.[177] In order to understand the tropes of experience, we must understand the transformation of "objective conditions" of action into cultural meanings in the context of everyday production and reproduction.[178]

Long hair proved to be a major issue of contention and concern for the regime, the students, and the media, which systematically treated this trend as an unacceptable sort of androgynous gender bending. Although initially a yé-yé feature, long hair soon became associated with a particular type of leftist politics as well. Colonel Ladas called it "the hirsute flag of nihilism," and the Junta associated it with abnormality ("men becoming women") and homosexuality, which were treated as identical.[179] As long hair became a fashionable means of defiance and a rival to the masculine ideal, a series of negative references started appearing in daily newspapers and pro-regime student journals. Similarly, when the majority of left-wing students wore beards, articles appeared with titles like, "Are beards anti-sexual?"[180] An article in the pro-regime student journal in Salonica criticized the role swapping between men and women that came about when men wore long hair, which supposedly resulted in a lack of decency. Another piece in the same issue rejected smoking pipes as part of a wider set of pretentious and grotesque behavior of left-wingers.[181] Policemen often called male students "poofters" and female students "whores" because of their appearance.

Long hair was not accepted by the traditional working class or hard-core communists either, and it "caused the condescending semi-ironic smile of the leadership of the pure left-wing youth," according to Kallivretakis.[182] Beards, apart from the aforementioned connection with the Greek partisan tradition, were a way of imitating Che Guevara, one of the student movements' mythical figures, omnipresent also in pictures and posters. According to Stergios Katsaros, by 1973 there was no student room in Athens without the poster of Che.[183] Che iconization was also a constant feature in the '68 movements, to the extent that the Libreria Feltrinelli, to take the Italian case, ran out of posters—underlining an awkward mixture of third-worldism, revolutionary iconography, and commodification.[184]

Another point of contention was that clothes such as suits and ties, the standard outfit of the overwhelmingly male-populated universities throughout the 1960s, went out of fashion among politicized students. Young people started redefining their apparel: turtlenecks, jeans, and freewheeling flared trousers became a clearly defined dress-code, while miniskirts and make-up were worn by women less and less. In the summer of 1971, the *Economist* reported that the Greek youth had "adopted the sartorial fashions of their age-groups in London, Paris, Amsterdam and Düsseldorf, though their sense of taste and their personal vanity ensure that they look cleaner, neater and more elegant."[185] In contrast to the article's conclusion, however, a new militant style came into fashion that featured military jackets—an international anti-Vietnam item—which became the necessary accessory of the young rebel's outfit, again suggesting a homeopathic subversion through the use of the military Junta's aesthetics. Kleopatra Papageorgiou describes how a well-known police torturer in Salonica ironically referred to her as a guerilla. She also makes a cultural identity statement when in order to describe her limited stock of blue jeans she refers to a popular rock song of the time:

> Imagine, I had two pairs of blue jeans.... "Cleopatra in blue jeans"! There was such a song at the time, incidentally a rock one. I had two pairs of blue jeans, I was interchanging them until I finished the Polytechnic. Some hobnailed boots from Monastiraki, and Tetradakos asked me, "Are you ready to take to the mountains with those boots?" He thought they were a provocation, that I did it on purpose. (Papageorgiou, interview)

In a more practical way, fashion choices acted as visual markers with subversive content, which facilitated recognition. Stelios Kouloglou observes: "In this period the military jacket was very much in fashion. There was something of Che Guevara in our look. It was a means of recognition. Namely, very few nonpoliticized people wore these kinds of clothes" (Kouloglou, interview). Similarly, Damofli comments on the semiotics of appearance: "I looked at you with your little glasses, you know, and the long hair and the beard and all this. It was something, the gaze, the clothes, all these were signs" (Damofli, interview).

Apart from its subversive character and social disapproval, attire linked the imaginary and the style of the student movements. By mimicking the aesthetics of students in France or the United States, Greek students felt that they were communicating with the movements abroad, even if unconsciously. Mandelou says: "Everyone was wearing a military jacket, and I remember a friend of mine who used to comment on the way I was dressed—she had studied in Paris: 'I think I will soon see you taking a petrol-bomb out of the jacket. You look like that, just like a girl I saw in Paris in May '68'" (Mandelou, interview). A humanities student at the time, Titika Saratsi is one of the few who confesses that she did not adopt these sort of aesthetics, hoping to avoid being a replica of revolutionary prototypes, in this case the iconic Palestinian guerrilla fighter Leila Khaled. Still, she did not follow the "Lenin-Levis" rule either, "out of pure respect for Vladimir Ilyich" as she writes: "I dressed and went around like a normal girl and not in a military jacket and threadbare jeans like some bad imitation of Leila Khaled—my jeans were always well ironed, with everything that this implies."[186] Katerina Detsika too is quick to add a *"comme il faut"* element in her self-representation, clarifying that apart from long hair and black clothes, "We were not shabby" (Detsika, interview).

The students' idiolect and their idiosyncratic conduct were shaped by their strong attachment to culture as a way of living. By 1973, progressive students started to be labeled *koultouriarides*, "artsy fartsies," a term that became inflated during the *Metapolitefsi*.[187] Artist Kostas Lachas describes in a poem the kind of atmosphere that reigned in the favorite haunt of "artsy fartsy students," a tavern named "Domna" in Salonica in the early 1970s: "Domna is thick with smoke and culture / the hullabaloo of empty words / and blasé architects hugging their Marcuse tight."[188] A highly illuminating article published in the newspaper *Thessaloniki* in mid-March 1973 enumerates many of the prejudices about but also the actual habits of young student intellectuals at the time, making specific reference to the dressing habits and the discourse of the "artsy fartsies:"

> The real *koultouriaris* believes that external appearance does not play a role in people's lives, that being occupied with it is something petty bourgeois. For that reason he goes to all the lengthy and often laborious efforts that would make him look as if he does not care about his appearance. In terms of clothing everything is allowed (up to this point rightly so), provided that certain basic rules are not violated, such as: the amount of filthiness should not reach the limits of unacceptability, and the amount of shabbiness should not degrade to a too-striking pennilessness. Prohibited are, of course, all sorts of hats, anything clean washed and ironed, any careful hairbrush or haircut, while, on the contrary, all variations of coats, weird socks

(black for funerals), zippers that come up and down in all directions are allowed (objectively useful only in order to satisfy the speed of a sexual act or the fulfillment of a physical need—but what happens when they get stuck?) and, finally, all folkloric fabrications: belts, skirts, bracelets. The full ensemble very often should be complemented by some trendy book (preferably tatty and grimy) or with an issue of some artsy magazine.[189]

The article goes on to assert that the *koultouriaris* "believes in free love" and adds sarcastically that "at least once in his lifetime he has to contract a venereal disease." Accordingly, "Artsy fartsy circles are impressed by those who suffer." Moving beyond their external appearance, the best way to spot a *koultouriaris,* the article suggests, is in their manner of talking. Being reductive, leaving out articles, and at the same time using intricate phrases to express simple notions were standard. In fact, in the early 1970s, Modern Greek scholar Georgia Gotsi argues, "the interrelation between discourses of censorship, urban life, consumerism, and a politicized version of the American Beat produced new themes and a new language."[190]

A series of semantic neologisms, including derivational prefixes, and a jargon peppered with sophisticated concepts became markers of an alternative and exclusive discourse that delineated a specific sort of identity. This elaborate slang was strongly influenced by the Marxist jargon of the time and constant references to the "process" (of production/history/revolution) as well as the "system."[191] It was further characterized by the frequent use of an excessive (revolutionary) demotic, that is, the use of ch [χ] instead of k [κ], which lent the students' discourse a grassroots flavor. The term διχτατορία, for instance, would be used instead of δικτατορία [dictatorship]. Through the careful appropriation of linguistic choices, the students created a distinctive lingo of their own, used both to define themselves and to mark off their symbolic territory against out-groups, particularly their parents and their "passive" peers. It is noteworthy, that even today former student militants still refer to themselves and their peers of the past as "the kids."

The appearance of a "revolutionary" everyday life based on style and behavior came in stark contrast to the conservative outlook of the previous student generation, whose members' attire and sexual rigidities did not differentiate them from ordinary adults. The new generation made a breakthrough in developing its own approach to socialization and aesthetics, which was reinforced by the difficulties of openly reacting against the regime. In other words, exterior appearance acquired enormous symbolic meaning, as did all the indirect, subterranean semantic codes and signals that implied an oppositional politics to the regime and its own aesthetics. To paraphrase Michel de Certeau, students used formal structures of practice to produce "everyday creativity."[192] This opposition culture provided a channel through which demands of freedom of expression could be voiced.[193] In that sense, "micro-resistances, which in turn found micro-freedoms, mobilize[d] unsuspected resources hidden among ordinary people."[194]

This was an entirely new habitus that created space for dissidence and dissonance, whereby alternative culture became the student's daily bread; young people were reading the political into everything and trained themselves to read between the lines in all forms of cultural expression. All this was about to come to a head in the ten months that shook Greece in 1973, resulting in the most spectacular act of collective resistance to take place during the seven years of the dictatorship.

Notes

1. For the concept of "information monopolies" see Bermeo, "War and Democratization," 392 (referring to Jack Snyder, *Myths of Empire*, 72).
2. Plaskovitis, "Years of Memory," 245.
3. Van Dyck, *Kassandra and the Censors*, 25.
4. Michel Foucault, *The History of Sexuality*, 27. For an elaboration of this notion, see Eugene Irschick's reflections on the British-Indian example in *Dialogue and History*, esp. 1–11.
5. Van Dyck, *Kassandra and the Censors*, 85. In her book Van Dyck offers an excellent overview of comic strip artists' techniques during the Junta years.
6. Andrews, *Greece in the Dark*, 176.
7. A-74 Confidential, American Consulate Thessaloniki (Brennan) to the Department of State, "Antonios Kourtis, Publisher of 'Thessaloniki,'" 24 October 1972, POL 6 Greece, USNA.
8. Iordanoglou, "Antidictatorship Student Movement," 278.
9. See, for example *Thessaloniki*, 13 January and 21 January 1972. The antiregime press used almost identical techniques in Franco's Spain. In October 1968, for example, a half-page image appeared in the newspaper *Madrid*, showing police beating protesting students under the tiny title "The Peruvian students protest against the Junta." PP, "Los estudiantes peruanos protestan contra la Junta," *Madrid*, 9 October 1968.
10. For a brief testimony by Kourtis, see "Resistance in Print through the Pages of the Newspaper *Thessaloniki*" in *Dictatorship 1967 1974. Resistance in Print*, 168–72. In the same volume also see Giorgos Anastasiadis, "The Printed Word of the Resistance against the Dictatorship (1967–1974): The example of the newspaper *Thessaloniki*," 128–32.
11. Immediately preceding the publication of the *Eighteen Texts* many of the contributors to the volume had signed a letter of protest against the intended publication of an anthology of prose by the regime, which undermined the premise that writers were resisting through silence. After the "Letter of the Eighteen," as it became

known, the anthology was withdrawn. See Van Dyck, *Kassandra and the Censors*, 26–27; and Papanikolaou, "Making Some Strange Gestures," 180.
12. Roufos, "Culture and the Military," 159.
13. Other collective publications such as *Neoi Poiites* [New Poets], *Katathesi '71* [Testimony '71], and *Katathesi '72* were also inspired by the need to be evasive or slippery for the sake of conveying a dissident message.
14. Anagnostakis, "Άγραφη Ιστορία" [Unwritten Story], *I Synecheia* 2 (April 1973): 3. Original emphasis.
15. Rigos, "Student Movement," 232.
16. Sotiropoulou, *Political Book*, 2.
17. Ibid., 4.
18. Sofoulis, "Social Sciences," 92–93.
19. Andrews, *Greece in the Dark*, 176.
20. The *Themelio* series was confiscated following the decree issued by the Junta on 12 May 1967 banning books by Marxist scholars, educational reformers, writers resident in Eastern Europe, and writers of "left-of-center" sympathies.
21. Sotiropoulou, *Political Book*, 4.
22. Ralos, "Μερικές σκέψεις για το κοινωνιολογικό βιβλίο" [Some Thoughts on Sociological Books]. I Synecheia 7 (Sept. 1973)
23. Ralos, "Παθήματα των βιβλίων στις μεταφράσεις και εισαγωγές άσχετες προς το περιεχόμενό τους" [Books' Misfortunes in Translations and Introductions Irrelevant to their Content]. I Synecheia 3 (May 1973): 189–90. A typical example was Th. Papadopoulos's introduction to a translation of Gramsci's Intellectuals, which attempts to find connections with the Greek War of Independence of 1821.
24. Sofoulis, "Social Sciences," 93.
25. Theodoridis, *Macedonian Rock*, 203.
26. Kotanidis, *All Together, Now!*
27. See Hamalidi et al., "A Second Avant-Garde without a First." In particular Leonidas Christakis, the idiosyncratic publisher of *Kouros* and *Panderma*, published on several occasions German antifascist photomontages on the front or back cover of his issues, drawing direct parallels between Nazism and the Greek dictatorship. Ibid, 10.
28. The editors of *Tram,* among whom was Panos Theodoridis, were tried in Salonica in 1972 for publishing "indecent" texts. The publisher of *Anti*, Christos Papoutsakis, in Athens managed to publish one issue in May 1972, causing a sensation, but then the journal was closed down by the authorities and he was arrested and tortured.
29. Cockburn et al., introduction to *Student Power,* 16.
30. Ibid., 7.
31. Fred Halliday, "Student Struggles: Spain," cited in *Protoporia* 2 (Jan. 1972). For a detailed analysis of the student resistance against Franco's regime in Spain see Maravall, *Dictatorship and Political Dissent* and Kornetis, "Student Resistance to the Greek Military Dictatorship." Also see Kornetis, "1968 in Spain and Greece."
32. Johnston, "Talking the Walk," 108.
33. Primo Moroni and Bruna Miorelli, "Storia e problemi della piccola editoria," *Ombre Rosse* 30 (Sept. 1979): 93–103, quoted in Lumley, *States of Emergency,* 39.
34. David Tonge, "Brecht Alienates Colonels," *Guardian,* 10 February 1972.

35. Axelos, *Publishing Activity*, 52. According to Axelos, these books offered students basic feedback on resisting not only the regime but also the old Left's arteriosclerotic stance—a common "biological" metaphor in Greek—and its traditional viewpoint. See also Lygeros, *Student Movement*, 69.
36. Kokkali, "Greek Cinema," 137.
37. *Ellinikos Kinimatografos*, 1967, 29–31, cited in Van Dyck, *Kassandra and the Censors*, 85.
38. Gounaridou, "Representations of Women in the Films of Pantelis Voulgaris," 151.
39. Petros Morozinis, *Kouros*, February 1971, quoted in Savvopoulos, *Sum Up*, 115.
40. From the television documentary by Stavros Kaplanidis *History of My Times*, dedicated to the making of Angelopoulos's first feature film *Reconstruction* (1970).
41. See Angelopoulos's personal site http://www.theoangelopoulos.com/daysof36.htm. Last checked 8 August 2013. In an interview to film critic Ulrich Gregor in 1973 Angelopoulos was even more outspoken: "What I was looking for was a certain climate. A reign of terror." See Fainaru, *Theo Angelopoulos*, 14.
42. Soldatos quoted in the documentary *We Have Decided and We Order*, by Eva Vernardou and Nikos Sarlis.
43. Komninou, "Television and Cinema."
44. Theodoridis, *Macedonian Rock*, 183.
45. Kaplanidis, *History of My Times*.
46. Kokkali, "Greek Cinema," 143–44.
47. Introduction to Darveris's *Night's Story*, 22.
48. These two films reached more than 150,000 admissions in the period of their release (1970), as *Woodstock* and the *Strawberry Statement* did in the same year. See Chrysanthi Sotiropoulou, *Greek Cinematography*, 140.
49. Miliex, "Continuous Vigilance," 347.
50. Papanikolaou, "Singing Poets," 153.
51. Kallivretakis, "Historicizing the Rock Phenomenon," 172.
52. Papanikolaou, "Singing Poets," 188.
53. Dimitris Psathas, *Ta Nea*, 29 November 1970.
54. See for example Ryback, *Rock around the Bloc*.
55. "Απαντήσεις του κ. Γεωργαλά σε ερωτήσεις των φοιτητών για την πολιτική κατάσταση της χώρας" [Mr. Georgalas's Responses to the Students about the Country's Political Situation], *Thessaloniki*, 1 December 1970.
56. Both *My Aunt, the Hippie*, directed by Alekos Sakellarios, and *A Hippie with Tsarouchia*, directed by Giorgos Papakostas, were released in 1970.
57. Vernikos, *Antidictatorship Student Movement*, 152.
58. "Swallows Winging South," *Economist*, 31 July 1971.
59. Ibid.
60. Bozinis, *Rock Globality and Greek Locality*, 346. Also see "Η δεκαετία του '70. Η Ελλάδα στα ράφια" [The 70s: Greece on the Shelf], in Papapolizos and Martzoukos, *Greece through Advertising*, 148–51.
61. Kunen, *Strawberry Statement*. The whereabouts of the revolt are purposely never mentioned in the movie.
62. Telegram from American Embassy, Athens, to Secretary of State, 6423, 24 November 1970, Tasca, POL 23–8 Greece, USNA.

63. Mulvey, "Visual Pleasure," 382.
64. Ortoleva, "Le culture del '68," 58. Cinema was regarded as an ideal middle way between literary elitism and flat television culture.
65. Andrews, *Greece in the Dark*, 177.
66. Grigoriou, *Memories in Black and White*, 124.
67. *Eleftheros Kosmos*, September 1970, quoted by Grigoriou, *Memories in Black and White*.
68. In Kotanidis's memoirs there are plenty of references to people using commercial tunes in everyday parlance, including fellow actor Periklis Korovesis responding to his torturers, "I am the almighty Vim" (a reference to a well-known detergent commercial) when asked if he was a communist during interrogation. *All Together, Now!*, 84. Interestingly, torturers themselves used the name of a well-known detergent (Tide) as a code name for a particular kind of "treatment." See Minuzzo, *Quando arrivano i Colonnelli*.
69. All references from an article by Gavriil Th. Lamtsidis, "Ο Ιπποκράτης, η δημοκρατία και η γαλαρία του Φεστιβάλ" [Hippocrates, Democracy, and the Back Seats of the Festival], *Thessaloniki*, 28 September 1972.
70. Ibid.
71. Papadogiannis, "Between Angelopoulos and the Battleship Potemkin," 19. Papadogiannis quotes film historian Janet Staiger, "Writing the History of American Film Reception."
72. The critic Natasa Bakogiannopoulou in the women's magazine *Gynaika* [Woman] in October 1973. Quoted in Kokkali, "Greek Cinema," 145.
73. Van Steen, *Venom in Verse*, 205.
74. "Athens Ban on Greek Classical Plays," *New York Times*, 28 June 1967.
75. Ibid.
76. Ibid.
77. Van Steen, *Venom in Verse*.
78. "Το Θέατρο, το Κοινό και άλλα. Γιατί επέστρεψε έπειτα από πέντε χρόνια απουσίας. Συνέντευξη της Άννας Συνοδινού στο BBC" [The Theater, the Audience and the Rest: Why She Came Back after Five Years of Absence; Interview of Anna Synodinou with the BBC], *Thessaloniki*, 14 November 1972.
79. *Anoichto Theatro*, editorial, 1 November 1971.
80. Mackridge, "Theater in the Colonels' Greece," 4.
81. Maravall, *Dictatorship and Political Dissent*, 137.
82. "Η «Νέα Σκηνή» του ΚΘΒΕ και οι φοιτητές" [The "New Scene" of *KThBE* and the Students], interview with G. Kitsopoulos, the general director of the State Theater of Salonica (KThBE), *O Foititis*, 4 December 1972.
83. *Protoporia* 1.
84. Lamtsidis, "Ο άντρας είναι άντρας" [A Man Is a Man], *Thessaloniki*, 18 November 1972.
85. Hager, "From the Margin to the Mainstream," 164.
86. Kotanidis, *All Together, Now!*, 87.
87. *To Vima*, June 1973.
88. Elefthero Theatro, "One Text," 193. Here I am using Hager's translation, "From the Margin to the Mainstream," 163.

89. Hager, ibid., 196.
90. See Markaris, *Repeatedly and Persistently.* For a detailed analysis of the play and its production see Hager, "From the Margin to the Mainstream."
91. Lakidou, "Theatrical Satire and Dictatorship," 6.
92. Ibid., 11.
93. Ibid., 13. Lakidou rightly notes that much of the subject matter was influenced by homosexual writer Kostas Tachtsis's bestselling novel *The Third Wedding* [To Trito Stefani] (1962), a very convincing depiction of the lower-middle-class discourse and mores at the time.
94. Varopoulou, "Theater 1974–2000," 227.
95. From Koumandos's preface to the published version of the play by Kambanellis, *Our Grand Circus,* 5. Quoted by Van Steen, "Joining our Grand Circus," 307.
96. See Kallimopoulou, *Paradosiaká,* 20.
97. Van Steen, "Joining our Grand Circus," 306.
98. Ibid., 309. Also see Hager, "From the Margin to the Mainstream."
99. Iakovos Kambanellis in Stavros Stratigakos's documentary *Nikos Xylouris and Three Poems,* ET1, 8 February 2005.
100. Giorgos Hadjidakis, "Ενός χρόνου" [One Year Old], *Anoichto Theatro* 12 (1972): 4–5.
101. Kotanidis, *All Together, Now!,* 194–207.
102. Hager, "From the Margin to the Mainstream," 108.
103. *Black-White* makes extensive references to pop culture in general, as one of the protagonists is a student of fine arts who spent his semester abroad in the United States. He mentions Pop Art and uses English words in his discourse, delineating the differences between Greek students at home and those studying abroad.
104. Kallivretakis, "Historicizing the Rock Phenomenon," 172.
105. Papanikolaou, "Singing Poets," 93.
106. Michael Wall, "A Hundred Days of Dictatorship," *Guardian,* 5 August 1967.
107. One result of this policy, according to the *New York Times,* was that Theodorakis's records became more expensive, even more than doubling in price. "The News Team Investigates the Fate of Greeks Who Fail to Conform: Even Football Is under State Supervision," 14 July 1967.
108. Papanikolaou, "Singing Poets," 94.
109. Ibid., 24.
110. See Kallimopoulou, *Paradosiaká.*
111. Interview with Dimitris Gionis, *Avgi,* March 1975.
112. Interview by Rena S., *Epikaira,* December 1970.
113. Karapostolis, *Consumerist Behavior,* 293.
114. See, for example, Giorgos Hadjidakis's editorial "One Year Old," *Anoichto Theatro.*
115. Gracia, García, and Carnicer, *La España de Franco,* 297.
116. This trend in Greece became, to borrow a description from Ron Eyerman and Andrew Jamison, "one of the main mediating forces, forms of translation, between the [student] movement's more obvious expressions—demonstrations, organizations, books and journals—and the wider population." See Eyerman and Jamison, *Music and Social Movements,* 119.
117. Ibid., 138.

118. Ibid., 124.
119. Interview by Rena S., *Epikaira*, December 1970.
120. Robert Shelton, *No Direction Home*, 15.
121. Giorgos Notaras, "Filthy Bread," 115.
122. Giorgos Karambelias, *For Savvopoulos* (Nicosia, 1985), 50. Quoted and translated in Papanikolaou, "Singing Poets," 218.
123. From the description of Kyttaro's history in the club's website. http://www.kyttaro live.gr/content/blogcategory/24/70/ Last accessed 8 August 2013.
124. From the jacket of the new edition of the *Live at Kyttaro* CD.
125. From the Antonis Boskoitis's documentary *Live at Kyttaro. Rock Scenes.*
126. Olga Bakomarou, "Μπουρμπούλια: Καινούργιοι δρόμοι" [Bourboulia: New Paths], *Fantasio*, 6 February 1973.
127. Stelios Elliniadis, "Ο πρίγκηπας της δισκογραφίας" [The Prince of the Record Industry], in *E-On Line*, 6 August 2002.
128. Theodoridis, *Macedonian Rock*, 322.
129. Kallivretakis, "Historicizing the Rock Phenomenon," 172.
130. Here, I am using Papanikolaou's translation. See "Singing Poets," 140.
131. "Οι συναυλίες της Μαρίζας Κωχ" [Marisa Koch's Concerts], *Thessaloniki*, 10 April 1973.
132. Theodoridis, *Macedonian Rock*, 241.
133. From the record sleeve of *Μαρίζα Κώχ. Στο 'πα και στο ξαναλέω. Παραδοσιακά— λαϊκά—προσωπικά. 40 ηχογραφήσεις 1970–1992* [Marisa Koch: I Told You Once, I'm Telling You Again: Folk Songs—Popular Songs—Personal Ones. 40 Recordings, 1970–1992].
134. Another major exponent of this tendency was the group Anakara.
135. Van Dyck, *Kassandra and the Censors*, 51.
136. Mitras, "Συζητώντας με το Διονύση Σαββόπουλο" [Conversing with Dionysis Savvopoulos], in *Chronicle 1972*, 215.
137. Marisa Koch's performance of a "harmed" folk song ["Armenaki"] in a video clip that was presented on television is quite telling of this conflation. Apart from the melding of electric bass guitars and the folk melody, Koch—dressed in perfect hippie fashion—was surrounded by an entirely psychedelic setting.
138. For an elaboration of this practice in the Spanish context, see Kaplan, *Red City, Blue Period.*
139. Cowan, "Popular Music." To Cowan's translation of *xasteria* as "clear skies," I prefer Andrews' "the season of starry nights." See *Greece in the Dark*, 56.
140. Another mythical song of the time containing references to revolutionary violence was Theodorakis's "A Solitary Swallow" [*Ena to chelidoni*] (1964). Based on Odysseus Elytis's *To Axion Esti*, the song concludes in an almost Jacobin way: "For the sun to turn it takes a job of work / It takes a thousand dead sweating at the Wheels / It takes the living also giving up their blood."
141. Van Boeschoten, *From Armatolik to People's Rule.*
142. Guffey, *Retro: The Culture of Revival*, 20.
143. Song entitled "Freedom Will Come Again to Our Poor Country" [Θάρθει, μωρέ, ξανά η λευτεριά στη δόλια μας πατρίδα] in Takis Mamatsis, "Οι αγώνες των φοιτητών" [The Student Struggles], *Neos Kosmos* (June 1973): 6.

144. Holst, *Road to Rembetika*.
145. Cowan, "Popular Music," 11. Here, I am using Cowan's translation.
146. See Clarke, et al., "Subcultures, Cultures, and Class," 10.
147. "Η Σωτηρία Μπέλλου συγκεντρώνει την προτίμησι των φοιτητών που ξετρελλαίνονται για ρεμπέτικο τραγούδι" [Sotiria Bellou Is Preferred by Students Who Get Mad about Rembetiko Songs], *O Foititis*, 9 April 1973. The same article continues, "*Rembetiko*, which touches a large part of the student world, finds in Bellou an 'authentic' interpreter and is applauded."
148. 'Καταδικάστηκαν οι 'χίππυς' που συμμετείχαν σε χασισοποτεία και όργια σε τεκέ στο Κουκάκι' [The "Hippies" Who Participated in Hashish Consumption and Orgies in a Dive in Koukaki Have Been Convicted], *Thessaloniki*, 12 October 1973.
149. See Eyerman and Jamison, *Music and Social Movements*, 42.
150. Interview with the nightclub's owner, K. Manioudakis, in Stratigakos's documentary *Nikos Xylouris and Three Poems*.
151. Cowan, "Popular Music," 3.
152. See Bakhtin, *Speech Genres*.
153. Hobsbawm, *The Age of Extremes*, 334.
154. Alberoni, *Falling in Love*, 3.
155. Ibid. Also see Peter Braunstein, "Possessive Memory and the Sixties Generation," *Culturefront*, Summer 1997, 66.
156. Kanellakis, "In Those Years," 49.
157. Papadopoulos, *Our Creed*, 134.
158. Eliou, "Those Whom Reform Forgot," 69. Still, women remained largely unrepresented in professional training colleges in the same year, numbering only 18,146 out of a total of 123,081 students, or 14.7 percent. Ibid., 67.
159. American Consul Thessaloniki to Department of State, "Follow Up on Rightist Student Demonstration, University of Thessaloniki, December 8, 1970," 14 January 1971, XR POL 13–2 Greece, USNA.
160. "Φοιτήτρια σε τρείς πράξεις" [Female Student in Three Acts], *Protoporia* 2 (Jan. 1972).
161. Ibid.
162. Valiant washing machine commercial titled "For the Emancipation of the Housewife," in Papapolizos and Martzoukos, *Greece through Advertising*.
163. Papapolizos and Martzoukos, *Greece through Advertising*. The shampoo's name was a translation of the Italian original "Libera e Bella."
164. Coerant, "On Their Own," 116.
165. Darveris, *Night's Story*, 130.
166. Donatella della Porta, Celia Valiete, and Maria Kousis, "Sisters of the South: Paths to Women's Rights in Southern Europe," unpublished paper, 7.
167. Tachtsis, *Terrible Step*, 288.
168. Ibid., 299.
169. Passerini, "'Utopia' and Desire," 14.
170. Historian Richard Clogg mentions an incident early on in the Junta years (1968) in which the then secretary-general of the Ministry of Public Order, Ioannis Ladas, "personally beat up the author of an article in the weekly magazine *Eikones*,

together with its editor, Panagiotis Lambrias, for having the temerity to suggest in an article on homosexuality that many of the worthies of ancient Greece had been homosexual." Clogg, "The Ideology of the Revolution of 21 April 1967," 41.
171. "Έρευνα της Μαίρης Πρινιωτάκη "Ο ρόλος της φοιτήτριας στην σημερινή κοινωνία" [Enquiry by Mary Priniotaki: The Role of the Female Student in Present Society], *O Foititis*, 1 March 1972.
172. Zannas, *Prison Notebooks*, 138.
173. Papachristos, *He Lived Life*, 29.
174. Herzog, "Between Coitus and Commodification," 281.
175. Darveris, *Night's Story*, 131.
176. Karatzaferis, *Polytechnic Slaughter*, 197.
177. Luedtke, "Historiography of Everyday Life," 38. I owe this reference to Dimitra Lambropoulou.
178. Ibid., 44, 52.
179. Van Dyck, *Kassandra and the Censors*, 104. See also special issue of *Epikaira*, "Μακριά μαλλιά. Από τον Αδάμ στους χίππηδες" [Long Hair: From Adam to the Hippies], Ibid.
180. *Thessaloniki*, 16 February 1973.
181. "Οι πίπες" [The Pipes], *O Foititis*, 16 September 1972; and "Βασίλης ή Κούλα" [Vassilis or Koula?], *O Foititis*, 16 October 1972.
182. Kallivretakis, "Historicizing the Rock Phenomenon," 172.
183. In Stelios Kouloglou, *The Children of Che in Greece*, television documentary.
184. Prestholdt, "Resurrecting Che: Radicalism, the Transnational Imagination, and the Politics of Heroes."
185. "Two-Headed Phoenix," *Economist*, 31 July 1971.
186. Saratsi, "For Epi," 102.
187. See Magia Lymberopoulou's illustrative comment of 1975: "Greeks conceptualize the word κουλτούρα [culture] as an illness." "Κουλτουριάρης, κουλτουρισμένος, κατά το ψωριάρης, ψωριασμένος" [Artsy Fartsy, Just Like Scabby], *Politika Themata* 72, no. 8 (29 Nov.–5 Dec. 1975).
188. Zafeiris, "Youth Hang-outs in the '60s," 58. I would like to thank Karen Emmerich for the translation of this short poem.
189. Atzil, "Ο δεκάλογος του κουλτουριάρη" [The Decalogue of the Artsy Fartsy], *Thessaloniki*, 14 March 1973.
190. Gotsi, Review of *Kassandra and the Censors*, 353.
191. See Bozinis, *Rock Globality*, 345–46.
192. Certau, *Practice of Everyday Life*, xiv–xvi.
193. Graham and Labanyi, "Developmentalism," 257.
194. Certeau, Giard, and Mayol, *Living and Cooking*, xxi.

Chapter 5

Ten Months that Shook Greece

Chapter 5 chronicles the events that led to the clash between the students and the regime, reconstructing the ten-month countdown to the climax of the student movement and its ultimate suppression. Further, this chapter explores the processes put in motion at the peak of the Junta's "liberalization experiment" and the main public expressions of the student revolt: the November 1973 Polytechnic occupations in both Athens and Salonica and their forerunners, the Athens Law School occupations in February and March of the same year. The chapter closes with the aftermath of the Polytechnic, including the brief interregnum of the Ioannidis dictatorship and the abrupt passage to the postdictatorship period in the summer of 1974, the so-called *Metapolitefsi*. It traces the continuation of the student movement with its parallel radicalization and disintegration, this time under democratic conditions.

The 1973 Reforms and Student Radicalization

By 1973, the Colonels' regime was approaching the apogee of its liberalization experiment. Georgios Papadopoulos had decided to personalize the regime (serving as regent, prime minister, minister of foreign affairs, minister of defense, and minister of government policy) and to some extent to enforce the Constitution of 1968.[1] Beginning in late 1972 with a counseling committee, or "miniparliament," as it came to be known, Papadopoulos urged his trusted men to speed up the process of restoring some form of parliamentarism. The state's attitude to protest had meanwhile been wavering. In the beginning, always in line with the normalization experiment, protest policing—the barometer of the political opportunities available for social movements—was milder, a situation that favors the diffusion of protest.[2] In contrast to the period of "clandestinity," public space became the object of contestation. As students were denied a private space (any indoor assembly of three or more people was prohibited), public spaces such as squares and avenues became the territory of open confrontation, and students began to favor collective action expressed in large demonstrations, gatherings, and clashes with the police.

The student movement acquired a greater following, higher visibility, and, occasionally, open support. This helped to render the conflict public, to turn it toward more successful forms of struggle, and ultimately to fuse it into a movement. During this time, the notorious Security Police were actively trying to decipher the mechanism of student mobilization by arresting and torturing those identified as the main student agitators and leaders. Once it became obvious that there was serious potential within the movement, Junta authorities again resorted to extreme forms of public violence. Confrontations between students and police forces became increasingly brutal.

Although Greek students did not respond to state-sponsored violence with violence, they did not remain entirely passive. Part of their repertoire was verbally attacking the policemen. An *Economist* report from the period describes one such incident:

> [T]his fairly parochial protest might have died down in a few days, but a government official (no one is certain who he was) sent squads of policemen to the campus to break up a meeting on the sub-engineer problem. Outraged by the "violation" of the university, students began taunting the invading cops with cries of "Fascists!" and "Gestapo!" For good measure, some also threw in two peculiarly Greek insults: *pustis,* meaning the passive partner in a homosexual relationship, and *malakas* (masturbator). The police responded by beating and dragging off a number of the student demonstrators; eleven of them were charged with "insulting authority." Eight students were later found guilty and given eleven-month suspended sentences.[3]

What is interesting to note here is that the students' confrontation with the police involved a performance of masculinity, not only on the side of the policemen, but notably on that of the activists as well—a tendency that has remained largely unaltered in terms of Greek protest culture up to the present day. Students habitually called policemen "Fascists," "Nazis," "lackeys," "starved out," and "sellouts." They were often accused of spitting on police and of using a slogan that irritated their adversaries and which was to become a motto: "Eleftheria" [Freedom].

Frequent clashes with the police, charged with adrenaline and risk, acted as rites of initiation for students, a necessary step toward radicalization and immersion in the movement. Giannis Kourmoulakis, himself of a "national-minded" family, describes the different stages of initiation, including the passage from passivity to action:

We passed the phase of noninvolvement, energetic involvement, and nonintense politicization, as far as the Junta's years are concerned; we started entering some events actively and politically minded. They summoned us to the police, they gave us warnings, during the first phase what happened was what I'm telling you: "You are from a good family, why do you get in trouble?" and so forth. Then they called us to the police station "for a private matter." (Kourmoulakis, interview)

Clashes constituted an "expressive behavior," insofar as they tended to be ends in themselves: part of their objective was the constitution of a new identity on the part of the students.[4] All testimonies stress that clashes were part of the everyday routine, a constant hide-and-seek. Dimitris Papachristos frames his decision to circulate a petition in the ASOEE School of Commerce in the context of his passage through the rite of conflict: "In any case they knew us. We had been caught; we had been beaten up; what more could they do to us?" (Papachristos, interview).

The twelve students of ASOEE who passed on the petition, a set of proposals on how to improve the functioning of the university, were summoned by the rector and were given severe warnings. In their plea, they talked about their need to be involved in the learning and educational processes in general, to prevent football and pool from monopolizing the media and "alienating the students' intellect," and to seek instead authentic knowledge:

> Our destination is not to become low-range professionals, little screws with preconceived roles within the social system. We did not climb up to Higher Education in order to remain passive listeners to dry knowledge.... We do not ask for truth to be served ready to us.... Formalized thought and expression, the lack of any imagination, any personal structure, gives us the creeps. We are struggling to improve our intellectual forces, even with mistakes, even under pressure.[5]

Contrary to the petition, which was articulated in formal and scientific language, this outburst is a very authentic text, probably the only one produced by students and made public at the time. It encapsulates in a particularly clear manner students' anger toward an educational system that did not meet their expectations. The reference to football as an element of manipulation is a recurrent one, but the demand for participation in all educational processes and the students' indignation with the unimaginative and static aspects of Greek intellectual life were strikingly novel. The publication of the plea created an unprecedented wave of solidarity with the twelve and took the movement another step forward toward becoming a truly mass movement.

At the same time, regime supporters were expressing their disgust with those who mouthed their opinions without knowing the "real student issues" at stake. According to their accusations, the antiregime students were patronizing professional trade unionists with no real knowledge of student problems and only went to the refectory and the assemblies but never attended classes. The resigned student council of electrical engineers—students who had been appointed by the regime—went further in expressing its rejection of the politics of antiregime students, arguing that there were issues more vital to student well-being than "the abolition of the disciplinary council, US or European imperialism, the solidarity of the building workers and the creation of a climate of anarchy and unaccountability in the higher educational institutions."[6] The contrast between the two preceding discourses, with both antiregime and pro-regime students becoming increasingly outspoken in terms of their prerogatives, delineates the growing radicalization of the two opposing spheres within the student body that consolidated the abyssal chasm between them.

The Movement Gains Prestige

In late January 1973, several students confronted raiding policemen in the area of the Athens Polytechnic, an incident that came to be known as the "little Polytechnic." Eleven were arrested and tried on several charges, including "insulting authority" and "teddyboyism." The little Polytechnic took place as a result of the students' decision to switch to the offensive: a student delegation had sent a memorandum to the rector of the Athens Polytechnic to inform him that students were struggling for intellectual freedom and academic dignity. The text concluded, "We struggle for the benefit of our nation."[7] Despite its careful wording, this text demonstrates the confidence that the students had in their "mission." The regime's immediate reaction was to stiffen its attitude by issuing decree 1347/73; it was the second decree authorizing the regime to forcefully conscript male students who acted in an "antinational" manner but the first one to be implemented.

In an unprecedented move, Polytechnic professors opted to oppose the decree. At the time, students were gathered in the courtyard of the Polytechnic staging an anti-Junta demonstration with slogans such as "Fascism shall not pass" and "Down with conscription." The students began chanting "Torturers out" as the building was encircled by police. Police forces entered the Polytechnic and beat the students, violating the asylum of the university and even attacking students inside professors' offices. Professors who dared oppose this behavior were equally harassed.[8] This helps to explain why the trial of the eleven arrested students that took place from 16 to 19 February 1973 turned into a political event.

A number of prominent political figures who opposed the Junta took on the defense of the arrested students. As a result, the trial received immense publicity, probably contributing to its brevity and the students' ultimate escape from punishment. For the first time, pictures of students with bruises caused by police beatings appeared in the papers, contributing to the rise of sympathy for the combatant youth. As Susan Sontag notes in her seminal book *On Photography*, "photographs shock insofar as they show something novel."[9] In the case of the beaten-up students the novelty lies in the fact that there was nothing banal about them: there was no familiarity of the public with such images, despite the clandestine press and the foreign reports, the dismissal of Greece from the Council of Europe on grounds of torture in 1969, and many people's first-hand experience of the regime's brutality. Above all, these photographs shocked the people who were not familiar with such practices or were reluctant to believe that the regime was indeed as harsh as some people were suggesting. More importantly, the faces of the students who were subjected to grievous bodily harm became, to quote Michel Foucault, the site of "political investment":[10] the political investment of the entire antiregime sphere against an authoritarian regime that was all too willing to resort to coercion in order to assert its authority (in spite of its supposed liberalization).

Figure 5.1. An antiregime student, Makis Balaouras, during the "Trial of the Eleven", with visible evidence of police brutality on his face. The fact that this photo was allowed to be published by a magazine such as *Epikaira,* alongside other images of arrested students with bruises, shocked the public but also indicated the controversial nature of the regime's "controlled liberalization." (Courtesy Olga Balaoura)

During the trial, Emmanouil Tzannetis, a Polytechnic student accused of "teddyboyism" and misconduct against policemen, accused the police in his turn of excessive brutality: "I have been dragged by the hair, like Hector by Achilles."[11] Apart from describing a violent scene, Tzannetis, by comparing himself to Hector, placed himself within a mythological paradigm with strong associational resonance. Elements of narcissism go hand-in-hand with violence and suffering in his graphic description. Long hair becomes a symbolic, almost heroic feature. As newspaper reports and student recollections confirm, it was a common police tactic to pull men and women alike by their hair. At the notorious "interview-interrogation" that the well-known television presenter and music producer of this period Nikos Mastorakis conducted with arrested students following the Polytechnic events that took place later on that year, one of the students stated bluntly on camera that his hair was cut off by policemen right after his arrest. Mastorakis, himself a long-haired man, expressed his great surprise.[12]

"Anything but May '68": The Law School Occupations

On 14 February 1973, on the eve of the "Trial of the Eleven", the first occupation of the Law School took place as a protest against police brutality. Several student issues were put forward, following the standard strategy of the movement at the time, which favored "student" over "political" demands. The great publicity that the little Polytechnic had acquired contributed to the students' decision to occupy the school, an event that lasted only a few hours. Still, the occupation was a qualitative leap for the movement, the result of growing radicalism and self-confidence, and Papadopoulos met it with a decisive move: 120 male students who were supposedly among the most active were given short notice that their suspension of military service for study reasons was no longer active and that they should appear in the army headquarters in order to "serve the patria." Deputy Minister Pattakos commented that being drafted to serve in the Greek Army was not punishment but good training, and if the students were hard working, they could still manage to graduate earlier than others. "Real students should not fear anything," he remarked.[13] Military conscription was a severe penalty, however, as it violently interrupted student life, and the army as an institution was the direct extension of the Junta and everything that it represented.[14] Compulsory drafting was being exercised at about the same time by the military regimes in Spain and, especially, Portugal, during its colonial wars in Africa.

The immediate student response was new mobilizations, this time to demand the return of the conscripted. The Junta's decision to show a tough face backfired when the draft threat proved to be a major rallying factor, just as it did in the United States during the Vietnam War. Moreover, the conscription of the Law School students acted as a springboard for the radicalization of the student movement, ensuring a lasting mobilization. Those who had been taken away acquired heroic status; their release became the standard objective of the whole movement. This pattern played out in the student mobilizations in Greece for the liberation of imprisoned and conscripted students under the slogan "Give us our brothers back!"[15]

Their action repertoire enriched by the experience of 14 February, anti-Junta students decided to remain inside the Law School building overnight the following week. On 21 February, some three thousand people barricaded themselves inside the Law School building in the center of Athens for about two days in an action organized by A-EFEE (and to a lesser extent by Rigas) and carried out mostly by law and humanities students. Physics and math students were by and large excluded because of the leftist character of their student leaders and their confrontational attitude, which aimed for the popular overthrow of the Junta. A-EFFE and Rigas wanted instead to restrict themselves to student demands, a focus that would soon be overtaken by the movement's own dynamics.[16] The student action was further enhanced by an occupation committee and a ritual: they made an oath that praised the student youth of Greece and rejected "the violence and terrorism" of the regime.[17] Ioanna Karystiani records this moment as one of the most vivid in her memory, as she was the one who drafted the oath, though she describes the text as insignificant (Karystiani, interview). Ex-student militant and present-day analyst Olympios Dafermos writes that the oath was awkward and out of tune with the character of the occupation.[18] The text referred to a relentless struggle on the part of the students for freedom and demanded the guarantee of asylum and the abolition of repressive laws. It further declared solidarity with the tormented students, rejected terrorization, and concluded: "Long live the student world of Greece." This epic gesture had no clear-cut purpose, but its declaration added to the theatricality and symbolic charge of the practice of occupation.

In addition to drafting the oath, the students appeared on the building's terrace, where they sang the classic *rizitiko* song "Xasteria" and shouted slogans about student matters, which soon turned to anti-Junta slogans despite the directives of the two main organizations behind the occupation. Karystiani recalls with emotion that it was on the Law School terrace that students wrote the first anti-American slogans, including "Americans Out." For the first time, slogans such as "Down with the Junta" and "Democracy" were uttered publically, aiming at more than one interlocutor—that is, at the police and all those who found themselves in the center of Athens. Similar slogans, including "No to football," were written on fliers and thrown down to the streets, and at some point large cartons marked with the letters F-R-E-E-D-O-M were placed along the terrace. This was the moment in which the students broke free from fear. Vera Damofli remembers:

> It had never happened before during the dictatorship period that a building was occupied and [protesters] shouted "Down with the Junta," "Long live Freedom," and other slogans, sometimes far-out ones as well, which were thrown and people picked them up. Because, you know, in the beginning there was a directive that we shouldn't say "Down with the Junta," we should say "Freedom," "Democratic Liberties," "Student Rights" instead. (Damofli, interview)

Soon, passers-by stopped to look up at the rare and unexpected spectacle. Many stopped out of curiosity, others out of solidarity. They did not rush to go home but instead stayed to watch. When the students called for solidarity, some dared to shout, "We stand at your side!" Motorists honked their horns. Soon, an immense traffic jam had begun all over Sina, Panepistimiou, and Solonos Streets, marking the first participation—albeit indirect—of private citizens in a student event. Stavros Lygeros, a student leader of the leftist OSE, describes this atmosphere: "We are talking about a situation of being besieged—we did not even have food, if you can imagine—and the people below [on the streets] were worrying. They were waiting at the bus stops intentionally, as an expression of solidarity." (Lygeros, interview). This was the moment in which the antiregime students ceased feeling like a "Generation of Robinsons," to use historian Jean-François Sirinelli's term, doomed to be isolated, with no one to hear or share their frustrations.[19] Sociologist Anna Mantoglou quotes a student at the time who remembers this change with enthusiasm: "The people were supporting us ... we knew it!"[20] Still, the Dutch reporter who covered the occupation recalls that people in the neighboring buildings were closing their windows from fear that they would be accused by the authorities of showing sympathy for the insurrectionists.[21]

In collective moments, people carry along their own expectations and frames. Stelios Kouloglou remembers that these moments brought with them a feeling of great uplift despite the relative deprivation caused by the lack of food and cigarette supplies. He describes the occupation experience as one of landing on a free island, a liberated space within an occupied city: "The best moments were when we went out to the terrace and talked, when we went out there. This was a niche of freedom, it was like being on a little island, which might have been encircled, but it was free—this is what I felt" (Kouloglou, interview). Damofli stresses that this was a most liberating moment after years of introversion. She imaginatively links freedom to a symbol from 1821, the Missolonghi, a Peloponnesian fortress where Greeks barricaded themselves in fear of the Ottomans and which was celebrated by nineteenth-century poet Dionysios Solomos in his unfinished poem "The Free Besieged": "A very strong image that I have, and a feeling, was the night on the law terrace when I felt really free. Freedom. We were up there, and beneath us there were people gathering all around. So I felt free, but in a very intense way.... This was something, man, a Missolonghi, you know, in scare quotes. This was something" (Damofli, interview). The intensity of feeling also reflected the fact that all these students were about to sleep overnight away from their homes—a new experience, especially for the women.

The strongest memory that *Katerina retains is of a strange, nonverbal communication code, which included a romantic evocation of exponents of the so-called Generation of the '30s, such as George Seferis, and the latter's icons, such as General Makrigiannis:

> It is a bit picturesque. There was the sleep-in inside an auditorium. Most of us didn't know each other, we were from various faculties, and most of us were snoozing on benches, on chairs, on tiers, and every now and then someone would stand up, anonymously from the crowd, and would write with chalk on the blackboard a verse of Seferis, something by Makrigiannis, don't think it was anything extreme, and then without saying her name, without saying anything she would return to her seat. It was the triumph of allusion again, which, however, said more than would a ten-minute oration, a stump speech. I'm telling you this was a very temperate, condensed way of communication. (*Katerina, interview)

The references to Makrigiannis, Seferis, as well as Solomos, indeed lacked any "extreme" content and rather seem very much aligned with the standard literary prototypes of previous generations. On top of this, according to some testimonies dissident students danced Greek folk dances in the Law School terrace during the occupation. Such features compromised the iconoclastic aura of the whole event. In the end, radical student action could go hand-in-hand with well-established ideas and standard practices regarding "Greekness."

The Law School occupation also marked the first appearance of a small group of anarchists. Nikos Balis and Christos Konstantinidis, in particular, were leading anarchists, who were not students but militant intellectuals with Parisian training. They were the first to translate Daniel Cohn-Bendit's *Leftism* and Guy Debord's *Society of the Spectacle* in 1972. Their journal *Pe-*

zodromio [The Gutter] was the first forum in which situationism was introduced to the Greek audience.[22] In his political autobiography student leader Nikos Bistis offers a very graphic description of how the communist majority, to which he belonged, treated anarchists like Konstantinidis during the occupation: with suspicion, condescension, and contempt.

> The order watch had identified a strange fellow, who dwelled for days amongst the Cretan students and was pretending to be an anarchist. He had all the external features, but there was something about him that bothered us: not so much what he was saying ... , but the way in which he was saying it. It was as if he had learned a poem by heart. His gaze was harsh, it did not have the romantic naiveté of the passionate ideologues, the anarchists of the '70s. But above all he stank. Anarchists have taken a divorce from reason, but not from soap. So this gentleman, called Konstantinidis, was going around the corridors, selling revolution and scaring people. "Be ready, there will be bloodshed, because they will storm in for sure. They might come in any minute now," he was saying gathering people around him, pretending to be a guru. Some were ready to follow him in the sacrifice, but most people froze, and you could see the fear in their eyes. Ad hoc people's court, and the verdict was carried out nevertheless. We isolated him on the first floor, we dragged him to the door and we threw him out before his newly baptized disciples realized what had happened to the prophet.[23]

Bistis ends this passage by concluding that Konstantinidis was surely a provocateur. This story underlines the physical intimidation, but even more, the discursive violence that was exercised by the hegemonic communist side over a few anarchists—a symbolic violence that has survived overtime, making inroads into Bistis's present-day memoirs.

During the evening, many of the people who stood outside the Law School staged a demonstration in solidarity across nearby Akadimias Street. The demonstrators held candles in Coca-Cola bottles in an unlikely, albeit functional, combination of antiregime sentiment, Orthodoxy, and the most recognizable American consumer product (this in spite of their critical attitude towards the US government). All this time, a mass of EKOF students was trying to force open the gates of the Law School to enter the building, despite shouts of disavowal from surrounding students and backers of the occupation. EKOF's aggressiveness is glossed over in police reports of the period, which exaggerate the intention of the barricaded students to use violence. Accordingly, an ESA lieutenant observed: "During the meeting of the

22 and 23-2-73, the students barricaded inside the building were spreading the rumor that they were armed and that lots of blood was going to be spilled if other people tried to enter the building. Indeed, many of them carried daggers, while women students carried design razorblades (which have a switchblade, capable of causing serious wounds), which they demonstrated threateningly to the national-minded students."[24]

By its own standards, the regime showed great self-control. Both the movement and the authorities were testing their limits. Professors sided with the students. Konstantinos Toundas, the dean of the University of Athens, offered the students assurances that they could leave unharmed and guaranteed them water and electricity until they evacuated the building. The students rejected this offer, however, as well as the University Senate's request that they leave peacefully. Instead, the occupiers insisted on the abolition of decree 1347 and expressed distrust regarding police guarantees.

On the second day of the occupation, things gradually changed, as many tired students decided to leave; indeed, some had been largely unprepared for a venture requiring such stamina. Most people in the occupation did not really know what their roles or aims were. Student leader Giorgos Vernikos illustrates this point in his writings, conveying with evident irony an image that largely deconstructs the "heroic" aura of the events: "Others were hungry, others got ill, others had their mom waiting, others were afraid."[25] As the dean had already promised to seek the withdrawal of the notorious decree within ten days and the recognition by the Senate of the councils elected by the students, the occupation committee decided to lead the students out of the building. This act was seen as a "victorious withdrawal" with great symbolic impact, though the conscriptions did not cease after all.

The Law School occupation marked the synchronization of the Greek student movement with the international one. The occupation, a newly imported practice in Greece, reflected practices of '68 and proved to be a powerful weapon in the hands of Greek students, who realized that concentrating their strength in a building could be more feasible and effective than a large open-air gathering. On 22 February, when Greek papers reported on the Law School occupation, they also cited the University of Barcelona as a "theater of student unrest," as well as "demonstrations of thousands of students in British cities," "students in Milan participating in illegal demonstrations," and "confrontations between police and students in Cairo."[26] In other words, 1973 was clearly another student year: from Barcelona to Milan and from London to Cairo, the student unrest was a globalized and constant phenomenon. Despite the contextual differences, the Greek uprising—at its height by this date—could finally be placed within this transnational context.

In parallel to the Athens occupation, some three thousand students gathered in Salonica outside the physics and math faculty in order to discuss the invitation of the appointed commission of Aristoteleion University, but they did not manage to conduct open talks. This was the largest meeting of anti-Junta students in the seven years of the dictatorship. The incident was marked by savage fighting between pro-regime and antiregime students. Student leader Chrysafis Iordanoglou justly castigates the otherwise accurate *Thessaloniki*'s lack of information on the extreme violence committed by EKOF's members, thanks to the authorities' intervention (Iordanoglou, interview). Many students were injured, some brought to the hospital, and others pressed charges in the following days, again using and upending the very system that oppressed them in order to obtain justice. The Polytechnic was shut down, and lessons were suspended for about three weeks (from 26 February through 14 March) in order to appease students:[27] a snowball effect was taking place in Salonica, too.

Despite its tactical retreat, the regime showed particular brutality right after the Law School events. Given the extensive media coverage of the occupation, Stylianos Pattakos threatened to close down any newspaper that promoted student issues from that time on. In his infamous talk to the University Senate, Georgios Papadopoulos took over the task of aligning professors with the regime. He contemptuously remarked: "Go stand in front of the mirror and have a look at your heads, because if they are not white they are grey. Think about your struggles until the present day, analyze your personality as teachers of the nation, and with consistency to yourselves, sirs, respond: is it possible that you cannot control your students? I don't believe it." In addition to intimidating the professors, Papadopoulos rendered them responsible for the student situation, assuring them that he would not intervene except at their request. He clarified that "nonstudent" demands would not be tolerated, but he committed to satisfy all student needs.[28]

Furthermore, Papadopoulos demonstrated a great lack of understanding of the real situation as he sought scapegoats by identifying outsider groups as responsible for the student unrest, identifying a retired officer as the leader of the Law School occupation and four communist students from Salonica as having forced the rest of the students to stay inside the building. He concluded that he would be ruthless if "riots and anarchy" persisted: "I will not allow anyone to set Greek society ablaze. I am well aware of the headquarters of ex-politicians and certain others who directed the student agitation and if necessary I will crush them."[29] At the same time, the education minister, Nikolaos Gandonas, was quick to announce new student loans, using the carrot and stick approach. In a change of mood, the recently considerate professors now sided with the regime in an attempt to appease the dictators' rage. They called for the students to cease their strikes, proclaiming that the university asylum and the independence of higher institutions were guaranteed but announcing that student gatherings would not be permitted on university premises.

The students' morale, however, boosted by their recent "outing," rendered them more demanding than before. Law school and humanities students continued to abstain from lectures and asked for a permit to hold a general assembly, opposing the ban on gatherings. At the same time that fifty thousand students were striking in Barcelona at Spain's largest university—unrest the authorities blamed on leftist groups—a high percentage of students abstained from the progress exams at the University of Salonica, especially in the department of architecture. In a resolution handed to the rector of the Athens Law School, a commission of students insisted that the general assemblies were the only way to bring the authorities in touch with the students: "General assemblies strengthen the dialogue on a democratic basis and set up the foundations for creating the recognition that students are socially thinking individuals."[30]

By contrast, in a telling article entitled "Anything but May '68," a French correspondent who reported the Law School events for *Le Monde* came to the conclusion that the Greek student movement was miles away from its counterparts abroad, and especially from the French agitators of the *événements*. The description he gave of a Greek woman militant was full of references to the fact that Greek students were mainly asking for basic rights, trying to separate their demands from further political vindications:

> They were fourteen or fifteen years old when the military took power in Greece on 21 April 1967. They have only a vague recollection of the disorders from the democratic period. Nevertheless, it is while screaming "Democracy!" that these students descend to the streets and confront the Colonels' police. The latter is searching for the "Communist leaders" that Mr Papadopoulos denounced with virulence in a long speech on March 2. Swarthy, with big round glasses, chewing gum while smoking. On 16 February, in the scuffle at the Law Faculty of Athens, she received a blow of bludgeons that has left her with eyesight problems even today: "We have not even heard Papadopoulos's speech. He does not talk about the things we're interested in." Very little politicized, she refuses to see anything in her action other than a protest against the "brutes," the counterdemonstrators, nationalist students, and plainclothes policemen who …

have insulted and beat her since the moment that she left the faculty: "They are the ones who provoked the scuffle. We just wanted our elementary rights."

Later on in the article, the French commentator unfavorably compared an unspecified unaffiliated Greek leader—probably Vernikos—to Daniel Cohn-Bendit, the *enfant terrible* of May 1968, pointing to the Greek leader's apparent lack of passion. In focusing on this specific unaffiliated student, the journalist underplayed the importance and influence of the communist groupings, to which most students belonged by that point. The French journalist noted:

> A law student with a big black moustache that poorly hides his still-juvenile lips. George attempts to analyze the revolt: "All we want, the rest of us students, is to show that the government doesn't accept even elementary demands such as the right to freely choose our representatives." When questioned about his political views, he says "I am a left-winger," pulling a face that excuses himself. Nothing in him of a strident Cohn-Bendit who was spitting vitriol at all sorts of requisitions. This is one of the "thinkers" behind the event, whereby leftists or Communists play a rather oblique role. "Naturally, the leftists have tried 'to politicize,' as they call it, the Law School occupation by making us shout: 'Down with the Junta!' ... But the majority refused and shouted instead 'Democracy!,' 'Freedom!,' and then he sings the Cretan song 'When will the dawn come!'"[31]

In contrast to *Le Monde*'s emphasis on the differences between the Greek and French cases, almost a week earlier, on 27 February, *Thessaloniki* had noted that "the recent student unrest" recalled "the French May of '68." While the headline referred to the student protest against the Debrais Law in France, it made indirect reference to the Greek student revolt.[32] At the same time, the president of the Free University of West Berlin expressed his support for the demands of the Greek students and his solidarity with the Senate of the Polytechnic. The president of the Student Union at the University of California, Berkeley, also expressed his solidarity with the demands of Greek students. This was a sign that the student conflict was being globalized and that despite *Le Monde*'s commentaries the post-'68 movements now looked to Greece: two of the hotbeds of student action were expressing their solidarity, Athens was finally heard, and the students were breaking their isolation.

After the Law School debacle, the dictators made it clear that they would resort to ruthless force to suppress similar incidents of protest. From this point on, however, more state violence would only produce more radicalization among the rebellious students. The recent successful experiment with occupation and the open popular support it had received created greater expectations on the part of the students, which made them less cautious. The Law School imbroglio led to more marches and demonstrations by students in Athens, often very combative ones. Ariadni Alavanou remembers that participating in such ventures had become her daily occupation: "We were always up for it! Do you know this? Such was our mentality in that period. Wherever there was an occupation, a demonstration, fuzz, we were in for it" (Alvanou, interview).

Already at the beginning of March 1973, police reports reflected the fears of the authorities that the next occupation was going to last longer due to the students' greater experience and enhanced organizational capacity: "It is being spread among the students that during the all-students meeting on Tuesday (6–3–73) those present will have food supplies for a week."[33] The next occupation did not take place when the authorities expected it but was launched two weeks later, on the one-month anniversary of the February events. This time, those mainly responsible for the initiative were the leftists, who insisted that the correct tactic was to seek a head-on confrontation with the regime. Kouloglou remembers, "I insisted that we had to remain there, but this was entirely spontaneous. We should do something. We have had a victory here, so we should do something more, out of impatience, in a way" (Kouloglou, interview).

Figure 5.2. Students barricaded at the terrace of the Law School building, Athens, March 1973. Notice the growing visibility of women among the protesters, partly due to the forced conscription of their male peers. (Photographer: Aristotelis Sarrikostas)

One of the protagonists of this new occupation of the Law School, Grigoris Kossyvakis, recalled in an interview taken shortly after the fall of the Junta: "At 4 o'clock a meeting took place at the Saripolos lecture theater. At that meeting the AASPE—the Chinese, as we called them—was in charge of coordination for the first time. Their representative, Dionysis Mavrogenis, stated that the committee of physics and math students was about to take over the building, regardless of whether the remaining faculty committees departed. Naturally, the other committees did not depart."[34] The occupation did not last long, as the university authorities asked for the intervention of the police, who invaded the Law School building, beating all the students. Most people who participated in those critical events retain very grim memories of the excessive violence used by the police—above all Angeliki Xydi remembered being "just saved from death" (Xydi, interview).

As political scientist Joachim Raschke argues, macrosocial conditions, or "dramatic events," can accelerate, retard, or break up the mobilization process, becoming full-fledged factors in the unfolding of a protest movement.[35] Pierre Bourdieu also argues for the innovative role of "critical events," which generate or result from general crises, with no relation to each other, casually bringing about a "synchronization effect."[36] In the Greek case, the events that marked the evolution of the student movement were the February and March 1973 Law School occupations, which fortified the students and widened their circles of support. The movement was already underway, having carved out a public space, an "opportunity structure,"[37] for the reinforcement of student cohesion. The Law School occupations was the turning point for the course of the events in Greece, just as the June 1967 killing of high school student Benno Ohnesorg in Berlin accelerated student agitation in West Germany, and the May 1968 "night of the barricades" led to the explosion of the *événements* in Paris.

The Greek Junta proved myopic, taken by surprise by the sudden rise of the student movement, having paid little or no attention to problems within educational institutions and the contagiousness of the protests in Europe and the United States. The ruthless suppression of the second Law School occupation just reinforced an entire cycle of protest that would end with the dramatic Polytechnic events half a year later. The open, brutal violence exercised by the police and experienced by the students was a radicalizing factor, reinforcing the students' potential for confrontation.

The first half of 1973 showed that apart from the students, others were also running out of patience with the regime. The self-exiled former prime minister Constantine Karamanlis heightened the tension when he released a statement in 23 April 1973 asking for an immediate transfer of power to the politicians. The dictators were also testing the patience of certain elites in the country, including several sections within the armed forces, a fact expressed bluntly in a mutiny within the Navy in late May 1973. The mutiny, organized by royalist officers, failed but managed to shake the regime;[38] for the first time since December 1967 and King Constantine's abortive countercoup, a branch of the country's armed forces questioned the dictators legitimacy. Reports about the arrested navy officers being brutally tortured in the dungeons of the notorious Interrogation Units of the Military Police (EAT-ESA) caused sensation at the time.

The Cost of Participation

Greek student protesters acted in the context of an authoritarian regime that maintained order through violence. A distinction should be made between students' willingness to participate in moderate versus militant forms of action, as well as in low- versus high-risk activities, due to the potentially high cost of certain forms of protest.[39] Still, it would be wrong to assume that the cost of clandestine action was significantly greater than that of open action, because the dangers, including prison and torture, were similar. Open action had the possibility of tangible results, however, which would be more visible than the results of covert actions. Open action was also dictated by specific, rather than abstract, demands, such as university unionism. Overall, participation in protest or resistance had a high cost in Greece, in contrast to Western countries where "resistance" meant street fighting with the police until arrested. Greater repression also led to the reinforcement of a common identity.[40] Stavros Lygeros suggests the unifying quality of high-risk resistance: "It was not like when you pass by a demonstration at present, or an occupation. ... This was a different thing, because risk was involved, they participated with risk. This thing marked it. It gave a nuance of gravity and drama to the whole movement" (Lygeros, interview).

Even as it was liberalizing in some ways, the regime resorted to violence to crush the presumed heads of the student movement, ignoring its polycephalous character. In spring 1973, two waves of arrests took place in which all the male student leaders who had not already been arrested or conscripted, along with some of the legendary women student leaders, were put in solitary confinement and tortured. The regime started using terror against the students when the ESA took over responsibility for addressing the student movement from the Public Security Forces, who had been blamed for failing to control it.[41] By 1972, a fifth of the 330 prisoners serving sentences for crimes against the regime were students.[42] On 8 May 1973, all identifiable leaders and those who defended them were arrested and tortured by the ESA. A civil war veteran commented to a foreign journalist: "They don't bother torturing us older communists, although they may knock us about a bit and make us feel impotent and helpless. They torture the young mainly. They want to break them."[43]

One of the most prominent members of the Law School occupations who got arrested on 8 May was Ioanna Karystiani, president of the Cretan Society and one of the most charismatic leaders of the movement. She argues that anyone who entered the movement knew well in advance that high and unpredictable risks were involved: "The ones who entered [the movement] knew that they were possibly taking a great risk of having, say, certain consequences, to be beaten up, to go to jail, and then to go to jail meant to be aware that they might charge you with Law 375, Law 509 on espionage [the anticommunist legislation introduced in the late 1940s], and if you were there in the front, you'd be given twenty years of prison." (Karystiani, interview).

Student leader Giorgos Vernikos was also arrested and tortured by the Military Police. In his view, he was tortured particularly harshly due to his upper-class background and his torturers' conviction that they were conducting a "popular struggle." He quotes his interrogator telling him, "We are struggling for the nation-saving revolution and you spoiled brats and rich kids are fomenting resistance."[44] As a result of physical and psychological mistreatment, Vernikos came close to suicide.

ESA was notorious for accompanying complete isolation and interrogation with ruthless torture; it relied heavily on the *falanga,* that is, beating prisoners with iron rods on the soles of the feet with their hands tied. Most of the time, interrogation served as nothing more than an opportunity to perform acts of domination on the prisoners. As the days people spent in the Military Prison were full of physical pain and psychological pressure, such a *rite de passage* gave its victims a credential. Dimitris Papachristos remembers, "We admired someone who returned from arrest on his feet; he had acquired prestige."[45]

Torture and psychological violence were even more intense for women due to the propensity of torturers to rape and to subject women to verbal assault with a sexual content. Xydi remembers: "It happened to me during a transfer from EAT-ESA to a military camp, to be taken out to the yard where there were colonels, the ones who were later on court-martialed of course, and all the EAT roosters gathered there, saying to me: 'Why did you get involved? Go back to your kitchen to wash your dishes'" (Xydi, interview). A twenty-two-year-old woman who was arrested during the demonstration of 4 November 1973 on the occasion of the fifth anniversary of George Papandreou's death told a foreign paper: "Policemen took hold of me, beat me on my private parts, and put me in a police car. One of them told me, 'We will put a black man in your cell to —— you.'"[46]

The use of deliberately and stereotypically sexist and offensive language was a standard means of humiliation and dehumanization. Tasos Darveris records one of the phrases capturing this spirit of hate mixed with a rapist drive: military officers during the Polytechnic uprising remarked, "We should take all the women students and tear their cunts apart with bayonets."[47] Accounts of direct sexual assaults are largely silenced in the verbal and written life stories of both male and female students of the time, however. The memoir of the young actress Kitty Arseni, written and published when she was already abroad, offers one example. Arseni described her extensive detention in detail for the most part, but she merely implied her rape without ever explicitly referring to it.[48] Christina Vervenioti was arrested and ruthlessly tortured by the Security Police while pregnant:

> Some days before I got caught I realized that I was pregnant. I was already together with my husband then, we were both students, and I was in trouble at home for all this. And of course I would go and have an abortion. When they were torturing me I didn't know that I had to say "Don't hit me because I am pregnant" and they would spare me the beatings, as another girl did whose mother had been exiled and so on, and so she knew that she had to act this way. I didn't say anything. On the contrary my concern was that my father shouldn't know about it, as that thing would have been a greater blow than being arrested. At the end of the day, they caught me because I was working against the dictatorship. Father would not be ashamed of this. While about having a baby in such a way ... he had different principles, although he was very open-minded. (Vervenioti, interview)

Vervenioti's recollection provides a graphic description of the ethics of the time, as her personal suffering was reinforced by her fear for the "shame" that an illegitimate child would cause her family. She nevertheless presents her father as quite open-minded, drawing a distinction between his attitude on "private" issues versus "public" ones. Though Vervenioti regrets not informing her torturers of her pregnancy in the hope of sparing herself some physical abuse, other incidents suggest that this would not necessarily have led to a more lenient treatment.

In the case of torture and its subsequent trauma, memories are often so poignant that narration becomes extremely difficult and sometimes impossible. More than once, when the life-story narration touched on an incident such as interrogation and torture, interviewees wished to continue speaking off the record, suggesting that making such a story public would degrade and humiliate them. In other cases, narration seemed to be part of a healing process, despite the trauma's long-lasting effects.[49] Alkis Rigos remembers the isolation and the impossibility of forgetting: "No, it is not claustrophobia. It is not the closed walls, it is ... the parting from the world, the violent parting from everything that exists, and I talk about the isolation cell. You were on your own. Entirely. Absolutely. These are sensations which remain with you ... forever" (Rigos, interview).

A notable theme in the narratives of imprisonment and torture is the division between those who "talked" during interrogation and those who did not.[50] This reflects an honor code of sorts and reveals something of the value system of the students of the time. Xydi attributes her refusal to talk to her determination. She explains that the visual image she had in her mind while in prison was one of emerging from captivity proud of having maintained her integrity: "It was very cold, outside and inside. Externally and internally. [I had] this determination, a determination that has followed me ever since. That I should withstand the interrogation and that I should go out holding my head high, in order to be able to look my comrades in the eye" (Xydi, interview). She asserted that the very thought of her comrades was a strong incentive for her to withstand and survive what she went through in prison, suggesting the comfort she took from collective belonging. This thought and the bodily memory of isolation made her break into tears, during the interview. For Xydi, the "collective experience" that Luisa Passerini describes as accompanying a "fatal sacrifice" was very much present.[51]

By contrast, unaffiliated students tend to attribute their greater frustration during their hours in prison to the fact that they did not have a collective structure, such as an organization or a party, in their mind: "The feeling of loss, the solitude, you didn't have anything to lean on. We had yet another handicap, we didn't have comrades. I did not see anything I could lean on, I had nothing to defend, no comrade to avoid betraying, I didn't have anything. This is why I remained in jail briefly, this is why I was probably tortured less than others" (Kourmoulakis, interview). The stakes were high for imprisoned students, whether they turned their comrades in or not. Most worked out individual strategies for dealing with their torturers, such as giving names of companions who were abroad or of persons who were already known or imprisoned. Despite the passage of time, distance, and the mental processing that accompanies them, Christina Vervenioti could not conceal her contempt for those who turned her in: "I was very much disturbed by the fact that they had talked. It disturbed me that so many kids were brought there after us. They could have stopped with us, without bringing in the rest of the kids." Later on, Vervenioti lamented that her group was small and inexperienced as compared to the depth and expertise of the Communist Party, a view that also marked her latter-day political choices:

> Maybe I was all tough toward them [the other members of her group]. They were older than me, supposedly more into, further up in the organization, and I expected better from them, that they wouldn't talk. They said it all, with the logic that they [the police] already knew everything, as we were all there. And they gave details.... I said, "Never again be involved in a small group." You should offer your life, do things, but at least there should be a party behind [you], a serious mechanism. I believed this, that there was no seriousness, they played at revolutionaries without being such. (Vervenioti, interview).

Kleopatra Papageorgiou similarly shows little respect for those who talked: "You see how the organizations collapsed, the clandestine ones when A-EFEE people got arrested. They gave into everything, they squealed, they ratted on everyone when they got caught. That's it, better not say names now. I know them, but let them be for the time being" (Papageorgiou, interview).

Giannis Kourmoulakis finds himself at the opposite end of the spectrum, as he recalls in despair the fact that he was forced to speak: "I think that they broke my spirit, despite all resistance. That is, I got scared. I did not say 'Fuck off, I'm not writing anything.' I sat down and wrote. What did I write? I sat down and wrote. It doesn't matter what I wrote, if I turned people in, if I didn't turn people in. I got scared—they broke my spirit—that they might kill me, that they might throw me out of the window" (Kourmoulakis, interview). Such coerced confessional writings reminded many of the notorious "statements," documents renouncing left-wing political beliefs that had been a thorn in the side of the Left ever since the interwar period. Consequently, a large number of people were stigmatized as traitors.

Makis Paraskevopoulos, a law student and Rigas member, wrote an account shortly after his long detention wherein, alongside a stirring description of his state of mind, he referred to the images of the relentless fighters of the Civil War years that came to haunt him: "You're always in your cell and the shortness of breath is inevitable. Terror has become a steady feature and at every sound you're scared to death. You're constantly trembling, so much that you're spilling the beans from your spoon, you are floundering in your words, you are incredibly cowardly, the most cowardly man in the world, and the people in Makronisos were made out of stone."[52] Kotanidis in his memoirs offers a similar testimony regarding the mythical courage of the fighters of the past and how they induced a sense of guilt regarding his own stance towards his torturers: "As if my sorry state was not enough, I kept on burdening myself with guilt." At a certain point he wonders: "What should I expect from myself, to be tough like Stalin? Probably."[53] Both Paraskevopoulos's idealized story of resilience about the left-wing inmates of the notorious "rehabilitation" camp on the island of Makronisos in the late 1940s[54] and Kotanidis's reference to Stalin demonstrate an internalization of the Greek communist moral standards of the past, according to which a "fighter" would never yield in duress.

A "Glocal" Movement

Papadopoulos meanwhile proceeded to implement the final steps of "liberalization," including the granting of a spectacular and full-fledged amnesty. He could have issued a pardon in order to satisfy criticism from abroad, mainly from the United States. Instead, he gave an amnesty that cancelled the criminal records of the accused. He further lifted the "state of siege" from the whole country and recognized all individual and collective freedoms for the first time since 1967.[55] Papadopoulos's decision to politicize and personalize the dictatorship—he concentrated so many powers in his hands that one could talk of "sultanism"[56]—greatly dissatisfied the hard-liners of the regime who thought that the "Revolution of 21 April" was being betrayed.[57] However, the regime's strong man was determined to accomplish his plan, as his attempts at *reforma* had been twice frustrated by the hard-liners in the past (1968 and 1971).

Papadopoulos also organized a referendum on the abolition of monarchy on the grounds that the exiled monarch had allegedly orchestrated the naval mutiny of May 1973, alongside the Paris based ex-prime minister Constantine Karamanlis. The referendum, which took place on 29 July 1973, gave Papadopoulos a 78.4 percent approval and made him the first president of the Republic. It caused great splits within the clandestine Left and the politicians of the predictatorship period, as did the announcement of forthcoming elections.[58] More importantly, on 8 October 1973 Papadopoulos moved for the first time to create a government around the old liberal politician Spyros Markezinis and other political figures from the past, the "interlocutors" or "bridge-builders" who were willing to engage in a dialogue with the Junta and take governmental positions.

Markezinis appeared to desire appeasement with the "student problem" and the fact that the students who protested in spring 1973 for the improvement of academic matters and more academic freedom had met with sup-

Figure 5.3. Junta's amnesty, summer of 1973. Political prisoners are returning home by boat from the remote islands to which they had been sent into exile. On their way out many praised the role of the students as a catalyst for their release. (Photographer: Aristotelis Sarrikostas)

pression, violence, arrests, and the suspension of their right to defer military service. The situation in October 1973 could not be compared to that of the spring of the same year, he said, when the "political question" (το πολιτικόν ζήτημα) was still open, reinforcing the unrest. He was confident that the liberalization process by now ought to have reassured the students, allowing reconsideration of their problems. Still, he said in an interview with the *New York Times*, "This does not mean that the channel of elections will make the problems of the student youth disappear, as these are of a general nature, meaning that they are also to be found outside the Greek borders." Markezinis thus placed the issue of student unrest in Greece within the wider context of international student agitation, implying that a single government could not possibly deal with student rebelliousness, no matter what measures it might take. Markezinis concluded the interview by hinting ironically that student revolt could be legitimate only when there was political repression, thus placing Greece's condition at that point in time in a different register. In other words, he stated overly optimistically that Greece no longer had a democratic deficit, thus making any student rebellion unjustified: "Only where democracy does not function should the universities protest on political grounds."[59]

Meanwhile, the students were diffident about the whole liberalization experiment, drawing on two other models of inspiration: the political unrest in Thailand and the shock generated by Pinochet's coup in Chile in September 1973. The latter led to a demonstration in late September in Athens. Rigas Feraios even passed a resolution on the Chilean case, linking it directly to the Greek case as part of the same US plot. While Chile's authoritarian twist reinforced Western left-wingers' lack of trust in the capacity of a democratic state to make socialist reforms without suffering a coup d'état, in Greece it was proof that American interests were ruthlessly pursued in the same manner all over the world, always at the expense of people's democratic rights. A Rigas leaflet read:

> For the Greek students, who have lived for six years now under the dictatorship of Papadopoulos, the scenario is well-known. Just like Papadopoulos in Greece, Pinochet in Chile talks about "a patient in a plaster cast," they have the same obscurantist ideology, they use the same rough-and-ready demagogy, the same lies. And it is not strange. Because the assassins of the Chilean people and the Greek Junta have been trained in the same centers of international subversion in the United States, the plans of the people behind the coups have been elaborated in the same offices of the American KYP. The two Juntas serve the same interests: they defend the privileges of native oligarchy and the strategic and economic positions of the popular movement that threatens directly or in the long term these privileges and positions. The Greek students are aware of all this, and this is why they shouted in the demonstration of 25 September in the center of Athens "Allende, Allende."[60]

Allende's name became a slogan and was later used during the Polytechnic, demonstrating the transnational attitude of protest among Greek students and their conviction that their struggle was part of a wider anti-imperialist front that was taking place worldwide. More importantly, drawing a parallel between the Greek and Chilean cases placed Greece firmly within a third-worldist paradigm. Similarly, in a speech in West Germany in early 1974, PAK's leader Andreas Papandreou summarized these ideas: "The bloody overthrow of Allende in Chile by the junta of Pinochet and the establishment of a military dictatorship in Greece express, just like Vietnam, Laos, Cambodia, Congo—and so many other cases—the violent course of modern capitalism. Therefore, for our struggle to be victorious it has to be conducted on a worldwide scale."[61] Another slogan that established the imaginary line of connection between the various oppressed countries went "Chile, Greece, and Spain, let's march on toward democracy," this time bringing the ailing General Franco's Spain to the picture.[62]

Thailand's unrest became a similar symbol. In October 1973, 200,000 protesters, mainly students, attacked and occupied a government building against the military Junta of Thanom Kittikachorn, a repressive regime dating from 1971 and thought to be corrupt and backed by the United States. After ten days of violent clashes and assaults between the Thai police and the crowd of protesters, a series of teargas explosions instigated riots, during which 66 students were shot dead and 876 participants injured. Kittikachorn had ordered the army to "do its duty" against student "terrorists" who were "destroying life and property."[63] This event was about to have striking similarities to Greece's Polytechnic bloodbath—more than the Polytechnic had had to the Parisian May '68. In contrast to the Polytechnic, however, the massacre of Thai students actually succeeded in bringing about the overthrow of the dictatorial government. The main slogan of Greek students, "Tonight there will be Thailand," was realized only in terms of violence.

The tendency to refer to and identify with international incidents betrays the students' perception of themselves as being part of a wider global struggle with international symbols, points of reference, and a common enemy: US imperialism. A positive identification emerged among Greek students with the repressed "other," also reflecting an orientalist certitude of possessing a privileged gaze that could distinguish between the positive and the negative elements in foreign experience. This was a trait that the Greek students had in common with many of their counterparts around the world. All in all, two different cultural images emerged, in which the Western Bloc's uprisings acted as a source of inspiration, while Third-World movements were a revolutionary guide.[64] What emerges clearly from all this is the link between the local and the international, in other words the "glocal" aspect of the Greek student movement: thinking "globally" and acting "locally"—long before that term became fashionable.

The Junta proceeded with its experiment and a carrot and stick attitude towards the student movement. By 18 October, all expelled students were permitted to return to the university thanks to decree 168/73 on amnesty. On the same day, however, the president of the Cretan local society in Salonica was arrested following a meeting of the society. Some days later, Chrysafis Iordanoglou, president of the Thrace Macedonian local society, launched a lawsuit against police pressure that had prevented the society from holding elections in accordance with law 937/1973, but the public prosecutor refused to discuss the case, saying it was beyond his responsibility.[65] Soon afterward, the Athenian local societies of Cretans, Patrans, Chiotes, Ilians, and Epirots called all students to mass registration and participation in student elections, due to the fact that the elected administrative councils wanted to hold elections with the existing small number of registered members. In their announcement, the societies repeated the classic demand of 15 percent of the budget for education, and they also called that the government rescind the decrees abolishing the deferral of military service and the holding of general assemblies until 1 November in order to elect committees that would hold elections in January 1974. Lastly, Law School students criticized the pro-regime–appointed student union Themis, which insisted on distinguishing between "strictly student matters" and political ones, ignoring conscription. By that time, 150 students had been conscripted.

At the same time, the prospect of elections was creating a new potential. The Markezinis experiment signaled an opening, a way out of stagnation that created new and greater expectations not about the Junta's intentions but about how civil society might exploit this opportunity. The undersecretary of public order, Spyridon Zournatzis, proposed a politics of oblivion premised on "forgetting and forgiving the past," even announcing the rehabilitation of Theodorakis's pre-Junta songs.[66] His appeal was not heard, however. In 1968, George Papandreou's funeral had provided one of the few big demonstrations in the first years of the dictatorship. On 4 November 1973, on the fifth anniversary of his death, his short memorial service provided terrain for the expression of more public protest.

Giannis Kourmoulakis remembers the violence that took place during the memorial between the two conflicting parties, demonstrators and policemen, with victims on both sides: "Papandreou's memorial took place. Something unprecedented happened there. Five hundred thousand people were gathered, and there was mayhem. Beatings, all hell broke loose! I was involved in the beatings too. There with the police. I hit some policemen too, over there, and then they searched for me all over Athens in order to find me and put me away. I really had a close shave there" (Kourmoulakis, interview). Seventeen people were brought to trial on the ground that they were "a few extremists committing anarchist acts and outrageous activities against the small police force maintaining order."[67] The trials caused renewed unrest around the University of Athens, where students shouted anti-Junta slogans and came into conflict with the police. In the meantime, Markezinis kept postponing his liberalization measures, creating even more tension. Prominent politicians, including Panagiotis Kanellopoulos and Georgios Mavros, defended the seventeen. A film used by the defense during the trial that recorded the most savage beating of students seen in public to date was later widely disseminated by the press, drastically undermining the image of a smooth transition to democracy. At the same time, the foreign press covering the incident reached a correct conclusion: "Greece is stretching out."[68]

By mid-November, the situation was turning explosive. Public tension escalated due to the 1973 oil crisis that was hitting the country. On 20 October, the government had announced new economic measures, one of which freed prices, which meant an automatic increase in the cost of bread and agricultural products. A politics of austerity was announced in order to keep inflation in check and prevent shortages. As the consumer index rose and inflation boomed during the period of the crisis, finances became tight; this is what the Polytechnic occupation slogan "Bread" would some weeks later refer to, underlining the students' conviction that they were talking on behalf of an entire nation in crisis.[69]

The Mission of the Youth

As a result of their frequent mobilizations over the previous two years, the students sensed that as an intellectual minority they had the mandate of the Greek people to act in their interest as a legitimate avant-garde aiming at a sociopolitical transformation. Alkis Rigos, a Panteios student and one of the movement's so-called grandfathers due to his relatively old age, describes this understanding: "We had the widespread sensation that all of society went in circles around us. There was a particular sort of authorization by society to us, that 'It is you.' Of course one could go off one's rocker through this, it had negative aspects too" (Rigos, interview). The sense students had of themselves as a nonconformist avant-garde in Greek society dated back to the Lambrakides but had strengthened by 1972 and above all after the Polytechnic events of early 1973.

The students' faith in their role stemmed in part from their positive representation in periodicals and other publications. Students were often characterized as millenarian carriers of change, reflecting the post-1968 mood. The publisher Nikolaos Psaroudakis said in 1972: "The revolutionary quality of this youth has a purity. Such a youth is the foundation of a free people. If a people goes ahead, this is owed to the youth's revolutionary spirit. Tomorrow's people will spring out of the youth with opinion and character. The rebellious youth is the foundation of the future."[70] The great dailies created parallels between the problems of youth, the students' world, and what was happening in other countries. The subject of youth as a whole was a heated topic of debate in the late 1960s and early 1970s, with such constant analyses of the role, function, and potential of youth, that it is often argued that youth itself became by and large a nonexistent category, "a pure construction of the media, a surface phenomenon only."[71]

Apart from being a valuable source for circulating information on international developments, newspapers also provided a means of bringing students closer to the spirit of protest movements abroad. Everyday reports in Greek newspapers analyzed the unrest in Spanish universities (with headlines such as "When the students dare, the dictatorship is shaken") as well as the situation in Portuguese universities and society when the parallel opening of Marcelo Caetano was taking place, referred to as "pseudo-elections." All this generated an obvious "transfer" and identification on the part of the readers.

The return of the students who had been violently conscripted had a major impact on the student movement. Considered a victory, their return encouraged and rallied the students, contributing to the growth of the mass movement. The return to the universities of the conscripted students, albeit shaved and with their long hair buzzed off, reinforced the self-confidence of the rest.[72] One returned conscript, Stelios Logothetis, recalled in an interview that, having been recently dismissed, "[we] still wore our military jackets."[73] The semiology of the military outfit and its homeopathic use was further enhanced by the Junta's own symbols, as at this time real Hellenic Army jackets came to replace the American ones, expressing a stark contrast to their wearers' actual political identity. Mimis Androulakis, a student leader at the time, recalls in his writings that the unification between the legendary students in uniform with their colleagues had explosive results:

> And you can imagine, a whole train full of left-wing soldiers, what a celebration, singing songs from the moment we left, and then we all met and this whole crowd entered the Polytechnic. In fact, I didn't change clothes, I went in with my military uniform. During all the days of the Polytechnic I was in military uniform, apart from a gabardine that someone brought me.... I insist on the chemistry that existed when the conscripted ones came and met the other movement which was in turmoil. This made the movement sprout up, it was a big mistake by the Junta to let us go.[74]

Androulakis describes the soldier-students' return to Athens in trains as "epic," and this adjective is often used in life histories regarding the trains that seem to be connected on an imaginary level with the Marxist icon of the "locomotive of history" and to Lenin's arrival in Saint Petersburg in 1917. Moreover, following the impact of May '68, which had posed the problem of defining the subjects of history, the role of the individual in historical procedures appeared to have shifted, and for the first time Greek students considered themselves vehicles of historicity and factors of social change.[75] Dafermos writes, "The people who participated in the movement ... were experiencing each moment with the feeling of History."[76] Others, such as the secretary of the Coordinating Committee at the Polytechnic occupation, argued that the function of a movement is to "eavesdrop on the people's historical consciousness."[77]

Students' image of themselves taking part in the process of history contributed to their conviction that they had been informally authorized by Greek society to lead the opposition on its behalf. As Stelios Kouloglou put it, "The students carried on their shoulders the weight of the whole of Greek society,"[78] acting as a counterweight to six years of apathy. Thus, it is no surprise that when the amnesty of the summer of 1973 had taken place, many attributed it to the effects of the students' mobilizations. While on their way out of prison, some political prisoners spoke of a "people's victory," most of them clearly referring to the students as the agents of the people. Nikos Konstandopoulos and Stelios Nestor, two prominent members of the clandestine resistance organization Democratic Defense in Athens and Salonica, thanked "our youth who struggled to bring us out of prison,"[79] adding that this was "their victory."[80] A third member of the organization, Dionysis Karagiorgas, an economics professor who lost four fingers in an explosion while trying to construct a bomb, concluded: "We owe everything to the youth and their struggles."[81]

This recognition of the student movement's ability to do what the underground political parties and resistance organizations failed to achieve is remarkable. However, it also increased the responsibility and sense of "national mission" that the students felt—a sense that they acted on behalf of the entire society rather than a focus on their own problems alone. The notion that the "mission" of youth was the vanguard of the antidictatorship movement differed greatly, however, from more traditional Marxist-Leninist notions of the party as the vanguard, since instead of wanting to be a tightly disciplined group of dedicated revolutionaries, the students sought to be part of a mass movement that involved the entire Greek society. This feeling was dramatically enhanced in November 1973, in the three days that marked the peak of the conflict between the student movement and the regime.

"This Is What Revolution Must Be Like": The Polytechnic Events

When writing of the Polytechnic occupation, it can be difficult to distinguish eyewitness testimony from hearsay.[82] This event has been memorialized and analyzed so thoroughly over the past forty years that the biographical memory in individual life stories often relies heavily on ex-post narratives. As a result, interviewees tend to exhibit a shifted perspective, "seeing" themselves through the eyes of an observer rather than as protagonists,[83] thereby reproducing the public discourse and its hermeneutical schemata. As a great shock creates the need to effectively identify its circumstances, causes, and consequences, namely, to find "adequate causation,"[84] people tend to formulate "objectified" conclusions based on their understanding of the nature of these three days and their significance instead of analyzing their own individual experiences.[85] Even conflated narratives and anecdotal recollections nonetheless constitute powerful transmitters of emotions, imagery, or silences, all of interpretative value.

By early November 1973, almost all corporate student issues had been satisfied by the Markezinis administration, including the restoration of the deferral of military service and the return of the conscripts. The thorny question of student elections remained, however. The latter were postponed to February 1974 instead of being scheduled prior to Christmas, as the students insisted. As this issue was not solved at the meeting between student representatives and Minister of Education Panagiotis Sifnaios on 13 November, a new impasse arose. A report by the newspaper *Thessaloniki* the following day openly attributed distinct student demands to the various political groupings. At first the spontaneous occupation of the Polytechnic that occurred on the same day, 14 November, superseded the divisions between different student lines, but in the end it exacerbated them.

14 November: Contingency

Though a climate of general discontent was solidifying, collective protest did not emerge automatically. The occupation started only three days prior to a scheduled and eagerly awaited press conference by Prime Minister Markezinis in which he was to delineate his government's strategy, announce the election day, and probably elaborate further on the "student issue." On Wednesday, 14 November, a false alarm impelled students who were already gathered at the Law School to rush to the Polytechnic in solidarity with their colleagues, who were supposedly being bullied by the police. More than three hundred enraged students created a clamorous demonstration stretching the length of the central Solonos Street. Although the students discovered upon their arrival that no beatings were taking place, the crowd that had gathered—almost two thousand strong—decided to enter the building despite police attempts to prevent them. Damofli describes the scene and stresses that there was a general feeling that something was about to happen:

> We had a meeting at the Law School, and some EKKE people came and said, "In the Polytechnic there is hell breaking loose." We stopped the assembly and went on foot to the Polytechnic, where no hell was breaking loose. But some people were shouting at the gate bars, and they were throwing some sour oranges, and some other people inside who were holding assemblies were saying "Hey guys,

stop it, we're having an assembly." In any case, people started coming, because anyway, I'm telling you, the wish, the climate for such assemblies to take place existed. (Damofli, interview)

The fact that the Polytechnic occupation took off because of a misunderstanding exposes the importance of contingency not just in the case of Greek students in 1973, but in historical processes in general.

The ensemble of students who accidentally found themselves in the Polytechnic decided to boycott classes and occupy the building in an entirely spontaneous takeover.[86] As Sidney Tarrow points out, "A few people who break away from the forms of collective action in unusual circumstances produce intensive mass movements at the peak of the protest waves."[87] Having already tested the tool of occupation, a highly symbolic performance, students felt they could control the situation. Social psychologist Anna Mantoglou quotes one individual who remembers the feeling of enthusiasm that characterized the decision to occupy the Polytechnic: "Then we went and locked the Stournara Street [gate]. This is where enthusiasm possessed us: OCCUPATION. When we were saying this, we really thought we had the POWER at this moment."[88]

The occupation largely bypassed the two main left-wing student organizations, and therefore there was no effective control of the direction that it took or of the students' demands for the first day and a half. The occupation was not within the scope of the leadership of the pro-Moscow communists, which considered it "an irresponsible and hasty move of an intense leftist character."[89] In fact, A-EFEE distanced itself from the venture from the very beginning, as it disliked unorganized action, which could get out of hand. Angeliki Xydi, who followed this line, recalled her past skepticism: "I wasn't sure, you know, about what we were going to do. I had far too many doubts, even a disagreement. Because I thought that it was too risky. From one point of view, yes, it was maturing; from another it was not organized. Not the least organized" (Xydi, interview).

Rigas more or less shared this attitude, although without expressing a clear-cut position, as it was not ready for such an eventuality. *Katerina, still in Rigas at this time, emphasizes that she was taken aback by the fact that an occupation could take place without a specific demand:

> The idea that one could organize an occupation, which is one of the advanced forms [of protest], and in fact without a specific student demand, a unionist one—this thought was shocking in the beginning.... So, beyond the surprise and the shock that this could happen even without a central student demand, and from the moment that we realized that this was possible, ... there was no issue,

everyone entered and stood on the first line, the dilemma didn't last long. (*Katerina, interview)

*Katerina's pragmatic attitude was widespread among the Greek students. Michalis Sabatakakis underlines this issue very clearly: "There we have a contradictory fact, which is that the protagonists of an insurrection do not believe in its insurrectionary character straight away" (Sabatakakis, interview). In fact, the smaller groups of leftists and even outsiders and marginal elements of the student movement, such as anarchists, led the way at first by writing antigovernment slogans on the walls and circulating leaflets containing anti-Junta messages. The Polytechnic gestalt was characterized by a constant tension between leftist and anarchist spontaneity and communist pragmatism.

In due time, the two main organizations tried to keep the situation under control by creating the first Coordinating Committee of Occupation (CCO), which exercised light control over the occupation until 15 November.[90] It was the leftists who supported the occupation throughout, however, as it was a form of direct provocation, and they took the lead during the early stages of the endeavor. Their declared line supported an anti-imperialist social upheaval, with slogans such as "People's rule," "People make the revolution," and "Workers-farmers government."[91] The then-orthodox communists refer in present-day life stories to the "stubbornness and frenzy" of the leftists.[92] The latter saw their desire for a direct confrontation with the regime becoming a growing possibility and antagonized the anarchists with their revolutionary zeal. The lurking or manifest differences within the entire microcosm of student resistance were rapidly coming to a head.

At first, the reaction of the regime to the occupation remained surprisingly measured. According to the memoirs of Prime Minister Markezinis, at a meeting on 14 November between himself, Papadopoulos, Minister of Education Panagiotis Sifnaios and Minister of Public Order Panagiotis Therapos, they made the decision not to interfere.[93] Naturally, the General Secretariat of Press and Information denounced student mobilizations as a result of anarchy. It particularly castigated political slogans, such as "Power to the people," "Down with the army," and "NATO out": "Groups of people [are] gathered in the premises and in front of the National Metsoveion Polytechnic, mainly composed of students streaming in from various Faculties, providing an admittedly improper spectacle, as they make noise and obstruct the movement of people and vehicles. None of the slogans that can be discerned from within this noise expresses a student demand, but they all without exception are of a political nature."[94] The declaration of the Junta stressed that the police also would restrain themselves from any involvement apart from making sure that no "peace-loving civilian" was harmed. It attributed the responsibility for the occupation not to student elements but to "other" circles, alluding to the leaders of the old political parties and the exiled KKE: "The government is firm in insisting on these lines, as it is certain that the entire student world denounces the deeds that are attempted by irresponsible elements and that it does not wish anything other than the smooth continuation of its studies. It knows with certainty that the Greek people and public opinion see the aims pursued by the irresponsible individuals mentioned before and will attribute the responsibilities to those to whom they actually belong."[95] The policemen who gathered outside the building never tried to break in, especially after the dean of the Polytechnic denied the police chief the right to storm the building to "restore order." The students interpreted the absence of police intervention as a weakness, and they acted to stimulate a particular framing of the existing conditions that enhanced mobilizational efforts.[96] The dictatorship was indeed experiencing a structural inner crisis, although it was not yet entirely visible.

15 November: Celebration

As the occupation went on for a second day, Thursday, 15 November, even more protesters entered the Polytechnic. The central streets around the Polytechnic were jammed with traffic, which the students exploited in order to distribute leaflets and write slogans on trolleys and buses, calling everyone to come and demonstrate against the dictators. At one point, an estimated ten thousand people were gathered around the Polytechnic, cheering and taking part in the celebratory atmosphere—a practice that enabled the collective expression of feelings. Most life stories describe this second day as a "celebration," blessed by a feeling of solidarity, companionship and participation. The individual was entirely absorbed by the collective, creating a huge "collective subject" that constitutes one of the favorite loci of this generation's memory.

The Polytechnic also tested the organizational efficiency of students. First and foremost, a short-wave radio transmitter was created ad hoc and broadcast with ever greater frequency as the occupation continued. While at first no control was exercised over the station, dubbed "The Radio Station of the Free and Fighting Students, the Free and Fighting Greeks," after the creation of the CCO it too came under central direction. The main message broadcast was that the students had barricaded themselves inside the Polytechnic building and were calling for the people to revolt. The station maintained that the student action was a blow against tyranny, and it issued statements concerning popular freedom, national sovereignty, exit from NATO, and above all opposition to foreign monopolies, "imperialist coalitions," and their domestic props.[97] Through its main announcer, A-EFEE member Maria Damanaki—a former student militant and present-day

Figure 5.4. 15 November 1973. An estimated ten thousand people gathered around the Polytechnic. This second day of occupation is typically described as a "celebration." (Courtesy Iason Chandrinos)

European Commissioner—set the main tone of the student mobilization and popularized, among other things, what was about to become the most famous slogan of the occupation: "Bread–Education–Freedom." And this alongside Mikis Theodorakis's songs that were played throughout the days of the occupation and heard on the megaphones that were positioned on the pillars of the Polytechnic gate. Radio proved to be the most significant means of propaganda in the hands of students and also their major means of disseminating information. To paraphrase Passerini, the students fully exercised the medium's power of turning individualism into collectivism and of involving people intimately.[98]

Dimitris Papachristos, one of the four main radio station announcers, argued that through the radio broadcasts "the poetic exaltation of an entire people found its expression," while "discourse rediscovered its meaning."[99] Another announcer, Tonia Moropoulou, remembers the initial embarrassment of the "cold announcement of dreams," including the students' proposals for modernization and for tackling the economic problems after the establishment of social democracy—all of which were propagated by radio.

When, on Thursday evening, more people took to the streets, the discourse became more "talkative." A fourth announcer, Lambros Papadimitrakis, recalls that as time went by, expression became "more poetical, freer, more human."[100] The Polytechnic radio station signified a "capture of speech," to use Michel de Certeau's celebrated term regarding the May '68 movement. Its potential in terms of communicative production was liberating, in so far as it freed the hitherto "imprisoned speech."[101]

Apart from the radio transmitter, the students created patrols, a first aid department, and a canteen, and they coordinated the writing and distribution of leaflets. Contrary to what was taking place outside, things were heating up inside the building regarding the control of the occupational components, such as the committees for the duplicator, the radio station, and the loudspeakers. In order to deal with this problem, assemblies were organized Thursday night supporting the creation of a robust coordinating structure.[102] The clashes within the thirty-one-member Coordinating Committee highlighted the vast conceptual differences between the various organizations. The system of allowing two representatives from each faculty with the right to one vote made apparent the overwhelming presence of A-EFEE and Rigas and of nonaffiliated students, as well as the underrepresentation of leftists. These latter were strong in influence but not coordinated enough to make their way into the students' organizational structure, and their flamboyant rhetoric was often castigated as unrealistic and somewhat grotesque.

The struggle for a majority vote tested the power and conviction of each organization. Ariadni Alavanou, an orthodox communist at the time and member of the CCO, recalls with bitterness the great hostility the leftists demonstrated against her organization: "They were very hostile toward us. That is, while there was a big event going on, you know, in which … hostilities and differences between the parties should soften in a way in order to promote the event, these ones were very much against A-EFEE" (Alavanou, interview). The conflict was intensified by the fact that the advent of the CCO signaled the first direct intervention exercised by "revisionists." The committee eradicated the far-flung anarchical and leftist rhetoric as dangerous, and from that point forward all slogans had to be permitted by the CCO, while anarchists themselves ran the serious risk of being thrown out of the building.

Angeliki Xydi confessed with some reluctance that these practices were undemocratic in character: "Probably we were doing certain things in a rather unorthodox way, namely, we imposed them in some way. Especially after Thursday, the control of emotions, what was being said from the radio station, what was coming out. Maybe from our side, which was the strongest one proportionally, some things were made by imposition, by force" (Xydi, interview). Anna Mantoglou quotes a participant who argues for the correctness of this decision:

> "Bread–Education–Freedom" was the right slogan.... Certainly, we should have antidictatorship, anti-imperialistic slogans then, and we tried to promote these ones. But I remember that slogans were written like "Sexual Freedom," "Down with the State."... We snuffed out these slogans and we put in a patrol group. We managed to promote anti-imperialistic, antimonopoly and antidictatorship slogans. ... One could say that the first Coordinating Committee ... put some order on the duplicators.[103]

The anarchists' role has long been contested by all sides, being alternately over- and underplayed. It is almost certain that their role during the 1973 Polytechnic occupation was marginal but highly controversial. The anarchists were accused of having a libidinal conception of politics that was harmful to the movement. Famously, one of their leading female figures, "Aretoula," is said to have written on the walls of the Polytechnic, "Long live the orgies!"[104] This bombastic demand for unlimited sexual pleasure was rejected as sheer provocation by all student groups and was effectively appropriated by the regime in order to smear the student occupation as a pansexual fiesta.[105] In such instances, the anarchists were immediately pigeonholed as *agents provocateurs*. A member of Rigas and the Coordinating Committee recalls this conflict: "The extreme and high-sounding slogans of the anarchists, such as 'down with the state,' 'sexual revolution,' etc. were extinguished, and they in turn howled at us as 'antiquated.'"[106] In contrast, Nikitas Lionarakis, another Rigas member, reacted to my assertion that the followers of the two communist parties were in search of provocateurs by arguing that only KNE, Rigas's rival organization, did so: "This is what KNE tried to do. We were more reasonable. We were aware of the fact that not everyone was a *provocateur*" (Lionarakis, interview).

The anarchists were quick to use antiestablishment slogans such as "Down with the authorities," "Social revolution," "State-repression," "Down with capital," "Down with the army," "General insurrection," "Down with salary jobs," and "Patriots are morons." They also spread pro-worker slogans, such as "Workers' councils" and "Workers have no motherland."[107] The hyperrevolutionary character of their slogans irritated communist students. The latter's attitude was partly dictated by the pragmatic estimate that the Polytechnic occupation was a serious situation that could hardly be linked to the libertarianism of May '68 in France. Those students who behaved too radically offered the Junta the advantage of accusing the students of being "anarchists". The anarchist students' slogans were daring and too "far out" for the caliber and aims of the student movement. The communists' idea was that revolutionism and counterculture had to be undercover and well hidden at a time when some student organizations were still advancing nonpolitical demands. A great sensation was created when a vast anarchist placard reading "Down with the State" appeared on the central gate of the Polytechnic, an act later used by the regime propaganda that dubbed the movement nihilistic.[108]

As the anarchists' slogans were in reality closer to those of the radical Left than to the anarchist tradition, leftist groups felt less hostile than the rest to this sort of radicalism. OSE leader Stavros Lygeros explains that the activists close to the KKE treated these anarchists in a violent way. He argues that the anarchists relied on him to defend them, implying a certain complicity: "I was protecting them. They were being beaten up, KKE people got them and beat them up within the Polytechnic, and they asked me for protection" (Lygeros, interview). Stergios Katsaros, a self-designated "professional revolutionary" of the previous generation who was released from prison just before the events, presents a different picture: "The slogans of the anarchists, such as 'down with the state,' were not adopted by anyone. They sounded somewhat weird, as the anarchist movement had no tradition in Greece. However, no one moved against them, even if some Stalinists tried to. Their attempts were absorbed within the wider tolerance of people."[109] However, this much more benign version of the events totally neglects the constant typecasting of anarchists as the *agents provocateurs* par excellence and their systematic harassment by the rest.

In many ways, the anarchists' voice—and especially their insistence on *jouissance*—expressed the provocative side of '68 against the more serious Greek student movement. The Greek movement's earnestness resembled the student uprisings in Third World and Eastern Bloc countries, all cases where protesters struggled for basic human and political rights, which were already firmly established in Western Europe. Seriousness in all these cases was largely dictated by the overtly repressive context, the high cost of participation, and the sense of "national mission" that students felt. This is why the CCO very quickly decided that slogans had to be direct, succinct, memorable, and ready to be copied and recounted, but deprived of any antihierarchical connotations.[110]

This does not mean that student slogans could not be burlesque: the cases of "We haven't got enough to eat, today it's them we'll gobble up," "Woe unto you, scribes and Pharisees, hypocrites," and "People do not want you, take the ape and go away" (this last referring to Markezinis's physical ugliness), were remarkable for their spontaneity and their almost surreal tone. "May '68," "Revolution now, now, now," "Women unite," and "The people are starving, Capital is chewing" were some more out-of-the-ordinary sound bites. The slogans often stressed economic deprivation, as the financial crisis and the currency devaluation had created an entirely different atmosphere than that of the relatively prosperous years of the late 1960s.[111] Maria Tzortzopoulou and Michalis Syrianos stress that the slogans calling for solidarity had a weird climax, starting from "People, you're starving, why do you bow to them?" and ending with the more radical "People, you're starving, why don't you hang 'em?" (Tzortzopoulou and Syrianos, interview). Some of the most heard slogans were anti-American ("USA out," "Throw the Sixth Fleet out") and anti-Atlanticist ("NATO out," "NATO-CIA, traitors"), expressing the students' certainty that the Americans were the major mainstays of the Junta and were therefore the Colonels' accomplices, if not their bosses. Other slogans referring indignantly to Papadopoulos's wife as a "laundress" received negative comments, as for example from *Le Monde*'s correspondent.[112]

In terms of different student strategies, A-EFEE soon stopped insisting on the evacuation of the building and the projection of student demands, while Rigas proposed the creation of a "government of national unity." This proposal highlighted a major problem concerning the objectives of the oc-

Figure 5.5. Students writing anti-Junta slogans on a bus in front of the occupied Polytechnic, 14–16 November 1973. The central streets around the Polytechnic were jammed with traffic, which the students exploited in order to distribute leaflets and write slogans on trolleys and buses, calling everyone to come and demonstrate against the dictators. (Photographer: Aristotelis Sarrikostas)

cupation: Was its real aim to bring down the Junta and return to the pre-1967 political situation, or was it to introduce something more radical? To what extent was this movement aspiring to pass from protest to revolution? Whatever the answer to that question might have been, the "workerism" of the students, endowed and indoctrinated with a solid Marxist background through which they framed events, was evident. It is no coincidence that alongside the Coordinating Committee, the students also formed a Workers' Committee composed mainly of construction workers with strong left-wing credentials, even though workers' trade unionism had barely existed up to that point. These construction workers, alongside the farmers from the region of Megara who happened to protest during the same days against the exploitation of their soil by a powerful industrialist, were the only ones who went out on strike. In its manifesto, the Workers' Committee asked for a general strike that never occurred. Its tone was more directly political than that of the students: it called for mixed student-worker assemblies, rejected the cost-of-living index, and praised the "working People."[113]

Giannis Felekis, a worker at the time and a member of the clandestine Trotskyist group Spartacus, remembers that the people repeated these slogans mimetically: "The people snapped up the slogans straight away, no matter what bullshit we were saying, no matter how far out these were. Just like the dry cane catches fire" (Felekis, interview). He further points out that in the assemblies the workers talked about a "Soviet Popular Democratic Workers-Farmers Government" and other unrealistic plans. Nikos Bistis shares this view from a somewhat different standpoint and adds with irony: "The ones who were turning political in those moments were willing to do everything you told them. Destroy the state and become Thailand" (Bistis, interview). There were many who recognized the possible danger of neglecting the rest of society as the students' conviction of being the national avant-garde reached its apogee. Stelios Papas, the secretary of the Coordinating Committee, notes, "When everyone is singing the national anthem, swinging Greek flags, you cannot be waving the sickle and hammer."[114] This precise contradiction indicates the limits of the revolt, which aspired to be simultaneously national and radical.

Nonetheless, the occupation seemed a first-class opportunity to bring about a "people's democracy." Political economist Albert O. Hirschman comments that humans are incapable of imagining different scales of social transformation and tend to aspire to "total," rather than modest changes in times of crisis;[115] this entirely fits the Polytechnic situation, where the tendency was reinforced by Marxist messianism. At this juncture when anything seemed possible, the perception of time itself was altered. As the waiting had come to an end, an immediate future seemed imminently close. The experience of collective liberation that brings along "the expansion of Eros," in Francesco Alberoni's words, is a source of unanimous group exaltation; the individual surpasses the self, feels that s/he is becoming a serious actor in history and forms the conviction that "everything is possible."[116] Leftist leader Dionysis Mavrogenis recalled in a latter day interview his sense that "this is what revolution must be like."[117] As in social movements, subjective perceptions matter as much as the objective situation on the ground—being in many ways "nested," and Mavrogenis's viewpoint offers us a valuable window to what was going on inside some of the actors' heads.

Recollections of the Polytechnic also often stress the density of experiences relative to time. Former student leader Giorgos Vernikos writes: "Under the increased danger and the tense situations you came to know the inner self of people in a very short time, something which in normal conditions takes years to discover. Fear, cowardice, bravery, sorrow for the wretchedness and other human capacities coexisted side by side, and were easily coming to the surface."[118] Historian Eleni Varikas's analysis of the ancient Greek division of time renders itself particularly useful here. Accordingly, whereas *chronos* stands for a temporal sequence referring to a continuous flow of time that "can be measured by the clock," *kairos* "points to a historical time in which each moment contains a unique chance for action, … an opportunity that might not recur."[119] The Greek student movement—just like its counterparts abroad in the '68 era—was poised by "the time of the now" attitude, a conviction that the moment could not be postponed and a faith in its ability to stop the methodical ticking of the world clock, to paraphrase Walter Benjamin's remark on the French Revolution.[120] The slogan "People, it's now or never" that was voiced when the collective coming-together at the Polytechnic was reaching its height, encapsulated the students' conviction that this was their only opportunity to inflict a fatal blow on the regime,[121] but was also a clear manifestation of their "hic et nunc" attitude.

The CCO's imposition of some order within the building was in stark contrast to what was taking place outside, where spontaneous demonstrations and enthusiasm ruled.[122] The occupation of the Polytechnic, located in the center of Athens, underlines the importance of performing acts of resistance on public stages, in addition to university campus yards.[123] The Polytechnic occupation possessed a favorable political opportunity structure, including sympathetic third parties and allies, and made use of a new set of tactics, all of which made it considerably more likely to succeed than earlier student actions. There is no doubt that it was an unprecedented event and an outlet for popular dissatisfaction, though the exact number of people who actually took to the streets remains unknown. Pictures and reels document a vast presence outside the closed gates of the building. People brought medicine, food, and cigarettes; many remained outside the gates and staged marches. Stergios Katsaros's reminiscences provide a biased but expressive analysis of the reasoning and typology of people who turned suddenly combative:

> The one who had been tortured and humiliated in the den of the Police ... was raising the fist to his torturers shouting "Tonight Fascism Will Perish." The "good Mr Vasilis" who sat down prudently for six years, with a little car or some prison-flat as a reward, tried to smother the guilty feelings for his subordination by showing the greatest intransigence in the clashes with the police. The one who was passing by just in order to satisfy his curiosity, was overtaken by the grandiose spectacle of the liberation of the masses and participated in the demonstrations. The worker, who for years felt inside his skin the alienation, the suppression and the barbarous exploitation was awaking from a lethargy and united his voice with the extremist provocateur: "Down with Capital."[124]

Despite the courageous and enthusiastic following that the occupation inspired, however, the popular response was not colossal. Contemporary reports refer to one hundred thousand people on site Friday morning, dwindling to fifty thousand by 7:00 Friday evening.[125] The daily *To Vima* and Athens Polytechnic's Rector Konofagos reported twenty thousand.[126] Ioanna Karystiani describes the failure of the occupation to mobilize the entire city, about 2.5 million people at the time, drawing an oppositional relation between students and people:

> Certainly, when I was inside the Polytechnic then, the last day, I had already inside me the impression that the Athenian people did not make their way down in solidarity. And I thought, nor have the parents come down, the ones who had come down there were few, there was a radio station which could mobilize the people, but there was fear. The people didn't make their way down, they got scared. (Karystiani, interview)

Activist-turned-novelist Maro Douka expressed a similar thought in her novel *Fool's Gold,* quoting Frantz Fanon's conclusion that "all spectators are cowards and traitors"—a standard reference among radical third-worldists in the "long 1960s":

> It occurred to me that if all the apartment blocks in the neighboring streets were to throw open their doors and windows, if all the

rooms and balconies were suddenly to be illuminated, then we could not be massacred this night. And I knew that whatever was to happen here tonight, would happen with the complicity of the apartment blocks—of the silent majority. And what Frantz Fanon says about cowards and traitors, could be applied with perfect truth here. I wondered what they could be doing in these flats. Surely not sleeping?[127]

Doukas's description of ordinary people experiencing the Polytechnic events without directly engaging with them—as a sheer representation of the reality that was actually unfolding before their eyes—apart from Fanon powerfully evokes Guy Debord's *Society of the Spectacle,* yet another 1960s favorite. Towards the late hours of Friday the students' desperate cries "Everybody to the Streets," "Descend to the Streets," and especially the dramatic appeal "Tonight they are killing your children" underline the real or perceived chasm between students and society.

In any case, by extending their demands beyond university concerns, students made it clear for the first time that university issues could not be separated from society as a whole. Through their slogans and repeated appeals, they sought an interlocutor beyond the Junta and the university authorities, and they expanded their social base. This was a crucial transition for the movement from pure student protest to a wider social conflict. As historian Jeffrey Wasserstrom says is the case for most major student movements, the Greek movement was "triggered by incidents with broader political implications, and struggles that began as conflicts over internal matters," and in the end it escalated into a protest that "involved social issues and social groups far beyond the walls of individual campuses."[128] For that reason, the Polytechnic was the first and only moment of genuine osmosis between different generations within the movement.

Nikitas Lionarakis comments on the private side of this public event about some of the parents who were standing at the Polytechnic gates: "[They] were outside not out of support but out of concern for their kids" (Lionarakis, interview). Leftist leader Mavrogenis describes how the presence of his mother, who had suffered greatly during his detention at the EAT-ESA headquarters, reversed his mood concerning the revolt:

My mom had come in order to take me out of there. She had experienced the whole story with EAT and she had come to pick me up. … She lay down there on the steps and remained until the evening, participating and listening to slogans. She was a young woman, together with other women over there. At a certain point, they brought her up to the CC and I saw her. She told me, "I know that you're not going to come." She wanted to put pressure on me and take me out of there. "I know, but try to get out of there, so that they won't bring you home dead," and she left. This thing influenced me."[129]

The affection conveyed in this description of the interaction between Mavrogenis and his mother creates an interesting contrast to his self-identification as an intransigent revolutionary and redefines the student militants of the period as twenty-year-old adolescents in a traditional family-based society.

The theme of worried parents is a common one in narratives of the Polytechnic. Kleopatra Papageorgiou remembers her father: "We had met in fact after my arrest, the next day, the one after, and he told me, 'Why do you get involved? Haven't I told you to protect yourself so that you get your degree and then you can do whatever you like?' And I told him, 'But no, it's now that it's needed.'" As this event took place shortly before her father died, Papageorgiou represents her bereavement as a catalyst that reinforced her determination to fight against the Junta, as she held the regime directly responsible for his death: "I even told them once, I told them, 'You put my father away. What else do you think you can do to me?'" (Papageorgiou, interview).

Xydi recalled with emotion her parents' dignity when they came to visit her in ESA and her father's understanding of her long-lasting absence from home:

> And I remember afterward when I got out of ESA, after some one and a half months without any communication with them all this time, and they didn't even know that I was coming home. When I went home, everything was so normal, that is, I knocked on the door, my father opened up, and I went in and he hugged me and said: "Come in, my child." (Xydi, interview).

Sabatakakis recalls that his father drove him back to the Polytechnic shortly before the tanks arrived, knowing that the regime would eventually violently suppress the movement: "What remains in me is the fact that in that moment my father knew that I returned to a place which would be shortly invaded by means of arms, and therefore it's a matter of life or death, and he didn't tell me 'Don't go'" (Sabatakakis, interview). In contrast, Dafermos remembers that his mother was entirely uncomprehending and preached in favor of the benefits of a pro-regime stance: "My mother, well, she was crying, she was screaming. At times they caught me, they released me, I was running, hiding, leaving, well, she didn't understand, she was saying, 'The smart ones now are with the regime'" (Dafermos, interview).

Left-wing parents were often more anguished about their children's political endeavors than those with other political affiliations. In her semifictional representation of the student movement, Maro Douka confronts the tense relationship between the female protagonist and her father, who ultimately succumbs to his daughter's will. Her heroine recognizes a major parental legacy in her father's instruction of verses by national poet Dionysios Solomos, marking a recurrent evocation of the romantic revolutionary past:

> I thought of my father—yesterday he'd come to look for me, I'd been much moved when he'd taken me unexpectedly in his arms, quoting in broken tones, *my eyes have beheld no land more glorious than this small battle ground,* and kissed my hair and the realization came to me once and for all that no matter how much or how wrongly I might judge this man, he was after all my father, and thank you, I said to him softly, for getting me to read Solomos and the *Free Besieged.*[130]

Lionarakis's description of parents outside the Polytechnic hints not only at their concern for the physical safety of their children but at a general distress, especially concerning women students (Lionarakis, interview). What had happened briefly and on a smaller scale in the Law School occupation was repeated now on a wider scale: women eighteen and nineteen years old stayed out of the house all day long and spent the night with their colleagues. The intensification of experience extended from daytime to night life. Naturally, the intimate aspects of the Polytechnic were censored by participants at the time in order to avoid offering the Junta more arguments about the "anarchist and pansexual" character of the occupation, but also because, officially at least, sexual liberation was not one of the movement's priorities. This hidden aspect is more visible in later recollections that expose the inevitable change that militancy and day-and-night symbiosis had on people's private lives. Dimitris Papachristos, the flamboyant radio announcer during the last hours of the occupation, remembers: "The three to four thousand people who found themselves barricaded awakened and realized another reality in front of the danger. The danger and the fear of conflict and death were generating eroticism, an atmosphere of love and coexistence. This was expressed by eating all together, singing all together. Even relationships were forged in there. This eroticism was overflowing in everyone's face, in men and women."[131]

Stavros Lygeros talks about the "orgasm of the feast" of the Polytechnic, an "element which is often neglected by political analysis,"[132] while Lionarakis equally argued that an enhanced sexual coming-together occurred during these days, aided by symbiosis and the intensity of the moment (Lionarakis, interview). Still, Kleopatra Papageorgiou clarifies that the "sexual revolution" aspect was a myth—also expressing a feeling of regret for this. She takes a very critical stance toward reports of promiscuity during the Polytechnic occupation, even though her own experience was that of the Salonica occupation: "[Conservative politician] Rallis had said too that inside the Polytechnic orgies had taken place. How stupid was that. Where? I wish this had happened" (Papageorgiou, interview). Regardless of these conflicting views concerning the libidinal economy of the occupation, and even though the "orgies" theory is unfounded, conservative circles within the army were enraged by the supposed "pansexual" nature of the occupation. In his autobiographical novel, Tasos Darveris convincingly reconstructs the dialogues between apparently sexually repressed officers and soldiers: "'Don't you know what the students were doing all those days at the Polytechnic? I'll tell you what they were doing. They were fucking. When the storm-troopers came in they found condoms in piles.'"[133]

Friday morning, 16 November, was marked by the embrace of the student venture by some illustrious political figures. This was, furthermore, the moment when A-EFEE decided to walk out of the building, as its "instruction" suggested that prolonging the occupation would only harm the aims of the movement. But A-EFEE's students left only to come back some hours later upon realizing that the dynamics of the occupation could not be controlled. This is why the third day inside the Polytechnic was crucial: although the slogans and radio announcements were fully controlled by the CCO by this point, the students entirely surpassed the organizations' lines.

The CCO continued to suffer greatly from the so-called line struggle, meaning the different strategies favored by the various student organizations. The declaration it issued on Friday manifested the difficulty of its members' task of finding a common ground and a compromise in formulating their demands and positions. Dimitris Hatzisokratis, a member of the committee and politician at present, laments this "political self-limitation" due to the fragile climate at the assemblies.[134] Maro Douka offers a quite powerful literary representation of the whole situation: "The invisible hand of the Coordinating Committee was everywhere—come on now, cut out the Velouchiotis stuff, come on you bloody anarchist, leftist, provocateur, bomber, petty bourgeois extremist, and all the rest of the shit."[135]

The CCO's statement of 16 November made it clear that the movement's aim was the overthrow of the regime within the framework of a national struggle.[136] Apart from this vague formulation, the manifesto made no mention of what conditions would follow the fall of the "tyrannical Junta," nor did it place itself within a wider political milieu that would include other political forces. It called on the people to support the ongoing revolt with all their means, mainly by going out on strike, and stressed the necessity of being detached from the so-called foreign factor, which the students held responsible for a great many things, including the coup itself. The manifesto initially contained an appeal for the creation of a "government of national unity," but this was rejected in the end due to the intransigence of the leftists, who threatened a walkout, considering any mention of "bourgeois" politicians to be totally out of tune with the subversive character of the revolt.[137] Accordingly, the manifesto, announced by the CCO at its first and only press conference in front of local and international journalists on Friday afternoon, was only approved after the removal of a call for solidarity between all antidictatorship forces and the old politicians. The call for "national independence and popular sovereignty" remained intact and was repeated on the radio station.[138]

16–17 November: Transcendence and Massacre

Friday was also the turning point that transformed the occupation into a massacre. On this third consecutive day without police intervention, people started to believe—in one of the major paradoxes in recent Greek political history—that this would be the event that would bring down the regime. In fact, Papadopoulos had not ordered the violent dissolution of the occupation by this point because the costs of suppression seemed to exceed the costs of toleration.[139] As the occupation proceeded, participants had the growing sensation that they were changing things and were sensing history in the making, framing the latter as a collective process that takes on the sense of an advent.[140] Ioanna Karystiani presents this in almost religious terms, as an instant of pure transcendence:

> In such elevated moments all people make crazy scenarios. … I think I saw it everywhere, everyone was determined, no matter how mad this seems to you, it was transcendence, from one point onward this takes you out of touch with reality. … In transcendence, how can I put it, one takes off. We had taken off, this did not touch us any longer. … Without knowing consciously that history was being written at this moment. (Karystiani, interview)

According to Dafermos, the widespread feeling was that the occupation was a unique opportunity that would never be repeated: "People were heated up, excited, saying, 'To hell with it, I cannot stand it anymore. Here, there are so many of us, now we're going to screw them'" (Dafermos, interview). Contrary to this view, Angeliki Xydi recalled having an awkward feeling of precariousness due to the lack of clear direction, which was in contrast to the "heroic" mood of the previous days:

On Friday I started asking myself where this entire thing was leading to and I had no answer either. And there was no one there to enlighten us. In contrast to that, on Thursday night I was very enthusiastic because I went out to the Patision Street and I saw that there were … I don't know if there were thousands of people, they must have been thousands. All these people were shouting, "Tonight Fascism is dying," and yes, I was very enthusiastic. But on Friday in the morning I had a … not exactly fear, but a freezing sentiment. That I don't know any more what I'm doing here and no one does.… From Friday onward I think that there was a generalized perplexity. Up to that it was, say, heroic. You know, we were organizing life, the crews which were writing the pamphlets, the CCO, the radio station, all of this. There was an excitement of everything, of the emotions, of the sensations, of all situations. I think that on Friday this thing started becoming perplexed and more difficult and, in the end, we had to organize pharmacies and surgeries. And it was getting onto another, entirely different track. (Xydi, interview)

At the same time, inside the building, the CCO faced a dilemma on which it could not reach consensus: whether to proceed to a "victorious" withdrawal without victims or to go on with the occupation on Saturday in order to "have the place put on fire."[141] As the first option was becoming increasingly unrealistic, the occupation steadily began to lose a coherent vision and became a series of emotional moments with no articulate philosophy, risking a devastating assault by government forces.

Contemporaneously, from about 6 PM onwards fever-pitch demonstrations started taking place in the center of Athens. A part of the crowd tried to march towards the central Syntagma Square and another one surrounded and attacked the Ministries of Employment and Education, and Attica's Municipality. As AASPE explained after the Polytechnic: "The people rushed in order to occupy public buildings, symbols of bourgeois state violence and oppression."[142] In several instances buses and trolleys were used as barricades while fires were lit throughout the central roads, which were closed. The police initially responded by sending teargas canisters into the crowd but soon resorted to opening fire. Shortly before 10 PM and while the news of the first casualties among the protesters started arriving, an angry unidentified crowd tried to make its way into the Ministry of Public Order. This particular instance marked a systematic use of cocktail bombs on the part of the protesters and an escalation of the confrontations with the police forces that reached unprecedented levels. Giorgos Kotanidis writes with emotion about the moment he launched his first Molotov cocktail, unprecedented throughout the seven years of dictatorship:

> I took my lighter outside my pocket, I checked it and went to the 3rd of September Street, where the armored vehicles were stationed and they were throwing teargas against a large group of young people.... I slowly approached them from behind, put fire to the wick, threw the Molotov cocktail to the last armored vehicle and saw its rear explode, setting it on fire. Success with the first blow.[143]

Kevin Andrews recalled in later years "the tang of combat in the nostrils: the smell of smoke, gas, gunpowder, and no more alternatives." His conclusion, however, that "years of collective boredom had given way to a few minutes of individual responsibility,"[144] paints the facts with too broad a brush. Though it may be applicable to the majority of the Greek society, it does not apply to the dissident few who had brought about the occupation and the conflict with the regime.

Despite the fact that this was the first and last time wide-scale riots occurred during the seven years of the Colonels' dictatorship (even a bank was attacked), the orders given by police headquarters were false and misleading, reporting that a thousand demonstrators were using weapons, policemen were being slaughtered by enraged workers, and crowds were isolating a phalanx of armed vehicles.[145] Capitalizing on this misinformation, Undersecretary of Public Order Zournatzis argued in a Pasolinian fashion, "If today there are violent clashes between protesters and policemen, who try not to use violent means, then the one who embodies the real revolutionary spirit should be the police and not the protesters."[146] When some major political figures, such as the right-wing intellectual Panagiotis Kanellopoulos, the last prime minister before the Junta, passed by the Polytechnic, Zournatzis expressed his surprise that respectable figures were coming out to support an entirely "anarchical" movement.

The government's description of the movement as anarchical was a conscious attempt to evoke memories of the constant social turmoil of "the anarchy," as the years prior to 1967 were frequently called. Zournatzis did not miss the chance, moreover, to draw parallels with December 1944, when British troops got involved in a bloody conflict with the Greek communist guerrillas over the control of Athens, leaving dozens of dead behind, ravaging the capital, and marking the official start of long-term civil strife. These so-called December events left a dark legacy of particular cruelty and a considerable number of civilian victims on both sides; the Junta aimed to create alarming associations with these memories in labeling the Polytechnic as "anarchy." Previously, rightist propaganda had equated the "Red December" with the popular unrest of July 1965. Interestingly, it was not just the regime that was drawing parallels to that key moment in Greece's recent political history. The Coordinating Committee of the Polytechnic occupation was warning the crowds not to use the word "people's rule" (*laokratia*) as it would "awaken bitter memories," since this had been a famous rallying cry of the communists in Athens in late 1944.[147]

Eventually, the regime dropped its passive stance toward the Polytechnic occupation and the movement that was unfolding in the streets of Athens and opted for measures of extreme repression. Snipers were placed on top of buildings surrounding the Polytechnic, and they started shooting protesters shortly before midnight. The students initially thought that the bullets were plastic, whereas later on rumors were spread that they were dum-dum bullets, as people who got hit bore unnaturally severe wounds. Ultimately, twenty-four civilians were killed outside the Polytechnic gates and in the nearby streets; none of the students barricaded inside were killed. Even though there was plenty of state violence and a number of casualties throughout the entire seven years of the dictatorship, this was the only time that the regime resorted to such extremes, attacking large crowds of unidentified people and causing widespread bloodshed. Andrianos Vanos, a student from Salonica who went to Athens in order to participate in the events, made contradictory statements about this last day of the occupation, initially describing it as "the most beautiful day of my life" but then calling the evening's clashes "the saddest demonstration I have ever been to" (Vanos, interview). The duality of his testimony reflects the biographical tension between exaltation and trauma, as well as the transition of the Polytechnic itself from a celebratory process to a massacre.

As tear gas was thrown from the Polytechnic up to Omonoia and Syntagma Squares and people lit fires in order to confront it, the radio station gave instructions on how to deal with the fumes. It also asked for help from the Red Cross for the wounded. *Katerina remembers, "In the School of Architecture they were pulling out the desks from the drawing tables and were making stretchers for the wounded" (*Katerina, interview). The radio announcers insisted, "We are unarmed," and the slogan of the day became "No more blood." A standard point of reference in life stories is overriding fear. Karystiani once more draws an opposition between the frightened "people" and the fearless "kids":

> I'm telling you, there were five thousand kids at the Polytechnic, and they were all ready to die. No one was afraid, there were tanks all around, if one only thinks of that moment, that there were tanks all around, it was dark, bullets were flying, some kids were already

killed, in the medical office they were bringing people, I remember they brought one whose leg was hanging from a slight piece of flesh, I saw killed ones, I saw ... and no one at that moment went away in order to save his skin. (Karystiani, interview)

When asked which were the strongest memories from the Polytechnic occupation, Sabatakakis portrayed a powerful image of chaos and fear: "The bullets were falling like haze, they were flying next to our heads, and we didn't know if we would die any second" (Sabatakakis, interview). As the number of people killed or wounded rose, things started getting out of hand. Damofli emphasizes the presence and massacre of high-school students as her strongest and most poignant memory: "The presence of high-school students and their action during the Polytechnic occupation was something sensational, I'll never forget it" (Damofli, interview). Karystiani also refers to the high-school students: "The kids were a bit further out, they were playing truant from their moms and the tutorials in order to come over there. It was easier and more barbaric to look at a child and shoot at it" (Karystiani, interview). In fact, several of the officially recognized Polytechnic dead happened to be schoolchildren. *Katerina argues that a couple of years earlier, many of these same kids were jumping into the Omonoia Square fountain to celebrate Panathinaikos's victory against Red Star Belgrade in football. In her view, most of them used to be apolitical youth who were involved in different everyday activities from the politicized students. She speculates about a radical change taking place inside them, transforming many of these "motorcycle freaks" into political activists overnight:

> Whereas before they used to have posters of motorcycles and women in their garages, now they tore them apart and made wallpaper out of hand-written slogans, "Down with the Junta of Papadopoulos" and so forth. That is, in a few days, all those, all this myth about the youth which was disoriented, football-friendly and this and that, collapsed. And I think that this means that no one should ever underestimate the young people, and not just during the Polytechnic. These kids knew nothing about Marcuse, Koligiannis, or Zachariadis, which we thought very important, but they came immediately, they got the spirit—and with less hesitation than many of us who were discussing the organized versus the spontaneous and so on. (*Katerina, interview)

This is a powerful, albeit impressionistic, rendering of these average youths' sudden metamorphosis. Moreover, *Katerina seems to underplay the importance of the intellectual panoply that student militants, like herself, enjoyed for joining the movement.

Armed vehicles began moving toward the Polytechnic shortly after midnight. Though the Junta reported that the students were armed with rifles and other weapons, the CCO had decided that no cocktail bombs or any sort of weapons should be used against policemen. Similarly, while the Polytechnic laboratories reportedly contained chemical substances that could have been used in order to create explosives, none were made. When the occupation gestalt was suspended between expectation and desperation, the strategy of pacific protest was chosen, marking a clear difference from the occupation's violent Thai prototype. Not everyone agreed with this judgment, of course. Exponent of the previous generation Stergios Katsaros laments the fact that he did not go to the Polytechnic in order to offer his solid theoretical knowledge of revolutionary insurrections and to turn over his explosives for the students' use. Like most of the people involved in the armed struggle, Katsaros was doubtful about the mass movement's dynamics and its decision to reject the use of violence. This line of thought is clear in his autobiographical account through the voice of an anonymous comrade who reproaches the students for serious distortions of Marxist thought: "'These brats,' he said, 'think of us elderly ones as cowards, but they themselves have nothing to do with the revolutionary Left. They have arrived, pretending to be revolutionaries. Their aim is to become leaders of the working class.'"[148]

Writer Maro Douka also belongs to the previous generation, and she too expressed her discontent through her fictional character, Myrsini, invoking the omnipresent shadow of civil strife: "Out in the courtyard we were asking for petrol from the labs to make Molotov cocktails, we're like sitting ducks here under fire, and we haven't even sticks for kindling. But the committees said no, they wouldn't endorse such tactics, we weren't to start another civil war." Referring to a standard phrase concerning the period of Ottoman rule and the servility of Orthodox religious zealots and implying that bravery is not necessarily a characteristic Greek feature, Douka adds with sarcasm: "Either way it was bound to end in violence. Morale among us was running high, we were on course of eternity—*thy murd'rous hand, oh Pasha, sends me to Heaven straight*, the chorus swelled, *thy murd'rous hand*, like an old *rebetiko* song of the city poor, *Pasha oh Pasha send me to the Pearly Gate*, in full cry, like a dithyramb, *thy murdr'ous hand, thy murd'rous hand.*"[149] In counterpoint, Douka presents people praising the barricaded students by shouting "Bravely done lads, well done you strugglers, like the heroes of 1821," arguing for a historical continuity in self-sacrifice.[150]

Lambros Papadimitrakis, one of the four radio announcers, also argues for this continuity, comparing the occupation to the recollections of students' parents from the period of Nazi occupation: "They were reminiscent of the stories from the National Resistance, the ones that our fathers were telling us."[151] This kind of framing drew on collective imaginary resources and positioned the Polytechnic firmly next to the wartime resistance of the 1940s and its vanguard organizations. EAM/ELAS were placed in an imaginary lineage with the student uprising that was later verbally consolidated in the slogan "EAM/ELAS, Polytechnic." Wartime resistance represented a model of the struggles antiregime students were envisioning and a glorious antecedent, as apart from their pedigree in the struggle against fascism, 1940s guerillas had allied themselves with options for radical social change. As Mark Mazower concludes, "the wartime resistance against the Germans became an inescapable analogue to the campaign against the Junta."[152]

National-religious symbols were also promptly appropriated. Most testimonies report that the church bells were ringing during the night of the tanks' raid. Certainly, this feature is connected in people's imagination to a legendary song by Theodorakis, "The Bells Will Ring" [Tha Simanoun oi Kampanes] (1966), in which communist poet Giannis Ritsos's verses announce a sort of apocalyptic revolutionary arrival, using a strongly Orthodox wording. Music analyst Panos Geramanis maintains that at the very moment that "the tanks broke into the grounds and attacked the people ... , [popular singer] Bithikotsis' voice was singing *Hush, the bells will ring any moment now.*"[153] Thus it is valid in this case to cite anthropologist Michael Herzfeld's claim that in Greece a common imaginary connects national insurrection with an orthodox "resurrection."[154]

The Greek flag, which people were waving at the gate, and the national anthem were other symbols widely used in the events. The Polytechnic's Rector Konofagos recalls with an evident sense of pride: "Over the Polytechnic gate at Patision Street the blue and white flag was waving. No other flag stood by its side. The blue and white flag remained the only symbol of the uprising for all four days. The Greek symbol of freedom."[155] Coordinating Committee member Dimitris Hatzisokratis's description of a man on a stretcher with his foot torn by a bullet is equally illuminating: "His foot was hanging by a thread and he was singing the National Anthem and raising his arm, making the sign of victory. These are unrepeatable things. To be like this, with your blood flowing like a river, while you are watching it, raising your arm like that and singing the national anthem is a scene that I shall never forget."[156] Once more, rather than rejecting national symbols, students, and the Left in general, were defending an "authentic" form of Greekness and patriotism. This reached a climax when, after a number of tanks lined up, obviously about to enter the Polytechnic, Dimitris Papachristos, the last radio announcer, began to chant the national anthem—a nineteenth-century revolutionary poem—in its full version with pomp and emotion.

The tank crashing the gate is recorded in life stories as the climax in the series of highly traumatic moments of the Polytechnic thriller: the flashing of a huge searchlight over the barricaded students was followed by a brief moment of uncertainty, the hasty negotiation between two student representatives and a general, and the final entry of the vehicle. The CCO had requested of the authorities that the students be allowed to evacuate the building at 6.30 AM in the presence of the Red Cross and of representatives of foreign embassies—a probably unrealistic scenario that was rejected on the ground that "the army does not negotiate." Thanasis Gaifilias, a well-known musician of the time who was barricaded inside the Polytechnic, remembers that most people laughed at what the general said, as he spoke with a heavy peasant accent.[157] His account demonstrates the thin boundaries between tragedy and farce in moments of tension, but it also underlines the sense of superiority young people felt toward the peasant, uncultivated militaries and their subordinates.

Andrianos Vanos recalled that he was the only one to stay in his position when the armored vehicle prepared to enter: "Everybody was on the floor. I said, 'What's the difference between up and down, at least I will see what's going to happen.' The tank turned, I see the soldier, the soldier sees me, I was

Figure 5.6. A tank is about to crush the Polytechnic gate where students are barricaded, morning hours of 17 November 1973. The bloody ending of the ten months that shook Greece. (Photographer: Aristotelis Sarrikostas)

staring at him, everybody down, I'm standing" (Vanos, interview). Kotanidis recounts in his memoir that the image of the tank approaching the gate reactivated the memory of a war film he had watched in his childhood:

> We saw the tanks coming in front of the Polytechnic. I remembered a movie that I had seen when I was little in Salonica, at the "Kentrikon" cinema, showing the Germans entering Prague, with their tanks and the SS parading, inducing fear in the few Czechs who were watching, I do not remember which movie it was, but this scene has stayed unaltered in my memory, as a silent duel between the fully armed conqueror and the unarmed people. This is what came to my mind when I saw the tanks approaching, ... and one of them stopping and pointing at the gate of the Polytechnic, with the soldiers and cops surrounding us.[158]

Long before the end of the ten minutes that were offered by the army officers, a M40 tank broke down the central gate and entered the Polytechnic, bulldozing the dean's Mercedes and crushing the legs of a female student, Pepi Rigopoulou. It was 3 AM. The tank was followed by the Marines, who entered with their bayonets pointed at the students, while a large number of policemen waiting outside arrested over a thousand of those who were leaving the Polytechnic en masse. Policemen and gendarmes hit the demonstrators on their heads with nail-studded beams.[159] An industrial school student testified in the trials, referring to films to help him understand the experience: "What happened can only be seen in movies. They were hitting me with clubs and with their feet on my head, on the stomach, wherever they could."[160] Damofli also likens these moments to a Western movie: "And that night Athens was like a Western, bang-bang-bang, you know" (Damofli, interview). On top of these accounts, the resemblance between the real events of the storming Marines inside the Polytechnic and the violent ending of Stuart Hagmann's semi-fictional signature film *The Strawberry Statement*—one of the Greek students' favorites—is quite striking.

Kotanidis and Lionarakis are among the few who remember a tragicomic incident in the middle of this havoc. Like Antonis Liakos's espousal of Brancaleone as his alter ego in the previous generation, they also adopt a "heroic-comic" register in order to narrate dramatic events. Self-irony becomes a means of distancing oneself from the lived experience and looking at things from without, with a certain detachment.[161] Incidentally, both stories involve tin cans. Accordingly, Kotanidis recalls that immediately prior to the tank's entry he saw a used tin can on the ground and referring to a well-known myth, that the communists used to slit their opponents' throats

Figure 5.7. After the Revolution. The crushed gate of the Polytechnic in daylight. Next to the bulldozed Mercedes of the school's dean, a gate column with the graffito "NATO Out." Other gate columns bore the inscriptions "USA out" and "Allende." (Photographer: Aristotelis Sarrikostas)

with open tin cans during the Greek civil war, he grabbed his newly acquired "weapon" and shouted "Prepare to attack!"; he records a female cadre of KNE shutting him off, pointing out that this was not an opportune moment for humor: "Really, how did I manage to use humor in the most difficult moments?" he wonders.¹⁶²

Lionarakis's most vivid memory of the building evacuation, on the other hand, was when he grabbed the cans and money that had been collected for the barricaded students: "Endless food, endless cans, you know, and I left with some 500,000 drachmas in my pockets, which was our money, the money that the people were giving us, you know. And I bagged several cans inside my coat and I had them in there." In this narrative Lionarakis depicted himself as a grotesque figure, more concerned about food than the tragedy that was unfolding. As Luisa Passerini notes, "Oral testimony draws a veil over more tragic elements—the dead and wounded, the pain and fear—and brings out the symbolic overturning of order characteristic of carnival."¹⁶³ Lionarakis's tone changed, however, as he recalled the shocking fact that when he found shelter in a basement upon his exit from the building, soldiers sang victory marches after their triumphant intervention: "After the evacuation operation, what was terrible was how the trucks were going away with the soldiers, who were singing in a style 'We screwed them,' you know, by singing songs, which is very frightening, in the middle of the night to listen to such songs, we didn't know how many were killed, didn't know anything at that point" (Lionarakis, interview).

Although this recollection is in accordance with other testimonies,[164] many remember the soldiers as scared and sympathetic adolescents who in fact helped the students get out unharmed, in contrast to the enraged and vulgar policemen. A number of accounts mention that during the students' frantic search for shelter, many doors were opened in order to briefly accommodate those who were persecuted by the police. Damofli remembers: "And in this condition that man opened up his door and said 'Guys, come in.' … Why did the rest of them not open up their doors? And he gave us blankets, there, they covered us, everything in the dark of course, see? Right across from the Polytechnic" (Damofli, interview). The most glorious moment of student resistance ended, in the best of cases, inside some stranger's house, in the dark.

The Copycat Occupation

The student mobilizations of mid-November were not confined to Athens alone. The students of Patras occupied that city's university soon after those of Athens, while Ioannina and Salonica students followed, mimicking what took place in the capital's universities. The most important of these three events was the one in Salonica, not least because the students there set up a radio station too. During the previous days, the students had gathered in order to protest the expulsion of four of their colleagues. After the Athens occupation began, they adopted a resolution expressing solidarity with their counterparts.[165]

It was not until Friday, 16 November, however, that the Salonicean students decided to act, largely due to the hesitation of Rigas and even more so of A-EFEE, whose leadership thought that the whole venture would backfire and would have a negative impact on the movement. Both *Pavlos and Kleopatra Papageorgiou remember that these organizations initially attempted to postpone the assembly until Monday, playing for time, in contrast to the Maoists, who were in favor of rapid, direct action. Petros Oikonomou, a Rigas member and one of the students who had been arrested in the past, thereby acquiring a sort of symbolic status, explains why his organization participated even though it was against the occupation:

We didn't have the luxury of remaining out of it and of denouncing it. It would have been stupid on our side because we would dissolve the student movement, we would cause fragmentation. Surely, we realized how wrong the tactic was and where it leads to and whose game it plays. ... I remember, we had an assembly before entering the Polytechnic, the team in which I participated, the clandestine one, and the conclusion we arrived at was that we were going to commit suicide. (Oikonomou, interview)

Oikonomou's insistence that for some people the entire venture seemed like a suicide mission highlights the fact that on behalf of these students, and despite the spontaneity of the moment and the willingness to reenact what was happening in Athens, there was a cost-benefit analysis. However, extreme pragmatism was abandoned in favor of not causing rifts inside the movement.

At this point, the Maoists took the initiative for an occupation, "being closer to the feeling of the moment."[166] The spontaneous entry of more students led to a gathering of around 2,500 students inside the School of Architecture. Later on, they set up a fourteen-member Coordinating Committee, which soon declared, "Today, the sixteenth of November, we students of Salonica have occupied the building of the Polytechnic in order to express our opposition to the Junta." *Pavlos points out that he and several of his companions preferred to stay out of the committee in order to "better guide" the occupation from outside: "If we had been inside, we wouldn't have been lucid enough" (*Pavlos, interview).

Unlike in Athens, the slogans that the students wrote were not filtered. They included typical incitements to an alliance with the workers ("Workers and farmers unite"), which never materialized, and anti-American ones like those used in Athens ("Americans out," "NATO out"), but also quite direct anti-imperialist ones ("People, strike the lackeys of the colonizers!"). Other slogans referred to the mythical Greek people who were finally going to act ("The people have awakened," "Freedom is not donated, it is conquered," "Long live people's power"), while yet another anticipated the arrival of the policemen and the pro-regime forces: "Informers, rub in order to expunge them [the slogans]."[167] In his account of the events, Chrysafis Iordanoglou, a member of the Coordinating Committee and a Rigas leader, expresses his bitterness at the fact that no control was allowed, nor was the possibility of a police raid discussed, while some leftists believed that they could overthrow the Junta here and now, and "maybe the capitalist system too."[168] Oikonomou shares this perception and castigates the extremist tendency that characterized the younger members of the movement: "Until the evening everyone was inside, everyone, even the little kids who were saying for the first time that 'we are going to fight against the Junta,' you know, who on the top were the most dangerous ones. Certainly they were thinking that they were starting the civil war" (Oikonomou, interview).

The statement that came out of the Coordinating Committee was that the takeover was an act designed "to express our antithesis to the Junta."[169] In Salonica, as in Athens, an ad hoc first aid center, press room, and refectory were created.[170] A radio station was set up as well, though its frequency was much weaker than the one in Athens. In between playing Theodorakis songs, the station denounced "Stayer" and "Esso Pappas," two prominent representatives of local and foreign "capital," as seeking to control university research through their funded programs. It further called for people's solidarity. Klearchos Tsaousidis, who alongside Thomas Vasileiadis was one of the "grandfathers" in the student movement, calls the demands immature, at least in retrospect:

> What we all said during the developments looks afterward a bit stupid and immature. Alright. So, when we invited people to come and express solidarity with us, we knew that they wouldn't come. Of course in Athens people went out. Here they didn't, also considering where we were. Yet another tragic mistake. How could people come over there? However, we showed our desire about where we wanted this thing to go: we wanted popular participation. (Tsaousidis, interview)

In fact, the physical distance from the rest of the city was a major limitation in attracting more people to express their solidarity at the Polytechnic School of Salonica, where the occupation took place. In contrast to Athens where simple passersby could stop by the occupied building in its central location, in order for someone to reach the barricaded students in Salonica, one had to cross the entire campus, in an unpopulated area.

It has often been argued that the radio station in Salonica was extreme in its articulation of the students' demands—perhaps an unsurprising development, as Kleopatra Papageorgiou, who was the main speaker at the station, was a radical. Vanos argued that no one expressed reservations at the time to those who had the courage to act: "Whoever had the guts took the microphone at the Polytechnic, and this is what made up the radio station, period. No one has ever doubted this. When she said, 'I am going to do it' … They knew Kleopatra, she was a pretty dynamic woman, she took the microphone and made a mess" (Vanos, interview). The Coordinating Committee did not seek to approve the texts that were announced, and by and large the speakers broadcasted all texts that they were given. Papageorgiou recalls: "We were saying everything, there was no censorship in our station, there was much freedom. You know what we were saying, all being communists. Of course in the station we didn't say for example, 'Down with capitalism' and stuff like that. We were saying more anti-Junta and anti-imperialist things." Though she boasts that the radio speakers enjoyed absolute freedom to announce any text that came before their eyes, Papageorgiou confesses that she imposed a censorship of sorts in order to reach a wider consensus:

> Well, okay, these slogans were a bit restricted because we wanted to preserve the mass form, not to chase away the more conservative ones—there were many of them inside—not at that moment to even clash with A-EFEE for example, which was totally against. These had entered and were throwing around leaflets saying, "Get out of here, these are provocations," "Who brought you together?" "You are playing the game of reaction with this action," this kind of crap. We didn't want to clash with them by saying overly extreme slogans on the station; we tried to express all streams in order to keep them inside too. (Papageorgiou, interview)

Here too, therefore, the sloganeering was conditioned by the announcer's judgment. She further notes: "Back then, we were distinguished from each other by subtle nuances. If, for example, you said 'Down with the Junta,' you were from KKE-Esoterikou. If you said 'Death to fascism and to imperialism,' you were a Maoist" (laughter).

Iordanoglou, in contrast, laments the fact that although the first radio program started in a moderate way,[171] it soon degraded into an anti-imperialist delirium ("the foreign enslaved fascist dictatorship," "struggle against the foreign capital and the American-European imperialists") and an argument against the "system," concluding that only with the final victory of the Greek people and the death of imperialism would the country be free again. To this end, the announcer declared, "Let's struggle by all means."[172] Klearchos Tsaousidis stresses that a committee effectively controlled the station's program after midnight:

> All texts passed through a particular committee and were filtered. There were no other things such as "down with the state" and so on ... that is the stuff that would worry petit-bourgeois people, at times also the democratic left-winger. From twelve o'clock onward, there was much filtering. Only the moment when the evacuation started and in which the kids from that particular radical Left group

controlled things did [Kleopatra] take back the microphone and say some hypercombative things. (Tsaousidis, interview)

As a climax of its appeal to the Greek people, the station proposed: "Greek intellectuals, enlighten the new struggles of our people with your spirit, express in your words the new struggles of our people. Communicate a faith for a better life. Stand next to the worker, the farmer, the student!"[173]

While the students were resting in the hours after midnight, news started to come in about the Athens bloodshed. Vourekas recalls the CCO's concern about the effect this news would have on the barricaded students' morale:

The night in which the Athens Polytechnic got hit, we got to know about it before we were encircled, that is, the Coordinating Committee was informed about it. And there it was decided not to tell anyone, in some way say, "Alright, the tanks appeared, let's not talk about the dead, so as not to let the people panic." But people had transistors which were transmitting foreign stations. Despite this, the people didn't break. (Vourekas, interview)

Starting at 3:30 AM, the Polytechnic of Salonica was encircled by army vehicles too. The committee members were given half an hour for the students to evacuate the building. At 4:30 on Saturday morning, 17 November, three armed vehicles and two units of commando/marine troops were standing by outside the Polytechnic. A little later, the Coordinating Committee negotiated with the university and military authorities for an unconditional evacuation, contrary to the students' wish. The radio station's final announcement that followed bears striking resemblances to the final dramatic appeal of the radio station in Athens:

We are talking to you from the radio station of the free University of Salonica. If the army strikes at us, if even one bullet gets fired, no one can be without responsibility for it.... We ask of the soldiers to understand that we are brothers, our enemy is a common one. ... We address the Greek people and the entire free world with an appeal to take a position. We ask the soldiers not to obey an order to shoot. We ask you to take a position. Don't turn it off. This is the last moment. The people want to listen.[174]

As with Papachristos, the radio announcer at the Athens Polytechnic, here too an appeal was made to the humanity of the soldiers and to the fact that they were "brothers." Similarly to the events in Prague during the Soviet invasion in August 1968 the students tried to convince the soldiers—to whom they were actually coetaneous—of the futility of their actions and their moral obligation to join their struggle by defying their orders; but to no avail.

Within half an hour, the students had started to come out. Descriptions of their exodus stress the savagery of the beatings they received and the immediate arrest of about two hundred people. Iordanoglou feels very proud that there were no fatalities, on the committee's responsibility,[175] while a former comrade of his, of Maoist inclinations, expresses a quite different opinion: "If in retrospect no one was killed, this is among the pros during a peaceful period. During a revolutionary period it is a con. In a revolutionary period you do not feel sorry for the dead people, you hate the ones who killed them" (*Pavlos, interview). There is a discrepancy between these two attitudes, clearly delineating disparate points of view on the past, a moderate and a radical one. *Pavlos's Jacobin analysis reflects the conviction of the time that this was a "revolutionary period" with specific characteristics and needs. Maoist and Trotskyist groups, such as EDE, effectively interpreted the student revolt of November 1973 as a "revolutionary situation." They lamented not having the necessary organizational structures to take advantage of this moment. One official document of the EDE warned: "Revolution has come, and we have got very little time left to build the Party."[176] *Pavlos expresses resentment at the occupation's lack of casualties, that the students did not struggle to the last drop of blood. This position is—once again—strongly reminiscent of the declaration of Simon, the protagonist of *The Strawberry Statement:* "If there's blood, I hope there are massive casualties."

After the evacuation many of the Salonica protesters, like those in Athens, went into hiding. Vourekas describes the prevailing effect of that time: "And I remember that feeling of fear, I remember noises out of sheet metal, because there were roofs made out of sheet metal, and every now and then I woke up in a nightmarish way, feeling that ... Because after [the occupation] repression was total" (Vourekas, interview). Arrested and tortured shortly after the occupation, he retains intense memories of the feeling of panic toward the unknown that possessed him, despite his belief that by that time he had "mastered" fear—a situation that many experienced.

In both cities, to most of the participants who were either arrested or went into hiding, it was still pretty unclear what the occupations had managed to achieve. However, apart from being the most massive acts of resistance against the military dictatorship—prompting for the first time thousands of people to actively protest—what the November 1973 occupations mainly achieved was far beyond student interests and aspirations: by exposing the dark underbelly of the Junta they practically canceled the "liberalization experiment" of Georgios Papadopoulos, which would have turned Greece to a "paternalistic democracy" under the tutelage of the army, just like 1970s Turkey or 1980s Chile. However, at the same time they had unwillingly opened the way for the hard-liners within the regime and for Papadopoulos's overthrow by one of his most trusted men: Brigadier Dimitrios Ioannidis, the notorious head of ESA.

After the Revolution

Prior to the Polytechnic, the student movement catalyzed state violence to reveal that the regime's liberalization was only a facade. With the storming of the Polytechnic, however, the regime went too far in continuing to try to keep up appearances. Consequently, although the movement and democratic civil society won a moral advantage at the Polytechnic, the tactical battle was already largely lost. Immediately after the morning of 18 November, decree 798/1971, which prescribed steps to be taken "in a situation of siege," was put into action. According to a later government announcement, Prime Minister Markezinis assumed responsibility for the "bloodless," as he called it, suppression of the popular uprising in his speech to the General Staff on 20 November.

Among the first things that the government did was to talk about the huge damage to the Polytechnic premises in both Athens and Salonica, estimated at several billion drachmas. In Salonica, pro-regime student newspaper *O Foititis* reported the events in a way that reflects how regime-friendly and apolitical students regarded the incident. It ran pictures accompanied by commentary expressing indignation about the disastrous state of the Polytechnic buildings: one caption remarked on "a sight of filthiness and misery," noting with sarcasm, "And then they tell you that they struggle for a better world, for beauty." In an article titled "They Abandoned Their Cars in order to Deliver the Proletariat," the paper castigated the "anarchist minority" that did not show proper respect to the people who paid for their education, and it expressed outrage about the anti-Western slogans written on the walls. Ironic comments were made about the misspellings and content of the students' slogans, such as "People, let's fight, they're sucking up your blood!":

> The Polytechnic is ravaged. The hordes of the defenders of academic freedom and popular sovereignty piled up in the auditoria and the labs of the buildings, mounted on the benches, broke the glass, tore down documents and drawings, turned the furniture upside down and covered the walls with misspelled slogans which they took from other epochs. Parading the walls of the Polytechnic were Allende,

Thailand, bread, the farmers, the Americans, "the People, whose blood has been sucked up." The "proletarians of all countries unite." Nothing remained intact. And why did all this happen? Not because no solution was given to student demands, but, on the contrary, because no considerable student problems have remained unsolved.

The article's main accusation was that students of left-wing sensitivities were the wealthier ones, who were driving their own cars—a definite luxury at the time—and therefore utterly hypocritical. *O Foititis* reproduced the usual polemic concerning left-wing rhetoric:

> And who were among the ones who "gave battle"? Those who leave their cars in the courtyard and enter the Polytechnic with their pockets full of banknotes, in order to pose as contestatory proletarians. These people, whose future is guaranteed. These people, to whom it does not make a difference whether free education exists or not. But the provocation of the "bourgeois proletarians" did not remain without a response. The wave of indignation from the rest of the students—regardless of faculty and social origins—resulted in their expulsion from the premises of the University of Salonica.[177]

Most of this damage the article cites was perpetrated by the Junta itself; in contrast to the Sorbonne in May 1968, which was left in a terrible state,[178] the Polytechnic in Athens—and to a lesser extent the Salonica Polytechnic—was preserved as clean and tidy as possible, as the Greek students did not wish to be smeared as "anarchists." Nevertheless, by governmental decree, twenty-eight local societies were disbanded in Athens, Salonica, and Ioannina, while their property was confiscated according to the decree 2636/1940 on "expropriation of enemy assets,"[179] which had been passed during the 1940 Greek-Italian War. This action, in other words, regarded the student associations as an internal enemy.

The Polytechnic occupation was the student movement's highest peak, during which the students managed to mobilize Greek society for the first time. The movement degenerated soon after due to the governmental cataclysm that followed, which included the overthrow of Papadopoulos by a group of hawks inside the Junta. A week later, on 25 November, Papadopoulos and his constitutional construct collapsed under the weight of another military coup by a group that would rule the country arbitrarily, with martial law in full operation. The Polytechnic events thus discredited the "liberalization experiment" that had aimed at a long-lasting authoritarian state with a democratic façade. Marxist theorist Nikos Poulantzas argued that the fact that the dictatorship was by and large dependent on violence in order to block dissent made it impossible for it "to direct its own transformation." "Controlled liberalization on the part of the state," he explained, created "a gaping hole through which the popular movement rushed in" as the Colonels failed to secure the "neutrality of the intelligentsia and the youth."[180]

The person pulling the strings behind the scene was Brigadier-General Ioannidis, head of ESA, nicknamed "the invisible dictator." With the transition from Papadopoulos to Ioannidis, the regime passed from a "personal" to an "impersonal" phase, as Ioannidis was hardly ever seen, instead letting the president of the republic, General Faidon Gizikis, do the job for him. Ioannidis, a hard-liner, decided to take the Junta back to the days of the iron fist and genuine authoritarianism.[181] He had already formed plans for a December 1973 coup that had to be rescheduled because of the Polytechnic uprising. Some analysts maintain that Ioannidis might even have allowed the Polytechnic to happen in order to gain support from the hard-liners by demonstrating the bankruptcy of Papadopoulos's experiment.

Ioannidis's period (25 November 1973–23 July 1974) brought about stagnation and a denouement to the student movement. During the eight months of its existence, no open action against the regime was recorded. Many student militants remained incarcerated, while others went into hiding. Most life stories portray this phase as the darkest of all. Nikos Bistis is adamant: "After the Polytechnic these were the worst days, the worst days, and psychologically also the worst days. A very tough Junta had arrived, and by looking at the facts those who had common sense were asking themselves whether we did well by pushing it so far" (Bistis, interview). In his memoirs too, Bistis defends his cautious stance during the days of the Polytechnic and debates the correctness of the decision to occupy the Polytechnic in November 1973.

Angeliki Xydi strongly remembered the disillusionment that she experienced when she got out of prison and tried to gain some new contacts in the university with no success. Contrary to Bistis, however, she was quick to note that the movement had gained respect thanks to its militancy: "I believe that the people that had mobilized before had a very high status, that is, they enjoyed a certain appreciation from the rest, be it the rest of the students or faculty members" (Xydi, interview).

The new regime decided to deal with student activism in a drastic way. Authoritarianism in its fullest form, as fantasized and practiced by Ioannidis, did not allow for any sort of student mobility. A social movement needs constant mobilization, however, in order to evolve and stay alive. When a movement's capacity to react and handle a crisis is weakened, stagnation and dissolution threaten.[182] Not only did the Greek student movement suffer the terrible blow of the night of the tanks in the Polytechnic, but it also experienced a dramatic regime change, accompanied by draconian measures. By February 1974, the main operational figures of A-EFEE and by May those of EKKE had been identified and arrested. This was a great blow, and the initiatives undertaken by remaining cadres who aspired to a massive demonstration or a general student strike were never realized.

To make things worse, the legacy of the Polytechnic divisions left the student movement as fragmented as ever. In the very aftermath of the uprising the general secretary of KKE-Esoterikou, Babis Drakopoulos, talked about "dark forces" that had infiltrated the students, trying to lead the occupation down a dangerous path. Not long after the events, KNE's mouthpiece, *Panspoudastiki*, in its infamous issue no. 8, more outspokenly castigated the three hundred and fifty students who incited the revolt as *agents provocateurs*, employed by the intelligence services.[183] Among them, the arch-*provocateur* was supposedly the Maoist leader Dionysis Mavrogenis, who was dubbed a government agent and had to hide for months both from the regime and from his communist denunciators. Stelios Kouloglou remembers feeling indignant at this injustice:

> When Mavrogenis was labeled a stool pigeon I entirely set myself apart from the group, I said that's it. I didn't say to anybody but I thought that these people were ... I knew Mavrogenis, I have seen him being beaten, we started off together. I said, no way it is him, because one knows some things, you cannot believe that someone who has been beaten up next to you, you have been scared together, you have been through.... Stool pigeons are not like this. (Kouloglou, interview)

The movement reached an impasse. No one knew the characteristics of the new regime, nor could they foresee how long it would last in its attempt to revive the true spirit of the "Revolution." A large number of students who had been involved in mass actions under Papadopoulos remained in strict clandestinity, passing their time in the houses of friends and relatives. Michalis Sabatakakis recalls: "I changed houses twenty-two or twenty-three times during the nine months from the Polytechnic to the *Metapolitefsi*. For a long time, ESA people were going to my place with rifles" (Sabatakakis, interview). Vera Damofli also remembers that she frequently changed hideouts and slept in all sorts of places. In the present, such recollections have an amusing aspect: "Alright, it was fun too," she says. Damofli argues that young people who provided accommodation were often people who had not participated actively in the movement and were thus paying tribute. She recalls one hideout:

> I remember another house that was full of comics [laughter]. A very beautiful flat, a student one too. These guys, you know, were at the fringes [of the movement]. They would come along sometimes too, but they hadn't come forward. And this was a flat with its bookshelves full of Mickey Mouse, you know, Lucky Luke, if it existed back then, I don't remember. And it was so nice, and they brought us roasted gourd-seed too. These are the memories, you see. (Damofli, interview)

In this example, the seriousness of the students' act of hiding is tempered by the frivolity of the flat's main feature: comics, a funny, popular culture item. In introducing this casual element in her interview, Damofli counterbalances her dramatic and charged description of the Polytechnic evacuation that immediately preceded it, underlining the fact that even in this bleakest of periods there could be moments of lightness.

In contrast to this ambivalence, *Katerina likens this period to the absolute darkness of a second German occupation where there could be neither escape nor escapism. In her narrative the dictators are presented not as real Greeks, but as foreign lackeys (a well-known trope of left-wingers at the time):

> I remember being spied on, many of my friends were being spied on. There were many friends of mine who were not in the Polytechnic who did not greet me when they saw me because they were afraid that I possibly knew someone. ... It was in general a period of German occupation. Then the great blow against KNE happened, and I think of the Political Bureau of the KKE in February '74, and the only activity we had were some contacts with the Deutsche Welle, with the BBC, with broadcasters abroad in order to learn about the news of the prisoners, to see if they died or if they were still alive and who else did they arrest, who else were they going to catch.

The only optimistic news that she recalls during Ioannidis's period were the anticolonial wars that led to the Carnation Revolution in Portugal: "The sole stimuli were Portugal, Angola, Guinea Bissau" (*Katerina, interview).

Whereas *Katerina's mind was set on Portugal, several students who were persecuted by the regime during this period tried to make their way to Great Britain. Others sought postgraduate grants for the same purpose. John Spraos, a Greek professor of economics at University College London, was an intermediary in these attempts, as he headed the London-based Greek Committee Against the Dictatorship. His correspondence with several British professors reveals that Greek student activists were often denied entrance and grants due to their low marks. A Greek professor contacted Spraos about a student named Emmanouil Tzannetis—one of the students that had been tried in February 1973 at the "Trial of the Eleven"—and was quick to explain: "Mr Tzannetis was actively involved in the student movement of recent years. Because of the persecutions that his family suffered, an inevitability after his involvement, this led to a fall in his performance, which is reflected in his marks."[184] Tzannetis's sister Evi, an architecture student, was reportedly warned after her release from EAT-ESA: "This academic year was lost. If you want to miss another one, keep on being involved in student issues."[185] In his own letters of recommendation, Spraos typically referred indirectly to Greek students' poor marks, saying that a particular student's "record is not brilliant," and he instead stressed other things, such as the "trials and tribulations" that the students had "undergone in the hands of the Greek regime." As Spraos noted in a letter to an English professor concerning student leader Giorgos Vernikos's anti-Junta activities, "This was a full-time occupation." Accordingly, Vernikos's "marks interpreted in the light of all this seem very creditable—even a genius could not be expected to have high examination marks under these circumstances."[186] Eventually, Vernikos made it out of Greece to Switzerland, though he never acquired postgraduate status.

All this became redundant, when Ioannidis's regime entered a precarious phase because of an ill-thought coup it masterminded in Cyprus on 15 July 1974 against President Makarios, which eventually led to its collapse. The subsequent invasion of the island by Turkey caught Ioannidis entirely unprepared. Interior struggles between the hard-liners and the soft-liners, taken together with the Cypriot adventure, brought the Junta to a stalemate. Guillermo O'Donnell and Philip Schmitter's assertion that a transition's beginning is the direct or indirect consequence "of important divisions within the authoritarian regime itself" is therefore absolutely accurate in the Greek case.[187] It was the members of the military themselves who decided that their regime had become dispensable and that it should be handed over to civilians in order to lead the country out of the crisis. With a demoralized army and a complete absence of coordination, the Greek military machine was not in a position to respond to what was considered to be a casus belli by Turkey, despite the general mobilization that General Faidon Gizikis ordered on 20 July. It was Gizikis himself, accompanied by the three heads of staff, who asked representatives of the "old politicians" to take over. They, in turn, asked the self-exiled Constantine Karamanlis to come and lead a civilian government; Karamanlis eventually formed a "government of national unity."

Vera Damofli offers an interesting metaphysical association between nature and political developments when she tries to recall 23 July 1974, the day the Junta fell:

And I think it hailed the previous day in Athens, though it was July. Crack-crack-crack. ... I was hidden in a basement back then. "What the hell is going on?" And yes, the Junta fell. It was terrific to go out in the streets. Surely, the police were chasing that day too, there was a panic, it was mad. On the one hand, the cars were beeping; on the other hand, people were dancing and jumping in the streets. It was very beautiful. (Damofli, interview)

Angeliki Xydi remembers that during these days of crisis and transformation she was on holiday on the island of Anafi, "for the very reason that life had everything, it had vacations too [laughter]." She continues: "And I urgently took the first caique that was leaving for Naxos in order to take the first boat to Athens, and there I found myself some days later under some balcony shouting 'two Ks and one E equals KKE'" (Xydi, interview). All these narratives underline the extreme abruptness of this unexpected regime change.

The ruthless regime of Ioannidis did not last more than eight months but, nevertheless, managed to leave a very intelligible trace of extreme repression, especially in the form of the Cyprus tragedy. However, if the students played an important role in the ultimate overthrow of the Papadopoulos regime by his former protégé, they did not have any involvement in the collapse of the Ioannidis regime, which happened by and large because of an imminent Greek-Turkish military conflict. Just like in Portugal in April 1974, it was events outside the country—in that case the African colonies, in this one Cyprus—that sealed the fate of the dictatorial regime.

Metapolitefsi and Beyond

When on 24 July 1974 the military decided to hand over power to the politicians, the period of the *Metapolitefsi,* or regime change, began. Although the majority of the people were ecstatic about this unexpected change, the core of the Left, including most students, remained skeptical. Most of them thought of the return of Karamanlis to power as a "change of NATO-ist guard," which stressed the element of continuity between the Junta and the government that succeeded it. Such continuity did not fulfill the Left's hope for radical sociopolitical change, which had partly fuelled the antidictatorship student movement. Former student dissident Panagiotis Xanthopoulos, for example, saw the transition as a major setback: "This was the least that could result from what we were experiencing as a movement all these years" (Xanthopoulos, interview).

Figure 5.8. Constantine Karamanlis is being sworn in as prime minister and head of a Government of National Unity in the morning hours of 24 July 1974 in the presence of General Gizikis. Certainly not the revolutionary outcome many of the Polytechnic protagonists had imagined. (Photographer: Aristotelis Sarrikostas)

The sudden collapse of the potential for utopia created vast disillusionment, as it looked like a return to the pre-1963 state of affairs (when Karamanlis was last time prime minister) instead of a step forward. Many students felt disoriented and frustrated. Olympios Dafermos recalls watching a televised version of the transition inside a coffee shop in his Cretan village. His distress was such that he fell into a heavy depression. Condensed events, extraordinary experiences, and high political expectations that were never fulfilled led to this emotional breakdown:

> I was not in Athens, I was in Axios, my village, where I watched the *Metapolitefsi* from the television and I saw thousands of people welcoming Karamanlis. I fell into depression, I left the coffee shop and I went home, and because I was playing the macho as I was young, I didn't cry. Now I would, I would let myself cry, because I said, "So much blood, so many sacrifices, so many struggles, in order to

have Karamanlis back?" From that point onward, I fell into a long depression, very long depression. (Dafermos, interview)

Ioanna Karystiani describes her own version of what she calls "a mind disorder":

> All of a sudden you feel that many things are exploding around you and inside you, do you understand? Because everything happened fast and the hopes for the country were too many, that it could gain the lost ground, that it would eradicate old wounds, different things could take place, all of which in the end were unfinished. Afterward, everything was measured and very petit-bourgeois and far away from the dreams that had nourished the twenty-year-old kids. (Karystiani, interview)

For *Katerina, a major problem was that the movement did not have enough strength to outbid the exponents of the old and discredited political cast:

> There emerged the most intense wave of politicization, I believe, in postwar history, which created possibilities of intervention from below. So the people had self-confidence; even though the change took place from the top, there was self-confidence in the youth and the people in general that "We can shape a new culture, different political correlations." Still, the so-called old political world proved to be more powerful. (*Katerina, interview)

These feelings were shared by exponents of the previous generation, as they watched "centrist and conservative politicians from the pre-dictatorial regime" take charge of "the founding of the new democracy" and occupy "its most important offices," to borrow Nancy Bermeo's description.[188] Christina Vervenioti was so shattered by the arrival to power of Karamanlis, the symbol of the pre-1967 Right, that she remembers bursting into tears:

> The day that I heard that Karamanlis was coming back, I remember, we were all at the Agia Paraskevi Square, many people, many, many, and all of us left-wingers, and I, who do not let myself cry easily, was in tears, because I considered it a defeat, that Karamanlis was coming back after so many sacrifices. Who? Karamanlis. For us, Karamanlis was the one who won the elections of '61 with violence and fraud, he didn't have a good reputation for us.... I said, "Is it

possible? Is it possible? After so many years, the one coming as a liberator is him?" (Vervenioti, interview)

At this point, these exponents of the antidictatorship student movement had shifted from voicing popular dissent to being out of tune with society as a whole. The vast majority of the Greek people expressed joy about the political change, even though that change had been imposed from above and without a popular uprising as its origin. An even greater disappointment for the students followed with the consolidation of Karamanlis in power in the 1974 elections, in which he won a landslide 54 percent majority. The elections were symbolically held on 17 November, the first anniversary of the Polytechnic—a move the students considered a rightist exploitation of a left-wing symbol. The electoral turnout from the recently legalized communist parties that ran united was miserable: 9.5 percent. Thodoros Vourekas remembers: "I had an illusion about real political correlations in society.... I had great illusions. Just to make you understand how lost in space I was, I believed that the Left would win around 25 to 30 percent of the vote" (Vourekas, interview). The slogan adopted by leftist groups and parties alike in the aftermath of the elections was "People, shame on you for your vote"; apart from being condescending, it practically blotted out the left-wing idealization of the people as bearer of authentic revolutionism.

The whole period of the *Metapolitefsi* was in fact characterized by growing disenchantment for the student movement, mainly due to the failure of the anticipated future transcendence of the Polytechnic's Utopia to arrive in any form.[189] For many people of this generation, the period signaled a traumatic reality check, in spite of spectacular moves by Karamanlis, such as the quick legalization of the Communist Party, the retreat of Greece from the military arm of NATO, significant measures that updated the university system, and the Language Reform (1976) that abolished the country's official diglossia.[190] Ioanna Karystiani's case is characteristic of this disillusionment:

> It is entirely different for the people who might have been fifty years old, let's say, and for the ones who were twenty. What we knew were the eight black years of Karamanlis, that was the only thing that we listened to back then, the accursed Right of this period and so on. The arrival of Karamanlis was of course an end to dictatorship, it was good that the dictatorship was over, but on the other hand we might have imagined that a "Government of National Unity" would be newer faces, more imperishable, whom you could trust because you wouldn't know about their past, their heavily charged criminal record. (Karystiani, interview)

Antonis Liakos recalls in his writings that during the *Metapolitefsi*, most people of his generation who had participated in the antidictatorship resistance "returned to their jobs and were sunk in psychological crises of varying depth and intensity": "There was a diffused feeling that the expected revolution had not come and its time had passed. The social hierarchies were restored. Our own efforts and plans had failed."[191] Kleopatra Papageorgiou has painful memories of this era too, which she attributes to the frustration that hardline communists felt of their millenarian expectations: "It was a very ugly period, very much so, probably because we communists had believed that it was natural determinism that capitalism would collapse and things like that" (Papageorgiou, interview). Millenarian or not, the majority of the student militants of the Junta years felt disillusioned by the fact that their surplus of expectations regarding a more just society following the fall of the regime was frustrated. This attitude had its counterpart in Spain—with the so-called *desencanto*, or disaffection regarding politics, characterizing a great part of the society in the immediate period following the transition to democracy.

In contrast to parliamentary elections, however, student elections favored the antidictatorship student organizations and rendered them the absolute protagonists of student unionism for the decade to follow and beyond. Student groupings increased their numbers but soon lost their supposedly independent character. Rigas, for instance, became the formal student section of KKE-Esoterikou. EKKE's AASPE won a mass following that caused even more hostility toward the hegemonic Panspoudastiki, A-EFEE's reincarnation. This would be the beginning of endless bickering and feuding factions within the student movement. Only the fervent process of cleansing the universities of the main pro-Junta professors, the so-called de-Juntification, temporarily reunited former dissident students. All of a sudden, the hitherto persecuted students became persecutors, often exaggerating the role of the avenger due to their revolutionary fervor. EKKE went so far as to demand People's Courts for professors who had collaborated with the regime.

The tendency of radical students to read the political into everything reached an extreme during the *Metapolitefsi* years. *Pavlos's description of a football match in 1975 conveys the level of ideological obsession among some leftists: "A Chinese football team came to Kaftantzogleio Stadium in '75. We saw the way they played football, and we saw them from an ideological point of view. They didn't make fouls; they tried to score with technique. Always for the benefit of the game and the team. It did not have the competitiveness of sports under capitalism" (*Pavlos, interview). Kleopatra Papageorgiou, another Maoist, used several football terms, such as "foul," "stopper," and "offside," to stress points during her interview, demonstrating a clear-cut shift in terms of the signifiers connected to such a discourse in comparison to the past—when football was the absolute off-limits zone for politicized students. Both use football at present as a privileged site for drawing anthropological conclusions, thus marking a clear rupture with the Junta period, during which left-wingers scorned the sport due to its association with the regime.

University politics in this period also favored endless discussions, capitalizing on the new feeling of the freedom of speech during the transition to democracy. Similar to the Spanish *transición*'s slogan "freedom–amnesty–status of autonomy," the Greek triptych of demands was "amnesty to political prisoners–punishment of perpetrators–new departure."[192] However, soon topics moved beyond Greece to touch on the Third World, the Soviet Union, and Spain in "long, endless, marathon-like student assemblies," according to Vourekas, whereby an almost logorrheic attitude, resembled the après-68 in France. Vourekas links this to the relativity of time for the student movement, depending on the context: "Was it all just two years? It looks as if these two years were centuries. There was a great difference between political action under the Junta and when was it, in '74, I was still in university for another one and a half years, and this seemed to me an endless period" (Vourekas, interview). The prevalence of *kairos*, the condensed, revolutionary, "hic et nunc" time of the student movement during the Junta years was clearly over, only to be succeeded by the restored postdictatorship *chronos* that seemed painfully slow.

To radicalized students, the *Metapolitefsi* era brought about fragmentation and internal confrontations, facilitated by the lack of a common objective and the hardening of people's commitment to rival political formations. Dimitris Fyssas remarked on the politicization of this era, "Without the Party … life was inconceivable."[193] Student radicalism was reinforced by a general societal impetus, an organizational explosion, and a growing mobilization and political participation that is typical of moments of transition and regime change. For those who remained unaffiliated, however, the excessive politicization that was becoming prevalent generated a feeling of marginalization in them. Olympios Dafermos was one of them: "In *Metapolitefsi* I did not have answers, I did not have opinions, I was confused. Because whereas we used to be the rulers of the game, we ended up being nothing" (Dafermos, interview).

In their memories, former militants often face difficulties in clearly distinguishing specific attitudes belonging to the dictatorship period from the attitudes that were bred during its aftermath. When a powerful event is followed by a period that might have had an equal or even stronger emotional impact, memory tends to cause overlaps between the two, usually favoring the cognitive predominance of the later period over the earlier. Lapses tend to be reinforced when the memory layer in question includes strenuous events.[194] The *Metapolitefsi,* a period marked by fragmentation, disillusionment, and lack of vision, which led to the gradual disintegration of the antidictatorship student movement, falls into this category. Even though most people conclude that the trigger for growing friction was the movement's sudden lack of a common goal, some maintain that radical newcomers to the movement mainly reinforced splits. Contrary to these "janissaries," as Nikitas Lionarakis contemptuously called them, students of the Junta period could not really step up hostility towards each other, thanks to that strongest of bonds that derived from common action in the all-too-recent past: "As we had been together through thick and thin, you couldn't say to the other, 'You're an asshole'" (Lionarakis, interview).

Interestingly, however, a discrepancy started emerging between the two cohorts that we have identified in this book, in terms of the first one becoming under- and the second one overrepresented by the media and in the emerging public memory. Up until recently, the historical generation of the first students involved in anti-Junta activities was not particularly present in public history, causing bitterness and resentment on the part of its members. Thanasis Athanasiou, a key figure of the clandestine organization Rigas Feraios, who was captured and imprisoned as early as 1968, expresses his bitterness about the contrast between the underrepresentation of the members of his generation in public memory, as opposed to the overexposure of the subsequent one. Athanasiou interprets this as the result of a conscious decision on behalf of himself and his peers to retain a low-key presence, in contrast to exponents of the Polytechnic Generation:

> None of the kids from that group of Rigas asked to buy off anything, we all stayed consciously in obscurity. We didn't want to buy off our resistance activity, which would be easy for us after such action and so many years in prison … in contrast to subsequent generations of youth, in which someone was becoming minister just because he was once slapped. (Athanasiou, interview)

Antonis Liakos too retains in his *ego-histoire* the deep alienation that people from his age group felt when prison made it impossible for them to maintain a high public profile and pursue a political path: "Few of us in the resistance against the Junta went on to pursue a political career. The new world which we faced coming out of the prison seemed strange to us."[195] Liakos's comrade, Tasos Darveris, who committed suicide in 1999, vividly depicts the gloomy mood of post-Junta conditions in his autobiographic novel, which is summarized as the end of collective endeavors and a return to individualism: "Each one decided to take one's own way: a political career, a doctorate, a professional promotion. And this was dividing the old comrades more and more; in the post-electoral, rather than celebrating, atmosphere of the New Year's Eve of '75 some people were already feeling lonely."[196]

Loneliness and hyperpoliticization led some people to embrace (or continue) the so-called armed struggle. Others did so out of the (widely shared) conviction that the newly born Third Greek Republic was in reality a prolongation of the dictatorship. "Change of guard" was the term socialist leader Andreas Papandreou had used to designate both Ioannidis's coup on 25 November 1973 and the *Metapolitefsi;* he regarded both as nothing more than different facets of US neocolonialism.[197] Even though Papandreou's claim was overtly exaggerated, it is a fact that authoritarian state structures remained intact for some time, while political discrimination did not disappear overnight. The secret services continued to spy on the parties of the Left, and the military kept a record of the political views of conscripts, while supporters of the Left still had troubles in obtaining public sector jobs.[198] Capitalizing on these facts and a general antiauthoritarian "structure of feeling," Papandreou—who would not abandon his third-worldist rhetoric until many years later—expressed the opinion that the dilemma "Karamanlis or tanks" that composer Mikis Theodorakis had rhetorically posed shortly before the 1974 elections was a pseudodilemma: there was no real choice, only a fait accompli, and that was "Karamanlis *and* tanks."

Feeling that nothing had changed, some extreme left-wingers decided to either begin or resume the armed struggle against the artificial transition imposed from above.[199] If the embrace of political violence by the most radicalized student wings was a perverse continuation of the 1968 movements "by other means,"[200] the opposite applies to Greece during the dictatorship: here, armed resistance was succeeded by a nonviolent mass movement of the early 1970s. But now, segments of the post-1974 generation of radicalized Greek youth, in combination with older radicals, flirted with ideological terrorism. The catalyst for this decision was the fact that, apart from the ringleaders of the coup, most Junta officers received light sentences in the 1975 trials. A number of torturers were treated by the judges during the so-called trials of the torturers in the second half of 1975 in a remarkably lenient way.[201]

Still, these public trials offered, among other things, a rare preliminary picture of the ways in which torturers were selected and trained in the Greek military police.[202] The particular jargon that had been used by the torturers to indicate specific types of corporal punishment—such as "tea party" or "tea party with toast"—were also revealed, causing sensation. Apart from the unsatisfactory verdicts and the aggressive and provocative stance of many torturers toward their past victims during the process, the judges themselves often showed a surprising lack of sensitivity toward the trauma of those victims and their need to talk about the violence inflicted upon them in detail. One of the most shocking moments for a present-day reader of the minutes of the trials is the fact that in several occasions the judges silenced trial testimony on the grounds that the details were "too pornographic," a fact that speaks volumes about the moral standards of the conservative Greek society of the time vis-à-vis issues such as sexual torture.[203] When some of the most notorious torturers received asymmetrically low sentences—some of them were even acquitted—many in the extreme Left became convinced of the fact that the democratization and de-Juntification processes were a facade. And this was precisely the moment in which terrorist organizations, such as "17 November," leveled up their action as "avengers." The killing of the notorious torturers Evangelos Mallios and Petros Bambalis, in 1976 and 1979 respectively, generated sympathy for the terrorists' cause and tolerance for their practices among vast segments of the Greek population—above all among the young. This was a powerful indication that for a considerable part of the society the post-1974 justice system had failed to right the wrongs.

Kleopatra Papageorgiou was one of those activists who faced the dilemma of whether or not to opt for the armed struggle in these new democratic conditions:

> I believed that violence could only be dealt with through violence. [But] it did not fit me as a person. And this is why I ended up having an enormous dilemma later on. Because on the one hand, I saw that only through violence could something be done.... On the other, as a person, violence did not suit me. Nor did I want to militarize my life and dedicate it to a specific cause. I wanted to have a private life too, other joys.... I did not want to become like that Palestinian hijacker, Khaled. [laughter] (Papageorgiou, interview)

In the end, Papageorgiou opted for nonviolence. Her discourse highlights the contradictions characteristic of the discrepancy between a holistic theoretical approach of violence and the practical difficulties that the latter involves in terms of the day-to-day realities. Stelios Kouloglou, on the other hand, is firm in his conviction that the Polytechnic generation did not use violence, as it had already "fulfilled" its mission:

> We, as a generation, did not generate terrorist, armed struggle, you know. Because we won, we succeeded in our aim that we had put together with the mass movement. And therefore there had never

been a serious intention to take up arms. But the ones who were either Lambrakides or the following generation, like Koufondinas, who did not spring out of the mass movement, they followed that path, in some way. (Kouloglou, interview)

Olympios Dafermos shares this view; interestingly, his discourse was emotionally charged by the arrests of the members of the terrorist group 17N and the media hysteria that took place shortly before our interview:

If we started beating or torturing or I don't know what, wouldn't we become shitty people? We would become "17 of November." And what did these assholes do? They killed twenty, thirty people, how many did they kill, what did they achieve? What did they achieve? But we were accomplishing things, I believe that we were accomplishing things. At least we saved the dignity of the Greek people, right? (Dafermos, interview)

In the universities, the *Metapolitefsi* was characterized by the rapid folklorization of the student struggle and the institutionalization of anti-Junta student activism as a landmark of revolutionism. By that time the word *student* had acquired not only social but also political significance, meaning the left-winger, the non-right-winger par excellence.[204] Dionysis Savvopoulos went so far as to argue that if you were young and not left-wing in those years, it was impossible to find a date. In addition to this, everyone wanted to capitalize on the pedigree of the antidictatorship movement. Even people who were not remotely connected to the Polytechnic events suddenly wanted to demonstrate that "they were there too." Actor and present-day writer Periklis Korovesis, who went through ruthless torture during the Junta years, sarcastically argued that "the mass resistance against the Junta appeared during the *Metapolitefsi.*"[205] Post-1974 was characterized by both awe and envy for the "Polytechnic Generation." A 1980s song by the popular pop band Fatme encapsulates this feeling, dubbing the mid- and late 1970s youth as "the lost generation of the *Metapolitefsi*" and concluding bitterly that in contrast to the anti-Junta activists, "History has given us nothing."[206]

Soon, new tendencies were born out of the growing radicalization of a new generation of students, who needed to express a much greater intransigence than their legendary predecessors. The new trends mainly included radical leftism, anarchism—a relative newcomer in Greek left-wing politics—and, to a lesser extent, feminism. From 1974 to 1979, writes sociologist Maro Pantelidou-Malouta, "the Greek experiences of the dictatorship, the euphoria of the return to democracy, the rise of the leftist protest, the development of a liberated logos, and the spread of women's struggles abroad, all contributed to the formation of a women's movement."[207] Among young women, however, a left-wing political identity against dogmatism and totalitarianism and in favor of democracy, freedom, justice, and social change prevailed over a more specific female identity. Accordingly, "left-wing parties stated that gender equality could be obtained only as a by-product of class exploitation."[208] A few large organizations, such as the Association for Women's Rights and the Movement for Female Liberation, that formed after the end of the military dictatorship played a significant role in the movement's history.[209] The slogan went, "I don't belong to my father, I don't belong to my husband, I belong to myself."

At the same time, the liberalization of mores was proceeding rapidly. The spirit of the *Metapolitefsi* opened the opportunity for tracing new limits in countercultural politics. The often antithetical and antagonistic poles of countercultural and political experimentation peaked in the late 1970s, and especially in the years 1978 and 1979 with the massive student occupations that resisted the Educational Law 815 introduced by Constantine Karamanlis's second tenure in office. Most prominently, the occupation of the Faculty of Chemistry in 1979 tried to reenact 1968 and, less so, the Polytechnic: indirectly, in terms of its open sexuality and situationist mood, and directly, through the reproduction of posters and slogans of May '68 in France.[210]

As far as the ritual commemoration of the Polytechnic was concerned, historical memory proved to be highly performative: on each 17 November, left-wing activists organized massive demonstrations in order to symbolically celebrate insurrection. By the late 1970s, these demonstrations often resulted in violent clashes with policemen. These commemorative clashes (which to some extent continue to occur on a regular basis on the premises of the Polytechnic) constitute a peculiar, almost theatrical staging of the "actual" events. While students were changing, however, many policemen were still the same who operated under the Junta. Just like in post-Franco Spain during the initial phase of the *transición*, the Greek police was the most persistent element of the old order that stubbornly refused to change its tactics.

The most notorious 17 November demonstrations of this period took place in 1978, when the increasingly powerful Maoist EKKE attacked the US embassy, provoking an extremely violent police reaction, and in 1980, when two youths, Iakovos Koumis and Stamatina Kanellopoulou, were clubbed to death by policemen. For Giannis Kourmoulakis, that became his last stop concerning political activism, as he realized that he could no longer stomach political persecution and the tension of such clashes with police. After all, the age difference between young policemen and the old guard of activists did not favor the latter anymore:

In 1980 there was a march to the American Embassy when Kanellopoulou was killed. We were sitting at the corner of Filellinon and Othonos Street and saw the people who were getting beaten there, and I left. I didn't want to get into trouble anymore. There I realized that I had matured, I became conscious of the danger. (Kourmoulakis, interview)

The police—an institution with a "long memory," to quote Kristin Ross's Balzacean conclusion[211]—was the last arm of the state to be democratized, and in activists' minds this stood as a synecdoche for the entire state. Vestiges of authoritarianism persisted in state practices throughout the late 1970s, tainting the image of the "model" transition but also the idea of the clean break with the past. Therefore, the decade-long sensitivity of the Greek state toward the so-called university asylum—the total ban of police from university premises unless a specific demand is voiced by the university authorities—should not come as a surprise, as it constitutes a direct offspring of the legacy of 1973.

Certainly, after 1981, with the advent of the socialist PASOK's rise to power, things changed radically. For most of the protagonists of the antidictatorship student movement and despite a common rejection of PASOK's populist tactics, 1981 marked the actual democratization of the country, as opposed to the interregnum of right-wing governments after 1974 that retained authoritarian residues. The fact that PASOK was a post-1974 incarnation of the third-worldist resistance organization PAK and did not really abandon much of its anti-neocolonial rhetoric until very late, had its own symbolic significance: it was seen by many as the moral victory of the entire generation that had mobilized against the Junta. It was not long after PASOK came to power that it institutionalized the "Polytechnic" as a national celebration.

Notes

1. Kouloumbis, "The Greek Junta Phenomenon," 359.
2. According to della Porta, "repressive and hard policing of protest results in the shrinking of mass movements but a radicalization of smaller protest groups." See della Porta, "Social Protest," 92.
3. "A Mosquito on a Bull," *Economist*, 12 March 1973.
4. For the notion of "expressive behavior" see Pizzorno, "Le due logiche dell'azione di classe," 13.
5. "Έξαρσις εις το Φοιτητικόν. Απελογήθησαν οι 12 της Εμπορικής [The student issue is booming: The twelve of the School of Commerce have presented their pleas], *Eleftheros Kosmos*, 6 February 1973.

6. "Παραιτήθηκε το ΔΣ των Σπουδαστών Μηχανολόγων" [The AC of the Mechanical Engineers' Society Has Resigned], *Eleftheros Kosmos*, 6 February 1973.
7. "Δίκη των 10 φοιτητών για τις ταραχές του "μικρού" Πολυτεχνείου [Trial of the Ten Students for the "Little" Polytechnic Riots], *Thessaloniki*, 19 February 1973. The pro-regime newspaper *Eleftheros Kosmos* referred to the events as reviving a climate reminiscent of EAM, the communist-led resistance during the German occupation. "Επεισόδια χθες εις το Πολυτεχνείο" [Riots Yesterday at the Polytechnic], 17 February 1973.
8. Dafermos, *Students and Dictatorship*, 107.
9. Sontag, *On Photography*, 19.
10. Foucault, *Discipline and Punish*, 25.
11. *Thessaloniki*, 19 December 1973.
12. With his long hair and military jacket, Mastorakis attempted to appear familiar to the students as one of them, a person from whom they had nothing to fear. The "interview-interrogation" took place on 18 November 1973.
13. *Thessaloniki*, 22 May 1973.
14. Dafermos, *Students and Dictatorship*, 113.
15. Luis Enrique de la Villa and Aurelio Desdentado Bonete's conclusion that "solidarity strikes and demands for the readmission of sacked workers are a historical constant which define the very identity of the labour movement" is applicable to any sort of social movement. See De la Villa and Desdentado Bonete, *La amnistía laboral*, 22. Quoted in Aguilar Fernández, "Collective Memory of the Spanish Civil War," 6.
16. Dafermos, *Students and Dictatorship*, 121–22.
17. "650–3000 Students Spent the Night "Barricaded" inside the Law School Building," *Thessaloniki*, 22 February 1973.
18. Dafermos, *Students and Dictatorship*, 123.
19. See Sirinelli, *Les baby-boomers*.
20. Mantoglou, *Polytechnic*, 165–66.
21. Coerant, "On their Own," 117.
22. See Hamalidi et al., "A Second Avant-Garde Without a First," 10.
23. Bistis, *Moving on and Revising*, 220. Even though Bistis mentions that this incident took place during the Law School occupation, his description applies equally, if not more, to the Polytechnic events.
24. Top Secret, EAT/ESA-TAS to AS/2nd EG-SDA, Athens, 1 March 1973, Dafermos Archive, EDIA.
25. Vernikos, "Personal Testimony," 149.
26. *Thessaloniki*, 22 February 1973.
27. Iordanoglou, "Antidictatorship Student Movement," 252.
28. *Thessaloniki*, "Οι δυο λόγοι του κ. Παπαδόπουλου" [The Two Speeches by Mr. Papadopoulos], 4 March 1973.
29. Ibid.
30. *Thessaloniki*, 20 March 1973.
31. P-J. Franceschini, "Tout sauf mai 68," *Le Monde*, 8 March 1973.
32. "Students: Yet Another Attempt," *Thessaloniki*, 27 February 1973.
33. Top Secret, EAT/ESA-TAS to AS/2nd EG-SDA, Athens, 1 March 1973, Dafermos Archive, EDIA.

34. Angelis and Dafermos, *Only a Dream*, 115.
35. Raschke, *Soziale Bewegungen*, 363.
36. Bourdieu, *Homo Academicus*.
37. Eyerman and Jamison, *Social Movements*, 104.
38. The commander and some thirty members of the crew of the destroyer Velos sought and were granted political asylum in Italy.
39. See Klandermans, "Mobilization and Participation," and McAdam, "Recruitment."
40. Della Porta, "1968," 139.
41. Dafermos, *Students and Dictatorship*, 132.
42. "Athens Students Quick to Rebel," *Guardian*, 27 October 1972.
43. Paul Rose, "'Vicious' Pressures from Police May Paralyze Opposition," *Chicago Tribune*, August 1972.
44. Vernikos, "Personal Testimony," 151. Vernikos recalls that those belonging to communist organizations blamed him for everything in order to protect their own comrades.
45. Papachristos, "Law School to the Polytechnic," 195.
46. "'Threat' to Greek Woman in Cell," *Guardian*, 14 November 1973. Deleted expletive in original.
47. Darveris, *A Night's Story*, 332.
48. Arseni, *Nelle carceri*. Almost forty years later this attitude has not entirely changed, which points to how persistent both the trauma and taboo remain. See, for example, the moving documentary by Alinda Dimitriou *Rain Girls* [Ta Koritsia tis Vrochis] (2011) on women tortured during the Junta.
49. On the issue of the extreme difficulty of dealing with the past trauma that involves (sexual) torture also see the interesting novella by Elias Maglinis, *The Interrogation*. In Maglinis's view the historical trauma is in some way inherited and transmitted from generation to generation.
50. Typically, organizations advised students to hold out for twenty-four hours to allow their comrades, who by then would be informed of the arrest, to change hideouts. See, for example, Kotanidis, *All Together, Now!*, 326.
51. Passerini, "Wounded Memory."
52. Paraskevopoulos, "Notes," 70.
53. Kotanidis, *All Together, Now!*, 379 and 475.
54. On this issue see Voglis, *Becoming a Subject*.
55. Alivizatos, *Political Institutions*, 294.
56. For an elaboration of this term see Fishman, "Rethinking State and Regime," 428. Also see Tzortzis, "The *Metapolitefsi* That Never Was."
57. See US Ambassador Tasca's report, USNA, Pol 15 Greece, American Embassy Athens, "The Papadopoulos-Markezinis Tandem: Prospects for the Return to Parliamentary Government in Greece," 17 October 1973.
58. Papadopoulos would be the uncontested president, with General Odysseus Angelis as vice-president, up to 1981. The president according to the new constitution was endowed with the right to create a legal context of his own liking for the first elections, reserving the right to appoint the ministers of defense, foreign affairs, and public order and to declare a "state of siege" on his own initiative. See Alivizatos, *Political Institutions*, 290–99.
59. Interview for the *New York Times*, 12 October 1973.

60. "Κάτω η χούντα του Πινοσέτ! Ζήτω η αντίσταση του χιλιανού λαού! Απόφαση του Κ.Σ. του "Ρήγα Φεραίου'" (1 October 1973) [Down with the Junta of Pinochet! Long Live the Resistance of the Chilean People! Decision of the C.C. of "Rigas Feraios"], *Thourios* n.s. 2 (November 1973): 63.
61. "PAK's leader at the congress of the Socialist Youth of West Germany—JUSOS, 25/1/74, Munich," Gogolou-Elefantis collection, PAK documents, box 5, file 4, ASKI.
62. Papazoglou, *Student Movement and Dictatorship*, 149. For a comparative analysis between the Greek and Spanish student movements under the Colonels and Franco see Kornetis, "Student Resistance to the Greek Military Dictatorship. Subjectivity, Memory, and Cultural Politics, 1967–1974."
63. Heinze, "Ten Days in October," 503. Also see Darling, "Student Protest in Thailand." For the connection with the Greek student movement, see Kallivretakis, "'Απόψε θα γίνει Ταϋλάνδη.' Η ερμηνεία ενός "εξωτικού" συνθήματος της εξέγερσης του Πολυτεχνείου" ["Tonight There Will Be Thailand": The Interpretation of an "Exotic" Slogan of the Polytechnic Revolt], *Tachydromos*, 13 November 2004.
64. See Varon, 'Between Revolution 9 and Thesis 11."
65. Iordanoglou, "Antidictatorship Student Movement."
66. *Thessaloniki*, 2 November 1973.
67. *Thessaloniki*, 6 November 1973.
68. *Thessaloniki*, 14 November 1973.
69. For an analysis of how social movements are reinforced by crises in the world economy, see Burke, *Global Crises*.
70. Interview of Psaroudakis by K. Tsaousidis and Zafeiris, "The Talk of the Publisher of the 'Christianiki,' Nikolaos Psaroudakis, with the Subject 'Education and Democracy,' Has Been Cancelled," *Thessaloniki*, 27 February 1972.
71. Clarke, et al., "Subcultures, Cultures, and Class," 10.
72. Dafermos, *Students and Dictatorship*, 153.
73. Logothetis, "Occupation," 209.
74. Interview, 2001, Audiovisual Archive, EDIA.
75. Passerini, "Le mouvement de 1968," 39–74. Cohn-Bendit himself commented several years later, "In May '68 we were in a certain way the engines of History, instead of suffering from it, we were making it." *Nous l'avons tant aimée*, 66.
76. Dafermos, "My Decade," 49.
77. Papas, "Juxtaposition of Opinions," 246.
78. *The Real 17N*, television documentary.
79. *Thessaloniki*, 22 August 1973.
80. *I Synecheia* 5 (July 1973): 291.
81. *Thessaloniki*, 22 August 1973.
82. For an elaboration of this issue, see Tonkin, *Narrating Our Pasts*, 87.
83. Brewer, "Recollective Memory," 24.
84. Portelli, *Death of Luigi Trastulli*, 15.
85. Van Boeschoten and Rosenthal argue, moreover, that when present public discourse is the prevailing component of a life story, it can indicate a particularly traumatized memory. See Van Boeschoten, *Troubled Years*, 220; Rosenthal, *Erlebte und erzaehlte Lebensgeschichte*, 90, 114.

86. Dafermos, *Students and Dictatorship*, 154.
87. Tarrow, *Democracy and Disorder*, 60.
88. Interview with anonymous source quoted in Mantoglou, *Polytechnic*, 186.
89. Report of the Central Committee of KKE, quoted in Dafermos, *Students and Dictatorship*, 158.
90. The committee comprised six to seven A-EFEE members, two to three affiliates, one Rigas and one affiliate, a leftist, and a member of PAK.
91. Christos Lazos, *Thourios*, 15 November 1975.
92. See Papas, "Juxtaposition of Opinions," 248.
93. Markezinis, *Reminiscences*, 415.
94. Kavvadias, *This Is Polytechnic Speaking*, 107, 88.
95. Ibid., 90.
96. As McAdam notes, the "dramatization of system vulnerability," that is, highlighting the supposed weakness of one's political opponents, is one of the main factors that set framing efforts in motion, spurring on protest activity. McAdam, "Culture and Social Movements," 41.
97. Chrisanthos Lazaridis, "Νοέμβρης '78. Ξεχασμένες ιστορίες για ένα επίκαιρο παραμύθι" [Forgotten Stories About an Opportune Fairy Tale], *Agonas* 4 (1978): 29.
98. Passerini, "Il programma radiofonico," 155.
99. *The Radio Station of the Polytechnic*, documentary by Lambros Papadimitrakis.
100. Ibid.
101. See Certeau, *The Capture of Speech and Other Political Writings*, 11. Also Roland Barthes famously compared the French university revolt's "taking of speech" to the 1789 "taking of the Bastille." See Barthes, "Writing the Event," 150.
102. Ibid., 161.
103. Mantoglou, *Polytechnic*, 187.
104. Felekis, interview by the author, January 2002. Also see Nikos Potamianos, "Η νύχτα του Πολυτεχνείου" [The Night of the Polytechnic], *Emfylios Typos* 59 (Apr. 2004).
105. Katsaros records that another slogan written by female anarchists rejected the universal dominance of the phallus. Katsaros, *I the Provocateur*, 219. In fact, Katsaros describes these female anarchists as "militant lesbians."
106. Logothetis, "The Occupation."
107. Quoted in anarchist newspaper *Allilengyi* 1 (15 November 1983).
108. The novelist Tachtsis recalls how shocked he was gazing at similar slogans while passing by the Polytechnic during the first day of the occupation. Tachtsis too thought initially that the whole thing may have been staged as part of a provocation. "Από τη χαμηλή προσωπική σκοπιά" [From the Low Personal Viewpoint], *I Lexi* 63–64 (Apr.–May 1987): 261.
109. Katsaros, *I the Provocateur*, 219.
110. A list of the most popular demonstrates the diversity in sloganeering during the Polytechnic days: "People show us solidarity," "All people with us," "Down with the Junta," "People break the collar." More radical ones were "Death to tyranny," "People make a revolution," and "Tonight it will be Thailand." The classics "1–1–4" and "The only leader is the sovereign people" made their way in, as well as the already popular "Democracy," "Freedom," "Tonight Fascism is dying," and

"ESA-SS, torturers." Others shouted "Free elections." See ibid., 191; Dafermos, *Students and Dictatorship*, 165. There were no "pure" student demands among the sloganeering.
111. See Kazakos, *Between State and Market*, 287–88.
112. Marceau, *Le coup d'Athenes*, 5.
113. Dafermos, *Students and Dictatorship*, 173.
114. Papas, "Juxtaposition of Opinions," 246.
115. Hirschman, *Felicitá privata*, 104.
116. Sommier, *La violence politique*, 37.
117. Angelis and Dafermos, *Only a Dream*, 177.
118. Vernikos, "Personal Testimony," 155. Lawyer and activist Kanellakis writes similarly concerning the potential of periods that involve great risks: "Sometimes I wonder whether there is some kind of natural determinism, according to which danger is a precondition for joy and delight." Kanellakis, "In Those Years," 49.
119. Varikas, "The Utopian Surplus," 102.
120. Kornetis, "Everything Links," 37.
121. Dafermos, *Students and Dictatorship*, 169.
122. Ibid., 162.
123. Wasserstrom, *Student Protest*, 23.
124. Katsaros, *I the Provocateur*, 226.
125. Kavvadias, *This Is Polytechnic Speaking*, 56.
126. *To Vima* quoted in Konofagos, *Polytechnic Uprising*, 51.
127. Douka, *Fool's Gold*. Here, I am using Roderick Beaton's translation, 262–63.
128. Wasserstrom, *Student Protest*, 23.
129. Audiovisual Archive, EDIA.
130. Douka, *Fool's Gold*, 262–63. Original emphasis.
131. Angelis and Dafermos, *Only a Dream*, 188.
132. Lygeros, "The Conjuncture," 204.
133. Darveris, *Night's Story*, 334. In her semificitonal account, Douka describes scenes of policemen and soldiers who upon their entrance to the Polytechnic insulted the female students: "Whores, been enjoying yourselves have you, all that time in the whorehouse?" Douka, *Fool's Gold*, 268.
134. Chatzisokratis, "Coordinating Committee", 218.
135. Douka, *Fool's Gold*, 264. Even though I am using Beaton's translation here, I chose to add some of the elements that he deliberately left out of the text for reasons of simplicity.
136. Dafermos, *Students and Dictatorship*, 166.
137. Ibid., 168.
138. Chatzisokratis, "Coordinating Committee," 217.
139. Here I am paraphrasing political scientist Robert Dahl's axiom. See Dahl, *Polyarchy*, 15.
140. Gagnon, "Life Accounts," 54.
141. Chatzisokratis, "Coordinating Committee," 219.
142. In *Two Years of Struggles*.
143. Kotanidis, *All Together, Now!*, 429.
144. Andrews, *Greece in the Dark*, 82.

145. See various testimonies in the Polytechnic trial as recorded by Karatzaferis in *Polytechnic Slaughter*.
146. "Καννελόπουλος, Μαύρος, Κ.Κ.Ε. και Ανδρέας Παπανδρέου συμπαρίστανται εις τους αναρχικούς" [Kanellopoulos, Mavros, K.K.E. and Andreas Papandreou Show Solidarity with the Anarchists], *Eleftheros Kosmos*, 17 November 1973. His point strongly resembles Pier Paolo Pasolini's controversial stance after the Valle Giulia "battle" in Rome of March 1968, when, after violent clashes between students and policemen, he sympathized with the latter for being the "real" proletarians. See Pasolini, "Il cerimoniale."
147. Andrews, *Greece in the Dark*, 78.
148. Katsaros, *I the Provocateur*, 223.
149. Douka, *Fool's Gold*, 263–64.
150. Douka, *Fool's Gold*, 1979, 226. My translation.
151. See D. Iatropoulos, *This Is Polytechnic Speaking*, documentary.
152. Mazower, "Appropriation of Memory," 224.
153. Panos Geramanis, "The Sensational Romiossini," on the sleeve of Η Συγκλονιστική Ρωμιοσύνη [The Sensational Romiossini], 1966, reissued 2004.
154. See Herzfeld, *Ours Once More*, 22–23.
155. Konofagos, *Polytechnic Uprising*, 32. In a conversation among protagonists of the movement a year after the restoration of democracy, it was stated that the flag was placed as a counterweight to anarchism. See the special issue by *Eleftherotypia*, 23–29 November 1977. Interestingly, Thai students also waved the country's flag while protesting as a sign of loyalty to the nation and its symbols. See Heinze, "Ten Days in October," 498.
156. Angelis and Dafermos, *Only a Dream*, 178.
157. *The Time Machine*, documentary.
158. Kotanidis, *All Together, Now!*, 431–32.
159. Kavvadias cites a progovernment testimony that he collected: "If it were during the first days the policemen would not have harmed the students, they would not have beaten up the kids, they had nothing against them. But so many days, they got enraged as well, they were human too, they were out of themselves, they didn't know what to do. It was a sudden chaos!" *This Is Polytechnic Speaking*, 131–32.
160. Vassilis Papadias, industrial school student, in Karatzaferis, *Polytechnic Slaughter*, 239.
161. Portelli, "Intervistare il movimento," 131.
162. Kotanidis, *All Together, Now!*, 432–33.
163. Passerini, *Fascism in Popular Memory*, 21.
164. The testimony of Laliotis agrees. Quoted in Karatzaferis, *Polytechnic Slaughter*, 298. Darveris, himself a soldier at the time, also comments that most soldiers felt a deep rage for the students.
165. See Iordanoglou's comprehensive account on Salonica's movement in "Antidictatorship Student Movement," 268.
166. Ibid.
167. See Άγνωστα Ντοκουμέντα του Πολυτεχνείου Θεσσαλονίκης [Unknown Documents of the Polytechnic of Salonica].
168. Ibid., 270.

169. Kavvadias, *This Is Polytechnic Speaking*, 111.
170. Zafeiris, "Clandestine Correspondence," 28.
171. "We find ourselves inside the third bastion of New Free Greece. We're transmitting to you the fighting pulse of thousands of students of Salonica. At this moment we are proving the tradition that wants us always to be in the first line of the struggle for popular sovereignty.... We demonstrate our opposition to the dictatorial regime that has repressed any sense of freedom, justice, and national sovereignty."
172. Iordanoglou, "Antidictatorship Student Movement," 272.
173. Kavvadias, *This is Polytechnic Speaking*, 112.
174. Quoted in Zafeiris, "Clandestine Correspondence," 28.
175. Iordanoglou, "Antidictatorship Student Movement."
176. *Protoporia*, December 1973.
177. "Άφησαν τα αυτοκίνητα και έκαναν προλεταριάτο!" [They Left Their Cars and Made a Proletariat], *O Foititis*, 19 November 1973.
178. Marwick, *The Sixties*.
179. "Διαλύονται 28 φοιτητικοί σύλλογοι και οργανώσεις" [Twenty-eight Student Societies and Organizations Are Dissolved], *Eleftheros Kosmos*, 22 November 1973.
180. Poulantzas, *Crisis of the Dictatorships*, 94–95.
181. In his article "The Greek Lesson" (*New Statesman*, 14 December 1973), Christopher Hitchens classified the three internal divisions within the ranks of the Colonels as the "gangsters," the "Puritans," and the "Quadafis." The first, like Papadopoulos and Pattakos, were only really interested in power; the second, like Ioannidis and Colonel Ladas, were fanatical believers in martial virtue and social discipline; and the third were lower-rank officers who were for the independence of Greece above all.
182. Holtey, "Die Phantasie an die Macht," 171, 187f, 79, 269.
183. *Panspoudastiki* dubbed these students as the "300 provocateurs of Roufogalis," the notorious chief of the Secret Services.
184. Dr. Ioannis Fikioris to John Spraos, Athens, 26 June 1974. Fikioris requested in his letter that Spraos burn his recommendation "right after reading it." Universities (Placing Junta Refugees), Greek Committee against the Dictatorship Files, League for Democracy in Greece (Modern Greece Archive), King's College London.
185. K. Tzannetis to Spraos, n.d., ibid.
186. Spraos to Professor R. G. Hines, Department of Economics, Birkbeck College, London, 12 July 1974. Ibid.
187. O'Donnell and Schmitter, "Uncertain Democracies," 56.
188. Bermeo, "Power of the People," 10.
189. On the evolution of the left-wing youth during the *Metapolitefsi* see further Papadogiannis, "Greek Communist Youth."
190. Sociologist Maria Eliou argues, however, that the government of the day left out the social dimension, "which would form the foundation of a bold attempt at reform." See Eliou, "Those Whom Reform Forgot," 60.
191. Liakos, "History Writing," 50.
192. Kousouris, "Temps de la défaite," 219.
193. Fyssas, *Polytechnic Generation*, 19.
194. Van Boeschoten, *Troubled Years*, 215, 222.

195. Liakos, "History Writing," 50.
196. Darveris, *Night's Story.*
197. Zoumboulakis, "One Night to the Next."
198. Siani-Davies and Katsikas, "National Reconciliation after Civil War," 567.
199. Zoumboulakis, "One Night to the Next."
200. Fraser, *1968,* 337.
201. See Alivizatos and Diamandouros, "Politics and the Judiciary and the Greek Transition to Democracy." Also see Graham and Quiroga, "After the Fear Was Over?"
202. On this issue see Haritos-Fatouros, "The Official Torturer" and T. Gibson and Haritos-Fatouros, "The Education of a Torturer."
203. See *The Trials of the Junta. Full Transcripts.*
204. Fyssas, *Polytechnic Generation,* 19.
205. Korovesis, *Guards of the Humans,* 17.
206. Also see Charisopoulou, *The Lost Generation of the Metapolitefsi.*
207. Maro Pantelidou-Malouta, "Για το φεμινισμό της κρίσης. Από τη διαφορά των φύλων στη(ν) (πολυκοίκιλη) Γυναικεία υποκειμενικότητα" [For the Feminism of Crisis: From the Difference of the Sexes to the Polymorphous Subjectivity of Women], *Dini* 8 (1995–96): 101–19. Quoted in della Porta, Valiete, and Kousis, "Sisters of the South: Paths to Women's Rights in Southern Europe," unpublished paper, 21.
208. Ibid., 22.
209. The total number of active members of the twenty most important women's organization in the late 1970s was estimated to range between 50,000 and 120,000—that is, 1.4 and 3.6 percent of the total female population. See Efi Kalliga, "Οργανωμένες Προσπάθειες Γυναικών" [Women's Organized Efforts], *Neoi Orizontes* 203–4 (1982): 49–52.
210. See Papadogiannis, "From Coherence to Fragments."
211. Ross, *May '68 and Its Afterlives,* 49.

Epilogue

"Everything Links"

In April 1968, almost exactly one year after the Colonels' 1967 coup, the actress Melina Mercouri gave an interview to the English newspaper *The Observer*:

> "I learn now of the shooting of Dutschke in Berlin and of Martin Luther King in America. I knew Martin Luther King, and I passed precious hours with him. I knew this boy who is lying gravely wounded in Berlin. I know what is happening in the world; the world is burning! ... I now have a feeling of what is happening in the world: I feel more for the Vietnamese or for the Negroes in America. I am less egocentric about Greece because everything is like that..." She joins her little fingers: "Everything links."[1]

This passage conveys to a large extent the "cultural and political mix" of the late 1960s and early 1970s: Melina Mercouri, a Greek exile, residing in Paris, speaks in London against the Greek Colonels, adding references to other movements and icons of the time, on the premises that one should not act in a myopic way, as "everything links." Interestingly, Mercouri herself was part of the student folklore that she described. Her speech against the Greek Junta at Trafalgar Square the same year, in which she passionately recited Lord Byron and the Greek communist poet Ritsos while wearing a scarlet dress, became an iconic moment of the 1960s. She too became part of the international palette of revolutionary references.[2]

Constant riots on university campuses and worker unrest all around the globe are among the most emblematic images of 1968, all evoked in Mercouri's interview. New collective actors articulated a synchronized critique of both the capitalist and communist systems and voiced demands for more liberalization in their respective bloc. The Prague Spring in Czechoslovakia, with its violent ending, and May 1968 in France are probably the most representative examples of these tendencies. At the same time, antiwar protests on American campuses as the Vietnam War reached its climax were accompanied by a growing sympathy for the escalating anti-imperialist struggles in Africa and Latin America.

Figure 6.1. Everything links. Antidictatorship rally in the United States in 1974, associating the Junta with the war in Vietnam. In the third-worldist frame of the "long 1960s," Greece and Vietnam were grouped together as victims of US imperialism. (Source: ASKI, Archives of Social and Cultural History)

What commonalties are there to be found in the nature and demands of the protest movements of these heterogeneous countries? The first is that they brought social actors to the fore who challenged old theories and ideologies. These actors were often influenced by romantic utopias, which proved instrumental in shaping their imaginary. They attacked authoritarianism, be it of the state, university, or family, and voiced demands for greater freedom in the political, intellectual, and sexual realms. Many rejected both capitalism and the "bureaucratization" of revolution by the Soviet Union, and they sought to acquire autonomy from political organizations. Alternative ideologies linked to mass politics positioned a new, radicalized subjectivity against the one-dimensionality of technical and scientific rationalism. In Western countries, young people started favoring "antiproductivity" over an economy-driven market society and its values of discipline, hierarchy, and obedience; they expressed their opposition to repressive social norms. Preconceived social roles were also rejected despite the fact that most of the people involved in the movements—those Pierre Bourdieu and Jean-Claude

Passeron call *les héritiers*—might have looked ahead to a more or less secure professional future.³ At the same time, they preferred sexual openness and promiscuity to monogamy and family microcosms.⁴

The year 1968 was not only Western and certainly not just European in nature. The global character of the revolts is therefore the major difference between '68 and the revolutions of 1848, to which they are often compared, or to the watershed events of 1989. The increased interaction in protest between various parts of the world was facilitated by a growing, globalized media communication infrastructure and a larger realignment of the Cold War world order. The cultural transfers that occurred in this period and the positive cross-identification between movements were also major factors for the creation of an osmosis.

The year 1968 also singles itself out by being a cultural as well as a political revolution. Much of the movements' iconoclasm derived from the fusion between the public and the private sphere. Art became part of everyday life. Within a growingly globalized culture industry, rock music became a powerful common reference through which people could communicate despite language barriers: Bob Dylan, the Rolling Stones, Jimi Hendrix, and Pink Floyd all contributed to the soundtrack of protest. Auteur cinema was another universal code and a means of "transmitting experiences." Street theater, music happenings, and subversive posters were massively diffused. A new "structure of feeling" was created whereby irony and collective imagination gave birth to irreverent posters, subversive poetry, and ironic writing on walls.⁵ According to Michael Loewy, artistic creation was informed by the "repertory of feast, play, poetry, 'liberation of speech,'" while its language [was] inspired by Marx, Freud, Nietzsche and Surrealism."⁶ Such attributes were particularly evident in small artistic "vanguard groups" like the Situationists in France or the Provos in the Netherlands, which promoted *détournement* and subversion as central elements of their artistic explorations. Attire and external appearance were part of a new socialization too and acted as a code, a way of life, and a cultural identity statement. A spectacular fusion took place between "high" and "low" culture, sophisticated intellectual items and popular consumer products. This dialectic between playfulness and seriousness, *engagé* political action and everyday iconoclasm, illustrates the dichotomies between—but also the pastiche and hybrid character of—the various movements.

As historians Martin Klimke and Joachim Scharloth have pointed out, "discontent with the Cold War was what united activists on both sides of the Atlantic," a discontent manifested in their shared opposition to the deterrence policy, the common threat of nuclear extinction, and "a deep-seated frustration with the apathy of their societies."⁷ The Vietnam War was both a point of reference and a source of inspiration for actors struggling against imperialism, and it became a connecting thread, cutting across the east, west, north, and south and eliminating continental differences. The New Left and neo-Marxism were also integral parts of the movements.[8] Political activists exercised new repertoires of action, including occupations, sit-ins, street theater, civil disobedience, and communes. In these "new social movements," students no longer had to wait for revolutionary conditions to mature but instead could create them themselves by accepting their role as revolutionaries.[9] For traditional Marxist thinkers, this posed insurmountable difficulties, not least due to student revolutionaries' not always harmonious coordination with workers. Revolutionary violence was yet another source of inspiration, and activists often adopted the theories of Frantz Fanon, Carlos Marighella, and Ernesto Che Guevara uncritically, transplanting the spirit of decolonization and "third-worldism" in often entirely irrelevant contexts.

The 1968 movements were also the product of the crisis in parliamentarianism, the expansion of universities, and the subsequent inability of states to accommodate rising student numbers. Growth of student populations, in turn, was in part the result of the postwar baby boom; the generational surplus produced a deep clash.[10] Age-group issues tended to be more crucial than conflicts of class, race, or political interests. In Western countries, affluent society and Americanization faced a new critique as a "postmaterialist" culture of protest with anticonsumerist undertones took center stage.

From a transnational perspective, 1968 was the first global protest movement. In the bipolar world of the Cold War era, surpassing borders and achieving synchronicity was not an easy task, and despite the cultural transfer, national particularities and political specificities determined the nature and outcome of the movements. Accordingly, while '68 became a fundamental moment in history in which national identities collided with and became subsumed by international ones, it was far from a homogeneous experience. While the movement in France was an antiauthoritarian revolt with strong anarchist undercurrents driven by activists in search of a new *Weltanschauung*, the New Left in Italy, primed by workerism, fought to abolish the "bourgeois state," often by violent means and as a response to "state-sponsored aggression." In West Germany, the radical movement was characterized by antimaterialism and a generational caesura, as young people asked emphatically, "What did you do during the war, Daddy?" expressing their disgust for the *Kriegsgeneration*. In the United States, the Berkeley free speech movement had given rise to a new generation of politicized anti-Vietnam youth who were mesmerized by the intransigence of the Black Power movement and eventually by the hippie counterculture as well. The difference between protest in Western democracies and in Southern and Eastern European and

Latin American countries under authoritarian regimes was stark. In the latter cases, "students fought for elementary civil rights, already possessed by their Western ... counterparts."[11]

It was necessary for the movements to communicate with one another through alternative channels and subterranean networks. Radical intellectuals started to be mutually influential for the first time: cultural transfer and projections started flowing from Latin America or Africa to Europe and the other way around. Students were convinced, according to Luisa Passerini, of the "relationship between the small, the local and the individual on one hand and the planetary level of oppression on the other."[12] Still, specific cultural logics and distinct social and political circumstances acted as filters. Commonalities between movements and the cross-national diffusion of movement ideas often consisted merely of decontextualized fragments that were filtered through specific cultural traditions.[13] Accordingly, even though the influence of the three Ms or the adoration of Che Guevara were attributed to a common cognitive orientation, the "uniformization" of the message did not necessarily imply a uniform reception of it. To paraphrase Stuart Hall, this is "the point where *already coded* signs intersect[ed] with the deep semantic codes of a culture and t[ook] on additional, more active ideological dimensions".[14] These were accordingly translated to a local "map of meaning," a "map of social reality" with a whole range of social meanings, practices and usages "written in" to it.[15]

Even though in pure temporal terms the events of 1968 were not synchronic all over the globe, the year has come to designate a series of movements with a similar ethos that occurred from the mid-1960s to the early 1970s. Accordingly, the Caputxinada in Barcelona in 1966 was dubbed an "early" '68, the Polytechnic uprising in Athens in 1973 was called a "late" one, and the 1960s in the States were divided into "low," "middle," and "high" subcategories. Arthur Marwick's already mentioned term the "long 1960s," designating an era starting in the late 1950s and stretching until the mid-1970s, is therefore useful when trying to reconcile these different dates, as well as their antecedents and aftermaths.

In this context, the Greek student movement under the Colonels was one of the last manifestations of the political and countercultural dynamism of the "global 1960s." Dimitris Papanikolaou argues that the Greek case under the dictatorship fits neatly into the general periodization, proposed among others by Fredric Jameson, which places the high 1960s in-between 1967 and 1974: a period of late capitalism characterized by a parallel hardening of global authoritarianism (coup d'etats, military interventions) and antiauthoritarianism (social movements, rise of counterculture).[16] The Greek transition to democracy fits well with yet another model, Samuel Huntington's famous "third wave of democratization," alongside Portugal and Spain in the mid-1970s—even though the student movements' strong anti-Americanism seriously undermines Huntington's conviction that social actors were supposedly "inspired and borrowed from the American example" of democratic pluralism.[17]

But is it correct to argue that the Polytechnic was a "Greek" or "belated" '68—or as some French scholars put it, part of what constitutes "les années 68"?[18] As social psychologist Nicole Janigro argues about the Yugoslav experience under Tito, the absence of democracy in Greece also made an institutional crisis of political parties and mechanisms of representation and a Dutschkean "long march through the institutions" impossible. What is more, Janigro's point that "the system was more rigid and inclined for a more brutal rendering of accounts with its adversaries" could well be an accurate description of the Greek situation.[19] On the other hand, mimesis, appropriation, and inversion of international models and transnational diffusion of protest culture played a major role in the making of the student movement and the shaping of new cultural identities.

To narrow my focus on this subject, I shall examine three temporal sequences, as Luisa Passerini suggests, in an almost Braudelian fashion: the relatively brief time span of the events, the medium-length period of the social movements, and the still lengthier period of cultural changes.[20]

Events

Structurally, the antitechnocratic objectives that for Alain Touraine were crucial to the French May '68 and Bourdieu's description of those events as a sign of crisis in social reproduction cannot be easily applied to Greece.[21] This was not a new social movement being bred by the postindustrial era, nor a movement having "broken with the traditional values of capitalist society and seeking a different relationship to nature, to one's own body, to the opposite sex, to work and to consumption."[22] In addition, Greek economic conditions were different from those in France, Italy, or West Germany, as was the country's post–World War II development, which elsewhere was the root of subsequent social agitation. Robert Inglehart's influential thesis that the 1968 movements were the product of a postmaterialist culture of protest[23] does not apply to the Greek student movement, as the Greek "consumer culture" was new but not strong enough to spark an antimaterialist youth frenzy.

Moreover, the fact that Western countries were experiencing a crisis of parliamentarism at the same time that Greece had been put in a "plaster cast" renders a direct comparison difficult. The Greek Communist Party had been outlawed since 1947, and the country's democracy was weak and "guided" even during the mid-1960s. Years after the end of the civil war, many people were still fighting for individual freedom and basic political rights. Therefore, Western students' slogans, such as *imagination au pouvoir,* often seemed out of place for Greeks, both inside and outside Greece. Being confronted with an arbitrary, brutal, and grotesque adversary such as the Junta, the students could not easily grasp protest activity of a bohemian or situationist character; this is partly the reason why the few anarchists inside the Law School and Polytechnic occupations were marginalized and suspected. Stavros Lygeros underscores that the distinct conditions in Greece led to different demands: "It has a specificity because it finds itself in an extraordinary situation, a dictatorship, it puts forward a demand that lies further back, it does not say 'All power to the imagination,' as May '68 does, it says 'Down with the Junta.' During the first phase it does not say it directly, because it wants to override fear, it says, for example, 'Free student elections'" (Lygeros, interview).

Just like the students of 1968, Greek students of the Polytechnic were the first generation to grow up under "less burdensome economic conditions and therefore were less subject psychologically to the disciplinary compulsion of the labour market" and "more sensitive towards the economization of life and individual costs of competitive society," to quote Bert Klandermans.[24] They dissociated themselves from the traditionalist home model and traditional social formations but not from the political ones. Furthermore, as in other underdeveloped countries, the students in Greece served as a catalyst for political change. Contrary to the experience of Western students, who had "no experience of political terror, economic crises [and] real political alternatives to the established order,"[25] they had considerable familiarity with these phenomena. In Greece, just like in Spain, the conflicts were more acute and conspicuous, reflecting the particular cleavages of a divided nation. Furthermore, a lot more was at stake and there was much more personal risk involved in protest in Greece than in France, Italy, or West Germany. These were democracies, albeit with a strong conservative state, while Greece was a repressive and authoritarian military regime. The fact that torture was an ongoing fact for the ones who were arrested during the dictatorship is a major differentiating factor that needs to be emphasized.

The 1973 Polytechnic occupation resembled 1968 insofar as the spirit of uprising inspired its emergence. Compared to other movements of the 1960s, however, neither the Polytechnic itself nor the Greek student movement as a whole was as messy or as unresolved. Accordingly, the controversial wisecrack that '68 was "an interpretation in search of an event" cannot be easily applied to the student movement in Greece. The primary ideology of

'68 was "contestation" with content, objectives, and enemies that were not always precise; in Greece meanwhile the huge weight of the military dictatorship and the special significance that acts of defiance such as the Polytechnic occupation acquired within this context unconditionally rendered it an event with clear interpretational cues. A rebellion against a dictatorship must be understood to be much more forthright than middle-class radicalism with the often ambivalent motivations of the Western movements of the late 1960s, which aimed to change society in general. As Catalan sociologist Salvador Giner has put it, regarding the Spanish case, antidictatorship students in the European South fought for "classical" liberal goals, such as free unions, a modern educational system, and the free circulation of ideas; radicals in Berkeley, Paris, Berlin, or Amsterdam rebelled precisely against this kind of liberalism.[26]

Though the self-organized structure of Greek students prior to 1973 shared similarities with the '68 ethos, the Polytechnic occupation broke the direct democracy precedent, introducing the principle of representative democracy in its extreme form. Nonmembers of the CCO, for instance, could not enter the room where the committee held its assemblies. Another interesting feature is the role played by the media. Students' pirate radio station in Athens was a very direct way of spreading influence and accessing a wider range of people. Konstantinos Konofagos, the former rector of Athens Polytechnic, argues correctly that the students in Paris in 1968 did not manage to find such a form of propaganda,[27] most likely because they did not want to. The Greek students did not employ radical tactics, however. Contrary to the 1968 movements, which relied heavily on the use of confrontational events, the Greek movement's repertoire was strictly nonviolent, although perhaps equally as disruptive, as the Law School and Polytechnic occupations proved to be.

Still, a semiotic study of the 1968 protest movements reveals a similarity to the anti-Junta student movement in terms of cultural significations (gestures, language, symbols) that formed their identity code: these cultural significations became a menace to the established order and incomprehensible to outsiders.[28] Elements of '68 were present at the Polytechnic, even if in disguise, including a common theoretical background, patterns of behavior, and the participants' placing of themselves in an imaginary chain of events in a global contestatory movement. What is more, the Greek student movement reacted against the pressure of a military dictatorship but was also strongly exposed to the general protest wave generated in 1968. Vourekas remarks: "In the discussions about political matters and so forth, May '68 was not absent, not at all. On the contrary, it seemed very close. Now think, the [Greek] student movement starts acquiring momentum in '72, there is a four-year time lag, it is not much" (Vourekas, interview). The temporal proximity between 1968 and 1972 that is mentioned here underlines the idea of the "long '68," once again relativizing the supposed synchronicity of the 1968 protest movements.

The political conscience of the student movement was also shaped by a set of cultural models and prototypes of resistance that originated abroad. "Foreign" models were quite subversive, as they included elements of defiance and linked the student movements' imaginary, experiences, and style together. This fits with Doug McAdam's observation that "the rash of student movements that flourished around the globe … in 1968 were clearly attuned to and influenced by one another, resulting in the development and diffusion of a 'student left master frame.'"[29] In contrast to the previous generation, the Polytechnic generation had experienced and learned from '68 as a past model, not a simultaneous event. Greek students had '68, and in particular the French experience, in the back of their minds. Solidarity, imagination, vitality, subversiveness, and hedonism were standard themes.

The distinct characteristics and ultimate demands of the Greek movement—a locally defined case—were determined not only by internal politics but also by a broader influx of information and semantic codes, such as dress, taste in music and literature, rhetoric and slogans, and the awareness that there were parallel student movements operating abroad. In this way, student mentalities, marked by both their domestic situation and an adversary as concrete as a military Junta, were nevertheless enhanced by an awareness of student movements elsewhere. This point evokes German historian Ingrid Gilcher-Holtey's comment on '68, that it was "the mimesis of all possible revolutions that united the students who were in revolt."[30] Greek students managed to accumulate many elements of the international protest movement alongside their distinct characteristics and despite structural incongruence. The general wave of '68 infiltrated Greece but it was "translated," "edited," and grafted according to the country's existing standards, conditions, and needs.[31]

In both the '68 and post-'68 movements, the revolutionary imagination was shaped by foreign experiences, including the international circulation of information about the student revolts and the strong influence of the liberation struggles in the Third World. Cross-national diffusion of protest led to the adoption of similar strategies concerning organization, action forms, and ideological frames.[32] In that sense, the fallout from '68 had a quasi-colonial cultural impact as "transmitter" countries influenced the politics of "receiver" nations, and this continued after the fall of the dictatorship through the work of a series of French-trained Greek scholars, some of whom arrived from Vincennes. Still, one could argue that a mutual influence took place.

The *tiersmondiste* tendency of Western students included positive identification with the Greek "underdog," and the campaigns that took place abroad against the Colonels' regime had rendered Mikis Theodorakis, Alekos Panagoulis, and Melina Mercouri parts of the pantheon of revolutionary folklore. This shifted the rules of the power game as well as the receiver and transmitter dynamics that had been linear and one-sided hitherto.[33] Here, I am not only arguing about a certain cross-fertilization and confluence between the different movements, but also about a destabilization of the symbolic geographies of transnationalism and their supposed asymmetric flow from the "center" to the "periphery."

Antiregime Greek students also shared the utopian vision of the '68 movements. Greek students could be described as visionary protesters, but with widely differing views on how to combat the regime and transform Greek society. None of them wanted to go back to the pre-1967 state of affairs. They did not, however, believe in aphorisms, such as the famous Italian dictum, "The bourgeois state should be smashed instead of changed." But the Junta's grip was not a static and impenetrable barrier; it proved to be surprisingly dynamic and porous, instead. It was a prism of sorts, which often privileged distortions instead of a clear viewpoint. The violence in the rhetoric and actions of Western protesters, for example, was translated into the peacefulness of the Polytechnic occupation, while consumption—rejected by the rebelling youth of the West—remained an ardent desire.

Finally, Greek students' public demonstrations were more serious and less irreverent and provocative than those organized by their Western counterparts, largely because they targeted the whole nation. Accordingly, although the Greek '73 was by definition antiauthoritarian, as it dealt with an authoritarian regime, it did not aspire to throw off authority altogether. While Greek students wanted to change things, alienated as they were both by the dictatorship and by the passivity of wider Greek society, they did not appear willing to be violently disruptive, perhaps because they did not have the conceptual and physical space to do so. Instead, they sought to create a national insurrection by appealing to ordinary people. Dimitris Hatzisokratis, for instance, stresses with pride that the greatest achievement of the Polytechnic was that it managed to isolate leftist radicalism and promote slogans that could be accepted and digested by most Greeks.[34] This was not a concern of '68 protesters, who could allow themselves to be as radical, libertarian, and anarchic as they wished.

An interesting testimony is provided by Rector Konstantinos Konofagos in a book published some years after the democratic transition in Greece. Since he had been to Paris shortly after May 1968, Konofagos had a firsthand opinion of what had happened during the *événements* and was in a position to compare this with the Greek case: "I compared the slogans of Paris with the ones in Athens. Much less humor in our people. But all the rest was equally multifarious. The anarchist slogans over here were fewer too."[35] So even if playfulness and hedonism were present in the Greek movement, they occurred on a strictly *private* level. As Claudie Weill has argued, there is a great difference between a joyous culture of revolt and a serious one,[36] and the French and Greek cases reflect this discrepancy. The strict guidance of Greek antiauthoritarian organizations, as well as their patrolling for "provocateurs" and out-of-line slogans at the Polytechnic, betray the seriousness that accompanied the Greek movement from the very beginning. All this differentiates it from the festivity and the *détournement* that, say, situationists expected from a social movement.[37] In Greece, by contrast, part of the repertoire of dissidence was acting with earnestness.

Medium-Length: Utopias and Outcomes

According to Italian political sociologist Giovanni Statera, there is a lag between utopia and ideology and an instantaneous conflict between the two in a social movement.[38] At some point in the 1968 movements, ideology superseded utopia, and the student movements "succumbed to reality as it was."[39] In the Greek case, it seems that the two were inextricably linked, and in all but a few cases ideology held paramount importance. Only in the Polytechnic uprising did the utopian feeling acquire a status of its own, aided by the circumstances. At that point, one could argue, paraphrasing Gareth Stedman Jones, that the Greek student movement became both "expressive" and "structural."[40] The spontaneous character of the revolt, the feeling that everything was possible and the momentary void, allowed for the creation of mini-utopias that were quickly dissolved when the movement was crushed under the tanks.

Romantic utopianism, based on the ambivalence between radical humanism and cold structuralism, was a common experience in '68 movements.[41] These movements began with a short period of complete freedom of imagination. The students' desires, their beliefs, and their rational expectations became temporarily intertwined, and the movement was not filtered through the prerogatives of ideology alone. The semantic content of their intentions and actions was dictated by the very rational preconditions set by the struggle, a fact that curtailed the space of the imagination, as the movement required cold and lucid thinking. On the other hand, ideological aspects were omnipresent: the frame that judged the conditions to be a "revolutionary situation" made people act in a specific way, proving its performative effect. Frames acquired a real basis, following André Breton's famous dictum that *"l'imaginaire est ce qui tend à devenir réel"* (the imaginary is that which tends to become real).[42]

Another defining factor was Greek political culture, which in many ways determined the claims that the Greek students did and did not make. This, to borrow the words of Lynn Hunt and Keith Barker, "ultimately provide[d] the logic of revolutionary action" by supplying most of the "discourses, values and implicit rules that express[ed] and shape[ed] collective action and intentions."[43] In terms of left-wing politics, even though the Greek students split into groupings, their attachment to communist orthodoxy remained intact. Though the Greek Communist Party itself condemned the 1968 uprisings as an opportunistic circus, the students were nonetheless very much attracted to the party. Their allegiance to basic communist principles, and even more so to the two communist parties as exponents of the only legitimate and authoritative alternative to Greek authoritarianism, remained unchallenged. To many young Greeks, nurtured as they were by the teachings of the traditional Greek Left, it was quite puzzling that communist parties tended to be excluded from and contested by the 1968 movements.

Although they shared the radicalism and flamboyance of their communist counterparts in rhetoric and action, Greek leftists did not aim at the "immediate mobilization of many individuals for the sake of mobilization itself," to use Habermas's phrase.[44] Maoists and Trotskyists were immersed in new actionism inspired by Mao and Castro and therefore sought mobilization at all costs, but not for its own sake. Moreover, although these people were, next to the anarchists, the closest in Greece to 1968 radicalism and internationalism, they were often the ones who rejected references to the international situation, opting for a more rigid focus on the Greek case and its special characteristics. A discrepancy, which partly derives from the above, is that while a certain neoanarchist tendency was born in the '68 movements, the word *anarchy* continued to bear negative connotations in Greece, not only for the ruling classes and the Junta but also for most sections of the Left, including the radicals.

The Greek student movement did not, in Andrew Feenberg and Jim Freedman's terms, lead to a change in the focus of opposition "from economic exploitation to social and cultural alienation," nor did it "prepare the rejection of Stalinist authoritarianism in the new social movements."[45] Greek students did it their own way, by incorporating the Communist Party and retro-Marxist Old Left as a leading player in contestatory action.[46] Given that "traditional values and forms of behaviour limit the actors' views on what is possible,"[47] the hegemonic communist ideology did not allow for major breakthroughs, given the imprinted traumatic memory of the civil war. The students' colorful cultural activism indirectly expressed "the demand for a different political rhetoric," which, however, did not "put in doubt ... the dominant left-wing ideology and practice," as writer Aris Marangopoulos maintains.[48]

The year 1968 was a revolt against bourgeois society, a revolt that felt the need to represent the working class and act in its name. The uprising in Greece was against a tangible oppression, and it happened to share some of 1968's tenets and points of departure: a general Marxist background that venerated the working classes and workers; the conviction that the ruling class in Greece was backing the dictators (as did the Right, the Church, and the Americans); and a rejection of Greek society's bigotry. The absence of a trade-unionist worker movement in Greece is striking,[49] in contrast, for example, to Francoist Spain, where the worker's movement under the communist-led Comisiones Obreras was becoming increasingly powerful, at about the same time. Despite all this, however, the so-called student-worker unity was a typical frame that antiregime actors used in Greece. The students' action repertoire was strongly influenced by their tendency to think of themselves as linked to the workers, even if there was a chasm between the two groups.

May 1968 also posed the problem of defining the subjects of history. This shift had an impact on Greek students too. Alkis Rigos stresses that they also believed in their capacity to change the world: "A thing into which we didn't fall as a generation was the mythology that the Great Powers do everything and therefore you are weak. Somewhere out there some foreigners decide, and you are weak. We believed that you could change the world" (Rigos, interview). This belief in the power of student agency over and against the official power structures was novel and quite unprecedented.

The Polytechnic can also be seen as a moment of collective madness, in which traditional barriers are broken and the perception of activists that they can intervene in history is changed.[50] The student activists of the Polytechnic shared the perception that they could change the world with other '68 movement actors, producing a type of account that explains how activists perceived the world order. Vernikos opts for a more limited version of this in the title of his book: *Once Upon a Time, When We Wanted to Change Greece*. It is significant that it is Greece, not the world, that is to be changed, and this lexical cautiousness, juxtaposed with the hyperbole of the Western (The Doors-inspired) slogan "We want the world, and we want it now" accurately encapsulates the Greek students' awareness of the limitations that they faced in contrast to some of their counterparts abroad. Even so, their conviction that they could change Greece, coupled with their certainty that they were part of a wider universal struggle, was enough to place them within the broader context of avant-garde protest. Michalis Sabatakakis describes it as a conviction that capitalism was in retreat at a global level:

> I believe that the main characteristic experienced by the young people in Europe and the young people in Greece was a feeling that capitalism was being replaced. Namely, this was the period of Vietnam, of movements of liberation in the whole world, Che Guevara, Chile. This is therefore a period in which the feeling was that capitalism was retreating, being replaced by a revolutionary movement. (Sabatakakis, interview)

Despite all those particularities and contradictions, the antidictatorship student movement shared many elements with the antihierarchical and antiauthoritarian character of the 1968 revolts and can fairly be considered a "revolt" (Touraine), a "quasi-revolution" (Morin), and a "cultural break" (Crozier).[51] But in Greece, part of the establishment backed the student struggle, including the "old" politicians and intellectuals and also those people who belonged to the old bourgeoisie and could not abide the coarseness of the dictators and their obscurantism. And they did so in part because the movement, despite its dynamism—and contrary to Sabatakakis's conclusion regarding the crisis of capitalism—was not a "tear-it-all-apart" fight but one that vindicated traditional values and thus was not intrinsically provocative. Even during the trial for the Polytechnic massacre that took place in 1975, a year after the Junta's fall, students refused to admit several facts, probably in order to avoid giving their opponents the right to argue that they wanted to stage an anarchist revolution.[52] They were "good kids," venerated by many people, because they shared healthy—if communist—attitudes. For some, they were "good kids" precisely because of their communist leanings. This was surely not the way they saw it; it was, after all, radical to be both middle-class and communist under a dictatorship. In the end, however, they were iconoclastic mostly in terms of everyday life: looser sexual mores, hippie appearance, declared political beliefs.

Future's Past: Cultural Changes

In the words of Carl E. Schorske, student revolts tends to pass over time from politics to culture due to "a gap that open[s] between generations in both moral and intellectual culture" that is "wider than in politics."[53] Cultural projections play a catalyst role as they remodel the imaginary and historical conscience of a generation.[54] Greek students mixed the high and low registers of culture, the "elite" and "popular" ones, as they appropriated both. They matched the characteristics of a countercultural movement of defiance with highly sophisticated book reading, and they immersed themselves in alternative cultural forms not only as producers/consumers of artifacts but also through their lived practices. In the end, ideology—supposedly the main characteristic of the time—went hand-in-hand with a deeper form of culture that was emerging, distinguishing this generation from any previous one, This was precisely what provided the movement with a strong sense of unity, despite the deep divisions among the students. It was a syncretic form of culture that had accumulated the international paradigm of youth radicalism as the Zeitgeist of the era and translated it into something new through the filter of Greek cultural tradition.[55]

The general antiauthoritarianism directed against all institutions (school, family, party, politics), which was closer to the original spirit of '68 than to Marxism,[56] was more implicit than explicit in the Greek case, however. Similarly, there was a striking absence of feminist, ecological, or homosexual components in the movement and its successors after the restoration of democracy. Overall, Greek students lay between innovation and tradition, a dualism reflected in their reluctance to attack the way in which power was being exercised in society at large. Still, in Greece, the uneven development of the student movement "exacerbated the experience of modernity as contradiction and crisis," as cultural historians Helen Graham and Jo Labanyi argue regarding the Spanish case, producing a more characteristic avant-garde than in the "more advanced capitalist nations where modernity was less problematic."[57]

This generation of Greek students was an avant-garde in terms of both its self-perception and its action repertoire. It accelerated the cultural modernization processes that took place at breakneck speed in the years following the Junta's collapse by linking political radicalism with everyday life practices. In this way, the student movement acted as incubator of new ideas and future behaviors, carving out new boundaries between the public and the private,[58] thus expanding the horizon of its possibilities. After all, student circles were privileged: they were the only site where alternative culture and politics were discussed, experimented with, and put into practice.

Overall, their relation to modernization, 1968, democracy, communism, and Europe were crucial in forging Greek students into a new elite that would accelerate and legitimize the transitional process. Finally, people belonging to this generation of activists acquired agency and drew important political lessons from their antidictatorship experience,[59] which they later employed in order to bring about social change and a new political culture in Greece, including a different *lingo politico* and a new cultural ethos. Moreover, they

Figure 6.2. A powerful *lieu de memoire*. Thousands of young people demonstrating within the Polytechnic yard one year later, November 1974. The democratic transition was already underway, and the Polytechnic acted as a legitimizing event of the entire process. (Photographer: Aristotelis Sarrikostas)

launched a culture of dissent that operated as a system of checks and balances for postauthoritarian politics throughout the transitional process.

Last, but not least, the Polytechnic was memorialized as the major act of resistance during the seven years of authoritarianism, thus serving as one of the founding myths of the post-1974 Greek Republic. If the standard way for a society to overcome a traumatic period is through the homogenization of collective memory,[60] in Greece this was done through the hagiography of student resistance and its epically bloody conclusion as a token of the Greek people's resistance to authoritarianism. In many respects, the Polytechnic was used to whitewash the lack of systematic dissent against the dictatorial regime of the Colonels. The relative consensus that the Junta enjoyed among some segments of the Greek population during the six-plus-one years of its existence was obliterated in this celebration and followed by collective amnesia.

The current economic crisis, however, has generated a new trend: that of complete dismissal of both the entire period of the transition to democracy and of the Polytechnic generation in particular, blaming them for all later ills of Greek society.[61] This threatens the very foundations on which postauthoritarian collective memory has been constructed. It remains to be seen in what ways the contestation of this hitherto quintessential national *lieu de mémoire* is going to affect the country's political culture and self-image in the years to come.

Conclusion

This book has attempted to trace the reasons behind the upsurge in student activity in Greece during the Colonels' dictatorship, which culminated in the most important public act of resistance against the Junta: the Polytechnic uprising. The student movement—the only form of social upheaval that took place during the dictatorship—exploited a series of cultural and ideological elements to disrupt the consensus created over the course of five years of dictatorial rule. Expressing the views of those elements of civil society that felt an ever greater discontent as the years passed, students demanded radical changes and ultimately created new meaning. By exploring the subjective element in their discourse and the identity of the Polytechnic Generation, this study has considered not only how new collective identities shaped student mentalities but also the ways in which the latter have changed over time and how individuals look back at their past militantism.

By promoting a dialogue between private microhistory and public events, this book has also explored both the political side of the events of the Greek antidictatorship movement and the everyday experiences of people, following Norbert Elias's invitation "to challenge the conventional antinomy between the study of social structures and that of the emotional ones but, at the same time, research and consider them together, dialectically."[62] By analyzing the discourse and action of some of the first antiregime student groupings, which exercised political violence with some restraint, I have further attempted to demonstrate the aspirations and imaginary resources of these students, but also their limited success.

Considering the student body from the early 1960s onward, I have traced the evolution of contentious politics in Greek university life over the "long 1960s," including the emergence of two distinct generational groups, and traced the continuities and ruptures in patterns and cultures of protest. Having already participated in the events of the first years of the 1960s, Generation Z was a force for change, even if it retained and reproduced many antiquated elements of old social life and aged militantism. However, the Lambrakides, despite their excellent organizational capacities, which included a wide infrastructure covering most of the country, proved unable to respond to the oncoming authoritarianism and did not manage to retain a structure for protest following the coup. With the political parties in disarray, these students did not react to the dictatorship in an efficient way, and they lost a great part of their rank and file to immediate detention. In general, Generation Z was conditioned by the past: it did not adapt to the new conditions created by the Junta, nor did it organize popular and successful forms of struggle, having already exhausted its creativity in previous years. All in all, the daring underground ventures of this generation proved unsuccessful.

The groupings that originated abroad often theorized the importance of the use of violence, bearing the clear marks of the third-worldist discourse of the time. For those in Greece, and as the '68 uprisings turned into a generational symbol, their counterparts abroad acquired a legendary status. This came into contrast with the opinions of many Greek émigrés, however, who regarded '68 as bizarre and even grotesque. Often, the seriousness with which Greek "revolutionaries" in France and Italy approached dissent made them suspicious of mass protest, as they expected armed struggle rather than peaceful marches.

Moving on to the 1970s, and with Generation Z out of the way, new collective identities were shaped by the very *experience* of the dictatorship, which in turn further politicized the members of the new generation, often in conflict with their class or ideological backgrounds. That these youths were not the ideological, cultural, or political clones of the civil war and post–civil war periods, as were various generations before them, including the Lambrakides, partly explains why the Junta did not succeed in either classifying or integrating them. New individual and collective behaviors, bred by a set of subversive everyday practices, greatly influenced the course of events. As in most dictatorial regimes, the private spaces that were preserved proved more significant than bombs set off, since they served as the necessary springboard for an initial "silent revolution" that would ultimately lead to a direct clash with the regime.

Furthermore, the regime's gradual liberalization offered the necessary political opportunities for the reinforcement of the mobilizing structures of this new generation. Collective platforms such as EKIN and the regional societies became points of reference and incubators of change, helping the dissident segments of the student body to acquire the coherence they were lacking. Resistance was oriented toward violent action in the years of the regime's harsher repression, persecution, and censorship; however, in the years following 1971 the first massive initiatives of the student body occurred. Students confronted the regime by using a legal platform to discuss university issues; at the same time, they transformed their everyday realities by drawing on cultural elements charged with symbolic meaning.

The preceding chapters further traced the forms of cultural warfare developed by Greek students, which bore its own stigma and was marked by a reappropriation of tradition against the regime's own conceptualization and promotion of Hellenic-Christian civilization in a succinct and subversive way. There was a renewal, enabled by the softening of censorship and provided by new readings, symbols, foreign prototypes of protest, and confidence that a break from the past was possible. A syncretic culture made out of music, literature, common political readings, cinema, theater, and style fostered student unity and recognition and served to counter threatening ideological rifts. These elements provided the means for the students' micro-resistances in everyday life, which eventually bred a full-fledged confrontation with the regime.

In addition, given the tough conditions, dissident male students started regarding their female companions as equals for the first time. This attitude was connected to the increased numbers of females in Greek universities, to the structural needs of the movement, and to a growing sexual emancipation and consciousness of parity. Even so, the battle of the sexes and gender prejudice remained a major issue in the Greek student movement, especially as they pertained to movement leadership, and despite the presence of a significant number of charismatic female leaders.

This book did not approach the Greek student movement only from within the scope of internal politics but also in the context of an ongoing radicalization of youth culture internationally. I have suggested that the Polytechnic Generation was an avant-garde in Greek society in general, and to a certain extent accelerated Greece's modernization, which took place at breakneck speed in the years following the Junta's collapse when a political radicalism merged with everyday life. However, the Polytechnic Generation was not as subversive and rejectionist, rebellious and contestatory as were its counterparts in other countries. The epic poetics of its politics were dictated by the romanticized communist past and conditioned by the overtly repressive context. The bloody conclusion of the Polytechnic underlines its resemblance to the experiences of Czechoslovakia, Mexico, Thailand, and Chile. In addition, despite the political rationalism and the general pragmatism that characterized the leadership of the mainstream student groups that seemed to be fighting for "classical" liberal goals, there was an underlying utopian frame regarding the radical transformation of the political environment. This was utterly frustrated by the experience of the *Metapolitefsi*, which students active in the movement often recall as a particularly traumatic moment.

With '68, a mimetic tendency was diffused among the students in an attempt to reenact the international protest movements. The influence of foreign and home-grown counterculture, facilitated by the opening of the regime, led to greater political and personal emancipation. The particular student culture that developed was marked not only by Greek internal politics but also by a strong international current of radical youth culture. Changes appeared in aesthetics and intellectual currents, as well as in the norms of social behavior. In addition, a mass consumerist youth culture *in statu nascendi* was coupled with political engagement, thus bringing the children of Marx and the dictatorship closer to the "Marx and Coca-Cola" model, even though protagonists reject this label with fury.

In terms of memory and subjectivity, former militant life stories are characterized by a certain homogenization by age group. While Generation Z stresses the continuity in suffering, the Polytechnic Generation presents itself as signaling a total rupture with the past. As far as the rivalry between the different components of the mass movement is concerned, I have revealed the "hardening" of subjectivity as ex-militants continue to use the analytical categories and to echo the ideological divisions of the past, such as the age-old ambivalence between strategy and spontaneity. Others, however, present a rather idealized image of student collaboration during the Junta years as an outcome of having a common goal, the overthrow of the regime. Rather than passing judgment, the book shares Ronald Fraser's conclusion that "what people thought, or what they th[ink] that they thought, also constitutes a historical fact." Even though I cannot know exactly what happened, the people I interviewed gave me "their truth," which is extremely valuable.[63]

It is not a given that the student movement in Greece took place because of the dictatorship or that without it the students would not have been radicalized as students were in much of the rest of the world. To paraphrase Raymond Carr and Juan Pablo Fusi's conclusion about Franco's Spain, judging by what happened in France, Germany, and Italy, there would probably have been student troubles with or without the Colonels.[64] The student movement that developed in Greece in the early 1970s not only constituted a reaction against the pressure of a military dictatorship but was also widely determined by the general wave generated in 1968. But it was the Junta itself that provided the complex framework for the specific evolution and climax of the Greek "long 1960s."

It was the response of the authoritarian regime that deepened the crisis and reinforced the students' combativeness and coherence. The conviction that this was a battle of life and death was further reinforced by the anger at the 1973 coup d'état against Allende in Chile and inspired by the contemporaneous student movement against the military dictatorship in Thailand—an identification that turned the movement "glocal." But the students did not really topple the regime, despite the Polytechnic bloodbath in November 1973 and present-day convictions about the contrary; it was the coup d'état against Makarios in Cyprus and the eventuality of a Greek-Turkish military confrontation that did so. As Jean-Paul Sartre argued regarding May '68 in

France, "A regime is not brought down by 100,000 unarmed students, no matter how courageous."[65] This is even truer, if the regime in question is a military one that does not refrain from resorting to violence in order to assert its authority.

Nevertheless, it was the student movement, bearer of the international protest movement's message of radicalism, which discredited the attempts of the regime to liberalize from within. The process of controlled liberalization failed miserably because, apart from helping to "educate" a new generation of students, its small concessions led to demands for still greater freedom of information, political pluralism, and democratization. This complex web of local and international references interpellated the students into specific social and political practices that became a major source of pressure on the Colonels' regime, to some extent defining its course but also laying the foundations for a total reshaping of Greek political culture in the following decades.

Notes

Previous versions of this chapter have been published in Kornetis, "'Everything Links'" and Kornetis, "68: Année symbolique."

1. John Gale, "Melina: What Those Colonels Told Me," *Observer,* 14 April 1968.
2. See for example the picture of that event in Ali and Watkins, *1968. Marching in the Streets.*
3. Bourdieu and Passeron, *Les Héritiers.*
4. Perry Anderson, "Renewals," 7.
5. Michael Loewy, "The Revolutionary Romanticism of May 1968," 97.
6. Ibid., 98.
7. Klimke and Scharloth, "1968 in Europe."
8. See, in this respect, John McMillian and Paul Buhle, eds. *The New Left Revisited.*
9. Mausbauch, "Historicising 1968," 183.
10. Flores and de Bernardi, *Il Sessantotto,* 91.
11. Jerzy Eisler, "March 1968 in Poland," 250.
12. Passerini, "Utopia and Desire," 25.
13. Della Porta, "1968," 141.
14. Stuart Hall, "Encoding, Decoding," 512–13. Original emphasis.
15. Ibid.
16. Papanikolaou, "Making Some Strange Gestures," 196. See also *Singing Poets* and Jameson, "Periodizing the Sixties."
17. Huntington, *The Third Wave,* 286. See Katsiaficas, *Asia's Unknown Uprisings, Vol. 2.*
18. See, for instance, Potamianos, "Ο "Ελληνικός Μάης'" [The "Greek May"], *Emfylios Typos* 59 (Apr. 2004).
19. Janigro, "Il '68 jugoslavo," 78–79.
20. Passerini, "Utopia and Desire," 12.

21. See the classics by Touraine, *Le communisme utopique* and Bourdieu, *Homo Academicus*.
22. Klandermans, "New Social Movements," 26.
23. Inglehart, *Silent Revolution*. While Habermas attributes "new social movements" to late modernity, Inglehart accounts for their appearance on the grounds of a postindustrial welfare and feeling of safety. The latter's theory about postmaterialism ascribes the rise of new social movements to changed values.
24. Klandermans, Ibid.
25. Habermas, *Toward a Rational Society*, 25.
26. Giner, "Power, Freedom and Social Change in the Spanish University, 1939–1975," 194.
27. Konofagos, *Polytechnic Uprising*, 51.
28. Sommier, *La violence politique*, 40.
29. McAdam, "Culture and Social Movements," 42. See in this respect Caute, *Year of the Barricades*, and Katsiaficas, *Imagination of the New Left*.
30. Gilcher-Holtey, "Die Phantasie an die Macht," 49.
31. I am grateful to Cornel Ban for drawing my attention to the importance of grafting in understanding how ideas travel. Also see Asimakoulas, "Translating 'Self' and 'Others'."
32. Della Porta, "1968," 136–37.
33. Ibid., 141.
34. Chatzisokratis, *Polytechnic '73. Rethinking a reality*.
35. Konofagos, *Polytechnic Uprising*, 115.
36. Discussion in terms of the paper "Fête ou révolution? Les perceptions diverses de mai 68 par les étudiants grecs," presented by the author within the framework of the Groupe d'études et de recherche sur les mouvements étudiants (GERME), Science Po, Paris, 17 December 2003.
37. See Knabb, *Situationist International Anthology*, 429.
38. Statera, *Death of a Utopia*.
39. Passerini, "Utopia and Desire."
40. Stedman Jones, "Significance of Student Uprisings," 33.
41. Della Porta, "1968," 131.
42. Bretón, preface to *Le Revolver à cheveux blancs*, 11.
43. Lynn Hunt and Keith Barker quoted in Wasserstrom, *Student Protest*, 10–11.
44. Habermas, *Toward a Rational Society*, 26.
45. Feenberg and Freedman, *When Poetry Ruled the Streets*, 68.
46. For the category of retro-Marxism see Berman, *Power and the Idealists*.
47. Feenberg and Freedman, Ibid.
48. Marangopoulos, "Children of Marx," 22.
49. It is important to note, however, that the workers in France around May 1968 did not always have clear-cut ideological prerogatives either, though they were constructed in the imaginary of the protesters as their mythical leaders. Cohn-Bendit conveyed this extreme workerism when he stated: "[The workers] were so present in our minds that we definitely had to get together some day." See Cohn-Bendit, *Nous l'avons tant aimée*, 63.
50. See on this Zolberg, "Moments of Madness."

51. See Gilcher-Holtey, *Die Phantasie an die Macht*, 40.
52. See *Trials of the Junta*.
53. Schorske, *Thinking with History*, 32.
54. Diouf, "Urban Youth," 63.
55. For an elaboration of the notion of the fusion between the paradigm of the international movement and national cultural tradition, see Gilcher-Holtey, "Mai 68 in Frankreich."
56. Sommier, *La violence politique*, 36.
57. Graham and Labanyi, "Culture and Modernity," 14.
58. Habermas, *Toward a Rational Society*, 29.
59. For the concept of the political lessons see Bermeo, "Democracy and the Lessons of Dictatorship."
60. Fernández, *Memoria y olvido*, 19–24.
61. See for example Kalyvas, "The 'December Insurrection.'"
62. Elias's text reads: "Pour expliquer le processus de civilisation, il faut procéder … à l'examen simultané des structures physiques et des structures sociales dans leur ensembles." *La dynamique de l'Occident*, 262.
63. Fraser, *Blood of Spain*, 3. Similarly, Hayden White has argued that "one can produce an imaginary discourse about real events that may not be less "true" for being imaginary." See *The Content of the Form*, 57.
64. Carr, et al., *Spain*, 94.
65. Jean-Paul Sartre, *Situations VIII: autour de 68*, Paris 1972, 194. Quoted by Ross, *May '68 and its Afterlives*, 65.

Bibliography

Interviews

Ariadni Alavanou, February 2002
Thanasis Athanasiou, October 2002
Nikos Bistis, March 2003
Zogia Chronaki, September 2003
Olympios Dafermos, October 2002
Vera Damofli, February 2001
Antonis Davanelos, October 2002
Katerina Detsika, January 2002
Giannis Felekis, January 2002
Anna Frangoudaki, February 2007
Chrysafis Iordanoglou, January 2001
Kostas Kalimeris, January 2002
Nikos Kaplanis, September 2002
Giorgos Karambelias, October 2002
Vasia Karkayianni-Karambelia, December 2003
Ioanna Karystiani, March 2003
Giorgos Kotanidis, March 2003
Stelios Kouloglou, January 2004
Giannis Kourmoulakis, February 2002
Nikitas Lionarakis, November 2003
Stavros Lygeros, March 2003
Anna Mandelou, February 2002
Maria Mavragani, March 2002
Triantafyllos Mitafidis, January 2001
Petros Oikonomou, September 2002
Dimitris Papachristos, February 2002
Kleopatra Papageorgiou, February 2002
Alkis Rigos, February 2001
Michalis Sabatakakis, February 2003
Kaiti Saketa, January 2003
Dionysis Savvopoulos, January 2004
Thanasis Skamnakis, February 2002
Michalis Spyridakis, March 2001
Rena Theologidou, March 2003
Ilias Triantafyllopoulos, February 2002
Agis Tsaras, March 2003
Klearchos Tsaousidis, January 2001
Maria Tzortzopoulou and Michalis Skyrianos, February 2002
Andrianos Vanos, March 2001
Eleni Varikas, May 2008
Christina Vervenioti, January 2002
Thodoros Vourekas, February 2002
Panagiotis Xanthopoulos, September 2002
Angeliki Xydi, February 2001
Myrsini Zorba, January 2004
*Georgia, January 2002
*Katerina, February 2003
*Pavlos, March 2003

Periodicals

Agonas	Emfylios Typos	Madrid	Protoporia
Allilengyi	Epikaira	Makedonia	Spartakos
Anti	Epsilon	Nea Estia	Spoudastikos Kosmos
Anoichto Theatro	Fantasio	Neoi Orizontes	Sunday Telegraph
Antistasi '68	Guardian	Neos Kosmos	Sunday Times
Apogevmatini	I Genia Mas	New Left Review	Ta Nea
Avgi	I Lexi	New Statesman	Tachydromos
Chicago Tribune	I Synecheia	New York Times	Thessaloniki
Culturefront	Kathimerini	Neoi Stochoi	Thourios
Dini	Kommounistis	Observer	Time
Economist	Kouros	O Foititis	To Kinima
Eleftheri Patrida	Krama	Politika Themata	To Vima
Eleftheros Kosmos	Le Monde	Poreia	Vradyni
Eleftherotypia			

Archives

Athens, Greece
Contemporary Social History Archives (ASKI)
Society for the Safeguarding of Historical Archives (EDIA)
Dafermos Archive

London, UK
League for Democracy in Greece (Modern Greece Archive), King's College London
    Greek Committee against the Dictatorship files
Info III–Info XVI, Correspondence Files I–VII, Chronological Files VI–IX, Press Cuttings, Circulars
Public Record Office (now the National Archives, PRO)
    FCO9 Greece, 1968–72

Paris, France
Historical Archives of the Fondation Hellénique

Washington, DC
United States National Archives (USNA)
NAR, RG 59, General Records of the Department of State (DS)
    Central Foreign Policy Files, 1967–1973
    Political and Defense, POL 2–1 to POL 23

Published Sources

Δύο χρόνια αγώνες (1972–1974). Πολιτικά κείμενα—Διακυρήξεις—Προκηρύξεις—Ντοκουμέντα—Υλικά της Αντιφασιστικής Αντιιμπεριαλιστικής Σπουδαστικής Παράταξης Ελλάδας Α.Α.Σ.Π.Ε. [Two Years of Struggles, 1972–1974: Political Texts,

Manifestos, Leaflets, Documents, Material of the Antifascist Anti-imperialist Student Party of Greece AASPE]. Athens, 1974.
Το ΚΚΕ. Επίσημα Κείμενα, 1961–1967 [KKE. Official Documents], Athens, 2002.
Ντοκουμέντα του ΠΑΚ 1972-1974 [Documents of PAK]. Athens, 1977.
Οι δίκες της Χούντας. Πλήρη πρακτικά. Δίκη Πρωταιτίων 21ης Απριλίου 1967 [The Trials of the Junta. Full Transcripts. The Trial of the Primarily Responsible for the 21st April 1967]. Athens, 1975.
Οι δίκες της Χούντας. Πλήρη πρακτικά. Η Δίκη του Πολυτεχνείου [The trials of the Junta. The Full Transcripts. The Polytechnic trial], Athens, 1975.
Οδηγητής, Παράνομο Υλικό της ΚΝΕ 1968–74 [Odigitis: Illegal Material of KNE, 1968–74]. Athens, 1976.

Secondary Sources

Adagio, Carmelo et al., eds. *Il lungo decennio: L'Italia prima del 68.* Verona, 1999.
Afentouli, Ino. *Μάης '68. 20 χρόνια μετά* [May '68: Twenty Years Later]. Athens, 1988.
Aguilar Fernández, Paloma. *Collective Memory of the Spanish Civil War: The Case of the Political Amnesty in the Spanish Transition to Democracy.* Madrid, 1996.
———. *Memoria y olvido de la Guerra Civil espagnola.* Madrid, 1996.
Alberoni, Francesco. *Falling in Love.* New York, 1983.
———. *Genesi.* Milan, 1989.
Ali, Tariq, and Susan Watkins. *1968. Marching in the Streets.* London, 1998.
Alivizatos, Nikos. *Οι πολιτικοί θεσμοί σε κρίση. Όψεις της ελληνικής εμπειρίας* [The Political Institutions in Crisis: Facets of the Greek Experience]. Athens, 1983.
———. *Μήπως το ταξίδι συνεχίζεται?* [Does the Journey Go On?], preface to *Ο Κομμουνισμός* [Communism], by Alex Adler, 9–47. Athens, 2004.
———, with Nikiforos Diamandouros. "Politics and the Judiciary and the Greek Transition to Democracy" in *Transitional Justice and the Rule of Law in New Democracies,* ed. James McAdams, 27–60. Notre Dame, 1997.
Altbach, Philip. "Students and Politics." In *Student Politics,* ed. Seymour Lipset, 74–93. New York, 1967.
Anagnostakis, Manolis. *Δεκαοχτώ Κείμενα* [Eighteen Texts]. Athens, 1970.
Anderson, Lynn R. *Προσωπικότητα και στάσεις των φοιτητών των ελληνικών Ανωτάτων Εκπαιδευτικών Ιδρυμάτων* [Personality and Stance of Students in Greek Institutions of Higher Education]. Athens, 1980.
Anderson, Perry. "Renewals," *New Left Review* 1 (Jan.–Feb. 2000).
Andreadis, Giagkos. *Η αντίσταση της μνήμης* [The Resistance of Memory]. Athens, 2004.
Andrews, Kevin. *Greece in the Dark ... 1967–1974.* Amsterdam, 1980.
Androulakis, Mimis. *Βαμπίρ και κανίβαλοι. Το ρίσκο μιας νέας σύγκρουσης των γενεών* [Vampires and Cannibals: The Risk of a New Conflict of Generations]. Athens, 2004.
Angelis, Vangelis, and Olympios Dafermos, eds. *Όνειρο ήταν: Το Αντιδικτατορικό Φοιτητικό Κίνημα και το Πολυτεχνείο με το βλέμμα των πρωτεργατών* [It Was Only a

Dream: The Antidictatorship Student Movement and the Polytechnic from the Point of View of the Protagonists]. Athens, 2003.

Arseni, Kitty. *Nelle carceri dei Colonnelli.* Rome, 1970.

Arseniou, Elizabeth, "The Emergence of a Hybrid Avant-Garde: The Response of the Magazine Pali to Greek Modernism," In *Greek Modernism and Beyond,* ed. Dimitris Tziovas and Nikos Stabakis, 271–80. Oxford, 1997.

Asimakoulas, Dimitris. "Translating "Self" and "Others": Waves of Protest under the Greek Junta." *The Sixties* 2, no. 1 (2009): 25–47.

Attias-Donfut, Claudine. *Sociologie des générations: L'empreinte du temps.* Paris, 1988.

Avdela, Efi. "Corrupting and Uncontrollable Activities: Moral Panic about Youth in Post-Civil-War Greece." *Journal of Contemporary History,* Vol. 43, no. 1 (Jan., 2008): 25-44.

Axelos, Loukas. Εκδοτική δραστηριότητα και κίνηση των ιδεών στην Ελλάδα [Publishing Activity and Circulation of Ideas in Greece]. Athens, 1984.

Bakhtin, Mikhail M. *Speech Genres and Other Late Essays.* Trans. Vern W. McGee. Ed. Caryl Emerson and Michael Holquist. Austin, 1984.

Barthes, Roland, *The Rustle of Language.* Oxford, 1986.

Becket, James, *Barbarism in Greece.* New York, 1970.

Bensaid, Daniel. *Les Trotskysmes.* Paris, 2002.

Berman, Paul. *Power and the Idealists: Or, the Passion of Joschka Fischer, and Its Aftermath.* New York, 2005.

Bermeo, Nancy. "Democracy and the Lessons of Dictatorship," *Comparative Politics* 24, no. 3 (1992): 273–91.

———. "Classification and Consolidation: Some Lessons from the Greek Dictatorship." *Political Science Quarterly* 110, no. 3 (1995): 435–52.

———. "The Power of the People." Working paper, Istituto Juan March de Estudios y Investigaciones. Madrid, 1997.

———. "War and Democratization: Lessons from the Portuguese Experience." *Democratization,* 14, no. 3 (2007): 388–406.

Bistis, Nikos. "Από το υπόγειο της Γιάννη Σταθά στην ταράτσα της Νομικής' [From the Basement of Giannis Stathas Street to the Law School Terrace], in Όταν θέλαμε να αλλάξουμε την Ελλάδα. Το αντιδικτατορικό φοιτητικό κίνημα: Η ΕΚΙΝ και οι καταλήψεις της Νομικής [When We Wanted to Change Greece: The Antidictatorship Student Movement; EKIN and the Law School's Occupations], ed. Giorgos A. Vernikos, 96–98. Athens, 2003.

———. Προχωρώντας και αναθεωρώντας [Moving on and Revising]. Athens, 2010.

Bourdieu, Pierre. *Homo Academicus.* Paris, 1984.

———. "L'illusion biographique." *Actes de la Recherche en Sciences Sociales* 62–63 (June 1986).

Bourdieu, Pierre, and Jean-Claude Passeron. *Les Héritiers: Les étudiants et la culture.* Paris, 1964.

Boyer, M. Christine. *The City of Collective Memory: Its Historical Imagery and Architectural Entertainments.* Cambridge, 1996.

Bozinis, Nikos. Ροκ παγκοσμιότητα και ελληνική τοπικότητα. Η κοινωνική ιστορία του ροκ στις χώρες καταγωγής του και στην Ελλάδα [Rock Globality and Greek Locality. The Social History of Rock in Its Countries of Origin and in Greece]. Athens, 2007.

Bretón, Andre. *Le Revolver à cheveux blancs.* Paris, 1932.
Brewer, William F. "What Is Recollective Memory?" In *Remembering Our Past: Studies in Autobiographical Memory,* ed. David C. Rubin, 19–66. New York, 1996.
Bude, Heinz. "The German Kriegskinder: Origins and Impact of the Generation of 1968." In *Generations in Conflict: Youth Revolt and Generation Formation in Germany, 1770–1968,* ed. Mark Roseman. Cambridge, 1995.
Burke, Edmund, ed. *Global Crises and Social Movements: Artisans, Peasants, Populists and the World Economy.* Boulder, 1988.
Cammelli, Andrea. *Studiare da Stranieri in Italia. Presenze e caratteristiche degli studenti esteri nelle Università italiane. Il quadro internazionale di riferimento (1954–1988).* Bologna, 1990.
Carr, Raymond, Fusi Aizpurua, and Juan Pablo. *Spain : Dictatorship to Democracy.* London, 1982.
Caute, David. *The Year of the Barricades.* New York, 1988.
Certeau, Michel de. *The Practice of Everyday Life.* Berkeley, 1984.
———. *La Prise de parole et autres écrits politiques.* Paris, 1994.
———. *The Capture of Speech and Other Political Writings.* Minnesota, 1997.
Certeau, Michel de, Luce Giard, and Pierre Mayol. *The Practice of Everyday Life, Volume 2: Living and Cooking.* London, 1998.
Chakkas, Marios. "Το ψαράκι της γυάλας" [The Fish Bowl]. In Άπαντα [Collected Writings], 166–69. 1972. Reprint, Athens, 1986.
Charalambis, Dimitris. Στρατός και πολιτική εξουσία. Η δομή της εξουσίας στη μετεμφυλιακή Ελλάδα [Army and Political Authority: The Structure of Political Authority in Post–Civil War Greece]. Athens, 1985.
Charisopoulou, Viky. «Της μεταπολίτευσης χαμένη γενιά» ["The Lost Generation of the *Metapolitefsi*"]. Athens, 2001.
Chatzisokratis, Dimitris. "Η συντονιστική επιτροπή" [The Coordinating Committee]. In Πολυτεχνείο '73. Ρεπορτάζ με την Ιστορία [Polytechnic '73: Reportage with History], ed. Giorgos Gatos, 214–19. 1983. Reprint, Athens, 2003.
———. Πολυτεχνείο '73. Αναστοχασμός μιας πραγματικότητας [Polytechnic '73. Rethinking a reality]. Athens, 2004.
Ciampi, N. Η ριζοσπαστικοποίηση της Νεολαίας στον Κόσμο. Ανώτατη Εκπαίδευση, φοιτητικό κίνημα και ταξική πάλη στη σημερινή αστική ελληνική κοινωνία [The Radicalization of Youth in the World: Higher Education, Student Movement and Class Struggle in the Present Greek Bourgeois Society]. Athens, 1973.
Clarke, John, Stuart Hall, Tony Jefferson, and Brian Roberts. "Subcultures, Cultures, and Class." In *Resistance through Rituals: Youth Subcultures in Post-War Britain,* ed. Stuart Hall and Tony Jefferson. London, 1986.
Clogg, Richard. "The Ideology of the 'Revolution of 21 April 1967,'" In *Greece Under Military Rule,* ed. Richard Clogg and George Yannopoulos, 36–58. New York, 1972.
———. *Parties and Elections in Greece: The Search for Legitimacy.* London, 1987.
Close, David. "The Road to Reconciliation: The Civil War as an Issue in the Politics of the 1980s." In *The Greek Civil War: Essays on a Conflict of Exceptionalism and Silences,* ed. Philip Carabott and Thanasis D. Sfikas. Surrey, 2004.
Cockburn, Alexander, and Blackburn Robin, eds. *Student Power. Problems, Diagnosis, Action.* Middlesex, 1969. Greek edition, 1973.

Coerant, Albert. "Ηταν μόνοι τους" [They Were on Their Own]. In Όταν θέλαμε να αλλάξουμε την Ελλάδα. Το αντιδικτατορικό φοιτητικό κίνημα: Η ΕΚΙΝ και οι καταλήψεις της Νομικής [When We Wanted to Change Greece: The Antidictatorship Student Movement; EKIN and the Law School's Occupations], ed. Giorgos Vernikos. Athens, 2003.

Cohen, Stanley. *Folk Devils and Moral Panics*. London, 2003, first publ. 1972.

Cohn-Bendit, Daniel. *Nous l'avons tant aimée, la revolution*. Paris, 1986. Greek edition, 1989.

Constas, Dimitri. *Η "Ελληνική Υπόθεση" στο Συμβούλιο της Ευρώπης 1967–69* [The "Greek Case" in the Council of Europe]. Athens, 1976.

Council of Europe, European Commission on Human Rights, *The Greek Case, Report of the Commission*, 4 vols. Strasbourg, 1969.

Cowan, Jane K. "Politics, Identity and Popular Music in Contemporary Greece." *Cambridge Papers in Modern Greek* 1 (1993): 1–23.

Dafermos, Olympios. "Η δεκαετία μου" [My Decade]. In *Εκ των υστέρων. 19+1* [Ex post: 19+1], ed. Dimitris Papachristos, 47–52. Athens, 1993.

———, ed. *Φοιτητές και Δικτατορία. Το αντιδικτατορικό φοιτητικό κίνημα 1972–1973* [Students and Dictatorship: The Antidictatorship Student Movement, 1972–73]. Athens, 1999.

Dahl, Robert A. *Polyarchy: Participation and Opposition*. New Haven, 1971.

Damofli, Vera. "Οι συνελεύσεις" [The Assemblies]. In *Πολυτεχνείο '73. Ρεπορτάζ με την Ιστορία* [Polytechnic '73: Reportage with History], ed. Giorgos Gatos, 197–201. 1983. Reprint, Athens, 2003.

Darling, Frank C. "Student Protest and Political Change in Thailand." *Pacific Affairs* 47, no. 1 (Spring 1974): 5–19.

Darveris, Tasos. *Μία ιστορία της νύχτας 1967–74* [A Night's Story, 1967–74]. Salonica, 1983. Reprint, Athens, 2002, first published 1983.

De la Villa, Luis Enrique, and Aurelio Desdentado Bonete. *La amnistía laboral. Una crítica política y jurídica*. Madrid, 1978.

Della Porta, Donatella. "Social Protest and the State: Thoughts on the Policing of Protest." In *Comparative Perspectives on Social Movements: Political Opportunities, Mobilizing Structures, and Cultural Framings*, ed. Douglas McAdam, John D. McCarthy, and Mayer N. Zald, 62–92. New York, 1996.

———. "1968: Zwischennationale Diffusion und Transnationale Strukturen." In *1968-Vom Ereignis zum Gegenstand der Geschichtswissenschaft*, ed. Ingrid Gilcher-Holtey. Goettingen, 1998.

Della Porta, Donatella, Celia Valiete, and Maria Kousis. "Sisters of the South. Paths to Women's Rights in Southern Europe." Unpublished paper.

Delveroudi, Elisa-Anna. *Ελληνικός Κινηματογράφος 1955–1965* [Greek Cinema, 1955–1965], in *1949–1967 Η εκρηκτική εικοσαετία* [1949–1967, the Explosive Decades], Scientific Conference, 163–88. Athens, 2002.

Dimaras, Giannis. *Εμπρός στον έτσι που χάραξε ο τέτοιος* [Toward the X Paved By Y]. Athens, 1981.

Dimitriou, Panos, ed. *Η διάσπαση του ΚΚΕ. Μέσα από τα κείμενα της περιόδου 1950–1975* [The Split within the KKE: Seen from within the Documents of the Period, 1950–1975]. 2 vols. Athens, 1975.

Diouf, Manadu. "Urban Youth and Senegalese Politics: Dakar, 1988–1994." In *Cities and Citizenship*, ed. James Holston, 42–66. Durham, 1999.
Douka, Maro. *Αρχαία Σκουριά* [Fool's Gold]. Athens, 1979.
———. *Fool's Gold*. trans. Roderick Beaton. Athens, 1991.
Doumanis, Nicolas. *Una faccia, una razza: Le colonie italiane nell'Egeo*. Bologna, 2003.
Dreyfus, Nicole. *Les étudiants grecs accusent: Dossier du Procès d'Athènes*. Paris, 1969.
Efthymiou, Petros. *Για όσους κάλυψε η λήθη και σκέπασε η σιωπή* [For All Those Covered Up by Oblivion and Stifled by Silence]. In *Εκ των υστέρων. 19+1* [Ex post: 19+1], ed. Dimitris Papachristos, 53–60. Athens, 1993.
Eisler, Jerzy. "March 1968 in Poland." In *1968: The World Transformed*, ed. Carole Fink, Philipp Gassert, Detlef Junker, and Daniel S. Mattern, 237–52. Cambridge, 1998.
ΕΚΝΕ. *Α' Συνέδριον Εθνικού Κινήματος Νέων Επιστημόνων* [First Congress of the National Movement of Young Greek Intellectuals]. Athens, 1972.
Elefandis, Angelos. "Εθνικοφροσύνη: Η ιδεολογία του τρόμου και της ενοχοποίησης" [*Ethnikofrosyni*: The Ideology of Terror and Incrimination], Sakis Karagiorgas Institute, *Η ελληνική κοινωνία κατά την πρώτη μεταπολεμική περίοδο 1945–67* [Greek Society during the First Postwar Period, 1945–67], 645–54, Athens, 1994.
Elefthero Theatro. "Ένα Κείμενο" [One Text]. In *Χρονικό 1971* [Chronicle 1971], 193–95. Athens, 1971.
Elias, Norbert. *La dynamique de l'Occident*. Paris, 1969.
Eliou, Maria. "Those Whom Reform Forgot." *Comparative and International Education Society* 22, no. 1 (Feb. 1978): 60–70.
Emanouilidis, Marios. *Αιρετικές διαδρομές. Ο ελληνικός τροτσκισμός και ο Β' Παγκόσμιος Πόλεμος* [Heretical Routes: Greek Trotskyism and World War Two]. Athens, 2002.
Eyerman, Ron, and Andrew Jamison. *Social Movements: A Cognitive Approach*. Cambridge, 1991.
———. *Music and Social Movements: Mobilizing Traditions in the Twentieth Century*. Cambridge, 1998.
Fainaru, Dan, ed. *Theo Angelopoulos. Interviews*. Mississippi, 2001.
Fakinou, Evgenia. *Έρως, θέρος, πόλεμος* [Eros, Summer, War]. Athens, 2003.
Fallaci, Oriana. *Un Uomo*. Milan, 1979.
Farakos, Grigoris. "Διεθνή Πλαίσια της ιδεολογικής πολιτικής πάλης του κόμματος μας. Μερικές Πλευρές" [The International Context of the Ideological Struggle of Our Party: Some Aspects]. *Neos Kosmos* 10 (October 1968): 15–31.
———. *Η νεολαία και το εργατικό κίνημα (σημειώσεις της φυλακής)* [The Youth and the Worker's Movement (Prison Notes)]. Athens, 1977.
Fatouros, Dimitris A. *Αλλαγή και Πραγματικότητα στο Πανεπιστήμιο* [Change and Reality in the University]. Athens, 1975.
Feenberg, Andrew, and Jim Freedman. *When Poetry Ruled the Streets: The French May Events of 1968*. New York, 2001.
Fehrenbach, Heide, and Uta Poiger, eds. *Transactions, Transgressions, Transformations. American Culture in Western Europe and Japan*. New York and Oxford, 2000.
Filias, Vassilis. *Τα αξέχαστα και τα λησμονημέα* [The Unforgettable and the Forgotten]. Athens, 1997.
Filippou, Filippos. *Οι Κνίτες* [The KNE Kids]. Athens, 1983.

Fischler, Claude. "Food, Self and Identity." *Social Science Information* 27, no. 2 (1988): 275–92.

Fishman, Robert M. "Rethinking State and Regime: Southern Europe's Transition to Democracy." *World Politics* 42, no. 3 (Apr. 1990): 422–40.

Flores, Marcello, and Alberto de Bernardi. *Il Sessantotto*. Bologna, 2003.

Foucault, Michel. *Discipline and Punish: The Birth of the Prison*. London, 1979.

———. *The History of Sexuality*. Vol. 1, *An Introduction*. New York, 1980.

Francovich, Lisa. "Le migrazioni intellettuali in Europa e in Italia." In *Migrazioni, Scenari per il XXI Secolo: Atti del Convegno Internazionale*, 621–74. Rome, 2000.

Fraser, Ronald. *Blood of Spain: An Oral History of the Spanish Civil War*. London, 1986.

———. 1968. *A Student Generation in Revolt*. New York, 1988.

Fyssas, Dimitiris. *Η γενιά του Πολυτεχνείου. 1973–1981. Ένα Βιογραφικό Λεξικό* [The Polytechnic Generation, 1973–1981: A Biographical Dictionary]. Athens, 1993.

Gagnon, Nicole. "On the Analysis of Life Accounts." In *Biography and Society: The Life History Approach in the Social Sciences*, ed. Daniel Bertaux, 47–60. London, 1981.

Geertz, Clifford. *Local Knowledge: Further Essays in Interpretive Anthropology*. New York, 1985.

Georgalas, Georgios. *Η Ιδεολογία της Επαναστάσεως* [The Ideology of the Revolution]. Athens, 1971.

———. *Η κρίσις της καταναλωτικής κοινωνίας* [The Crisis of Consumerist Society]. Athens, 1971.

Giannaris, Giorgos. *Από την ΕΠΟΝ στο Πολυτεχνείο* [From EPON to the Polytechnic]. Vol. 2 of *Φοιτητικά Κινήματα και Ελληνική Παιδεία* [Student Movements and Greek Education]. Athens, 1993.

Giataganas, Xenofon. "Δυναμικές ενέργειες ή μαζική δράση; Παρανομία ή νομιμότητα" [Dynamic Acts or Mass Action? Clandestinity or Legality?]. In *Όταν θέλαμε να αλλάξουμε την Ελλάδα. Το αντιδικτατορικό φοιτητικό κίνημα: Η ΕΚΙΝ και οι καταλήψεις της Νομικής* [When We Wanted to Change Greece: The Antidictatorship Student Movement; EKIN and the Law School's Occupations], ed. Giorgos A. Vernikos, 60–62. Athens, 2003.

Gibson, Janice T., and Mika Haritos-Fatouros. "The Education of a Torturer," *Psychology Today* 20, no. 13 (November 1986): 10–13.

Gilcher-Holtey, Ingrid. *"Die Phantasie an die Macht": Mai 68 in Frankreich*. Frankfurt am Main, 1995.

———. "Mai 68 in Frankreich." In *1968: Vom Ereignis zum Gegenstand der Geschichtswissenschaft*, ed. Ingrid Gilcher-Holtey, 131–50. Goettingen, 1998.

Giner, Salvador. "Power, Freedom and Social Change in the Spanish University, 1939–1975." In *Spain in Crisis. The Evolution and Decline of the Franco Régime*, ed. Paul Preston, 183–233. Sussex, 1976.

Giourgos, Kostis, Takis Kambylis, and James Becket. *Athènes*-Presse Libre. *Η ταράτσα της Μπουμπουλίνας. Καταστολή και βασανιστήρια στην Ελλάδα του '67–69* [The Terrace of Bouboulina Street. Repression and Torture in Greece, '67–69]. Athens, 2009.

Gotsi, Georgia. Review of *Kassandra and the Censors* by Karen Van Dyck. *Byzantine and Modern Greek Studies* 23 (1999): 353–57.

Gounaridou, Kiki. "Representations of Women in the Films of Pandelis Voulgaris: *Acropole, The Stone Years*, and *The Engagement of Anna*," *Journal of Modern Greek Studies* 18 (2000): 151–60.
Gourgouris, Stathis. *Dream Nation: Enlightenment, Colonization, and the Institution of Modern Greece*. Stanford, 1996.
Gracia, Jordi, Miguel Ángel García, and Ruiz Carnicer. *La España de Franco (1939–1975): Cultura y vida cotidiana*. Madrid, 2002.
Graham, Helen, and Jo Labanyi. "Culture and Modernity: The Case of Spain." In *Spanish Cultural Studies*, ed. Helen Graham and Jo Labanyi, 1–20. Oxford, 1995.
———. "Developmentalism, Mass Culture, and Consumerism, 1960–1975: Editors' Introduction." In *Spanish Cultural Studies*, ed. H. Graham and J. Labanyi, 257–58. Oxford, 1995.
Graham, Helen and Alejandro Quiroga. "After the Fear Was Over? What Came after Dictatorship in Spain, Portugal and Greece," In *The Oxford Handbook of Post-war European History*, ed. Dan Stone, 502–25. Oxford, 2012.
Grigoriadis, Solon. Ιστορία της Δικτατορίας [History of the Dictatorship]. 2 vols. Athens, 1975.
Grigoriou, Grigoris. Μνήμες σε άσπρο και σε μαύρο. Η ιστορία ενός επαγγελματία [Memories in Black and White. The Story of a Professional]. Athens. 1996.
Gris, Ilias, ed. Το μελάνι φωνάζει. Η 17ῃ Νοέμβρη 1973 στη λογοτεχνία [The Ink Screams: 17 November 1973 in Literature]. Athens, 2003.
Guffey, Elizabeth. *Retro: The Culture of Revival*. London, 2006.
Habermas, Jürgen. *Toward a Rational Society: Student Protest, Science, and Politics*. Trans. Jeremy Shapiro. London, 1971.
Hager, Philip. "From the Margin to the Mainstream: The Production of Politically Engaged Theater in Greece during the Dictatorship of the Colonels (1967–1974)." Unpublished PhD thesis, Royal Holloway, University of London, 2008.
Hall, Stuart. "Επανανακάλυψη της Ιδεολογίας: Η Επάνοδος του απωθημένου" [Rediscovering Ideology: The Revival of the Suppressed]. In *Κοινωνία, Εξουσία και ΜΜΕ* [Society, Power and the Media], ed. Maria Komninou and Christos Lyrintzis, 139–44. Athens, 1988.
———. "Encoding, Decoding," in *The Cultural Studies Reader*, ed. Simon During, 507–17. London and New York, 1993.
Halliday, Fred. "Η ιστορία του φοιτητικού συνδικαλιστικού κινήματος σ' όλο τον κόσμο" [The History of Student Movements Worldwide]. Athens, 1972.
Hamalidi, Elena, Maria Nikolopoulou, and Rea Wallden. "A Second Avant-Garde Without a First: Greek Avant-Garde Artists in the 1960s and 1970s." In *Regarding the Popular: Modernism, the Avant-garde, and High and Low Culture*, ed. Sascha Bru et al., 425–45. Berlin, 2012.
Haritos-Fatouros, Mika. "The Official Torturer. A Learning Model for Obedience to the Authority of Violence." *Journal of Applied Social Psychology* 18, no. 13 (1988): 1107–20.
Hart, Janet. *New Voices in the Nation: Women and the Greek Resistance, 1941–1964*. Ithaca, 1996.
Hatzinikolaou, Nikos. "Ο δικός μας Μάης του '68" [Our Own May '68]. *Archeiotaxio* 10 (June 2008): 92–119.
Hebdige, Dick. *Subculture: The Meaning of Style*. London, 1991.

Heinze, Ruth-Inge. "Ten Days in October: Students vs. the Military: An Account of the Student Uprising in Thailand." *Asian Studies* 14, no. 6 (June 1974): 491–508.
Herzfeld, Michael. "The Horns of the Mediterranean Dilemma." *American Ethnologist* 11 (1984): 439–54.
———. *Ours Once More. Folklore, Ideology and the Making of Modern Greece.* New York, 1986.
———. "Towards an Ethnographic Phenomenology of the Greek Spirit," *Mediterranean Historical Review* 16, no. 1 (2001): 13–26.
Herzog, Dagmar. "Between Coitus and Commodification: Young West German Women and the Impact of the Pill." In *Between Marx and Coca-Cola. Youth Cultures in Changing European Societies, 1960–1980,* ed. Axel Schildt and Detlef Segfried, 261–86. New York, 2006.
Hirschman, Albert O. *Felicitá privata e felicitá pubblica.* Italian translation of *Shifting Involvements: Private Interest and Public Action.* Bologna, 1983.
Hobsbawm, Eric. *The Age of Extremes. A History of the World, 1914–1991.* New York, 1994.
———. "Revolution and Sex." In *Revolutionaries,* 256–60. 1973. Reprint, London, 1999.
Holst, Gail. *Road to Rembetika: Music of a Greek Sub-culture; Songs of Love, Sorrow and Hashish.* Limni and Athens, 1977.
Holtey, Gilcher. "Die Phantasie an die Macht." In *Soziale Bewegungen: Ein historisch-systematischer Grundriss,* ed. J. Raschke. Frankfurt, 1985.
Huntington, Samuel P. *The Third Wave: Democratization in the Late 20th Century.* Oklahoma, 1993.
Inglehart, Robert. *The Silent Revolution.* Princeton, 1977.
Iordanoglou, Chrysafis. "Το αντιδικτατορικό φοιτητικό κίνημα στη Θεσσαλονίκη" [The Antidictatorship Student Movement in Salonica]. In *Φοιτητές και Δικτατορία. Το αντιδικτατορικό φοιτητικό κίνημα 1972–1973* [Students and Dictatorship: The Antidictatorship Student Movement, 1972–73], ed. Olympios Dafermos, 237–81. Athens, 1999.
Irschick, Eugene. *Dialogue and History: Constructing South India, 1795–1895.* Berkeley, 1994.
Jameson, Fredric. "Periodizing the Sixties." In *The Ideologies of Theory,* 2 (The Syntax of History), 178–210. Minneapolis, 1988.
Janigro, Nicole. "Il '68 jugoslavo: Vent'anni di bisbigli per un movimento di sette giorni." In *Il Sessantotto: L'evento e la storia,* ed. Pier Paolo Poggio, 77–92. Brescia, 1988–89.
Johnston, Hank. "Talking the Walk: Speech Acts and Resistance in Authoritarian Regimes." In *Repression and Mobilization,* ed. Christian Davenport, Hank Johnston, and Carol Mueller, 108–37. Minneapolis, 2002.
Jones, Gareth Stedman. "Η σημασία της φοιτητικής εξέγερσης" [The Significance of Student Uprisings]. In *Φοιτητική Δύναμη* [Student Power], ed. A. Cockburn, G. S. Jones, D. Adelstein, L. Tinkham, T. Fawthrop, T. Nairn, J. Singh-Sandou, D. Wouigry, D. Triesman, H. Marcuse, and D. Cohn-Bendit, 31–74. Athens, 1973.
Josselson, Ruthellen. "Imagining the Real: Empathy, Narrative, and the Dialogic Self." In *The Narrative Study of Lives,* ed. Ruthellen Josselson and Amia Lieblich. Thousand Oaks, 1995.

Junco, José Álvarez. *Movimientos Sociales en España: Del modelo tradicional a la modernidad post-Franquista*. Madrid, 1995.
Kallimopoulou, Eleni. *Paradosiaká: Music, Meaning and Identity in Modern Greek*. Athens, 2009.
Kallivretakis, Leonidas F. "Προβλήματα ιστορικοποίησης του Rock φαινομένου. Εμπειρίες και στοχασμοί" [Problems of Historicizing the Rock Phenomenon: Experiences and Thoughts]. *Ta Istorika* 20 (June 1994): 157–74.
———. "Επώνυμοι νεκροί του Πολυτεχνείου" [Eponymous Dead of the Polytechnic]. In *Η στρατιωτική δικτατορία 1967–1974*, ed. Vangelis Karamanolakis, 197–202. Athens, 2010.
Kalyvas Stathis, "Η 'εξέγερση του Δεκέμβρη' ως σύμπτωμα της κουλτούρας της Μεταπολίτευσης" ["The 'December Insurrection' as a Symptom of the *Metapolitefsi* Culture"]. *Athens Review of Books* 2 December 2009.
Kambanellis, Iakovos. *Το μεγάλο μας τσίρκο* [Our Grand Circus]. Athens, 1975.
Kanellakis, Panagiotis. "Τω καιρώ εκείνω" [In Those Years]. In *Όταν θέλαμε να αλλάξουμε την Ελλάδα. Το αντιδικτατορικό φοιτητικό κίνημα: Η ΕΚΙΝ και οι καταλήψεις της Νομικής* [When We Wanted to Change Greece: The Antidictatorship Student Movement; EKIN and the Law School Occupations], ed. Giorgos A. Vernikos. Athens, 2003.
Kaplan, Temma. *Red City, Blue Period*. Berkeley, 1992.
Karambelas, Dimitris. *Διονύσης Σαββόπουλος* [Dionysis Savvopoulos]. Athens, 2003.
Karakasidou, Anastasia. Book review of *Historein*, special volume on "Heterodoxies: Construction of Identities and Otherness in Medieval and Early Modern Europe," *Journal of Modern Greek Studies* 21, no. 1 (2003): 145–47.
Karakatsanis, Neovi M. *The Politics of Elite Transformation. The Consolidation of Greek Democracy in Theoretical Perspective*. London, 2001.
Karapostolis, Vassilis. *Η καταναλωτική συμπεριφορά στην ελληνική κοινωνία 1960–1975* [Consumerist Behavior in Greek Society, 1960–1975]. Athens, 1984.
Karatzaferis, Spyros. *Η σφαγή του Πολυτεχνείου. Η Δίκη* [The Polytechnic Slaughter: The Trial]. Preface by P. Kanellopoulos. Athens, 1975.
Katris, Giannis. *Η γέννηση του νεοφασισμού στην Ελλάδα* [The Birth of Neofascism in Greece]. Athens, 1974.
Katsapis, Kostas. *Ήχοι και απόηχοι. Κοινωνική ιστορία του ροκ εν ρολ φαινομένου στην Ελλάδα, 1956–1967* [Sounds and Echoes. A Social History of the Rock 'n Roll Phenomenon in Greece, 1956–1967]. Athens, 2007.
Katsaros, Stergios. *Εγώ ο προβοκάτορας, ο τρομοκράτης* [I the Provocateur, Me the Terrorist]. Athens, 1999.
Katsiaficas, George. *The Imagination of the New Left*. Boston, 1987.
———. *Asia's Unknown Uprisings Volume 2: People Power in the Philippines, Burma, Tibet, China, Taiwan, Bangladesh, Nepal, Thailand, and Indonesia, 1947–2009*. Oakland, 2013.
Kavvadias, Filippos A. *Εδώ Πολυτεχνείο, Εδώ Πολυτεχνείο* [This Is Polytechnic Speaking]. Athens, 1974.
Kazakos, Panos. *Ανάμεσα σε Κράτος και Αγορά. Οικονομία και οικονομική πολιτική στη μεταπολεμική Ελλάδα, 1944–2000* [In between the State and the Market: Economy and Fiscal Policies in Postwar Greece, 1944–2001]. Athens, 2001.

Kilekli, Vassiliki. "Πτυχές της γαλλικής πολιτικής απέναντι στην εγκατάσταση των Ελλήνων στη Γαλλία και τον αντιδικτατορικό αγώνα" [Aspects of the French Policy vis-à-vis the Installation of Greeks in France and the Antidictatorship Struggle]. *Archeiotaxio* 10 (June 2008): 66–83.

Kitschelt, Herbert P. "Political Opportunity Structures and Political Protest." *British Journal of Political Science* 16 (1986): 57–85.

Klandermans, Bert. "Mobilization and Participation: Social Psychological Expansions of Resource Mobilization Theory." *American Sociological Review* 49 (1984): 583–600.

———. "New Social Movements and Resource Mobilization: The European and the American Approach Revisited." In *Research on Social Movements: The State of the Art in Western Europe and in the USA*, ed. Dieter Rucht, 17–44. Frankfurt am Main, 1991.

Kleitsikas, Nikos. *Το ελληνικό φοιτητικόν κίνημα και ο αντιδικτατορικός αγώνας στην Ιταλία* [The Greek Student Movement and the Antidictatorial Struggle in Italy]. Athens, 2000.

Klimke, Martin, and Joachim Scharloth. "1968 in Europe: An Introduction." In *1968 in Europe: A History of Protest and Activism, 1956–77*, ed. Martin Klimke and Joachim Scharloth. New York, 2008.

Knabb, Ken, ed. *Situationist International Anthology*. Berkeley, 2006.

Kokkali, Angeliki. "Ελληνικός Κινηματογράφος και Αντιδικτατορικό Φοιτητικό Κίνημα" [Greek Cinema and the Antidictatorship Student Movement]. In *Epitheorisi Koinonikon Ereuvnon* 92–93 (1997): 127–50.

Komninou, Maria. "Τηλεόραση και κινηματογράφος: η διαμάχη για την ηγεμονία στην περίοδο της δικτατορίας 1967–74" [Television and Cinema: The Battle for Hegemony in the Period of the Dictatorship, 1967–74]. In *Η Δικτατορία. 1967–74. Πολιτικές πρακτικές, ιδεολογικός λόγος, αντίσταση* [The Dictatorship, 1967–74: Political Practices, Ideological Discourse, Resistance], ed. Gianna Athanasatou, Alkis Rigos, and Serafeim Seferiadis, 174–83. Athens, 1999.

———. *Από την αγορά στο θέαμα. Μελέτη για τη συγκρότηση της δημόσιας σφαίρας και του κινηματογράφου στη σύγχρονη Ελλάδα, 1950–2000* [From the Market to the Spectacle: Study on the Construction of the Public Sphere and Cinema in Contemporary Greece, 1950–2000]. Athens, 2002.

Konofagos, Konstantinos. *Η εξέγερση του Πολυτεχνείου* [The Polytechnic Uprising]. Athens, 1982.

Kornetis, Konstantinos (Kostis). "¿Un 68 periférico? Reflexiones sobre un análisis comparativo de la resistencia. estudiantil en los regímenes autoritarios de la Grecia de los Coroneles y de la España tardofranquista." *Studia Historica. Historia contemporanea* 21 (2003): 83–112.

———. "Student Resistance to the Greek Military Dictatorship: Subjectivity, Memory and Cultural Politics, 1967–1974." PhD diss., European University Institute, Florence, 2006.

———. "Una diaspora adriatica: La migrazione degli studenti universitari greci in Italia." In *Immaginare l'Adriatico*, ed. Gerardo Minardi and Emilio Cocco, 151–68. Milan, 2007.

———. "1968 in Spain and Greece." In *1968 in Europe: A History of Protest and Activism, 1956–1977*, ed. Martin Klimke and Joachim Scharloth, 253–66. London, 2008.

———. "68: Année Symbolique." In *Revolution, I Love You. 1968 in Art, Politics and Philosophy*, ed. Ruben and Maja Fawkes, 17–23. Manchester, 2008.

———. "'Everything Links'? Temporality, Territoriality and Cultural Transfer in the '68 Protest Movements." *Historein* 9 (2009): 34–45.

———. "No More Heroes: Rejection and Reverberation of the Past in the 2008 Events in Greece." *Journal of Modern Greek Studies* 28, no. 2 (2010): 173–97.

———. "Les premiers mètres carrés de territoire grec libre: La Fondation Hellénique pendant la dictature des Colonels (1967–74)". In *La Fondation hellénique de la Cité internationale universitaire de Paris : lieu de vie, lieu de mémoire*. ed. Maria Gravari-Barbas, Dimitri Bacharas, Hélène Fessas-Emmanouil et al. Paris, 2013.

———. "The Greek 'New Wave' Music of the 1960s." In *The Continuum Encyclopedia of Popular Music of the World*, ed. John Shepherd, David Horn, and Dave Laing. London, forthcoming.

Korovesis, Periklis. *The Method: A Personal Account of the Tortures in Greece*. London, 1970.

———. *Οι ανθρωποφύλακες* [The Guards of the Humans]. Athens, 1997.

Kotanidis, Giorgos. *Όλοι Μαζί, Τώρα!* [All Together, Now!]. Athens, 2011.

Kotzias, Alexandros. *Αντιποίησις Αρχής* [Usurpation of Authority]. Athens, 1979.

Kouloumbis, Theodoros A. "The Greek Junta Phenomenon." *Polity* 6, no. 3 (Spring, 1974): 345–74.

———. *... 71 ... 74: Σημειώσεις ενός πανεπιστημιακού* [... 71 ... 74: Notes of an Academic]. Athens, 2002.

Kousouris, Dimitris. "Temps de la défaite: Parcours d'un oubli mémorable; Représentations du temps chez les vaincus de la guerre civile grecque (de 1949 à 1967)." D.E.A. thesis, E.H.E.S.S., Paris, 2003.

Kranaki, Mimika. *Οι φιλλέηνες. Είκοσι τέσσερα γράμματα μιας Οδύσσειας* [The Philhellenes: Twenty-four Letters from an Odyssey]. Athens, 1998.

Krimbas, Kostas. "Ανώτατη Εκπαίδευση τον καιρό της Χούντας" [Higher Education at the Time of the Junta]. In *Η Δικτατορία 1967–1974. Πολιτικές πρακτικές, Ιδεολογικός λόγος, Αντίσταση* [The Dictatorship, 1967–1974: Political Practices, Ideological Discourse, Resistance], ed. Gianna Athanasatou, Alkis Rigos, and Serafeim Seferiadis, 135–52. Athens, 1999.

Kunen, James Simon. *The Strawberry Statement: Notes of a College Revolutionary*. New York, 1969.

Kyparisis, D. "Το αντιδικτατορικό φοιτητικό κίνημα" [The Antidictatorship Student Movement]. M.A. thesis, University of Athens, 1999.

Ladas, Ioannis. *Λόγοι* [Speeches]. Athens, 1970.

Ladis, Fontas. *Μίκης Θεοδωράκης. Το χρονικό μιας επανάστασης 1960–1967. Η ιστορία της γενιάς του 1-1-4 και των «Λαμπράκηδων»* [Mikis Theodorakis: The Chronicle of a Revolution, 1960–67; The History of the 1-1-4 Generation and of the "Lambrakides"]. Athens, 2001.

Lakidou, Ilia. "Theatrical Satire and Dictatorship: The Case of the "Eléfthero Théatro" and the Show ...kai sí chtenízesai, Summer 1973." Unpublished paper.

Lambropoulou, Dimitra. *Οικοδόμοι. Οι άνθρωποι που έχτισαν την Αθήνα 1950–1967* [Construction Workers. The People Who Built Athens 1950–1967]. Athens, 2009.

Lane, Robert E. *Political Life: Why People Get Involved in Politics*. Glencoe, 1959.

Lazos, Christos. *Ελληνικό Φοιτητικό Κίνημα 1821–1973* [Greek Student Movement, 1821–1973]. Athens, 1987.
Lefebvre, Henri. *Le droit à la ville*. Paris, 1968.
Lefort, Claude. *L'invention démocratique: Les limites de la domination totalitaire*. Paris, 1983.
Lendakis, Andreas. *Οι νεοφασιστικές οργανώσεις στη Νεολαία* [The Neofascist Organizations within the Youth]. Athens, 1963.
Levitt, Cyril. *Children of Privilege. Student Revolt in the Sixties: A Study of Student Movements in Canada, the United States, and West Germany*. Toronto, 1984.
Liakos, Antonis. *Η εμφάνιση των νεανικών οργανώσεων. Το παράδειγμα της Θεσσαλονίκης* [The Appearance of Youth Organizations: The Case of Salonica]. Athens, 1988.
———. "Σκέψεις πάνω στην Ιστορία του Φοιτητικού Κινήματος" [Thoughts on the History of the Student Movement]. In *Πανεπιστήμιο. Ιδεολογία και Παιδεία. Ιστορική Διάσταση και Προοπτικές* [University: Ideology and Education; Historical Dimension and Perspectives], 1:327–33. Athens, 1989.
———. "History Writing as the Return of the Repressed." *Historein* 3 (2001): 47–58.
———. "Το χαμένο ραντεβού" [The Lost Date]. *Archeiotaxio* 8 (May 2006): 47–49.
Linardatos, Spyros. *Από τον Εμφύλιο στη Χούντα* [From the Civil War to the Junta], vol. 5, 1961–64. Athens, 1986.
Linde, Charlotte. *Life Stories: The Creation of Coherence*. Oxford, 1993.
Livieratos, Dimitris, and Giorgos Karambelias. *Ιουλιανά '65. Η έκρηξη των αντιθέσεων* [July Events '65: The Explosion of Contradictions]. Athens, 1985.
Loewy, Michael. "The Revolutionary Romanticism of May 1968," *Thesis Eleven* 68 (2002).
Logothetis, Stelios. "Η κατάληψη" [The Occupation]. In *Πολυτεχνείο '73. Ρεπορτάζ με την Ιστορία* [Polytechnic '73: Reportage with History], ed. Giorgos Gatos, 207–13. 1983. Reprint, Athens, 2003.
Luedtke, Alf. "The Historiography of Everyday Life: The Personal and the Political." In *Culture, Ideology and Politics*, ed. Raphael Samuel and Gareth Stedman Jones. London, 1982.
Lumley, Robert. *States of Emergency: Cultures of Revolt in Italy, 1968–1978*. London, 1990.
Lygeros, Stavros. *Φοιτητικό κίνημα και ταξική πάλη στην Ελλάδα. Από τις προσφυγές στα πρωτοδικεία στην εξέγερση του Πολυτεχνείου* [Student Movement and Class Struggle in Greece: From the Appeal to the Courts of First Instance to the Polytechnic Uprising], vol. 1. Athens, 1978.
———. "Η συγκυρία" [The Conjuncture]. In *Πολυτεχνείο '73. Ρεπορτάζ με την Ιστορία* [Polytechnic '73: Reportage with History], ed. Giorgos Gatos, 202–6. 1983. Reprint, Athens, 2003.
Mackridge, Peter. "Theater in the Colonels' Greece: Impressions of an Eyewitness." Unpublished lecture given at Archive for the Performance of Greek and Roman Drama, Oxford, 6 June 2011.
Maglinis, Elias. *Η Ανάκριση* [The Interrogation]. Athens, 2009.
Manitakis, Nicolas. "Struggling from Abroad: Greek Communist Activities in France during the Civil War." In *The Greek Civil War: Essays on a Conflict of Exceptionalism and Silences*, ed. Philip Carabott and Thanasis D. Sfikas. Surrey, 2004.

Mannheim, Karl. *Essays on the Sociology of Knowledge*. London, 1952.
Mantoglou, Anna. *Η εξέγερση του Πολυτεχνείου. Η συγκρουσιακή σχέση ατόμου και κοινωνίας* [The Polytechnic Uprising: The Conflictual Relationship between the Individual and the Society]. Athens, 1995.
Marangopoulos, Aris. "Παιδιά του Μαρξ και της Κόκα-Κόλα" [Children of Marx and Coca-Cola]. *O Politis* 99 (April 2002): 21–24.
Marangopoulos, Dimitris. "Οι άγνωστοι στρατιώτες" [The Unknown Soldiers]. In *Όταν θέλαμε να αλλάξουμε την Ελλάδα. Το αντιδικτατορικό φοιτητικό κίνημα: Η ΕΚΙΝ και οι καταλήψεις της Νομικής* [When We Wanted to Change Greece: The Antidictatorship Student Movement; EKIN and the Law School's Occupations], ed. Giorgos A. Vernikos, 51–56. Athens, 2003.
Maravall, José María. *Dictatorship and Political Dissent: Workers and Students in Franco's Spain*. Cambridge, 1978.
Marceau, Marc. *Le coup d'Athenes*. Paris, 1974.
Marcuse, Harold. "The Revival of Holocaust Awareness in West Germany, Israel and the United States." In *1968: The World Transformed*, ed. Carole Fink, Philipp Gassert, Detlef Junker, and Daniel S. Mattern, 421–438. Cambridge, 1998.
Markaris, Petros. *Κατ' εξακολούθηση* [Repeatedly and Persistently]. Athens, 2006.
Markezinis, Spyros. *Αναμνήσεις 1972–1974* [Reminiscences 1972–1974]. Athens, 1979.
Maronitis, Dimitris N. *Ανεμόσκαλα και Σημαδούρες* [Rope-Ladder and Buoys]. Athens, 1975.
Marwick, Arthur. *The Sixties: Cultural Revolution in Britain, France, Italy, and the United States, c. 1958–c. 1974*. Oxford, 1998.
Marx, Karl. *The Eighteenth Brumaire of Louis Bonaparte*. London, 2002, first edn. 1852.
Mausbauch, Wilfried. "Historicising '1968.'" *Contemporary European History* 2, no. 1 (2002): 177–87.
Mavris, Giorgos. "Κρίση του Πανεπιστημίου και φοιτητές" [University Crisis and Students]. *Kritiki* 9/10 (Athens, 1985): 31–41.
Mayakovsky, Vladimir. *The Bedbug: and Selected Poetry*, ed. Patricia Blake. Bloomington, 1966.
Mazower, Mark. "The Cold War and the Appropriation of Memory: Greece after Liberation." In *The Politics of Retribution in Europe: World War II and Its Aftermath*, ed. István Deák, Jan T. Gross, and Tony Judt, 212–32. Princeton, 2000.
McAdam, Doug. *Political Process and the Development of Black Insurgency*. Chicago, 1982.
———. "Recruitment to High-Risk Activism: The Case of Freedom Summer." *American Journal of Sociology* 92, no. 1 (July 1986): 64–90.
———. "Culture and Social Movements." In *New Social Movements: From Ideology to Identity*, ed. Enrique Laragna, Hank Johnston, and Joseph R. Gusfeld, 36–57. Philadelphia, 1994.
McAdam, Doug, John D. McCarthy, and Mayer N. Zald, eds. *Comparative Perspectives on Social Movements: Political Opportunities, Mobilizing Structures, and Cultural Framings*. New York, 1996.
McMillian John, and Paul Buhle, eds. *The New Left Revisited*. Philadelphia, 2003.
Meletopoulos, Meletis. *Η Δικτατορία των Συνταγματάρχων. Κοινωνία, Ιδεολογία, Οικονομία* [The Colonels' Dictatorship: Society, Ideology, Economy]. Athens, 1996.

Metaxas, Anastasios-Ioannis. *Πολιτική Κοινωνικοποίηση* [Political Socialization]. Athens, 1976.
Miliex, Roger. "Αγρυπνία διαρκής στην Κύπρο (1967–1971). Σελίδες από ημερολόγιο" [Continuous Vigilance in Cyprus, 1967–1971: Pages from a Diary]. *I Lexi* 63–64 (Apr.–May 1987): 339–49.
Minuzzo, Nerio. *Quando arrivano i Colonnelli: Rapporto dalla Grecia*. Milan, 1970.
Mouzelis, Nikos. *Modern Greece: Facets of Underdevelopment*. London, 1978.
Mulvey, Laura. "Visual Pleasure and Narrative Cinema." In *Visual Culture: The Reader*, ed. Jessica Evans and Stuart Hall, 381–89. London, 1999.
Murtagh, Peter. *The Rape of Greece: The King, the Colonels and the Resistance*. London, 1994.
National Statistical Service of Greece (ESIE). *Statistical Yearbook of Higher Education for the Academic Year 1968–69*.
Neidhardt, Friedhelm, and Dieter Rucht. "The Analysis of Social Movements: The State of the Art and Some Perspectives for Further Research." In *Research on Social Movements: The State of the Art in Western Europe and the USA*, ed. Dieter Rucht, 421–64. Frankfurt am Main, 1991.
Nikolaidou, Magda. "Η εργαζόμενη γυναίκα στην Ελλάδα" [The Working Woman in Greece]. *Greek Review of Social Research* 25 (1975): 470–506.
Nikolinakos, Marios. *Αντίσταση και Αντιπολίτευση. 1967–74* [Resistance and Opposition, 1967–74]. Athens, 1975.
Notaras, Gerasimos. "Δικτατορία και Οργανωμένη Αντίσταση" [Dictatorship and Organized Resistance]. In *Η Δικτατορία 1967–1974. Πολιτικές πρακτικές, Ιδεολογικός λόγος, Αντίσταση* [The Dictatorship, 1967–1974: Political Practices, Ideological Discourse, Resistance], ed. Gianna Athanasatou, Alkis Rigos, and Serafeim Seferiadis, 187–98. Athens, 1999.
Notaras, Giorgos. "Τους Έλληνες δεν τους ενδιέφερε η αισθητική, τους ενδιέφερε η ζωή" [Greeks Did Not Care about Self-Criticism, They Cared about Life]. In *Είκοσι Πρόσωπα Ζητούν την Ελλάδα. Απόπειρα μιας ελληνικής αυτοβιογραφίας* [Twenty People Seek out Greece: An Attempt at a Greek Autobiography], ed. Rena Aggouridou, 127–46. Athens, 1999.
———. "Βρώμικο Ψωμί. Ένα test drive ουτοπίας" [Filthy Bread: A Test Drive for a Utopia]. In *Η Σούμα* [The Sum Up], ed. Dionysis Savvopoulos. Athens, 2003.
O'Donnell, Guillermo. *Modernization and Bureaucratic-Authoritarianism*. Berkeley, 1979.
———. "Tensions in the Bureaucratic-Authoritarian State." In *The New Authoritarianism*, ed. David Collier. Princeton, 1979.
O'Donnell, Guillermo, and Philip Schmitter. "Tentative Conclusions about Uncertain Democracies." In *Transitions from Authoritarian Rule*, ed. G. O'Donnell, P. Schmitter, and Lawrence Whitehead. Baltimore, 1986.
Olick, Jeffrey K. "Collective Memory: The Two Cultures." *Sociological Theory* 17, no. 3 (Nov. 1999): 333–48.
Ortoleva, Peppino. "Le culture del '68." In *La cultura e i luoghi del '68*, ed. Aldo Agosti, Luisa Passerini, and Nicola Trafaglia, 38–61. Milan, 1991.
Paloukis, Kostas. "Η αριστερή αντιπολίτευση στο ΚΚΕ κατά την περίοδο του Μεσοπολέμου: αρχειομαρξιστές και σπαρτακιστές [Left-Wing Opposition to the KKE during the Interwar Period: Archive Marxists and Spartacists]." In Ιστορία της Ελλάδας στον

20º αιώνα [History of Greece in the 20th Century], ed. Christos Hadjiiosif, vol. B2. Athens, 2003.

Panourgiá, Neni. *Dangerous Citizens. The Greek Left and the Terror of the State.* New York, 2009.

Papachelas, Alexis. *Ο βιασμός της ελληνικής δημοκρατίας. Ο αμερικανικός παράγων. 1947–67* [The Rape of Greek Democracy: The U.S. Factor, 1947–67]. Athens, 1997.

Papachelas, Alexis, and Tasos Telloglou. *Φάκελος 17 Νοέμβρη* [The 17 November File]. Athens, 2002.

Papachristos, Dimitris, ed. *Εκ των υστέρων. 19+1* [Ex post: 19+1]. Athens, 1993.

———. "Από τη Νομική στο Πολυτεχνείο" [From the Law School to the Polytechnic]. In *Πολυτεχνείο '73. Ρεπορτάζ με την Ιστορία* [Polytechnic '73: Reportage with History], ed. Giorgos Gatos, 192–96. 1983. Reprint, Athens, 2003.

———. *Ζούσε τη ζωή σα να τη θυμόταν* [He Lived Life As If He Were Remembering It]. Athens, 2003.

Papadimitriou, Despoina. "George Papadopoulos and the Dictatorship of the Greek Colonels, 1967–1974." In *Balkan Strongmen. Dictators and Authoritarian Rulers of South Eastern Europe*, ed. Bernd J. Fischer, 393–424. London, 2007.

Papadogiannis, Nikolaos. "From Coherence to Fragments: '1968' and the Making of Youth Politicisation in Greece in the 1970s." *Historein* 9 (2009): 76–92 (83).

———. "Between Angelopoulos and The Battleship Potemkin: Cinema and the Making of Young Communists in Greece in the First Post-dictatorship Years (1974–1981)." Unpublished paper presented at the University of Cambridge, 2009.

———. "Greek Communist Youth and the Politicisation of Leisure, 1974–1981." Unpublished PhD diss., Cambridge, 2010.

Papadopoulos, Georgios. *Το Πιστεύω μας* [Our Creed]. Athens, 1968.

Papandreou, Nikos. *Ανδρέας Παπανδρέου. Η ζωή σε πρώτο ενικό και η τέχνη της πολιτικής αφήγησης* [Andreas Papandreou: Life in First-Person Singular and the Art of Political Narration]. Athens, 2003.

Papanikolaou, Dimitris. "Singing Poets. Popular Music and Literature in France and Greece (1945–1975): Reading Brassens, Ferré, Theodorakis and Savvopoulos." PhD thesis, University College London, 2002.

———. "Σχηματίζοντας τη Νεολαία. Ο Θεοδωράκης, ο Σαββόπουλος και 'του '60 οι εκδρομείς" [Shaping the Youth: Theodorakis, Savvopoulos, and the "Travellers of the '60s"]. Unpublished article, 2005.

———. *Singing Poets. Literature and Popular Music in France and Greece, 1945–1975.* Oxford, 2007.

———. "'Making Some Strange Gestures': Culture in the Years of Dictatorship." In *Η στρατιωτική δικτατορία 1967–1974* [The Military Dictatorship 1967–1974], ed. Vangelis Karamanolakis, 175–96. Athens, 2010.

Papapolizos, Filimon, and Kostas Martzoukos. *Hellads. Η Ελλάδα μέσα από τη διαφήμιση (1940–1989)* [Hellads: Greece through Advertising, 1940–1989]. Athens, 1998.

Papas, Stelios. "Αντιπαράθεση θέσεων" [Juxtaposition of Opinions]. In *Πολυτεχνείο '73. Ρεπορτάζ με την Ιστορία* [Polytechnic '73: Reportage with History], ed. Giorgos Gatos, 244–48. 1983. Reprint, Athens, 2003.

Papathanasiou, Ioanna. "Η Βουλή εμανταλώθη. … εκτροπή ολοκληρώθη. … Αριστερές αυταπάτες τις παραμονές του πραξικόπημα της 21ης Απριλίου" [The

Parliament Is Shut Down. ... The Putsch Has Been Carried Out. ... Leftwing Illusions on the Eve of the 21 April Coup d'état." In *Η «σύντομη» δεκαετία του '60. Θεσμικό πλαίσιο, κομματικές στρατηγικές, κοινωνικές συγκρούσεις, πολιτισμικές διεργασίες* [The "Short" Decade of the '60s. Institutional Context, Party Strategies, Social Conflicts, Cultural Processes], ed. Alkis Rigos, Serafeim I. Seferiadis, and Evanthis Chadzivasileiou, 183–203. Athens, 2008.

Papathanasiou, Ioanna, et al. *Η Νεολαία Λαμπράκη τη δεκαετία του 1960. Αρχειακές τεκμηριώσεις και αυτοβιογραφικές καταθέσεις* [Lambrakis Youth in the 1960s. Archival Documentation and Autobiographical Depositions]. Athens, 2008.

Papazoglou, Minas. *Φοιτητικό Κίνημα και Δικτατορία* [Student Movement and Dictatorship]. Athens, 1983.

Papoutsis, Kostas. *Ο Ματρίκολας* [The Freshman]. Athens, 1992.

———. *Το μεγάλο 'Ναι'* [The Great "Yes"]. Athens, 1996.

Paradeisi, Maria. "Η παρουσίαση της νεολαίας στα κοινωνικά δράματα της δεκαετίας του εξήντα" [The Depiction of Youth in the Social Dramas of the 1960s]. *Τα Istorika* 22 (June 1995): 205–18.

Paraskevopoulos, Makis. "Σημειώσεις μετά την αποφυλάκιση" [Notes after Prison Release]. In *Όταν θέλαμε να αλλάξουμε την Ελλάδα. Το αντιδικτατορικό φοιτητικό κίνημα: Η ΕΚΙΝ και οι καταλήψεις της Νομικής* [When We Wanted to Change Greece: The Antidictatorship Student Movement; EKIN and the Law School's Occupations], ed. Giorgos Vernikos, 63–72. Athens, 2003.

Pasolini, Pier Paolo. "Diario per un condannato a morte." 7 December 1968. Reprinted in *Il caos*, ed. Gian Carlo Ferretti. Rome, 1999.

———. "Il cerimoniale della violenza." In *Il caos*, ed. Gian Carlo Ferretti. Rome, 1999.

Passerini, Luisa. *Torino Operaia e Fascismo*. Bari, 1984.

———. "Le mouvement de 1968 comme prise de parole et comme explosion de la subjectivité: Le cas de Turin." *Le mouvement social* 143 (April–June 1988): 39–74.

———. "Il programma radiofonico come fonte." *Storia e soggettività: Le fonti orali, la memoria*, 155–73. Florence, 1988.

———. *Storie di donne e femministe*. Turin, 1991.

———. "La memoria europea fra totalitarismo e democrazia." In *Politiche della memoria*, ed. Gianpaolo Calchi Novati, Luciano Canfora, Enzo Collotti, Marcello Flores, and Nicola Gallerano. Rome, 1993.

———. *Autobiography of a Generation: Italy 1968*. Middletown, 1996.

———. "Youth as a Metaphor for Social Change in Fascist Italy and America in the 1950s." In *A History of Young People. Stormy Evolution to Modern Times*, vol. 2, ed. Levi Giovanni and Jean-Claude Schmitt. Massachusetts, 1997.

———. "Πληγές της Μνήμης. Γυναικεία Ταυτότητα και Πολιτική Βία» [Wounded Memory: Female Identity and Political Violence]. In *Σπαράγματα του 20ου Αιώνα. Η Ιστορία ως Βιωμένη Εμπειρία* [Fragments of the Twentieth Century: History as a Lived Experience], 213–70. Athens, 1998.

———. "'Utopia' and Desire." *Thesis Eleven* 68, no. 1 (2002): 11–30.

———. *Fascism in Popular Memory: The Cultural Experience of the Turin Working Class*. Cambridge, 2009.

Peponis, Anastasis. *1961–1981. Τα γεγονότα και τα πρόσωπα* [1961–1981: Events and People]. Athens, 2002.

Pimblis, Manolis. *Το φοιτητικό κίνημα και η πάλη του Λ.Δ.Μ.Ε.* [The Student Movement and the Struggle of L.D.M.E.]. Salonica, 1974.
Pizzorno, Alessandro. "Le due logiche dell'azione di classe." In *Lotte operaie e sindacato: Il ciclo 1968–72 in Italia,* ed. A. Pizzorno, E. Reyneri, M. Regini, and I. Regalia, 6: 7–45. Bologna, 1978.
Plaskovitis, Spyros. "Χρόνια Μνήμης και Αμνημοσύνης" [Years of Memory and Oblivion]. *I Lexi* 63–64 (Apr.–May 1987): 240–49.
Polichronopoulos, Panos. Παιδεία και Πολιτική στην Ελλάδα. Κριτική Ανάλυση και Αξιολόγηση των Ιδεολογικών και Γνωστικών Λειτουργιών του Σχολικού Συστήματος 1950–1975 [Learning and Politics in Greece: A Critical Analysis and Evaluation of the Ideological and Cognitive Functions of the School System]. Athens, 1980.
Portelli, Alessandro. "Intervistare il movimento: Il '68 e la storia orale." In *Il Sessantotto: L'evento e la storia,* ed. Pier Paolo Poggio, 125–32. Brescia, 1988–1989.
———. *The Death of Luigi Trastulli and Other Stories: Form and Meaning in Oral History.* New York, 1991.
Poulantzas, Nikos. *The Crisis of the Dictatorships: Portugal, Spain, Greece.* London, 1976.
Prestholdt, Jeremy. "Resurrecting Che: Radicalism, the Transnational Imagination, and the Politics of Heroes," *Journal of Global History* 7, no. 3 (November 2012): 506–26.
Psyroukis, Nikos. *Ιστορία της Σύγχρονης Ελλάδος (1940–74)* [History of Contemporary Greece, 1940–74]. Athens, 1983.
Raftopoulos, Rigas. "Between Italy and Greece: Resistance, Dictatorship, and the Unfreezing Cold War, 1967–74." Unpublished paper, Second Ph.D. Symposium on Modern Greece, London School of Economics, 10 June 2005.
———. *Φοιτητές και δικτατορία στην Ιταλία μέσα από τα έγγραφα του ιταλικού υπουργείου εσωτερικών (1967–1970)* [Students and Dictatorship in Italy through the Documents of the Italian Ministry of the Interior (1967–1970)]. In *Η ελληνική νεολαία στον 20° αιώνα. Πολιτικές διαδρομές, κοινωνικές πρακτικές και πολιτισμικές εκφράσεις* [Greek Youth in the 20th Century. Cultural Itineraries, Social Practices and Cultural Expressions], ed. Vangelis Karamanolakis, Evi Olympitou, and Ioanna Papathanasiou. Athens, 2010.
Raschke, Joachim. *Soziale Bewegungen: Ein historisch-systematischer Grundriss.* Frankfurt, 1985.
Rigas Feraios. *The Rigas Feraios Album.* Athens, 1974.
Rigos, Alkis. "Φοιτητικό κίνημα και δικτατορία" [Student Movement and Dictatorship]. In *Η Δικτατορία. 1967–74. Πολιτικές πρακτικές, ιδεολογικός λόγος, αντίσταση* [The Dictatorship, 1967–74: Political Practices, Ideological Discourse, Resistance], ed. Gianna Athanasatou, Alkis Rigos, and Serafeim Seferiadis, 224–54. Athens, 1999.
Rigos, Alkis, Serafeim I. Seferiadis, and Evanthis Chadzivasileiou, eds. *Η «σύντομη» δεκαετία του '60. Θεσμικό πλαίσιο, κομματικές στρατηγικές, κοινωνικές συγκρούσεις, πολιτισμικές διεργασίες* [The "Short" Decade of the '60s. Institutional Context, Party Strategies, Social Conflicts, Cultural Processes]. Athens, 2008.
Romvos, Teos. "Η Φωνή της Αλήθειας" [The Voice of Truth], in Nikos Theodosiou (ed.), Μάης του '68. Οι προκηρύξεις [May '68. The leaflets] in Makedonia, special section, Epiloges, May 1998.
Rosenthal, Gabriele. *Erlebte und erzaehlte Lebensgeschichte.* Frankfurt, 1995.

Ross, Kristin, *May '68 and its Afterlives*. Chicago, 2002.
Roszak, Theodore. *The Making of a Counter Culture: Reflections on the Technocratic Society and Its Youthful Opposition*. Berkeley, 1995.
Roufos Kanakaris, Rodis [the Athenian, pseud.]. *The Truth about Greece*. London, 1971.
———. "Culture and the Military," In *Greece Under Military Rule*, ed. Richard Clogg and George Yannopoulos, 146–62. New York, 1972.
Ryback, Timothy W. *Rock Around the Block. A History of Rock Music in Eastern Europe and the Soviet Union*. Oxford, 1990.
Saint Martin, Catherine. *Λαμπράκηδες. Ιστορία μιας γενιάς* [Lambrakides: History of a Generation]. Athens, 1984.
Samatas, Minas. "Studying Surveillance in Greece: Methodological and Other Problems Related to an Authoritarian Surveillance Culture." *Culture and Society* 3, no. 2–3 (2005): 181–97.
Sánchez Vidal, Agustín. "El cine español y la transición." In *Del Franquismo a la Posmodernidad: Cultura española 1975–1990*, ed. José B. Monleón, 85–98. Madrid, 1995.
Saratsi, Titika. "Για τη φίλη και συναγωνίστρια μου Έπη, που κοιμήθηκε νωρίς" [For My Friend and Comrade Epi, Who Passed Away Too Soon]. In *Όταν θέλαμε να αλλάξουμε την Ελλάδα. Το αντιδικτατορικό φοιτητικό κίνημα: Η ΕΚΙΝ και οι καταλήψεις της Νομικής* [When We Wanted to Change Greece: The Antidictatorship Student Movement; EKIN and the Law School's Occupations], ed. Giorgos A. Vernikos. Athens, 2003.
Savvopoulos, Dionysis, ed. *Η Σούμα* [The Sum Up]. Athens, 2003.
Schildt, Axel, Detlef Siegfried, and Karl Christian Lammers, eds. *Dynamische Zeiten: Die 60er Jahre in den beiden deutschen Gesellschaften*. Hamburg, 2000.
Schildt, Axel and Detlef Siegfried. "Youth Consumption, and Politics in the Age of Radical Change." In *Between Marx and Coca-Cola. Youth Cultures in Changing European Societies, 1960–1980*, ed. Axel Schildt and Detlef Siegfried. New York, 2006.
Schorske, Carl E. *Thinking with History: Explorations in the Passage to Modernism*. Princeton, 1998.
Schuman, Howard, and Jacqueline Scott. "Generations and Collective Memories." *American Sociological Review* 54, no. 3 (June 1989): 359–81.
Scott, James C., *Domination and the Arts of Resistance: Hidden Transcripts*. New Haven, 1992.
Serdedakis, Nikos. "Διαδικασίες παραγωγής και συγκρότησης των κοινωνικών κινημάτων. Τα νέα κοινωνικά κινήματα στον ελληνικό κοινωνικό σχηματισμό [Processes of Social Movement Production. New Social Movements within Greek Society]." Ph.D. diss., University of Rethimnon, 1996.
———. "Political Violence in Post-War Greece: The Origins of Greek Terrorism." Unpublished paper, September 2003.
Sfikas, Thanasis D. Review of *New Voices in the Nation: Women and the Greek Resistance, 1941–1964. Journal of Modern Greek Studies* 16, no. 2 (1998): 378–81.
Shelton, Robert. *No Direction Home. The Life and Music of Bob Dylan*. New York, 2003.
Siani-Davies, Peter, and Stefanos Katsikas. "National Reconciliation after Civil War: The Case of Greece." *Journal of Peace Research*, no. 46 (2009): 559–75.
Siegfried, Detlef. "Understanding 1968: Youth Rebellion, Generational Change and Postindustrial Society." In *Between Marx and Coca-Cola: Youth Cultures in Changing*

European Societies, 1960–1980, ed. Axel Schildt and Detlef Siegfried. Oxford and New York, 2005.
Sirinelli, Jean-François. *Les baby-boomers: Une génération 1945–1969*. Paris, 2003.
Skocpol, Theda. *States and Social Revolutions: A Comparative Analysis of France, Russia, and China*. Cambridge, 1979.
Skroumbelos, Thanasis. *Οι κόκκινοι φίλοι μου. Μια ιστορία της οργάνωσης Ρήγας Φεραίος* [My Red Friends: A History of the Rigas Feraios Organization]. Athens, 2004.
Snyder, Jack. *Myths of Empire: Domestic Politics and International Ambition*. Ithaca, 1991.
Sofoulis, Kostas M. "Κοινωνικές Επιστήμες. Απορίες για τις ελληνικές εκδόσεις" [Social Sciences: Some Questions about Greek Publications]. *I Synecheia* 2 (Apr. 1973): 92–94.
Solzhenitsyn, Alexander. *The First Circle*. London, 1968.
Sommier, Isabelle. *La violence politique et son deuil: L' après 68 en France et en Italie*. Rennes, 1998.
Sontag, Susan. *On Photography*. London, 1979.
Sotiropoulou, Chrysanthi. *Ελληνική Κινηματογραφία. 1965–1975. Θεσμικό πλαίσιο—Οικονομική κατάσταση* [Greek Cinematography, 1965–1975: Institutional Context, Financial Situation]. Athens, 1989.
Sotiropoulou, Mariana. *Το πολιτικό βιβλίο στη διάρκεια της δικτατορίας, 1967–74* [The Political Book during the Dictatorship, 1967–74]. Athens, 1997.
Staiger, Janet. "Writing the History of American Film Reception." In *Hollywood Spectatorship. Changing Perceptions of Cinema Audiences*, ed. Melvyn Stokes and Richard Maltby, 19–32. London, 2001.
Statera, Giovanni. *Death of a Utopia: The Development and Decline of Student Movements in Europe*. Oxford, 1975.
Stockton, Bayard. *Phoenix with a Bayonet. A Journalist's Interim Report on the Greek Revolution*. Georgetown, 1971.
Swanson, Gillian. "Memory, Subjectivity and Intimacy: The Historical Formation of the Self and Writing of Female Autobiography." In *Memory and Methodology*, ed. Susannah Radstone. Oxford, 2000.
Tachtsis, Kostas. *Το φοβερό βήμα* [The Terrible Step]. Athens, 1989.
Tarrow, Sid. *Democracy and Disorder: Protest and Politics in Italy, 1965–75*. Oxford, 1989.
———. *Power in the Movement: Social Movements, Collective Action, and Mass Politics in the Modern State*. New York, 1994.
Theodorakis, Mikis. *Μελοποιημένη Ποίηση. Τραγούδια* [Poetry Put into Music: Songs], vol. 1. Athens, 1997.
———. *Το Μανιφέστο των Λαμπράκηδων. Ποιοι είμαστε. Τι θέλουμε. Γιατί μας πολεμούν* [The Lambrakides' Manifesto: Who We Are; What We Want; Why They Are Fighting Us]. Athens, 2003.
Theodoridis, Panos. *Το ροκ των Μακεδόνων* [The Macedonian Rock]. Salonica, 1998.
Tilly, Charles. *From Mobilization to Revolution*. Reading, 1978.
Tonkin, Elizabeth. *Narrating Our Pasts: The Social Construction of Oral History*. Cambridge, 1992.
Touraine, Alain. *Le communisme utopique: Le mouvement de mai 1968*. Paris, 1968.

Tsirkas, Stratis. Prologue to *Αρχείο Παράνομου Αντιστασιακού Εντύπου. ΚΚΕ Εσωτερικού, ΕΔΑ, ΠΑΜ, Ρήγας Φεραίος* [Archive of Clandestine Resistance Journals: KKE Interior, EDA, PAM, Rigas Feraios]. Athens, 1974.

———. *Η Χαμένη Άνοιξη* [The Lost Spring]. Athens, 1976.

Tsoukalas, Konstantinos. "Η ελληνική δεκαετία του '60: «σύντομη ή μακρά»;" [The Greek 60s: 'short' or 'long'?] In *Η «σύντομη» δεκαετία του '60. Θεσμικό πλαίσιο, κομματικές στρατηγικές, κοινωνικές συγκρούσεις, πολιτισμικές διεργασίες* [The "Short" Decade of the '60s. Institutional Context, Party Strategies, Social Conflicts, Cultural Processes], ed. Alkis Rigos, Serafeim I. Seferiadis, and Evanthis Chadzivasileiou, 41–46. Athens, 2008.

Tzortzis, Ioannis. "The *Metapolitefsi* That Never Was: A Re-evaluation of the 1973 'Markezinis Experiment.'" Paper presented at the First LSE Symposium on Social Science Research in Greece, London, June 2003. http://www.lse.ac.uk/europeanInstitute/research/hellenicObservatory/pdf/1st_Symposium/TheMetapolitefsiThatNeverWas.pdf, accessed 9 August 2013.

Van Boeschoten, Riki. *From Armatolik to People's Rule: Investigation into the Collective Memory of Rural Greece, 1750–1949*. Amsterdam, 1991.

———. *Ανάποδα Χρόνια. Συλλογική μνήμη και ιστορία στο Ζιάκα Γρεβενών (1900–1950)* [Troubled Years: Collective Memory and History in Ziakas, Grevena]. Athens, 1997.

Van Dyck, Karen. *Kassandra and the Censors: Greek Poetry since 1967*. Ithaca, 1998.

Van Steen, Gonda. *Venom in Verse: Aristophanes in Modern Greece*. Princeton, 2000.

———. "Joining Our Grand Circus." *Journal of Modern Greek Studies* 25, no. 2 (October 2007): 301–32.

———. "Rallying the Nation: Sport and Spectacle Serving the Greek Dictatorships." *International Journal of the History of Sport* 27, no. 12 (2010): 2121–54.

Varikas, Eleni. "The Utopian Surplus." *Thesis Eleven* 68, no. 1 (2002): 101–5.

Varon, Jeremy. "Between Revolution 9 and Thesis 11." In *The New Left Revisited*, ed. John McMillian and Paul Buhle, 214–40. Philadelphia, 2002.

Varopoulou, Eleni. "Το Θέατρο 1974–2000. Ένα σύγχρονο καλλιτεχνικό επίτευγμα" [Theater 1974–2000. A Modern Artistic Achievement]. In *Η Ελλάδα της ομαλότητας 1974–2000. Δημοκρατικές κατακτήσεις. Οικονομική ανάπτυξη και κοινωνική σταθερότητα* [Greece of Normality, 1974–2000: Democratic Conquests; Economic Growth and Social Stability], vol. 10 of *Ιστορία του Νέου Ελληνισμού 1770–2000* [History of Modern Hellenism], ed. Vasilis Panayotopoulos. Athens, 2003.

Vavizos, Giorgos. *Έτσι δενόταν ... η καρμπονάρα. Μαρτυρίες ενός αριστεριστή για την αντιχουντική δράση των Ελλήνων φοιτητών στη Νότιο Ιταλία* [How ... Carbonara Was Tempered: Testimonies of a Leftist on the Anti-Junta Action of Greek Students in Southern Italy]. Athens, 2002.

Venturas, Ekaterini. "Identité féminine, identité culturelle et migration. Continuités et changements dans la vie et le vecu des migrantes: la coupure de l'immigration." In *International Oral History Conference VII: Memory and Multiculturalism, Siena-Lucca, 25–28 February 1993*, 810–18. Siena, 1993.

Vernardakis, Christoforos, and Giannis Mavris. *Κόμματα και κοινωνικές συμμαχίες στην προδικτατορική Ελλάδα. Οι προϋποθέσεις της μεταπολίτευσης* [Parties and Social

Coalitions in Predictatorship Greece: The Preconditions of the *Metapolitefsi*]. Athens, 1991.

Vernikos, Giorgos A., ed. *Όταν θέλαμε να αλλάξουμε την Ελλάδα. Το αντιδικτατορικό φοιτητικό κίνημα: Η ΕΚΙΝ και οι καταλήψεις της Νομικής* [When We Wanted to Change Greece: The Antidictatorship Student Movement; EKIN and the Law School's Occupations]. Athens, 2003.

———. "Προσωπική Μαρτυρία" [Personal Testimony]. In *Όταν θέλαμε να αλλάξουμε την Ελλάδα. Το αντιδικτατορικό φοιτητικό κίνημα: Η ΕΚΙΝ και οι καταλήψεις της Νομικής* [When We Wanted to Change Greece: The Antidictatorship Student Movement; EKIN and the Law School Occupations], ed. Giorgos A. Vernikos, 143–55. Athens, 2003.

Vlachou, Helen. *House Arrest.* London, 1970.

Voglis, Polymeris. *Becoming a Subject. Political Prisoners during the Greek Civil War, 1945–1950.* Oxford, 2002.

———. "'The Junta Came to Power by the Force of Arms, and Will Only Go by Force of Arms.' Political Violence and the Voice of the Opposition to the Military Dictatorship in Greece, 1967–74," *Cultural and Social History* 8, no. 4 (2011): 551–68.

Wasserstrom, Jeffrey N. *Student Protest in Twentieth-Century China: The View from Shanghai.* Stanford, 1991.

White, Hayden V. *The Content of the Form: Narrative Discourse and Historical Representation.* Baltimore, 1987.

Williams, Raymond. *The Long Revolution.* 1961. Reprint, London, 1971.

Wilson, James Q. *Political Organizations.* New York, 1973.

Yiannopoulos, Georgios. "Οι αντιστασιακές δυνάμεις μετά το στρατιωτικό πραξικόπημα" [Resistance Forces after the Military Coup d'état]. In *Η Ελλάδα κάτω από στρατιωτικό ζυγό* [Greece under Military Rule], ed. Richard Clogg and George Yiannopoulos, 256–92. Athens, 1976.

Zafeiris, Christos. *Εμείς του '60 οι εκδρομείς* [We, the Travelers of the '60s]. Athens, 2000.

———. "Μια παράνομη ανταπόκριση για το δικό μας Πολυτεχνείο" [A Clandestine Correspondence on Our Own Polytechnic]. In *Η μνήμη της πόλης. Κείμενα και σπάνιες φωτογραφίες για τη Θεσσαλονίκη* [The Memory of the City: Texts and Rare Photographs of Salonica], ed. Christos Zafeiris. Salonica, 2004.

———. "Νεανικά στέκια του '60, καφενεία και ταβέρνες" [Youth Hang-outs in the '60s, Coffee-Houses and Taverns]. In *Η μνήμη της πόλης. Κείμενα και σπάνιες φωτογραφίες για τη Θεσσαλονίκη* [The Memory of the City. Texts and Rare Photographs of Salonica]. Salonica, 2004.

Zannas, Pavlos A. *Ημερολόγια Φυλακής* [Prison Notebooks]. Athens, 2000.

Zei, Alki. *Η αρραβωνιαστικιά του Αχιλλέα* [Achilles' Fiancée]. Athens, 1987.

Zolberg, Aristid. "Moments of Madness." *Politics and Society* 2, no. 2 (1972): 183–207.

Zoumboulakis, Stavros. "Ο πολιτικός ριζοσπαστισμός στη δεκαετία του "60" [Political Radicalism in the 1960s]. *O Politis* 99 (Apr. 2002): 12–15.

———. "Από νύχτα σε νύχτα" [From One Night to the Next]. *Nea Estia* 154, no. 1758 (July–August 2003).

"Δικτατορία 1967 1974. Η έντυπη αντίσταση" [Dictatorship 1967 1974. Resistance in Print]. Salonica, 2010.
"Η δικτατορία των Συνταγματαρχών. Το Απριλιανό καθεστώς" [The Colonels' Dictatorship: the April Regime]. In *Ιστορία του Ελληνικού Έθνους* [History of the Greek Nation], 265–86. Athens, 2000.
Χρονικό 1971 [Chronicle 1971]. Athens, 1971.
Χρονικό 1972 [Chronicle 1972]. Athens, 1972.

Film

Anderson, Lindsay. *If...*. UK, 1968.
Angelopoulos, Theo. *Αναπαράσταση* [Reconstruction]. Greece, 1970.
———. *Μέρες του '36* [Days of '36]. Greece, 1972.
Antonioni, Michelangelo. *Blow Up*. UK/USA, 1996
———. *Zabriskie Point*. USA, 1970.
Bertolucci, Bernardo. *Il Conformista* [The Conformist]. Italy, France, West Germany, 1970.
———. *Strategia del ragno* [The Spider's Stratagem]. Italy, 1970.
Brooks, Richard. *Blackboard Jungle*. USA, 1955.
Dadiras, Dimis. *Ο Ιπποκράτης και η Δημοκρατία* [Hippocrates and Democracy]. Greece, 1972.
Dalianidis, Giannis. *Τεντυμπόη Αγάπη Μου* [*Teddyboy, My Love*]. Greece, 1965.
———. *Μαριχουάνα Στοπ* [Marijuana Stop]. Greece, 1971.
Godard, Jean-Luc. *Masculin Féminin*. France, 1966.
Hagmann, Stewart. *The Strawberry Statement*. USA, 1970.
Hopper, Dennis. *Easy Rider*. USA, 1969.
Melville, Jean-Pierre. *Le Doulos*. France, 1962.
Montaldo, Giuliano. *Sacco e Vanzetti*. Italy, 1971.
Nichols, Mike. *The Graduate*. USA, 1967.
Papadatos, Gerasimos. *Οργισμένη Γενιά* [Raging Youth]. Greece, 1972.
Papakostas, Giorgos. *Ένας Χίπης με Τσαρούχια* [A Hippie with Tsarouchia]. Greece, 1970.
Rentzis, Thanasis, and Nikos Zervos. *Μαύρο-Άσπρο* [Black-White]. Greece, 1973.
Sakellarios, Alekos. *Η Θεία μου η Χίπισα* [My Aunt, the Hippie]. Greece, 1970.
Stamboulopoulos, Giorgos. *Ανοιχτή Επιστολή* [Open Letter]. Greece, 1968.
Voulgaris, Pandelis. *Το Προξενιό της Άννας* [The Matchmaking of Anna], Greece, 1972.
———. *Ο Μεγάλος Ερωτικός* [Magnus Eroticus]. Greece, 1973.
Williams, Paul. *Out of It*. USA, 1969.

Documentaries

Theos, Dimos, and Fotos Lambrinos. *Οι εκατό ώρες του Μάη* [The 100 Hours of May]. Athens, 1963.
Boskoitis, Antonis. *Ζωντανοί στο Κύτταρο. Σκηνές Ροκ* [Live at Kyttaro. Rock Scenes]. Athens, 2006.

Television Documentaries

Iatropoulos, D. *Εδώ Πολυτεχνείο* [Here Is Polytechnic Speaking], ERT Archive.
Kaplanidis, Stavros. *Ιστορία των χρόνων μου: Θόδωρος Αγγελόπουλος. Αναπαράσταση 1970* [Story of My Years: Thodoros Angelopoulos. Reconstruction 1970]. ET1, 2005.
Kouloglou, Stelios. *Η "αληθινή" 17 Νοέμβρη* [The "Real" 17 November]. NET, *Reportage without Frontiers*, 17 November 2003.
———. *Τα παιδιά του Τσε στην Ελλάδα* [The Children of Che in Greece], NET.
Papadimitrakis, Lambros. *Ο ραδιοφωνικός σταθμός του Πολυτεχνείου* [The Radio Station of the Polytechnic], ERT1 Archive, 17 November 1984.
Stratigakos, Stavros. *Νίκος Ξυλούρης και τρία ποιήματα* [Nikos Xylouris and *Three Poems*], ET1, 8 February 2005.
Theologidou, Rena. *Το πολιτιστικό έγκλημα της χούντας* [The Cultural Crime of the Junta]. ET1, *Rimeik*, 21 April 1997.
Vernardou, Eva, and Nikos Sarlis. *Αποφασίσαμεν και διατάσσομεν* [We Have Decided and We Order], ERT Archive.
Η μηχανή του χρόνου [The Time Machine], NET, 17 November 2000.

Sound

Music

LP *Τα Μικροαστικά* [Petty Bourgeois Songs], by Loukianos Kilaidonis (music) and Giannis Negropontis (lyrics), 1973.
LP *Παραδοσιακά—λαϊκά—προσωπικά. 40 ηχογραφήσεις 1970–1992 Στο 'πα και στο ξαναλέω* [I Told You Once, I'm Telling You Again. Folk Songs—Popular Songs—Personal Ones. 40 recordings] by Marisa Koch.
LP *Το περιβόλι του τρελλού* [Fool's Garden] & *Μπάλλος* [Balos] & *Βρώμικο Ψωμί* [Filthy Bread] by Dionysis Savvopoulos [1969, 1970, 1973].
LP *Ριζίτικα* by Giannis Markopoulos, 1971.
LP Collection *Ο Σαββόπουλος στη Λύρα* [Savvopoulos at Lyra], 1998.
LP *Τα Τραγούδια του Αγώνα* [Songs of the Struggle] & *Ρωμιοσύνη* [Romiossyni] by Mikis Theodorakis, 1966, reissued 2004.
LP *Ζωντανοί στο Κύτταρο. Η Ποπ στην Αθήνα* [Live at Kyttaro. Pop Music in Athens], Lyra, 2003, first edn. 1971.

Sound Documents

CD *Άγνωστα Ντοκουμέντα του Πολυτεχνείου Θεσσαλονίκης* [Unknown Documents of the Polytechnic of Salonica], EDIA.

Index

114 Movement, 15, 30, 78
15 percent, 16
17 November (organization), 70, 82, 135, 300–301, 302
1968 revolts. *See* events of 1968
"3 M's," 162

AASPE, 138–39, 144, 156n146, 296
abortion, 208, 243
adultery, 208
A-EFEE, 85, 131–33, 141–42, 144, 146, 231, 280, 283, 289, 296
    role of KKE's history in, 142
    role in Polytechnic occupation, 255, 257, 259, 262, 269, 307n90
Aeschylus, 182
Agapiou, Kostas, 80, 82
Agnew, Spyro, 65
Albanian model, 136, 137
Alkimoi, 97
Alkyonis (cinema), 178
Allende, Salvador, 248, 279f, 286, 331
Althusser, Louis, 163, 164
American College of Athens, 110
amnesty for accused, 246, 247f, 249, 253
Anagennisi (journal), 24
Anagnostakis, Manolis, 51, 157n172, 161, 182
anarchism, 91n94, 233–34, 261, 301, 323
anarchists and the Polytechnic occupation, 256, 260–61, 307n105, 307n108
"anarchists," for antiregime students, 125, 256, 260–61, 272–73, 286, 325
Anastasiadis, Themos, 157n173
ancient Greece, Junta references to, 97
Androulakis, Mimis, 2

Angelis, Vice-General Odysseus, 39, 48, 305n58
Angeloni, Maria Elena, 67, 80–81, 82
Angelopoulos, Theo, 170, 173
Anoichto Theatro (journal), 182–83, 184, 189
antartika songs, 200, 202
Antidictatorship EFEE. *See* A-EFEE
Anti-Espionage Law of 1947, 59
Anti-fascist, Anti-Imperialistic Student Front of Greece. *See* AASPE
Anti (journal), 218n28
Antonioni, Michelangelo, 174
apathy. *See* student apathy
Archaeological Museum demonstration, 122
ARF, 80–82
Aris. *See* Velouchiotis, Aris
Aris-Rigas Feraios. *See* ARF
Aristeristes. See Leftists
Aristophanes, 182
Aristotelian University of Thessaloniki. *See* Salonica University
arms
    restrictions on, 39–40
    transfer to Greece, 67, 80
Army, role of in coup, 38
artsy fartsies, 131, 215–16
ASPIDA conspiracy, 38
assembly, restrictions on, 113, 117, 152n60, 225
assistants, teaching, 128
Athens, as primary center of student resistance, 114
Athens Law School, 123, 146, 206, 230–40, 250
    and beginning of Polytechnic occupation, 254

conscription of students of, 230–31, 235
demand for general assemblies at, 237
first occupation of, 230
second occupation of, 231–35, 236–39
solidarity with students of, 232, 239
third occupation of, 240
weapons at, 235
Athens, University of
construction during Junta, 50
first demonstration at, 122
student life at, 96
Averoff, Evangelos, 43
Avgi (newspaper), 29, 43

baby boom, effects of, 315
Baez, Joan, 190
Bakunin, Mikhail, 162
Balaouras, Makis, 229f
Balis, Nikos, 233
Bambalis, Petros, 300
Baran, Paul, 162
Barcelona student strike, 237
Basque separatists, 86–87
Bazin, André, 169
beards, 213
Beatles, The, 18, 34n26, 54, 190
Beckett, Samuel, 183
Bellou, Sotiria, 201, 222n146
Berliners, 65
Bertrand Russell Youth Committee for Nuclear Disarmament, 16, 19, 24
birth control, 207–8
Black-White (film), 173, 174f, 190, 221n103
Blue jeanists, 26
boîtes. See music halls
"Boliguay," 161
books
blacklist of, 161, 218n20
discouraged list of, 168
role in resistance, 160–69
sale and purchase of, 168

bookshops, 168
boredom and student life, 96
Bost, 185, 186
Bostanzoglou, Mendis, 185, 186
Bourboulia, 94n173, 195
Boy Scouts. *See* Alkimoi
Brassens, Georges, 192
Brecht, Bertholt, 182, 184–85, 186
Brillakis, Antonis, 47
bullying by pro-regime students, 96

Caetano, Marcelo, 252
Carnation Revolution, the. *See* Portugal
cartoons, 159
Cavafy, Constantine, 51
censorship
attempts to appear liberal despite, 182
and film, 169, 170, 173
in interwar period, 200
journalists' protest of, 159
during Junta, 39, 57, 84, 158, 198
of music, 198, 200, 202–3
results of, 159
of sexually explicit material, 148
softening of, 116, 152n60, 158, 161, 182, 330
of theater, 181–82, 188
Center Union. *See* EK
certificate of civic mindedness, 14, 22, 50, 116
Chile, 68, 247–48, 331
"Chinese." *See* PPSP
Chinese Cultural Revolution, 172
Christakis, Leonidas, 218n27
cinema. *See* film
cinema clubs, 170–72, 173
cinema halls, 178, 180
cities, modernization of, 114
civil disobedience, 315
civil rights movement (US) 24
Civil War
Greek, Junta references to, 97
references to, 245–46
class and politicization, 108–9
class division, 138

classical Greek drama, 181–82
Coca-Cola, 58–59, 234
Cohn-Bendit, Daniel, 56f, 64, 134, 233, 238
colonels' regime. *See* Junta
comics. *See* cartoons
commercials, television, 180, 193, 220n68
    women in, 205–6
Communist Organization of Students. *See* KOS
Communist Party of Greece. *See* KKE
conscription, forced, 228–29, 230, 250, 252, 254
Constantine II, King of Greece, 26, 28, 241
    countercoup of, 42
Constitutional Charter for Education, 128
consumer culture, 12, 18, 46, 58, 180, 193, 314, 317, 331
    in Greek music, 193
contraception. *See* birth control
controlled liberalization, 116, 186, 225, 229f, 246, 247, 250, 286, 287–88, 329, 332
    and student resistance, 116, 160, 286
Coordinating Committee of Occupation. *See under* Polytechnic University, Athens: CCO at
Council of Europe, 118
coup d'état, 21 April 1967
    background to, 37, 43
    condemnation of by political leaders, 42–43
    passive response to, 43–45
    student response to, 64
    tolerance of, 45–47, 50
Cretan Society of Athens, 117–18, 242
Cretan Society of Salonica, 249
Crete, as symbolic of resistance, 200
Crete, University of, 50
Crosby, Stills, Nash and Young, 190
Cuba, 134
cultural revolution, 138

Cyprus
    coup of 1974, 291–92, 331
    unification with Greece, 15

DA, 47
Dallas, Vasilis, 94n173
Damanaki, Maria, 257–58
Damon and Feidias, 190, 195
dance as political message, 105, 198, 199f, 233
Darveris, Tasos, 71–73
Day of the Student, 97
DEA, 52
de Beauvoir, Simone, 212
Debord, Guy, 233, 266
Debray, Regis, 163
December Events, the, 272
Decree 1010, 30
Deep Purple, 190
deferment of military service, 124, 250, 254
    revocation of as punishment, 230
de-Juntafication. *See under* universities: de-Juntification of
Democratic Committees of Resistance. *See* DEA
Democratic Defense. *See* DA
dictatorship, Greek. *See* Junta
diglossia, 115, 295
Dimaras, K. Th., 24
dimotika songs, 192, 196
dimotiki Greek, 14, 216
Doors, the, 190
dress, traditional, and resistance, 117–18
drug use, 54, 85, 94n173, 177, 202
    references to in music, 190, 200
Dylan, Bob, 190, 192, 193, 194, 314

EAM/ELAS, 79, 167, 276, 304n7
EAT-ESA, 40, 188, 241–42, 266–67, 286, 291
economic crisis of 2009–, Greek, 1, 327–28
economic prosperity, 33n6, 45–46, 88n30, 318

economy after civil war, 11
EDA, 10, 15, 23, 28, 33n4, 48
    and response to coup, 38, 43, 47
EDA Youth, 26
EDE, 135, 136, 285
EDIN, 48
educational reform, 13–14, 101
    abolishment of, 50
    demands for, 132, 227–28, 249–50
    in universities, 128, 154n91, 254, 295
EEC, 118
EFEE, 78, 125, 132
Eighteen Texts, 161, 217n11
Eisenstein, Sergei, 174
EK, 11, 14, 15, 74, 101, 139
    defectors from, 27, 28
    youths of, 23
EKIN, 110, 116, 118–19, 120–22, 137, 186, 206, 329
    recruitment efforts of, 119
EKKE, 65, 109, 137–39, 144, 148–49, 156n147, 185, 195, 289, 296, 302
    and violence, 138, 302
EKNE, 99
EKOF, 23, 96–97, 114–15, 234, 236
ELA, 82
elections, national, 116, 246, 247, 250, 295
    guided, 131
elections, student, 117, 124, 249, 254, 296
    boycott of, 125–26
    as catalyst for generalized protest, 123
    demand for, 132, 249
    legal battle for, 123, 249
    organized protest for, 116, 124, 125
    recommendations against, 139
Elefthero Theatro (Free Theater), 185–87
Elliniadis, Stelios, 195
Ellinikos Kinimatografos (journal), 169
Elytis, Odysseus, 191, 222n139
EMEP, 119, 121–22
EMP, 125

entertainment by Junta, 96, 98
EPES, 91n90
Epoches (journal), 24
EPON, 142
ERE, 15
EREN, 48
ESA. *See* EAT-ESA
ESESI, 92n118
ethnikofrosyni, 10
ethnokratia, 99
Eudes, Dominique, 167
Euripides, 182
Euro-Communism, 166
European Economic Community. *See* EEC
events of 1968, 53–58, 312–17, 320, 324
    and Greece, 1, 2–3, 6, 7, 27, 53–58, 61–65, 68–69, 105–6, 109, 125, 172, 190, 203, 209, 214, 235–39, 261, 264, 299, 302, 312–22, 324–25, 329
    KKE view of, 133, 323
Exadaktylos, 190, 195
expression, freedom of, 153n77
extreme right, 1, 23

falanga, 242
falling in love, 203
family
    and communism, 106–7, 108
    pressure on students, 95
    and reluctance of students to become politicized, 107
Fanon, Frantz, 315
Farakos, Grigoris, 61, 133
fashion, 17, 26, 42, 84, 117–18, 136, 140, 176, 177, 193, 207, 210, 213–16, 314
Fasis, Manousos, 157n172. *See also* Anagnostakis, Manolis
Fatouros, Dimitris, 49, 96, 115, 204
FEA, 123–24, 129
fear
    as response to coup, 50–51
    and role in resistance, 78, 95

feminism, 212, 301–2, 311n209, 326
  organizations related to, 302, 311n209
  rejection of by pro-regime students, 99
film
  audience's dialogue with, 181
  banning of, 175
  and discussions of, 170–71, 173
  juvenile delinquency in, 34n25
  mainstream genres of, 170
  and politicization of, 170
  popularity of, 148
  role in resistance of, 73, 169–81
  as universal code, 175
  See also New Greek Cinema
"five days of May," 19
flag. *See under* Polytechnic University, Athens, occupation: national symbols in
Foititikos Palmos (journal), 99
folk culture as resistance, 117–18
football, 189, 227, 232, 296–97
  role in Junta, 96, 98
Ford Foundation, the, 189
Fourth International. *See* Trotskyism
Franco, Francisco, comparisons to, 43, 86–87. *See also* Spain, comparisons to
Frangatos, Gerasimos, 128
Frankfurt School, the, 163
Frederica, Queen Mother of Greece, 28
French May (1968), 55–58, 61–64, 238, 239, 260, 302, 312

Galbraith, John Kenneth, 162
Gandonas, Nikolaos, 236
Gauchistes. *See* Leftists
Gavras, Costa, 20
Gay, John, 186, 187f
General Confederation of Greek Workers. *See* GSEE
Generation Z, 20–23, 191, 328–29, 331
Genet, Jean, 183
Georgakis, Kostas, 66–67
Georgalas, Georgios, 48, 54–55, 176

Gerali, Margarita, 83
German occupation of Greece, 25
  comparisons to, 290
  resistance to, 79
Giotopoulos, Alexandros, 70, 82
Giovine, Umberto, 67
Girl Guides. *See* Alkimoi
Gizikis, General Faidon, 288, 291, 293f
Glezou, Despoina, 195
global revolt, 314, 315
"glocalism," 249
Godard, Jean Luc, 6, 18, 58, 169, 171
Golden Dawn, 1–2
Gousgounis, Kostas, 181
Government of National Unity, 293f
graffiti, 77
Gramsci, Antonio, 163, 166, 191
Grass, Günter, 120, 153n77
Grateful Dead, the, 190
Great Britain, involvement in Greek civil war, 10
Greek Committee Against the Dictatorship, 290
Greek Left, history of the, 166–67
Greek Pavilion, Cité Universitaire, occupation of, 63–64
Greek War of Independence (1821
  referenced by resistance groups, 118, 275
  referenced by Rigas Feraios, 77
  use by Junta, 77, 87n2
GSEE, 75
guerilla songs. *See andartika*
Guevara, Che, 24, 59, 65, 74, 133, 134, 213–14, 315

Hadjidakis, Manos, 172, 201
Hagmann, Stuart, 177
hair, length of, 213, 230, 252, 304n12
  and role in police brutality, 230
Halliday, Fred, 167–68
Hellenic European Youth Movement. *See* EKIN
Hendrix, Jimi, 190, 195, 314
hideouts of antiregime students, 289–90

Hikmet, Nazim, 165
hippie culture, 12, 54, 59, 174, 175, 176–77, 190, 202, 222n136
Hitler, Adolf, 79
Ho Chi Minh, 24
homosexuality, 23, 208–9, 213, 223n169, 326
Hymn to Freedom, 112, 122, 276–77

Ibárruri, Dolores, 206
IDEA, 38
I Genia Mas (Lambrakis Youth paper), 22
Iliou, Ilias, 43
Indignados, 2
industrial production, 33n6
inflation, 88n30, 251
International Commandos for Greece, 67
International Fair of Salonica, bomb plot on, 71
"invisible dictator, the." *See* Ioannidis, dictatorship of
Ioannidis, Brigadier Dimitrios, 286, 288, 310n181
Ioannidis, dictatorship of, 288–92
    and Cyprus coup, 291
Ioannina, University of, 13, 280
Ionescu, Eugène, 183, 184

Jancso, Milos, 174
Jefferson Airplane, 190
Jimmy the Tiger, 192
jokes, role in resistance of, 45
Joplin, Janis, 190
Juan Carlos de Bourbon, 16
July Events (1965), 26–27, 56f, 207
Junta
    crisis within, 257, 287, 291, 310n181
    as defining experience of youth, 100
    and emotional response to, 101–2
    fall of, 291–92
    military coup within, 287
    on silent approval of, 76, 88n31
    tolerance by professors of, 49–50
    trials of, 299–300

K29M, 70, 73
Kalambokias, Konstantinos, 48
Kaldaras, Apostolos, 201
Kambanellis, Iakovos, 187–88
Kanellakis, Panagiotis, 121
Kanellopoulos, Panagiotis, 25, 27, 42, 43, 250
Kanellopoulou, Stamatina, 302–3
Karamanlis, Constantine, 12, 19, 43, 123, 240, 246, 291, 292–95
Karezi, Jenni, 187, 188
Karpeta, Eleni, 183
Karystiani, Ioanna, 206, 231, 242
katharevousa Greek, 14, 50
Katsaros, Stergios, 28, 75, 85–86
Kazakos, Kostas, 187
Khaled, Leila, 215, 300
Kitsopoulos, Georgios, 183–84
Kittikachorn, Thanom, 249
KKE, 11, 15, 26, 28, 34n33, 53, 61, 80, 133, 138, 142, 145–46, 149, 156n147, 164, 323
    and inflexibility of, 131, 145
    legalization of, 295
    resistance to Junta by, 47, 69–70
KKE-Esoterikou (Interior), 53, 61, 80, 84–85, 156n147, 289
kleftika songs, 200, 202
KNE, creation of, 131
    sexual mores in, 149
Koch, Marisa, 196–97, 222n136
Kommounistis (journal), 138
Konstantinidis, Christos, 233–34
Korovesis, Periklis, 220n68, 301
KOS, 131
Kotanidis, Giorgos, 185, 189
Koufondinas, Dimitris, 82, 83, 301
koultouriarides. See artsy fartsies
Koumis, Iakovos, 302
Koun, Karolos, 183
Kourtis, Antonis, 160
Kyriopoulou, Paki, 68
Kyrkos, Leonidas, 34n39, 43
Kyttaro Club, 192f, 194, 195

Ladas, Colonel Ioannis, 16, 54, 213, 223n169, 310n181
Laiki Pali (organization), 71–72
Lambrakis, Christos, 24
Lambrakis, Grigoris, 19–21, 28
    funeral of, 19, 20f, 34n33
Lambrakisses, 23, 25
Lambrakis Youth (Lambrakides), 19–26, 28–30, 48, 60, 74, 155n131, 190, 251, 328
    and KNE, 131
    and Rigas Feraios, 78
    women and, 23, 24–25
language question. *See* diglossia
Language Reform, 295
Law 4000, 16, 17f
Law School occupation. *See* Athens Law School
LEA, 65, 82
leaflets, 77–78
Led Zeppelin, 190
Leftists, 64–65, 133–34, 280–81
    attitude toward violence of, 133–34
    and Polytechnic occupation, 256, 259, 307n90
legal action against Junta, 121, 123
Lenin, Vladimir Ilyich, 162, 252
Liakos, Antonis, 71–73
liberalization policy. *See* controlled liberalization
Lidra (nightclub), 202
"little Polytechnic," 228–30, 304n7
Linaios, Stefanos, 183
Llach, Lluís, 193
Loizos, Manos, 190
"long 1960s," the, 4, 8n12, 147, 316
Lúkacs, Gyorg, 162, 184
Luxemburg, Rosa, 162

Machitis (journal), 47
machoism, 149, 209
magazines
    avant-garde art, 167
    protest, 167
Magnus Eroticus (film), 172
Makarezos, Colonel Nikolaos, 40

Makarios III, President of Cyprus, 291
Makrigiannis, General, 79, 233
Makrigiannis (organization), 91n107
Makronisos, 245
Mallios, Evangelos, 300
Maoism and culture, 172, 173
Maoists. *See* Leftists *and* EKKE
Marcopoulos, Giannis, 199
Marcuse, Herbert, 137, 149, 163–64, 168
marcusism, 137
Marighella, Carlos, 315
Markaris, Petros, 186
Markezinis, Spyros, 1, 85, 246, 250
    and Polytechnic occupation, 256, 261, 286
    and the "student problem," 246–47, 254
marriage, 208
martial law during Junta, 39–40, 287
    end of, 116
Marxism, 129, 164–65
Marxist-Leninists, 136–37, 156n146
Marxist texts, appearance of, 162–63
Marx, Karl, 162
masculinity
    challenges to, 213
    constructions of, 74, 149
Mastorakis, Nikos, 230
Mavrogenis, Dionysis, 289
Mavros, Georgios, 43, 250
May 29th movement, the. *See* K29M
Mercouri, Melina, 44, 312, 321
metapolitefsi, 146, 147–48, 165, 189, 212, 292–99, 301–3
    disappointment over, 293–97, 330
    mythologizing of Polytechnic occupation during, 327
    student protests during, 302
Metaxas, Ioannis, 79
    in film, 170
Michailidis, Giorgos, 184
middle class and resistance, 127
military jacket, symbolism of, 141, 215, 252, 304n12
"miniparliament," 225

Mitafidis, Triantafyllos, 71–72
modernization, 11
monarchy, abolition of, 246
Montaldo, Giuliano, 174
Moropoulou, Tonia, 258
Mourselas, Kostas, 186, 193
music halls, 194–96
music of resistance, 189–96, 196–202
    Cretan history in, 199–200
    folk, 196–99, 199–202
    Greek, 190–94, 196–99, 199–202
    militant, 199–200
    rock and the, 190
    students and, 200–202
    traditional instruments in, 192, 196
Mussolini, Benito, 79, 125
mythology, references to, 230

Nasser, Gamal Abdel, 87n2
national anthem of Greece. *See Hymn to Freedom*
National Metsoveion Polytechnic. *See* Polytechnic University, Athens, occupation
national-mindedness, 10
National Movement of Young Scientists. *See* EKNE
National Radical Union. *See* ERE
National Social Student Union. *See* EKOF
National Society of Hellenic Students of Italy. *See* ESESI
National Student Union. *See* EFEE
NATO, 70, 80, 257, 262, 295
Navy, mutiny of, 241, 246, 305n38
Nazism and the Greek dictatorship, 218n27
Nea Keimena (publication), 161
Neoi Stochoi (publishing house), 163
    and suspicion of provocation, 163
neo-Marxism, 315
Neruda, Pablo, 165
New Greek Cinema, 169
    and attack on by Maoists, 173
    and rift with mainstream film, 170

New Left, 131, 163, 315
New Wave of Greek song (Neo Kyma), 191–92
Nostradamus, 195
Nouvelle Vague, 174
November 17th (organization). *See* 17 November (organization)

Ochs, Phil, 193
October 20th movement, 64, 65, 67, 75
Odigitis (journal), 133
O Foititis (journal), 99, 286–87
Ohnesorg, Benno, 239
oil crisis of 1973, 250
OMLE, 136–37, 155n133
Organization of Marxist-Leninists of Greece. *See* OMLE
Otto, King of Greece, 79, 188

Pablo. *See* Raptis, Michalis
paganism, 151n12
PAK, 47, 67, 139–40, 303, 307n90
Palamas, Kostis, 112
Pali (journal), 23
PAM, 47, 110, 135
Panagoulis, Alekos, 67, 112, 321
Panarmonia, 140
Pan-Hellenic Antidictatorship Front. *See* PAM
Pan-Hellenic Resistance Movement. *See* PAK
Panspoudastiki (journal), 35n45, 35n54, 132
Panspoudastiki (organization), 296
Panteios School, 176
Papachristos, Dimitris, 258
Papadimitrakis, Lambros, 259
Papadopoulos, Colonel Georgios, 40, 42, 45, 50, 67, 71, 79, 85–86, 97, 102, 116, 131, 225, 230, 236, 246, 248, 262, 310n181
    overthrow of, 287–88
    personalization of dictatorship by, 246, 288, 305n58
    and Polytechnic occupation, 256

referendum for, 246
Papageorgiou, Kleopatra, 206, 282–83
Papageorgiou, Thanasis, 183
Papandreou, Andreas, 37, 39, 47, 139, 299
Papandreou, George, 11, 12, 26, 30, 37, 42, 43, 101
　funeral of, 111–12, 113f, 250
　memorial of, 250
Papanoutsos, Evangelos, 13, 101
Papaspyrou, Dimitrios, 121
Papastathis, Lakis, 192
Papazoglou, Minas, 159
Papoutsakis, Christos, 218n28
Paris
　as center of Greek émigrés, 60
　rebellions (May '68). *See* French May
Paris, James, 180
partisan songs, 167
PASOK, 140, 303
Patras, University of, 13, 50, 280
Pattakos, Brigadier-General Stylianos, 40, 45, 77, 230, 236, 310n181
Petroulas, Sotiris, 28, 29f, 134, 155n131
Pezodromio (journal), 233–34
phoenix as symbol, 41f, 42, 102
Pietrangeli, Paolo, 193
Pink Floyd, 174, 190, 314
Pinochet, Augusto, 247
Pinter, Harold, 183
Pirandello, Luigi, 183
Ploumbidis, Nikos, 144
poetry, 165
police brutality, 32, 79, 171–72, 175, 179, 226, 228–30, 237–38, 240, 250, 278, 285, 302
　in film, 177
　images of, 217n9, 229, 250
　in music, 201
　as rite of passage, 121, 226–27
　targeting women, 211f, 242–43
politicization of students. *See* student politicization
Poll, 190
Polytechnic Generation, 2–4, 8n3, 20, 298, 300–301, 330, 331
　as small minority, 4
Polytechnic University, Athens, occupation, 122, 140, 253–80, 286–87
　aftermath of, 279f, 286–89
　allegations of provocation at, 289
　apologists, 1
　as archetype, 2
　army response to, 275, 276, 277–78, 280, 309n164
　casualties of, 273–74
　CCO at, 256, 257, 259–60, 261, 269, 273, 275, 277, 307n90, 319
　conflict among various political groups at, 256, 259–61, 269–70
　damage to facilities due to, 286
　effects of on urban environment, 257, 264
　and events of December 2008, 8n6
　high-school students at, 274
　memory of, 253–54, 257, 264, 273–74, 278
　as myth, 8n5
　national celebration for, 303
　national symbols in, 276, 309n155
　organization of services at, 259
　parents and, 266–68
　police response to, 257, 271, 272, 273, 278, 309n159
　political organizations and, 255–56, 259, 262
　radio transmissions from, 257–59, 270, 273, 319
　reaction of Junta to, 256–57, 260, 261, 270, 272, 273
　reenactments of, 302, 327f
　sexual implications of, 268–69
　solidarity of citizens with, 257, 258f, 264–66, 271, 280
　Solonos St. demonstration, 254
　Syntagma Sq. demonstration, 271
　use of weapons by protesters, 271–72, 275, 279
　women's involvement in, 268
　Workers' Committee at, 263

See also "little Polytechnic"
Polytechnic University of Salonica, copycat occupation at, 280–85, 286–87, 310n171
Pop 11, 195
Popular Revolutionary Resistance. *See* LEA
Popular Struggle. *See* Laiki Pali (organization)
Portugal, 290, 292
    conscription in, 230
    universities of, 252
PPSP, 136, 144, 149, 155n131
Prague Spring, 312
pregnancy, 243
price controls, abolishment of, 250–51
prisoners, political, 40, 43, 48, 59, 77, 78, 85
    amnesty for, 116
    informing of, 244–46
professors
    firings of, 89n50
    manipulation of, 49
progressive rock, 174f
Progressive Student Unionist Party. *See* PPSP
"Prometheus" plan, 39
propaganda during Junta, 54, 76
    against antiregime students, 125
    using War of Independence, 77
protest in early Junta, 111–12
protest, varying forms of around the world, 315–16
Provos, 314
Psychogios, Dimitris, 75
public sector, growth in, 13
Public Security Forces, 241
publishing houses, 161

radical leftism, 301
radio. *See under* Polytechnic University, Athens, occupation: radio transmissions from; Syntagma Sq. demonstration. *See* Polytechnic University of Salonica
rape, 242–43, 300, 305n49

Raptis, Michalis, 65
rebellion against parents' political beliefs, 109–10
"Red December." *See* December Events, the
refugees and communism, 106
Reich, Wilhelm, 163
rembetika songs, 189, 200–201, 202
rembetomania, 201
resistance to Junta
    by clashes with police and pro-regime students, 126, 226–27
    costs to protesters of, 92n119, 241
    financial support of, from France, 62
    financial support of, from Italy, 67
    and folk culture, 117
    initial attempts, 47–48
    lack of, during Ioannidis dictatorship, 288
    through open demonstrations, 117, 122, 230–40, 241
    and press response, 76, 159
    return to clandestinity and, 289
    and role of journalism in, 159–62
    as social interaction, 120
    status gained through, 288
    student attempts, 52, 59–60, 230–39
    by students in France, 60–65, 91n90
    by students in Germany, 65
    by students in Italy, 66–68
    support from foreign universities for, 238
    unifying quality of, 241
    by violent means, 69–71, 72, 74–76, 78, 80–81, 82, 139, 329
    and violent reactions to, 226, 239, 240–41
    by writers, 158
    See also Athens Law School; "little Polytechnic"; Polytechnic University, Athens, occupation; Polytechnic University of Salonica; Salonica University

Revolutionary Communist Movement of
    Greece. See EKKE
Revolutionary Internationalist Union.
    See EDE
Revolutionary Organization November
    17th. See 17 November (organization)
Rigas Feraios, 68, 77–81, 83, 131, 142,
    144, 280–81
    in Athens Law School occupation,
        231
    and earlier resistance movements,
        79
    evolution of, 131
    founding and naming of, 77
    and KKE-Esoterikou, 80, 296
    and Polytechnic occupation,
        255–56, 259, 262, 307n90
    and popularity among students of
        high social class, 110, 142
    response of to Chile coup, 248
    and sexual mores in, 149–50
    trial of leadership of, 78
    and violent resistance, 78
    women's involvement in, 83, 150,
        157n173
rights, restoration of, 152n60
Rigopoulou, Pepi, 278
Ritsos, Giannis, 191, 276
rizitika songs, 199–200, 202, 231, 238
Robespierrism, 133
Robinson, Joan, 153n77
rock and roll, 18, 19, 34n22, 59, 99,
    190, 314
Rodeo (music hall), 194, 196
Rolling Stones, 32, 190, 314
rural Greece in film, 169–70

Sacred Bond of Hellenic Officers. See
    IDEA
Salonica
    antiregime journalism in, 159
    copycat occupation at. See
        Polytechnic University of
        Salonica
    and differences from Athens, 115

    Film Festival of, 172, 173, 179–80,
        181
    political climate in, 114–15
    urban space of, 115
Salonica University, 32, 115, 124, 236
Savvopoulos, Dionysis, 19, 82, 85,
    94n173, 189, 190, 191–95, 196–97,
    198, 201
Seferis, George, 24, 161, 191, 233
    funeral of, 111, 112
SEP, 135
Servan-Schreiber, Jean-Jacques, 162
sexual assault. See rape
sexual harassment, 308n133
sexuality
    in Greek society, 148, 208–9
    and marriage, 149, 208
    as political resistance, 208, 260
sexual revolution, 208, 269, 314
Shakespeare, William, 183
short decade, the, 4
Sifnaios, Panagiotis, 256
silence of writers, 158–59
Situationists, 314, 322
Skourtis, Giorgos, 186
Skylodimos, Nikos, 186
slang. See speech, peculiarities of
slogans
    role in protest, 112, 228, 231–32,
        238, 248, 250, 281, 283, 322
    in Polytechnic occupation, 256,
        258, 259–62, 262f, 263, 264,
        266, 273, 307n105, 307n108,
        307n110
smoking, 135
soccer. See football
Socialist Revolutionary Struggle. See SEP
Society for the Study of Greek Problems.
    See EMEP
Society of National-Minded Students of
    the Polytechnic. See EMP
Socrates (rock group), 190, 195
Sofia, Princess of Greece, 16
solitary confinement, 241–42, 244
Solomos, Dionysios, 233, 268
Sophocles, 183

Spain, comparisons to, 107, 112, 157n168, 183, 193, 209, 212, 217n9, 230, 248, 251–52, 296, 302, 318, 324
Spartacus, 135
Spatharis, Evgenios, 192
Special Interrogation Unit—Military Police. *See* EAT-ESA
speech, peculiarities of, 216
sport. *See* football
Spoudastiki Pali (organization). *See* Laiki Pali
Spraos, John, 290–91
Stalin, Joseph, 138, 246
Stalinists, 61, 109, 131, 135–36, 139f, 261, 323
Stamatopoulos, Byron, 125, 153n77
State Theater of Salonica, 180, 183
Stoa Theater, 183
Strawberry Statement, The (film), 177, 178f, 278, 285
street theater, 185, 314
student apathy and passivity, 95–96, 97, 115–16, 119, 123
Student Committees of Struggle. *See* FEA
student journals
    limitations on, 130
    pro-regime, 99
    of resistance, 35n45, 130, 132, 136–37, 138
student organizations
    allegations amongst, 143–44
    apathy of, 97
    clandestine, 129–30, 131–33, 136–39
    dismantling of, 48, 88n43, 287, 289
    diversity of opinion among, 129–30, 144
    as enemy of the state, 287
    fragmentation between various, 143–44, 146, 150, 289, 296
    and friendship, 147
    hierarchical nature of, 130, 132, 140, 142, 148–49
    imitation between, 143
    lack of, 96
    lasting identification with, 144–45
    during *metapolitefsi,* 296
    physical appearance and, 140
    pro-regime, 96–99
    recruitment to antiregime, 104, 132, 141–42
    and refusal to expose members, 244–45, 305n44, 305n50
    regional and local societies, 116–17, 118, 249, 287, 329
    rejection by, 144
    repression of sexuality within, 148–49
    role of in social identity, 140
    sexuality in, 148–50
    solidarity and collaboration between, 145, 146–47
    theatricality of, 140
    tradition and, 132
student politicization, 103, 105, 121
    and diversity of, 129
    and unity despite ideological differences, 123–24, 145
student resistance to Junta. *See* resistance to Junta
student unrest abroad, 249
    references to in press, 159–60, 167, 251
students
    as avant-garde of society, 251, 253, 263, 326
    as capable of fomenting change, 324
    as elite citizens, 127, 129, 251, 326
    emergence of antiregime, 99–100, 103–4
    mass imprisonment of, 241, 288
    oppression of, 105
    pro-regime, 96
subengineers, 127
surveillance on citizens, 40, 49
Sweezy, Paul, 162
Synchroni Epochi (publishing house), 164
Synchrono Elliniko Theatro (theater), 183
Synchronos Kinimatografos (journal), 169

Synecheia, I (journal), 161
Synodinou, Anna, 182

Ta Nea (newspaper), 159
tavernas, 201, 202–3
"technocratization," 128
teddy boys (*tediboides*), 16–17, 54, 228, 230
television, 12, 189, 193
    and contrast with film, 171
terrorism, 82, 299–302
    emergence of in *metapolitefsi*, 299
Thailand, 247, 248–49, 331
theater, 181–89
    journals of, 184, 188
    revue genre, 186–87
    in Salonica, 184
    student interaction with, 181, 183–86, 187–88
    as venue for dissent, 182–83, 185–86, 189
Theatrika (journal), 184
Theatriko Ergastiri (Theatrical Workshop), 184–85
Theatro Technis, 183
Themelio (publishing house), 163, 218n20
Themis (student union), 250
Theodorakis, Giannis, 22
Theodorakis, Mikis, 19, 21, 24, 26, 28, 190–91, 193, 194, 201, 222n139, 282, 321
    banned music of, 68, 84, 112, 189, 191, 221n107, 250
    and Polytechnic occupation, 258, 276
    response to coup of, 43, 45, 191
Theodoridis, Panos, 218n28
Theotokas, Giorgos, 24
Therapos, Panagiotis, 256
Thessaloniki (city). *See* Salonica
Thessaloniki (newspaper), 159
third-worldism, 133, 140, 144, 214, 248–49, 313f, 315, 321
Thourios (journal), 78, 80
Thrace Macedonian Society, 249

Thymeli (cinema), 178
tiersmondisme. See third-worldism
torture, 76, 77, 79, 83, 218n28, 220n68, 226, 229, 241–44, 285, 299–300, 318
    and the Council of Europe, 118, 229
    memory of, 243–44, 305n49
    in music, 201
    as rite of passage, 242
    students' sensitivity to, 103
    of women, 242–43
torturers, trials of, 299–300
Toundas, Konstantinos, 235
tourism, development of, 12, 46
tradition
    rediscovery of through music, 196–99
    and role of censorship in, 198
Tram (journal), 167, 218n28
transvestitism, 209
"Trial of the Eleven," 229–30, 291
trial transcripts, publication of, 159
Trotskyism, 52, 65, 134–36
    and printing, 135, 163
trousers, adoption by women of, 207, 210
Tsembelidou, 83
Tsikouris, Giorgos, 80–81, 82
Tsitsanis, Vassilis, 201
tuition fees, 13
Turkey, invasion of Cyprus by, 291, 292
Tzannetis, Emmanouil, 230, 291

unemployment, 128–29
United Democratic Left. *See* EDA
United States
    as cause for Junta, 82, 163, 262
    imperialism of, 139–40, 163, 248–49, 299, 313f
    involvement in Greek government, 10, 70, 79–80
    popular culture of, 58–59
    radio station of, 34n30
    student protest against, 231, 262, 281
    violence directed against, 70, 80–82, 302

universities
  administration, reorganization of, 128
  and asylum, 132, 303
  attempts at reform at, 128
  de-Juntafication of, 296
  demographics of student body in, 14
  entrance into and political beliefs, 50
  foreign, and asylum for antiregime students, 290–91
  increase in enrollment at, 12–13, 315
  intensification of studies at, 128
  See also educational reform in universities
urbanization, 11

Valaoritis, Nanos, 23
Vamvakaris, Markos, 201
Varikas, Eleni, 62
Vassiliadis, Thomas, 84
Velos. *See* Navy, mutiny of
Velouchiotis, Aris, 74, 80, 269
Vietnam War, 312, 314–15
  references to, 160, 181, 190, 214, 313f
violence as inspiration, 315
Vlachou, Helen, 25, 30, 46

War of Independence. *See* Greek War of Independence
weapons. *See* arms
Weiss, Peter, 183
welfare state, attempts to establish, 12
Williams, Paul, 174
women
  adoption of male practices by, 206, 209
  feminist organizations for, 302, 311n209
  and Lambrakis Youth, 23, 24
  and leadership role in student organizations, 117, 206, 212, 330
  men's attitude toward, 210, 211, 330
  at Polytechnic occupation, 268, 307n105, 308n133
  and restrictions on, 42, 208
  and right to vote, 25
  role in clandestine organizations of, 74, 83, 207
  role in student resistance of, 52–53, 68, 69, 74, 83, 206, 211–12, 239f, 268
  and segregation from men, 25, 204
  sexist attitudes toward, 157n173
  and sexual openness, 17, 204, 207, 208, 268
  students, treatment of by male students, 205, 210–11, 330
  traditional roles of, 204, 243
  in university enrollment, 14, 25, 204, 223n157
  use of profanity by, 209–10
Woodstock (documentary film), 175–76, 190
Woodstock festival, 175, 190, 195
World War II, references to, 272, 276

Xarhakos, Stavros, 188
Xylouris, Nikos, 188, 199–200, 202

Yé-yés, 18, 19, 32, 34n26, 55, 195–96, 213
youth, as social class, 251
Youth Directory, 97

Z, as symbol for Lambrakis Youth, 19–20
Zappa, Frank, 174f, 190
Zournatzis, Spyridon, 250, 272

www.ingramcontent.com/pod-product-compliance
Lightning Source LLC
Chambersburg PA
CBHW072141100526
44589CB00015B/2041